Closed Shop: An employer agrees that all workers must belong to the union to keep their jobs; and he further agrees that when hiring new workers he will hire only members of the union. The closed shop is more strict than a union shop.

Union Shop: An employer agrees that all workers must belong to the union to keep their jobs. He can hire whom he wants; but the workers he hires must join the union within a specified time (usually 30 days) or lose their jobs.

Maintenance-of-Membership: An employer agrees that all present and future members of the union must remain in the union for the duration of the contract in order to keep their jobs.

Yellow-dog Contracts: An employer requires of each non-union employee a signed agreement which prohibits membership in a union as a condition of employment.

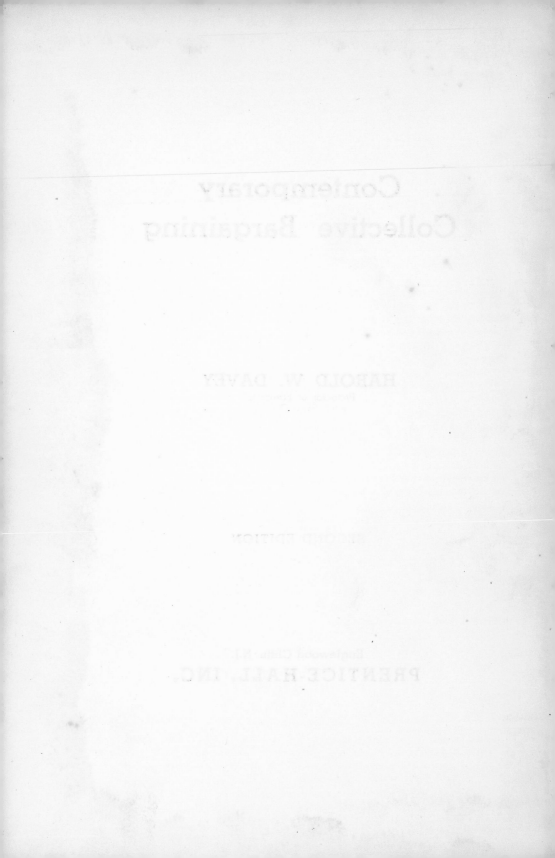

Contemporary Collective Bargaining

HAROLD W. DAVEY
Professor of Economics
Iowa State College

SECOND EDITION

Englewood Cliffs, N.J.
PRENTICE-HALL, INC.

PRENTICE-HALL INDUSTRIAL RELATIONS AND PERSONNEL SERIES

DALE YODER, editor

BELCHER • *Wage and Salary Administration*
BELLOWS • *Creative Leadership*
BELLOWS • *Psychology of Personnel in Business and Industry, 2nd ed.*
CARPENTER • *Case Studies in Collective Bargaining*
DANKERT • *Contemporary Unionism in the United States*
DANKERT • *Introduction to Labor*
DAVEY • *Contemporary Collective Bargaining, 2nd ed.*
DUBIN • *Human Relations in Administration*
GALENSON • *Comparative Labor Movements*
GOMBERG • *A Trade Union Analysis of Time Study, 2nd ed.*
HABER AND COHEN • *Readings in Social Security*
HARDMAN AND NEUFELD • *The House of Labor*
HENEMAN AND TURNBULL • *Personnel Administration and Labor Relations: A Book of Readings*
LINDBERG • *Cases in Personnel Administration*
MILLER • *American Labor and the Government*
OTIS AND LEUKART • *Job Evaluation, 2nd ed.*
PFIFFNER • *The Supervision of Personnel, 2nd ed.*
SHARTLE • *Occupational Information, 2nd ed.*
SMITH • *Collective Bargaining*
TAYLOR • *Government Regulation of Industrial Relations*
THOMPSON • *Personnel Management for Supervisors*
YODER • *Personnel Management and Industrial Relations, 4th ed.*
YODER • *Personnel Principles and Policies*

Second printing—December, 1959

PRENTICE-HALL, INC.
ENGLEWOOD CLIFFS, N.J.

LIBRARY OF CONGRESS CATALOG CARD NO.: 59-6884. PRINTED IN THE UNITED STATES OF AMERICA.

16974

Preface to Second Edition

In many respects this is a new book. I have changed the chapter organization materially. Most of the chapters have been rewritten completely and several new ones have been added. These fundamental changes are a tribute to the dynamic quality of the subject matter and to greatly appreciated critical comment on the first edition.

In preparing this revision I have considered carefully the suggestions of friends and reviewers. Some wanted more theory. Others wanted more practical, applied analysis. I have tried, in a measure, to satisfy both schools of thought. As in the first edition, I have sought to achieve a judicious blending of theoretical and applied analysis. In preparing the manuscript, however, I found myself unavoidably influenced by my own experience and predilections. Thus, it is fair to state that the emphasis in this second edition remains on problems, policies, and procedures in union-management relations at the plant level. However, those who are primarily interested in the theory and economics of collective bargaining will find that the treatment of wage determination has been expanded.

The major organizational change involves the consideration of public policy and procedures for contract negotiation and administration before dealing with the principal substantive issues in collective bargaining. This appears to be a more logical approach. In several chapters I have used recent arbitration decisions to illustrate recurring problems in contract administration. An effort has been made to treat more fully the "non-factory" areas of collective bargaining.

The basic approach remains primarily analytical rather than descriptive. I have avoided detailed factual analyses that tend to become dated rather rapidly. At the same time, major recent developments have been treated if they are likely to have a continuing impact on collective bargaining in the years ahead. I refer here to such matters as automation, the AFL-CIO merger, initial experience with SUB plans, the impact of McClellan Committee disclosures, the wage inflation controversy in its newest phase, current problems in "health and welfare" bargaining, recent changes in NLRB policy, and so on.

No single book can possibly do justice to the rich and varied patterns of contemporary bargaining relationships. This book is intended to serve as a comprehensive introduction and framework for more intensive study of particular problem areas in collective bargaining and for appraisal of bargaining performance in specific union-management situations. It should be of value to management and union representatives as well as to teachers and students of industrial and labor relations.

Fortunately, the reader who wishes to inform himself more completely will find that a great deal of productive theoretical and empirical research has been completed in recent years. The chapter bibliographies for this edition were designed to be of value for further study of particular problems.

Many questions discussed in this book are highly controversial and have no scientifically correct answers. In all such cases (e.g., union security, management prerogatives, causes of inflation), I have not hesitated to express my personal views. However, I have tried to label all value judgments as such, and to present fairly conflicting viewpoints on debatable policy issues.

The book's readability has been improved by the elimination of lengthy quotations from other writers and by the minimal use of footnotes.

This edition has been in the writer's mind for some years. The actual writing had to be done at unorthodox hours in the midst of a rather hectic program of teaching, arbitration, and editorial chores on another volume. Therefore, in my acknowledgements I wish to express first my deep appreciation to my wife, Mary, and to my son, Bill, for their patience and forbearance over a period of several years. Without their understanding support and willingness to tolerate a certain amount of temperament, this task would never have been completed.

No book is in any proper sense a one-man project. I am deeply indebted to a number of individuals for their frank criticisms of the first edition and their suggestions for improvement. In particular, I should like to thank my colleagues Howard H. Hines and Madelynne K. Chandler at Iowa State. I am also grateful to Herbert Heneman, John Turnbull and Dale Yoder of Minnesota, J. J. Kaufman of Penn State, Gladys W. Gruenberg of St. Louis University, and Arthur W. Saltzman of the Ford Motor Company for their helpful suggestions and to Mrs. Margaret McWilliams for typing the manuscript.

One debt that is difficult to acknowledge properly is that to the many management and union representatives whom the writer has met during the past fourteen years in connection with grievance arbitration. Whatever practical merit and usefulness this book may have is due in large measure to the knowledge gained from this experience. In particular, I should like to express gratitude to Ralph S. Clifford and Robert S. Wolff of Deere & Company and to Morris Field and Sam L. Grogg of the UAW for many illuminating insights and observations on the problems of negotiating and administering collective bargaining contracts in a multi-plant enterprise.

It is perhaps unnecessary to add that none of the individuals mentioned above is responsible for the ensuing analysis. Any errors or shortcomings therein are entirely the writer's responsibility.

Harold W. Davey

Ames, Iowa

To Bill

Contents

1

Collective bargaining today: definitions and problem areas

Some years ago it was fashionable to assert that collective bargaining as a medium for achieving worker benefits was approaching the saturation point. It was alleged that business unionism stressing short-run gains through collective bargaining was old-fashioned and that it was now time for American unions to shift their emphasis to the legislative and political arenas in their search for "more."

The march of events in recent years has demonstrated conclusively that these reports of the imminent decline of collective bargaining were premature and greatly exaggerated. Collective bargaining remains the principal instrumentality through which American unions seek to improve the economic position of their membership. Furthermore, notwithstanding the increasing maturity of many union-management relationships today, there are few signs that collective bargaining has lost its resilience and capacity to adjust to rapidly changing economic circumstances. Collective bargaining remains an ingenious mechanism for simultaneously promoting stability and change in employer-employee relationships.

Major developments since 1950 have underlined the abilities of union and management leaders through private negotiation to face and solve new problems not contemplated in the earlier years of their relationship. Long-term contracts were a novelty in 1950. They are accepted in many areas of industry today. In 1950 private efforts to deal with the problems of employment security and retirement were comparatively limited. In recent years we have seen an amazing extension and proliferation of novel approaches to the solution of these problems through collective bargaining. In 1950 only a few attempts were made to utilize collective bargaining as a medium for grappling with the knotty problem of adjustment to basic technological change. Today, the rapid spread of automation in highly unionized industries has made adjustment to technological change a major policy issue in many collective bargaining relationships.

In recent years union and management leaders have been required to adjust their policies and planning to such new developments as the impact of the AFL-CIO merger, fundamental jurisdictional and policy changes by the NLRB, and growing resentment by some skilled trades at the alleged inadequacy of their representation by industrial unions. The familiar controversy over the relationship between managerial authority and the scope of collective bargaining is still with us in somewhat revised form, as is the perennial issue of union security. So too is the continued concern over the alleged inflationary impact of collective bargaining in a full employment economy.

In short, the dynamism of our economy represents a continuing challenge to the parties in collective bargaining to adjust contracts to changing requirements. We have some fundamental new problems to appraise and analyze. We also have many familiar problems such as wages, seniority, and discipline whose pragmatic requirements have shifted somewhat, even in a few short years. In other words, while most union-management relationships show evidence of increasing stability and maturity, there is a continuing need for reappraisal in the light of changed circumstances. In many cases yesterday's solutions are inadequate for contemporary needs.

EXTENT AND IMPORTANCE OF COLLECTIVE BARGAINING

Collective bargaining today is unquestionably the principal method of determining wages and other conditions of employment for those who earn their living by working for others. By conservative estimate there are more than 100,000 collective labor agreements in force in the United States today. Membership in *bona fide* unions is currently estimated at around 18 million. Approximately 20 million workers are covered by collective bargaining contracts.

These bare figures do not properly convey the real importance of collective bargaining to the economy as a whole. The policies and procedures of many nonunion employers are directly and significantly influenced by collective bargaining. Unorganized clerical workers and supervisory employees in many manufacturing plants owe improvements in their economic status to the gains achieved through collective bargaining in the organized sectors of employment. Many small firms in a variety of industries stay nonunion either because it is uneconomical for the appropriate union to attempt to organize their employees or because the managers of such firms have unilaterally instituted employment terms and conditions comparable with, or superior to, those negotiated in the organized portion of their industry.

Although unions have not made substantial progress in organizing new territory in recent years, it seems probable that our economy will become more highly unionized than it is today. Having effectively organized most of manufacturing, transportation, communication, and the extractive industries (mining of coal, iron ore, etc.), unions are now turning to the clerical, retail, service, and distributive occupations, and professional employees, most of whom are not yet organized.

One of the primary objectives of the new AFL-CIO federation is to complete the task of organizing the unorganized. No conspicuous successes along these lines can be noted to date. It is logical to assume, however, that the federation will continue to give high priority to new organization to the extent that somewhat limited funds permit. The resistance of many southern employers continues to be strong, particularly in textiles. Also, the labor movement has made only slight progress in unionizing small firms in small towns.

WHAT IS COLLECTIVE BARGAINING?

It is not easy to define a complex, institutional process like collective bargaining in one meaningful sentence. Yet it is important at the outset to have a clear understanding of what collective bargaining is and what it is not. *As used here, the term collective bargaining is defined to cover the negotiation, administration, interpretation, application, and enforcement of written agreements between employers and unions representing their employees setting forth joint understandings as to policies and procedures governing wages, rates of pay, hours of work, and other conditions of employment.*

When laymen think of collective bargaining, they frequently picture shirt-sleeved men in a smoke-filled room at midnight with a strike deadline staring them in the face, trying desperately to reach agreement on the terms of next year's contract. This melodramatic picture is true in particular cases, but it serves to obscure the paramount significance of day-to-day contract administration in the success or failure of the particular relationship.

Contract negotiation is undeniably an important phase of collective bargaining. It is well to keep in mind, however, that when a company and a union negotiate a contract, they are reaching a joint understanding on a written statement of policies and procedures under which they will have to live together for at least a year and, in many cases today, for three to five years or longer.

It is the process of living together under the written agreement that gives real meaning and significance to the contract. As Neil Chamberlain and the late Harry Shulman pointed out some years ago, the negotiation of a contract is to labor relations what the wedding ceremony is to domestic relations. In their view, ". . . the heart of the collective agreement—indeed, of collective bargaining—is the process for continuous joint consideration and adjustment of plant problems." [1]

The term "collective bargaining" was reputedly coined by Sidney and Beatrice Webb, the famed historians of the British labor movement.[2] It was first given currency in the United States by Samuel Gompers and has long been an accepted phrase in our vocabulary. It is an extremely useful shorthand term for describing a continuous, dynamic, institutional process for solving problems arising directly out of the employer-employee relationship.

The definition of collective bargaining used here is deliberately elastic, in order to cover the entire range of organized relationships between unions and management. This is essential to underline the important fact that collective bargaining provides a system of a *continuous* nature. It is customary, however, to distinguish between the *negotiation* of union contracts (the "legislative" phase of the union-management relationship), the *administration* of contracts (the "executive" phase), and the *interpretation* or *application* of contracts (the "judicial" phase).

There are admittedly fundamental differences between collective bargaining in its legislative and in its executive and judicial aspects. The legislative phase of contract negotiation creates an instrument governing the relationship between the parties for a given period of time, usually one to five years. If the relationship between the parties is to be a stable and constructive one, the existence of such a legislative instrument must be held to preclude the possibility of continuous bargaining for change in

[1] Harry Shulman and Neil W. Chamberlain, *Cases on Labor Relations* (Brooklyn: The Foundation Press, Inc., 1949), p. 3.

[2] See Vernon H. Jensen, "Notes on the Beginnings of Collective Bargaining," *Industrial and Labor Relations Review*, IX (January, 1956), 225–34.

→ The true nature of the institution of col barg is better portrayed—although less spectacularly—in those situations where relationships were being worked out on a man-to-man basis. Conflict was the manifestation of lack of acceptance or frustration, whereas the humble structural and procedural developments were the promise and the hope of the future. The latter were basic, the former transitory.

its terms. Such bargaining must be confined to specified contract negotiation periods. Of course, the parties by mutual consent may choose to modify an unworkable provision or may meet a specific contingency that arises after the signing of the contract through a "memorandum of understanding."

Too rigid an insistence upon a separation between negotiation and administration obscures the continuous nature of the organized relationship between the parties to the contract. It tends to magnify unduly the importance of contract negotiation as contrasted with administration.

Collective bargaining is an institutional process of representation. The chief participants in collective bargaining do not act for themselves. They are representatives of their respective institutions, the workers organized into a trade union and the collective entity of the corporation or business firm.

The American trade union is a body politic. It is an institution with a life of its own. It has its own survival and growth requirements that in some cases may be independent of those of the workers who compose its membership.

If the growth requirements or the survival of the union are threatened, union leaders may take actions or adopt policies that an economist might consider unwise or irresponsible. Some strikes, for example, are politically rather than economically motivated when the union feels that management is threatening its institutional security. As Arthur Ross has demonstrated so forcibly, the trade union is a political institution operating in an economic environment.[3]

The rank-and-file workers' interests in collective bargaining are represented by an institutional hierarchy of trade union officials, ranging from the shop steward and the local union bargaining committee to the top officers of the national union with which the local union is affiliated.

In collective bargaining the employer does not deal directly with his workers. He deals with an institution authorized to represent the workers for purposes of negotiating and administering the terms and conditions of employment. It is important to note that this representative nature of the organized union-management relationship applies to contract administration as well as to negotiation. Even in the handling of grievances, the shop steward and other union functionaries usually take a hand at an early stage.

It is from this representative nature of the bargaining process on the labor side that the term "collective" derives its prime significance. In many cases those who bargain for the employer also perform a representative function. Of course, there are still many owner-managers who

[3] See Arthur Ross, *Trade Union Wage Policy* (Berkeley: University of California Press, 1948), *passim.*

deal directly with labor organizations representing their employees. In the main, however, the structure of American business has evolved to the point at which the corporation is the dominant form of business unit. The corporation is the employer, with professional managers handling the employer's interests in collective negotiation. In such situations, the employer negotiators represent the actual owners of the business, the stockholders. Bargaining then becomes collective on the employer as well as on the labor side. The representative nature of bargaining on the employer side is seen most clearly in the increasing number of centralized bargaining relationships involving more than one employer.

Collective bargaining thus involves organized group relationships on both sides of the bargaining table, rather than individual dealings between principals. It is an institutionalized representative process. Further, as already noted, collective bargaining provides a mechanism for continuous organized relationships between management and unions.

THE SUBJECT MATTER OF COLLECTIVE BARGAINING

Collective bargaining is concerned with the core of the employment relationship. When basic issues relating to wages, hours, and working conditions are *not* open to joint negotiation, we have something less than genuine collective bargaining. The best example of this is furnished by the company unions or employee representation plans of the 1920's and early 1930's. Many of these plans were directly or indirectly under employer influence and control. They were frequently effective mechanisms for handling individual employee grievances. However, there was seldom genuine two-way bargaining concerning the heart of the employment relationship. When efforts were made to bargain directly over the price of labor, the unilateral nature of such plans usually became clear. The employer refused to entertain demands or to accord union recognition in the sense demanded by affiliated unions or independent unions free from employer influence.

The actual content of collective bargaining varies considerably from industry to industry and from plant to plant. Some collective agreements are little more than price lists for labor. Others are lengthy, detailed documents covering a wide range of problems. But virtually all collective bargaining today embraces the two fundamental aims of independent trade unionism, "wages and human relations on the job." [4] All unions are interested in the former objective; most of them are concerned also with the latter.

The nonincome objectives of unionism (such as human relations on the

[4] The phrase is John M. Clark's. See his *Guideposts in Time of Change* (New York: Harper & Brothers, 1949), p. 148. "Wages" is here used in the broadest sense to embrace a host of money issues in collective bargaining beyond wages as such.

job) have received increasing attention in recent years.[5] In this connection many employers who accept trade unionism look upon collective bargaining as a mechanism for continuous adjustment of problems arising out of the administration of the union contract. In other words, they regard collective bargaining as a feasible *method of management.* They accept the union as an integral part of the industrial relations framework. Such an attitude has special relevance to the controversial questions of management prerogatives and the scope of collective bargaining, discussed more fully in Chapter 8.

The modern union also regards contract administration as a means of giving flesh-and-blood significance to those sections of the contract that establish a system of "industrial jurisprudence," a useful term first given wide currency by Sumner H. Slichter. As used by Slichter and as used here, industrial jurisprudence encompasses the function of collective bargaining as a "method of introducing civil rights into industry . . . of requiring that management be conducted by rule rather than by arbitrary decision." [6]

Collective bargaining is a complex process. It involves "psychology, politics and poker." [7] It is a process of tough-minded economic calculus and horse-trading. It is also a collective manifestation of individual and group drives for status and power. It frequently involves a contest between sovereign institutional entities whose survival requirements are sometimes related and sometimes independent of, or in conflict with, one another. The substantive and procedural problems with which collective bargaining wrestles become more complex as the interdependence of our economy becomes more pronounced.

To summarize, collective bargaining is carried on typically by representatives of institutions on behalf of constituents. The constituents are the rank-and-file workers on the one hand and the stockholders on the other. Collective bargaining is a continuous process, embracing both the negotiation and administration of union contracts. The subject matter of collective bargaining includes all matters directly relating to terms and conditions of employment.

ALTERNATIVE ATTITUDES TOWARD COLLECTIVE BARGAINING

At the outset it is important to appreciate the variety of approaches and attitudes toward collective bargaining that may be adopted and to

[5] For a comprehensive survey of significant recent research in the "human relations" field, see Conrad M. Arensberg and others, editors, *Research in Industrial Human Relations: A Critical Appraisal,* Industrial Relations Research Association Publication No. 17 (New York: Harper & Brothers, 1957), *passim.*

[6] Sumner H. Slichter, *Union Policies and Industrial Management* (Washington: The Brookings Institution, 1941), pp. 1–2.

[7] John M. Clark, *op. cit.,* p. 151.

make clear the frame of reference within which collective bargaining is considered in this book. How collective bargaining is treated depends a great deal on the interests and preconceptions of the analyst.

An economist is primarily interested in collective bargaining as a method of determining the price of labor. A political scientist is interested in collective bargaining as a mechanism of industrial government. The psychologist, the sociologist, and the social psychologist view collective bargaining as a special form of dovetailing individual and group interests. Employers regard collective bargaining in a variety of ways, but tend to view it primarily as an economic factor influencing their cost picture. Union leaders regard collective bargaining primarily as the most effective means of satisfying the desires of their members for short-run economic gains. Workers themselves regard collective bargaining primarily from a "bread and butter" standpoint, but also as a vehicle for achieving status and dignity on the job through the grievance procedure.

Each of these approaches and attitudes has validity in terms of the special interests of those adopting it. Collective bargaining is not a simple, unitary phenomenon. It is a complex, many-faceted process. To see it whole requires greater breadth and perception than can be encompassed by any one individual. Therefore, a choice of emphasis becomes essential. The treatment of collective bargaining in this book reflects the writer's academic training as a political scientist and practical experience as an economist and an arbitrator of labor disputes. His particular combination of training and experience leads him to view collective bargaining primarily from a functional point of view as a "way of life" in industrial relations.

From a functional standpoint, collective bargaining may properly be regarded as an institutional process for: (1) fixing the price of labor services; (2) establishing a system of industrial jurisprudence; and (3) providing machinery for representation of the individual and group interests of employees (and also employers) under the contract. It is possible to consider the third function as an integral part of the second, if we regard grievance and arbitration machinery as a procedural device for insuring equal treatment under the collective bargaining "law" that is the system of industrial jurisprudence. However, the machinery for representation of individual and group interests under the contract is of sufficient importance in contemporary contract administration to warrant its listing as a separate and distinct function of collective bargaining.

The foregoing statement should make clear that this volume treats collective bargaining as a means of joint decision-making on economic aspects of the employment relationship and, equally important, as a means of instituting and maintaining democratic industrial government. All of the author's value judgments in this and ensuing chapters are conditioned by a basic predisposition in favor of collective bargaining as the most logical and equitable method for deciding upon the terms and conditions of employment in a capitalistic democracy.

SOME FUNDAMENTAL PROBLEMS

Collective bargaining in a highly unionized economy poses fundamental problems that constitute a formidable challenge to social scientists and to practitioners on both sides of the bargaining table. From a research standpoint, many of these problems cut across disciplinary lines. Their understanding and solution require a more effective pooling of research efforts than has yet been achieved in most cases. There is an urgent need to develop an integrated appraisal of a constantly expanding body of empirical evidence. Also, since collective bargaining is a highly dynamic process, the research responsibility is both challenging and endless.

Our task is somewhat simplified today in comparison to a few years ago because of the growing stability and maturity in a number of key bargaining relationships that were formerly at a critical stage. Many union-management relationships have "shaken down" enough in recent years to permit somewhat greater confidence in appraisal and prediction. At the same time, even in a mature and constructive relationship, new problems constantly arise and old problems still press for more satisfactory solution. Few collective bargaining relationships can accurately be described as being in a state of static equilibrium.

In the first edition of this book, attention was centered on three major problem areas defined in terms of goals or objectives, as follows: (1) how to achieve full employment without inflation while maintaining free collective bargaining; (2) how to achieve an effective democratization of industrial relations, although faced with an increasing amount of centralization in bargaining structures and in union and management organizations; and (3) how to achieve a stable and equitable condition of industrial peace without undue compulsion. These three goals still command our attention, with the treatment necessarily revised to accommodate the impact of recent developments.

We shall outline each of these continuing problem areas briefly here, followed by a summary exposition of significant recent trends in collective bargaining that require examination in ensuing chapters.

COLLECTIVE BARGAINING IN A FULL EMPLOYMENT ECONOMY

For more than twelve years, we as a nation have been committed by the Employment Act of 1946 to achieving and maintaining a maximum of employment opportunities through policies consistent with the private enterprise system. There is widespread agreement that this objective should be achieved without inflation and with private discretion over wage bargains preserved. Such a goal is a real challenge to public and private policy formulators. There are many who argue persuasively that we cannot "have our cake and eat it too." It remains an open question whether unregulated collective bargaining can be compatible with a national objective of maintaining full employment [8] with a stable general level of prices.

Some economists contemplate a steadily rising inflationary spiral under full employment conditions, stimulated by a persistent drive for wage flexibility upwards by increasingly powerful trade unions. They discount the effectiveness of self-restraint based on fear of government control and argue that it is unreasonable to anticipate that those who have economic power will not use it. Without accepting this pessimistic view of the alleged impact of unregulated collective wage determination, it must nevertheless be recognized that collective bargaining under full employment conditions has a built-in inflationary bias. In itself collective bargaining offers no solution to (and may contribute toward) price inflation on both the cost side and the demand side. Anti-inflationary measures lie outside the scope of effective control by private employers or trade unions.

The success or failure of a non-inflationary full employment policy will be *primarily* dependent upon the nature and timing of federal government action and the impact of such federal action on private initiative. The critical measures lie in the fields of monetary and fiscal policy. It has frequently been pointed out that collective bargaining as a process is not suited to the solution of such major organic problems as substantial involuntary unemployment, checking of inflationary pressures, and more equitable distribution of national income. At the same time, the parties to collective bargaining can accelerate the pace of either a cost or demand inflation by substantial wage boosts accompanied by equivalent or (in some cases) more than equivalent price increases. For example, the multiplier effects of a price increase in steel on costs of all products using steel is well-known and has been widely discussed. Under certain conditions, then, collective bargaining can be a powerful stimulus to inflation.

At the same time, it must be recognized that there is nothing inevitable in this pattern of potentially inflationary collective bargaining. If the need for "restraint" in key wage bargains is fully understood, there

[8] As used throughout this book, the term "full employment" assumes a minimum percentage of unavoidable unemployment appropriate to an essentially private enterprise economy that wishes to remain dynamic. Assuming the dividing line between normal and abnormal unemployment at approximately 5 percent of the labor force, a more semantically correct phrase would be "high and stable levels of employment."

is no reason why collective bargaining cannot be employed to facilitate rather than disrupt governmental efforts at maintaining full employment without inflation. Collective bargaining *can* be used to insure a rational, equitable balance among wages, prices, and profits. Progress along these lines is dependent in large measure, however, on the development of a mutually acceptable formula for sharing the fruits of increased productivity. If the parties in the decision-making are fully cognizant of the fundamental relationship in the long-run between productivity and real wages, there are grounds for solid optimism about the potentialities of private planning in aid of full employment.

As a nation we are committed to maintaining a maximum of free play for private decision-making as to capital investment, price policy, and wage determination. If we are to retain the profit motive as an integral driving force in our economy, considerations of realism and political feasibility demand that, if possible, we avoid governmental determination of the wage bargain. It is certainly not inconsistent or unrealistic to be prudently aware of the inflationary potential in large-scale bargaining aggregates while at the same time working toward the development of collective bargaining as an instrumentality for improvement rather than distortion of wage-price-profit relationships. The beneficial (as well as disruptive) effects of collective bargaining can flow far beyond the confines of the industry in which the bargaining takes place.

By way of illustration, three different examples of how private decision-making can aid a full employment, higher real wage objective may be cited briefly. One is the recent negotiation of various forms of supplemental unemployment benefit plans designed to cushion the impact of involuntary unemployment. Such plans have a clear counter-cyclical effect, since funds that otherwise might have gone into direct wage increases in good times are earmarked for payment to laid-off employees during periods of declining economic activity. Thus, in general, SUB plans have a counter-inflationary effect during periods of high economic activity and a counter-deflationary effect during periods of low economic activity through their demand-sustaining effect as reinforced by state unemployment insurance benefits. Both the newer SUB plans and the more orthodox guaranteed annual wage or employment stabilization plans must necessarily be tailor-made to the needs of the particular plant or industry in question. There can be no model plan for all firms or all types of employment. This is a type of decision-making or planning that is inescapably *private* in nature.

A second illustration of private planning through collective bargaining is the continuous improvement that is being made in the rationalization of occupational wage rate structures to eliminate interplant and intraplant inequities. The development of equitable hierarchies of occupational rates within a particular firm, within an industry, or within a particular labor market area is difficult if not impossible to accomplish by national controls, as the World War II experience under the National War Labor Board amply demonstrated. The important values of flexibility and adaptability can best be achieved through private negotiation rather than through governmental directives.

A third illustration of how private planning through collective bargaining can support rather than disrupt a national policy objective of full employment without inflation is the development of joint efforts to increase productivity and reduce costs. The writer is not as sanguine about the potential of joint union-management production committees to increase productivity and reduce costs as he was when writing the first edition of this book. The challenge here is necessarily one that is *private* in nature. Although formal arrangements of a joint nature do not seem to be increasing appreciably, there is considerable evidence of an increasing private awareness of the necessity for abandoning policies which interfere with productivity gains and cost reductions. Many of the building trades unions, for example, encouraged by the tremendous volume of construction activity in recent years, have given up their restrictive opposition to the use of new techniques. Industrial unions, although alarmed at the employment implications of automation, have generally not opposed the introduction of fundamental technological changes. Their efforts have been largely in the direction of planning such changes so that their impact can be cushioned as much as possible.

The goal of having our cake and eating it too cannot be reached unless we have a tremendous *private* effort accompanying such governmental fiscal, monetary, and other policies as may be found necessary. Full employment without inflation in a democracy can only be achieved by a *shared effort* on the part of government, business, and labor. Collective bargaining can prove to be a powerful instrumentality for the development of sound economic policies. Irresponsible collective bargaining can wreck governmental efforts at maintaining full employment without inflation. The key here is a constant cognizance by employers and union leaders of the integral nexus between productivity and real wages.

DEMOCRATIZATION OF INDUSTRIAL RELATIONS

A second major question is whether in a highly unionized economy collective bargaining can achieve the democratization of employer-employee relations that historically has been one of its major objectives. The successes and failures of collective bargaining as a mechanism for achieving industrial self-government is an area in which political scientists have been particularly concerned. Increased research attention to problems of internal trade union government and internal management organization is a recognition of the importance of this problem area.

The basic question concerns the effectiveness of collective bargaining in satisfying the nonincome objectives of workers who join trade unions. Studies dealing with why workers join unions (and why many do not) indicate that economic improvements are not always uppermost in the workers' minds. Aspirations toward status, personal dignity, and sense of individual worth and accomplishment are frequently powerful motivations for joining trade unions. Such motives frequently operate independently from the economic gains that may be anticipated from union membership. The force of these egocentric drives for worker citizenship in industry can be testified to by anyone familiar with the problems of day-to-day contract administration.

The most dramatic achievement of collective bargaining in this area of worker rights in industry is the contractual protection extended to the individual worker against arbitrary discharge or lesser discipline. Other illustrations include the contractual regularizing of layoff and recall procedures, the elimination of intraplant inequities in occupational rates, rights to equitable distribution of overtime opportunities, and so on. Although many of these problems have an economic aspect, their basic importance to the worker flows from the standardization of policy and procedure in a contract that insures equality of treatment.

The foregoing illustrations are representative of the types of noneconomic, egalitarian service performed by collective bargaining that bring it substantial support from many students of the process who find no justification for it on economic grounds. Those who argue that wages would be just as high in the absence of unionism and collective bargaining will justify the process as the best practical medium for insuring democratic conduct of industrial relations.

Certainly it can be said that the "economic man" concept does not fully explain the union member's loyalty to trade unionism and collective bargaining. He may well support the union because he believes it puts more money in his pay envelope. He also envisages the trade union, however, as a medium for securing individual status and dignity, and for protecting on-the-job rights in the shop.

In stressing the importance of collective bargaining as an instrumentality for achieving industrial self-government it is hardly necessary to add that we are not employing the concept of industrial democracy in the socialist sense of worker control of industry. Rather, the collective bargaining process is viewed as an agency through which both management and union can develop and utilize a democratic procedure of joint decision-making for equitable solution of the vexing problems of day-to-day labor relations.

Realism compels recognition that there are many collective bargaining relationships that fall far short of this rosy ideal of democratic self-government. One important, sobering fact is that there are many management and union organizations that are internally undemocratic in practice. In some tightly centralized and controlled unions, it must be said that the rank-and-file worker has exchanged one type of dictatorial control for another in seeking to escape the arbitrariness of unilateral, managerial decision-making. Certain provisions of the Taft-Hartley Act designed to protect the individual worker are a recognition that some unions are undemocratic in their operations. The internal organization and structure of many business firms also fall far short of any democratic rationale.

In addition to the foregoing considerations, we must note the development of centralized bargaining structures in many industries that some feel is sapping the vitality of local unions and drastically curbing the initiative and discretion of local plant management. Close attention needs to be given here to the achievement of an effective balance between the needs of organizational efficiency and responsibility on the one hand and the requisites for maintaining democracy within industry on the other. This basic problem is fully treated in Chapter 16. The generic bureaucratic problem of size, i.e., reconciling the conflicting requirements of democracy, efficiency, and responsibility, is one that needs constant attention by many American unions.

At the present writing, considerable pressure is developing in favor of stringent governmental regulation of the internal affairs of unions. The ostensible aim of such proposed legislation is to guarantee democracy in unions. The union answer is that the trade union movement is far more democratic in practice than most voluntary private organizations and that there is no need for extensive public control. This is not the place to debate the pros and cons of proposed legislation in this area. The mounting pressure for such controls, however, is at least *prima facie* evidence that room for improvement exists.

On the other side of the bargaining table, the periodic interest of foremen in unionization in recent years and the current interest among engineers and other professional employees in unionizing are clear indications that management must also face a growing demand for more democratic procedures.

INDUSTRIAL PEACE

Collective bargaining may be regarded as a method of institutionalizing inherent conflict elements in the labor-management relationship. It would be a serious oversimplification to equate successful collective bargaining with complete industrial peace. Collective bargaining involves elements of real conflict. It will not always be successful in preventing resort to economic pressure as the ultimate means of resolving such conflicts. The right of organized workers to strike and the right of the employer to close his plant when negotiation reaches an impasse are essential to the effective working of the collective bargaining process. *The most important sanction tending to produce agreement in collective bargaining is the ability of the parties to bring economic pressure to bear on one another, if necessary.*

While recognizing these basic considerations, most responsible union leaders and employers seek to achieve and maintain industrial peace as a positive end of policy. They recognize that interruptions of production as a result of a breakdown of contract negotiations or contract administration are costly and should be avoided whenever possible. In addition to a recognition of the economic loss and suffering entailed by a shutdown of production, there is a joint awareness of the adverse impact on the community at large that may stimulate pressures for public control of the bargaining process.

In a number of industries formerly characterized by considerable conflict, substantial progress has been made in recent years toward achieving continuous production by the elimination of many former causes of industrial strife. Long-term contracts, nearly universal adoption of arbitration as the terminal step in contract grievance procedures, progress by the labor movement in eliminating jurisdictional strikes, the continued importance of NLRB election machinery as a peaceful alternative for union recognition strikes—these are a few of the positive developments that can be cited. However, much progress can still be made.

Genuine industrial peace may be said to exist when union-management relationships have developed to the point where continued production is usual and the resort to economic force as a means of producing agreement is exceptional. Reaching this goal involves continuous joint effort to settle all conflicts that arise within the framework of the relationship by negotiation, compromise, and accommodation, rather than by "pulling the pin" or "hitting the bricks."

In a sensitively interdependent economy such as ours, resort to economic force as a method of dispute settlement is an expensive luxury that should only be used when all other approaches have proved fruitless. If we are to regard the strike and the lockout as rare techniques for dispute settlement, satisfying alternatives must be available. It is important to bear in mind that economic force cannot be eliminated by merely wishing it away or by attempting to legislate it out of existence. Experiments with various forms of compulsory arbitration have demonstrated conclusively that constructive peace cannot be imposed from the outside by governmental decree. Obviously, then, the best possible *voluntary* machinery must be developed to insure as far as possible the peaceful settlement of those disputes that inevitably arise and seemingly cannot be negotiated successfully.

A democratic society such as ours stresses freedom of private action.

In such a society, conciliation, mediation, and voluntary arbitration are the three most acceptable *external* procedures for promoting industrial peace where differences cannot be resolved through negotiation. All three should be viewed as supplements to the collective bargaining process, not as substitutes for it. As long as they remain *complementary* to collective bargaining, their appropriate utilization will strengthen rather than weaken private bargaining processes.

It is extremely unlikely that research in human relations will ever reveal any universally applicable formula for constructive management-labor relationships. Where the human equation is involved, differing economic, political, and personal circumstances are likely to require different prescriptions for industrial peace. If one general maxim is justifiable, however, it might be stated that constructive relationships need to be developed *internally*. They cannot be imposed from without. For this reason, attention to machinery for maintaining industrial peace needs to be concentrated on the development and perfection of *voluntary* dispute-settling facilities.[9]

RECENT TRENDS IN COLLECTIVE BARGAINING

We have had the experience of many years of collective bargaining since the end of World War II. Although this period includes the "hot" war in Korea and has been influenced by the constant pressures of the continuing cold war with the Soviet Union, it is appropriate in some respects to regard the post-World-War-II period as one of peacetime bargaining between unions and management. In that span of years some issues that were critical at the end of World War II have now largely disappeared as focal points of conflict at the bargaining table. For example, the use of arbitration for peaceful settlement of unresolved grievances during the term of an existing contract was vigorously resisted by many employers (and some unions) at the end of World War II. Today, this process is virtually universal and, consequently, resort to economic force during the life of a contract has become exceptional. In many sectors of the unionized area of our economy the fires of controversy over union encroachment on managerial authority have been extinguished by the development of a mutually satisfactory allocation of functions. The union security issue is still a critical one in some sectors, but the rapid growth of union shop contracts in recent years has narrowed considerably the boundaries of this conflict. Also, union opposition to job evaluation and incentive methods of wage payment and restrictive union practices in relation to technological change appear to have been reduced substantially in recent years.

[9] The foregoing considerations are developed more fully in Chapter 17. See also Harold W. Davey, "Government Intervention in Labor Disputes," *Labor Law Journal*, V (November, 1954), 739–42, 800.

At the same time, some of the most important current and prospective issues in collective bargaining are brand new, or, if not new, are assuming new forms and shapes. It is these trends that it is appropriate to note briefly in this introductory chapter. One of the significant trends is the intensified union interest in utilizing collective bargaining as a means of promoting a greater degree of employment security. The drive for supplemental unemployment benefit plans, the pressures to utilize collective bargaining as a means of regulating the introduction of fundamental technological change in industries that are automating, the prospective bargaining push for a shorter work week—all reflect the current interest on the part of the key industrial unions in greater employment security through private channels. The emphasis on protection against involuntary unemployment is not so marked as yet in the bargaining demands in the areas of what Kennedy has termed "non-factory unionism." [10] Employment is generally expanding in such areas, and the need for protection is not as pressing as in the more technologically dynamic manufacturing area.

Another recent trend is the constant union pressure to enlarge and broaden the fringe benefit items in contemporary contracts. Virtually no negotiation occurs without some demands for improving the present fringe mix or adding some new items to it. Constant attention is paid to liberalizing paid vacation plans, paid holidays, shift bonuses, and the like. Perhaps more important, however, is the accelerated pace of the drive for improved negotiated pension plans and other forms of insurance such as hospitalization, surgical, prepaid medical care, disability, maternity care, and so on. The increase in negotiated pension plans and the scope of health and welfare funds has been remarkable in recent years.

Current union emphasis on employee security is also reflected in recent demands on the part of some industrial unions for interplant or industry-wide seniority. While such demands are encountering vigorous employer resistance, the union interest in such proposals appears to be serious.

Since the merger of the AFL and CIO in December, 1955, there appears to have developed an increasing degree of coordination of bargaining demands and joint action by unions in related fields. For example, the UAW and the Machinists, formerly serious rivals in the aircraft industry, are cooperating with one another in this industry. To the extent that such coordination of bargaining demands becomes a reality instead of a promise, it will give comfort to those opponents of the AFL-CIO merger who view it as a step toward national bargaining by huge aggregates of union power.

[10] See Van Dusen Kennedy, *Nonfactory Unionism and Labor Relations* (Berkeley: Institute of Industrial Relations, University of California, 1955).

Long-term contracts of two, three, and five years in duration have become standard practice in a variety of industries. When the General Motors-UAW five-year pact was negotiated in 1950, many observers felt that this pioneering move would not catch on elsewhere. Yet, contracts of two or three years' duration are common in an impressive number of key relationships today.[11]

Another trend worth noting is the increasing professionalization of the industrial relations function. It cannot be successfully disputed today that intelligent collective bargaining demands specialized training. The increasingly technical complexity of the collective bargaining agenda of today makes it mandatory that those in charge of negotiations and contract administration have the benefit of expert, professional advice. The intensified factualization of wage bargaining has revealed the need for professional economists to supply, interpret, and, sometimes, present data in bargaining. Widespread introduction of pension plans, SUB plans, and health and welfare programs has sharply increased the demand for professional expertise. There is little room left for the gifted amateur in contemporary collective bargaining.

PUBLIC POLICY AND COLLECTIVE BARGAINING

The impact of public policy on collective bargaining has been of critical importance in recent years. The current trend appears to be clearly in the direction of increasing governmental regulation of private decision-making. Although the Eisenhower Administration has advocated a hands-off policy in labor disputes and has stressed the role of voluntary conciliation and mediation, the current pressures for more stringent legislative control appear to be mounting. It is somewhat ironical to note that while many employers and unions seem to be enjoying increasingly stable and mature relationships, others are experiencing more difficulties and hostility. Those who have advocated greater governmental control have received considerable comfort from the disclosures of the Senate Select Committee on Improper Activities in the Labor or Management Field (the McClellan Committee) as to corrupt or unethical practices by certain union leaders and as to collusive activities between management and union leadership in certain industries. The McClellan Committee findings, coupled with other Congressional investigation reports showing corrupt or loose handling of union health and welfare funds, have stimulated the drive for new legislation regulating the internal affairs of unions and the

[11] For a thoughtful evaluation of the current status and future prospects of long-term agreements, see Jack Stieber, "Evaluation of Long-Term Contracts," Ch. 7 in Harold W. Davey, Howard S. Kaltenborn, Stanley H. Ruttenberg, eds., *New Dimensions in Collective Bargaining*, Industrial Relations Research Association Publication No. 21 (New York: Harper & Brothers, 1959).

adoption of federal "right to work" legislation. It is impossible to assess precisely the impact of recent disclosures on union-management relationships generally. Certainly, however, there can be little comfort for those who have looked forward to a decreasing amount of governmental restriction of private discretion.

CONCLUSION

The reader of a book in a controversial field has a right to know the writer's fundamental value judgments that condition his analysis. Therefore, by way of concluding this introductory chapter and as a preface to the substantive chapters to follow, it is proper to set forth in summary form the author's basic beliefs as to the role and challenge of collective bargaining in a free society.

In the first place, a strong, independent, and responsible trade union movement is indispensable to a healthy, productive, private-enterprise economy and a vigorous political democracy. Secondly, excessive public control of labor relations tends to weaken or destroy private bargaining relationships. The best interests of the community as well as of the parties themselves require that we work diligently toward a goal of what George Taylor has termed "free collective bargaining," wherein the scope of the relationship, the procedures for negotiation and joint dealing, and the substantive terms of employment are all private matters to be worked out by employers and the unions with whom they deal without government interference.[12] In line with this thinking, the trend toward increased public regulation must be reversed if we are to make enduring progress in union-management relationships.

Finally, the public interest and the interests of both management and organized labor will be best insured by adoption of a positive, dynamic approach to collective bargaining. Such an approach requires unremitting effort to increase productivity, reduce costs, and effectively allocate and utilize available manpower. It involves a joint recognition of the perils of inflation and a realization of the need for responsibility and restraint in wage bargaining under full employment conditions. It involves full recognition of the crucial importance of solving the human equation by diligent attention to improved methods of living together under a contract. Finally, it involves a willingness to experiment and a receptiveness to innovation in order that collective bargaining may realize its full potential as a flexible instrumentality for intelligent accommodation to changing economic and industrial circumstances.

[12] See George W. Taylor, *Government Regulation of Industrial Relations* (Englewood Cliffs, N. J.: Prentice-Hall, Inc., 1948).

SELECTED BIBLIOGRAPHY

NOTE: The chapter bibliographies in this volume consist primarily of recent articles, books, and monographs that have been helpful in writing this book. Considerations of space have compelled the exclusion of many excellent references cited in the first edition in favor of more recent publications. A considerable number of legal periodical references have also been omitted, since these sources are not as readily available to the general reader.

The reader will note that a considerable percentage of the journal references are to articles in the *Industrial and Labor Relations Review* and the *Labor Law Journal.* These two journals are the most consistently useful for one who is professionally interested in the labor relations field. The reader who is interested in staying current in this dynamic field should familiarize himself with the wide range of excellent publications by the various divisions of the United States Bureau of Labor Statistics, most of which are noted or summarized in the Department of Labor's *Monthly Labor Review.* Prentice-Hall's current reporting service, *Union Contracts and Collective Bargaining Practice,* is extremely useful. So is the Bureau of National Affairs' *Labor Relations Reporter* service.

Also recommended are the annual proceedings volumes of the Industrial Relations Research Association and the special research volumes sponsored each year by the Association. References to numerous papers from these sources will be found in the bibliographies.

In the references for Chapter 1 are most of the pertinent general purpose books and articles bearing on contemporary collective bargaining. The bibliographies for the remaining chapters are more specialized and relate directly to the subject matter of the chapter in question.

Arensberg, Conrad and others, eds., *Research in Industrial Human Relations,* Industrial Relations Research Association Publication No. 17. New York: Harper & Brothers, 1957.

Bakke, E. W., *Mutual Survival.* New Haven: Yale Labor and Management Center, 1946.

——— and Clark Kerr, eds., *Unions, Management and the Public.* New York: Harcourt, Brace and Co., Inc., 1948.

Barbash, Jack, *The Practice of Unionism,* 1st ed. New York: Harper & Brothers, 1956.

Barkin, Solomon, "Management Personnel Philosophy and Activities in a Collective Bargaining Era," *Proceedings of the Sixth Annual Meeting, Industrial Relations Research Association.* Madison: IRRA, 1954, pp. 324–35.

———, "Organization of the Unorganized," *Proceedings of the Ninth Annual Meeting, Industrial Relations Research Association.* Madison: IRRA, 1957, pp. 232–37.

———, "The Industrial Impact of the American Trade Union Movement," *Labor Law Journal,* VII (April, 1956), 216–24.

Bell, Daniel, "The Next American Labor Movement," *Fortune,* XLVII (April, 1953), 120–23, 201–2, 204, 206.

———, "Where Does Labor Go From Here?" *Fortune,* LVI (December, 1957), 153–55 ff.

Bortz, Nelson M. and Alexander Moros, "Characteristics of 12,000 Labor-Management Contracts," *Monthly Labor Review*, LXXIII (July, 1951), 35.

Brooks, George W., "Reflections on the Changing Character of American Labor Unions," *Proceedings of the Ninth Annual Meeting, Industrial Relations Research Association.* Madison: IRRA, 1957, pp. 33–43.

Brown, Douglass V. and Charles A. Myers, "The Changing Industrial Relations Philosophy of American Management," *Proceedings of the Ninth Annual Meeting, Industrial Relations Research Association.* Madison: IRRA, 1957, pp. 84–99.

Chamberlain, Neil W., Frank C. Pierson, and Theresa Wolfson, *A Decade of Industrial Relations Research, 1946–1956*, Industrial Relations Research Association Publication No. 19. New York: Harper & Brothers, 1958.

Chase, Laura C. and Ernestine M. Moore, "Characteristics of Major Union Contracts," *Monthly Labor Review*, LXXIX (July, 1956), 805–11.

Clark, John Maurice, *Economic Institutions and Human Welfare*, New York: Alfred A. Knopf, Inc., 1957.

Cohany, Harry P., "Membership of American Trade Unions, 1956," *Monthly Labor Review*, LXXX (October, 1957), 1205.

Cole, David L., "Improving Labour-Management Cooperation: A Proposed Program of Action for the International Labour Office," *International Labour Review*, LXXIII (May, 1956), 483–500.

Cooke, Morris L. and Philip Murray, *Organized Labor and Production.* New York: Harper & Brothers, 1940.

Davey, Harold W., Howard S. Kaltenborn and Stanley H. Ruttenberg, eds., *New Dimensions in Collective Bargaining*, Industrial Relations Research Association Publication No. 21. New York: Harper & Brothers, 1959.

Derber, Milton, "Research in Union-Management Relations: Past and Future," *Proceedings of the Ninth Annual Meeting, Industrial Relations Research Association.* Madison: IRRA, 1957, pp. 292–305.

de Schweinitz, Dorothea, *Labor and Management in a Common Enterprise.* Cambridge: Harvard University Press, 1949.

Dolnick, David, "Major Collective Bargaining Trends," *Proceedings of the Eighth Annual Meeting, Industrial Relations Research Association.* Madison: IRRA, 1956, pp. 31–37.

Dunlop, John T., "Research in Industrial Relations: Past and Future," *Proceedings of the Seventh Annual Meeting, Industrial Relations Research Association.* Madison: IRRA, 1955, pp. 92–101.

———, "Structural Changes in the American Labor Movement and Industrial Relations System," *Proceedings of the Ninth Annual Meeting, Industrial Relations Research Association.* Madison: IRRA, 1957, pp. 12–32.

Douty, H. M., "Labor Status and Collective Bargaining," *Monthly Labor Review*, LXXIX (June, 1956), 647–53.

Forkosch, Morris D. and Ernest Fleischmann, "Objectives in Labor-Management Relations," *Labor Law Journal*, VII (May, 1956), 286–96.

Goldberg, Arthur J., *AFL-CIO: Labor United.* New York: McGraw-Hill Book Co., Inc., 1956.

Golden, Clinton S. and Harold J. Ruttenberg, *The Dynamics of Industrial Democracy.* New York: Harper & Brothers, 1942.

Gruenberg, Gladys W., "Unionism at the Crossroads: Retrospect and Prospect," *Social Order*, V (January, 1953), 3–12.

Gulick, Charles A. and Melvin K. Bers, "Insight and Illusion in Perlman's Theory of the Labor Movement," *Industrial and Labor Relations Review*, VI (July, 1953), 510–31.

Haber, William and others, eds., *Manpower in the United States: Problems and Policies*, Industrial Relations Research Association Publication No. 11. New York: Harper & Brothers, 1954.

Harbison, Frederick H. and John R. Coleman, *Goals and Strategy in Collective Bargaining*. New York: Harper & Brothers, 1951.

Hardman, J. B. S., "The Power Motivations of the American Labor Movement," *Monthly Labor Review*, LXXVI (March, 1953), 258–60.

Henderson, John P., "The Impact of the NLRB upon Union Growth," *Labor Law Journal*, VII (May, 1956), 276–85.

Henle, Peter, "Are Unions Running Out of Collective Bargaining Proposals?" *Labor Law Journal*, VIII (September, 1957), 622–27.

Heron, Alexander, *Beyond Collective Bargaining*. Palo Alto: Stanford University Press, 1948.

Hickman, C. Addison and Manford H. Kuhn, *Individuals, Groups, and Economic Behavior*. New York: The Dryden Press, 1956.

Hoxie, Robert F., *Trade Unionism in the United States*. New York: D. Appleton Co., 1917.

Imberman, A. A., "Labor Leaders and Society," *Harvard Business Review*, XXVIII (January, 1950), 54–60.

Kennedy, Van Dusen, *Nonfactory Unionism and Labor Relations*, (West Coast Bargaining Systems). Berkeley: Institute of Industrial Relations, University of California, 1955.

Laski, Harold J., *Trade Unions in the New Society*. New York: Viking Press, 1949.

Leiter, Robert D., "The Meaning of Collective Bargaining," *Labor Law Journal*, VI (December, 1955), 835–42.

Lens, Sidney, "Will Merged Labor Set New Goals?" *Harvard Business Review*, XXXIV (March-April, 1956), 57–63.

Loftus, Joseph, "The McClellan Committee Hearings and Labor," *Michigan Business Review*, X (July, 1958), 8–12.

Lucy, George E., "AFL-CIO: One Year After," *Social Order*, VII (January, 1957), 2–11.

Marting, Elizabeth, ed., *Understanding Collective Bargaining: An Executive's Guide*. New York: American Management Association, 1958.

McConnell, Campbell R., "Institutional Economics and Trade Union Behavior," *Industrial and Labor Relations Review*, VIII (April, 1955), 347–60.

Millis, Harry A., ed., *How Collective Bargaining Works*. New York: Twentieth Century Fund, Inc., 1942.

——— and Royal E. Montgomery, *Organized Labor*. New York: McGraw-Hill Book Co., Inc., 1945.

Mills, C. Wright, *The New Men of Power*. New York: Harcourt, Brace and Co., Inc., 1948.

2

Approaches to collective bargaining: an essay on variety

The principal business of American unions has been and remains collective bargaining. Unions that are successful must satisfy the aspirations of their membership over any period of time. The rank and file have abundantly demonstrated their pragmatic interest in concrete improvement in their economic and status position on the job. The continuing ability of the American economy to expand the total quantum of goods and services has fortified and supported the unions' ability to deliver short-run gains to the membership. This explains, in brief, the primary emphasis that has always been placed on the collective bargaining front in the American union's table of priorities.

As noted in the first chapter, all unions are concerned with wages (broadly defined) and with human relations on the job. There is a tremendous diversity, however, in the approaches to the attainment of these broad objectives and in the specifics of each area. The present chapter is an effort to convey some appreciation of these patterns of diversity that are characteristic of union-management collective bargaining relationships in the United States. Many students of labor relations, including the writer, are inclined to emphasize collective bargaining developments in manufacturing and to overgeneralize on the basis of that experience. In actuality, the area of "nonfactory unionism" deserves more attention than it customarily receives and is likely to become increasingly important in ensuing years. What collective bargaining looks like depends very largely on what trade, industry, service, or profession you are examining. The variety and diversity in approaches and objectives are so great that it is difficult to draw a balanced picture of the over-all scene.

Historically, certain basic crafts were the first to organize and the first to form stable and durable national unions. The fundamental objectives of craft unions in building and construction have remained similar over a long period of time. They have sought to control employment for union members exclusively and to increase steadily the direct compensation of craftsmen for their labor. Characteristically, the construction craft unions have displayed little interest in using collective bargaining to control employer discretion on the job. They have no interest in an elaborate apparatus of principles and procedures governing on-the-job conditions. The business agent of a craft union in the construction trades handles and adjusts grievances as does a shop steward in a manufacturing plant. But the type of policing that a business agent engages in is limited to making sure the union scale is being observed and that no nonunion labor or itinerant journeymen without a work permit are employed on any project. In some crafts the business agent may also be concerned with the enforcement of fairly specific sets of working rules and practices. But his main job in contract administration is enforcing the union scale and the closed shop.[1]

In contrast, unions representing employees in a manufacturing plant with several hundred or several thousand employees necessarily pay a great deal of attention to incorporating into the contract a detailed set of uniform principles and procedures concerned with on-the-job rights and relationships. An industrial union cannot control entrance to the trade or the supply of labor in a particular labor market. It therefore directs its attention to *job security on the job* by hedging the employer's right to discipline and utilizing seniority wherever possible as the primary if not sole criterion governing layoffs, recalls, transfers, and promotions. Contract administration in a large factory is likely to be highly formalized and legalistic in contrast to the informal and flexible adjustment of grievances in nonfactory employment.

[1] A thorough study of labor relations in the building trades is that of William Haber and Harold M. Levinson, *Labor Relations and Productivity in the Building Trades* (Ann Arbor: Bureau of Industrial Relations, University of Michigan, 1956). See also Gordon W. Bertram and Sherman J. Maisel, *Industrial Relations in the Construction Industry* (Berkeley: Institute of Industrial Relations, University of California, 1955).

What issues are regarded as of central importance in collective bargaining will vary greatly from one industry to another and one union to another. Most unions in basic manufacturing will place strong emphasis on seniority. Unions whose members work short periods of time for a variety of employers, as in the construction industry and the needle trades, display little interest in seniority. Unions in the hotel and restaurant field are especially interested in hours of work and split shift problems. Most manufacturing unions face no particular problems in this regard. Unions that effectively control the supply of labor and handle the employment function do not attempt to control the employer's right to discipline. On the other hand, protection against arbitrary discipline is regarded as a prime problem by most industrial unions. Spell-out time or relief time every few hours is of particular importance in meat packing. Wash-up and clothes-changing time may be a critical issue in the foundry industry. Setting and changing of piece rates will be regarded as the most important perennial problem in industries such as the garment trades, shoes, or textiles where labor cost is a substantial percentage of total cost. In industries characterized by casual employment such as longshoring, the most important problem is likely to be insuring fair and equitable allocation of scarce employment opportunities among the membership. Employee safety and regulations governing hazardous assignments may be of critical importance in chemical plants or oil refineries.

Perhaps enough has been said to point up the fact that there is no ideal prototype of the collective bargaining relationship. The most cursory exploration of the contemporary union-management scene will reveal an amazing variety in the range of subjects covered by collective bargaining and in the thoroughness with which they are treated.

The pattern of variety may also be illustrated when we attempt to classify union-management relationships in terms of a continuum with open conflict on one end and full cooperation on the other. Again, if we seek to classify collective bargaining in terms of the structural bases on which it takes place, an amazing variety of forms will be found. Each of these approaches to classification will be considered briefly.

BARGAINING RELATIONSHIPS CLASSIFIED BY DEGREE OF CONFLICT OR COOPERATION

Benjamin Selekman, in a stimulating essay on variety in the labor relations scene,[2] has sought to distinguish eight principal structures of union-management relationships as follows: (1) the structure of containment-aggression; (2) the structure of ideology; (3) the structure of conflict;

[2] Benjamin M. Selekman, "Varieties of Labor Relations," *Harvard Business Review*, XXVII (March, 1949), 175–99.

(4) the structure of power bargaining; (5) the structure of deal bargaining; (6) the structure of collusion; (7) the structure of accommodation; (8) the structure of cooperation.

Selekman's structures are not mutually exclusive. In practice several of them might shade into one another. In American experience generally, the five most significant structures are containment-aggression, conflict, power bargaining, deal bargaining, and accommodation. Structures based on ideology, collusion, or cooperation are comparatively rare in the United States.

Bargaining relationships dictated directly or indirectly by left-wing ideological considerations have become comparatively insignificant since the isolation of eleven allegedly Communist-led former CIO affiliates from the main stream of the labor movement in 1949 and 1950.[3] Such unions have lost ground steadily in competition with AFL-CIO affiliated unions in most cases. It is worth noting also that even unions led by extreme left-wingers are usually fairly orthodox in their approach to collective bargaining. In most cases they have had to follow conventional business union tactics in order to maintain the contractual relationships they still enjoy.

Similarly, bargaining relationships based on a structure of collusion between management and union leadership have been comparatively rare in American experience. Illustrations can be found, however, of two types of collusion, each of which is representative of what Jack Barbash has termed the pathology of collective bargaining.[4] One type is where union leaders and employers have unblushingly combined to freeze out "unfriendly" or noncooperating employers or have passed on the excessive costs of lucrative contractual agreements to the consumer. A second type is where the unsuspecting union member has been the victim of contractual agreements providing pay scales and benefits below that which the condition of the business and the economy requires. Also, some illustrations can still be found of what Hoxie many years ago termed predatory unionism, describing those situations in which a *bona fide* union is taken over by racketeers who proceed to exact tribute from both the employer and the union members. The common technique here is to sell "strike insurance" to the employer and to keep the rank-and-file terrorized by violence or the threat of violence while exacting kickbacks from those who wish to work.

Excluding the structures of collusion and ideology, the remainder of Selekman's bargaining types arrange themselves on a continuum with

[3] For a readable account of the expulsions and their significance see Max M. Kampelman, *The Communist Party vs. the CIO: A Study in Power Politics* (New York: Frederick A. Praeger, 1957).

[4] See his *The Practice of Unionism* (New York: Harper & Brothers, 1956).

open conflict on one end of the scale and wholehearted cooperation between union and management on the other. The overwhelming majority of union-management relationships in the United States fall somewhere between the extremes of conflict and cooperation. It is probably accurate to generalize that the number of conflict relationships is on the decline, but it would be hazardous to say that the number of "cooperation" relationships is on the increase. As the latter term is used by Selekman, it contemplates a relationship in which union and management go beyond the conventional framework of collective bargaining and concern themselves jointly with such matters as productive efficiency, solvency of the business, elimination of waste, and advancement of technology. The structure of cooperation as thus described is most closely allied to the requirement for greater productivity-consciousness and cost-consciousness in a full employment economy. However, instances of positive union-management cooperation along such lines remain unusual on the American scene.

Outright conflict relationships still exist in some industries and areas where employers continue to deny union recognition and collective bargaining rights. As will be noted in greater detail in Chapter 3, it is probable that the Taft-Hartley Act has in some cases accentuated rather than alleviated conflict situations. The National Labor Relations Board's docket of employer unfair labor practice cases continues to be crowded, but the unions complain bitterly that certain policies of the board in recent years deny employees the effective protection of the Act. Perhaps the most famous illustration of open conflict in recent years is the war of attrition between the Kohler Company of Wisconsin and the UAW. The resistance of many southern textile employers to unionization has also been well-publicized. When one contrasts the current scene with the turbulent 1930's or the strike-studded post-war year of 1946, however, it seems evident that the proportionate importance of direct conflict relationships is declining.

If we add open conflict and full cooperation to our previous exclusion of the structures of ideology and collusion, this leaves the preponderant majority of union-management relationships to be classified as: (1) containment-aggression; (2) power bargaining; (3) deal bargaining; or (4) accommodation.

In the containment-aggression pattern, the employer assumes a firm defensive position in an attempt to "contain" a militant, aggressive union. In those situations where the pattern shades into a conflict situation, the relationship is little more than an armed truce where an uneasy peace, marred by wildcat stoppages, prevails between bitter contract negotiation periods. The prerogative issue, or the alleged encroachment by the union on managerial authority, is likely to be prominent in such a relationship. Even after the parties have largely eliminated resort to economic force as a method of producing agreement the struggle is likely to continue with considerable intensity at the level of contract administration, with management typically seeking the narrowest possible construction of the contract and the union aggressively attempting to "milk" the contract for all that it can. Such patterns of containment-aggression are found in a wide variety of industries.

Power bargaining involves a structure of "orthodox" union-employer negotiation in which the parties accept one another and accept the legitimacy of relative economic strength as the prime determinant of the terms of the agreement. In such a pattern both the union and the employer are usually strong and well-established and likely to be fairly evenly matched in bargaining ability and economic power. Bargaining in bituminous coal and in many sectors of trucking and transportation is illustrative of this pattern. So also would be negotiations between craft locals in the building trades and contractor associations in urban labor markets.

Deal bargaining, as the structure is pictured by Selekman, involves a semisecretive type of negotiation between top management and top union leadership. The word "deal" has obviously unfavorable semantic connotations that are not necessarily justified. A famous example that comes to mind is the pioneer agreement in the basic steel industry reached in 1937 in secret session by John L. Lewis, representing the Steel Workers Organizing Committee, and Myron C. Taylor, then chairman of the board of the United States Steel Corporation. Many times the requirements of bargaining will dictate the desirability of confining the negotiation to the principals involved rather than conducting proceedings in a climate of publicity that might freeze the positions of the parties in such a way as to make agreement impossible. Union leaders vary widely in their negotiation practices. Some industrial union negotiators will operate only in the presence of the full shop committee. In other cases the international representative in charge of negotiations will go it alone until an agreement is reached, subject to membership ratification. The latter is frequently little more than a formality. Some craft union business agents negotiate their contracts solely on their own initiative and responsibility. Others will check repeatedly with their executive boards before making commitments. The fact remains, however, that a substantial number of contracts are negotiated in virtual privacy by top leadership on both sides.

Finally, the structure of accommodation requires mention as a pattern that appears to be becoming more widespread in contemporary bargaining relationships. It involves a relationship in which employer and union work cooperatively within the conventional framework of collective bargaining. The employer accepts the union as an integral part of the industrial relations scene, but will negotiate only on the *conventional* subjects of wages, hours, and other conditions of employment. The structure of accommodation may be regarded as a more mature state than either power bargaining, containment-agression, or deal bargaining. It is not, however, as affirmatively oriented as the structure of cooperation.

STRUCTURAL CLASSIFICATION OF BARGAINING RELATIONSHIPS

Another approach to visualizing the current collective bargaining scene is to classify bargaining relationships in terms of the principal structural bases on which collective bargaining takes place.

Still the most common type of structural arrangement is the bargain between a single firm and a single local union, either craft or industrial. If a craft union is involved, the agreement normally covers only those workers whose jobs fall under the jurisdiction of the particular craft, i.e., machinists, electricians, or pattern makers. If the local union is of the industrial type, the bargaining unit will typically include all production and maintenance employees exclusive of clerical and supervisory personnel. In the building and construction field, the hotel and restaurant industry, and local trucking, the typical bargaining structure may involve an association of employers in negotiation with several local unions acting jointly for this purpose.

In addition to single plant-single union bargaining, the most common structural types include multi-employer bargaining, multi-union bargaining with a single employer, company-wide bargaining or multi-plant bargaining, and industry-wide bargaining. We must also take account of the importance of pattern bargaining. The growth of multi-employer bargaining and the prevalence of pattern bargaining pose important problems that will be treated in subsequent chapters.

MULTI-EMPLOYER BARGAINING

Bargaining units embracing the employees of more than one concern have increased in recent years.[5] This phenomenon, although commonly referred to as industry-wide bargaining, is more accurately termed *multi-employer bargaining*. As will be noted in Chapter 4, very few examples of pure industry-wide bargaining exist. However, there has been a rapid growth of bargaining arrangements covering more than one employer within a region or local community.

[5] For a comprehensive recent analysis, see Neil W. Chamberlain, "The Structure of Bargaining Units in the United States," *Industrial and Labor Relations Review*, X (October, 1956), 3–25.

In some instances the bargaining unit covers most employers in an industry within a given geographic area. Well-known examples are the paper and pulp manufacturers of the Pacific Northwest and the Waterfront Employers' Association. In other instances the bargaining unit is confined to a local area but includes employers from a variety of industries, for example, the San Francisco Employers' Council. In the latter situation the contract is a master agreement covering wages and other major issues, but it is flexible enough to permit the establishment of particular provisions for individual cases.

Associational groupings by industry are also increasingly common on a local basis. For example, in the building and construction trades, master agreements frequently cover all contractors in the local area. Similar arrangements are also common in the printing industry, hotels and restaurants, trucking, and many others.

A few cases of nearly pure industry-wide bargaining may be noted briefly. Precisely defined, industry-wide bargaining calls for a single master agreement negotiated by all associated employers in an industry with a single union representing all workers in the industry. In recent years, in the absence of splits between northern and southern operators, bituminous coal bargaining fits such a definition. Industry-wide bargaining is also practiced in industries such as wallpaper, stoves, glass and glassware, pottery, elevator installation and repair, and installation of automatic sprinklers.

The main concentration of multi-employer arrangements continues to lie in the area of nonfactory unionism. Probably more than one-third of all unionized employees today operate under some variant of multi-employer bargaining. Since the union gains of the future are likely to develop in the retail, service, and distribution trades, it seems logical to expect a continued growth in multi-employer bargaining arrangements. In manufacturing employment the significant phenomenon is likely to remain pattern bargaining.

PATTERN BARGAINING

Frederick Harbison, Robert Dubin, and Robert Burns have attempted to classify all union-management relationships into: (1) generating types; (2) satellite types; and (3) semi-isolated types—in their search for the determinants of a generalized theory of union-management relationships.[6] We are not exploring here the merits of the Harbison-Dubin-Burns ap-

[6] See Frederick H. Harbison, Robert K. Burns, and Robert Dubin, "Toward a Theory of Labor-Management Relations," in Richard A. Lester and Joseph Shister, eds., *Insights into Labor Issues* (New York: The Macmillan Company, 1948), pp. 3–24.

proach. Their distinction between generating and satellite types, however, has an interesting application to the pattern bargaining phenomenon.

Although it is easy to exaggerate the influence of a key settlement on other contracts, there is no doubt that *many union-management negotiations today are conducted within the framework of policies established in bargaining outside their industry.*

Pattern bargaining refers to the development of a particular wage or fringe benefit package negotiated between a union and a major employer in a particular industry, the substance of which then becomes the basis for negotiation in other firms in that industry or related industries. For example, although bargaining technically takes place on an individual firm basis in such industries as steel, automobiles, and meatpacking, it has been a familiar phenomenon in recent years for negotiations with most firms in these industries to be carried on pursuant to a contract pattern established by negotiations with one of the leading firms in the industry. In automobiles one of the Big Three is the pattern setter.[7] In steel it is usually United States Steel. In meat packing the pattern traditionally is set by negotiations with one of the Big Four, usually either Swift, Wilson, or Armour.

Another manifestation of pattern bargaining is the type engendered by a union such as the UAW with bargaining relationships in a variety of industries. This giant union has its basic roots in three industries: automobiles, aircraft, and agricultural implements. Its key bargain is usually made first with one of the major automobile concerns. Then a strenuous effort is made to extend the salient features of that pattern to contracts in farm equipment and aircraft, not to mention a large number of small firms in a variety of industries.

Other multi-industrial unions such as the International Association of Machinists, the International Union of Electrical Workers, and the International Brotherhood of Teamsters frequently seek a uniform pattern of collective bargaining demands in a variety of industrial settings. Such strategy has important consequences in terms of centralization of policy determination and the gradual erosion of local union and local management discretion.

We have now illustrated the fundamental characteristic of variety in contemporary collective bargaining by discussing briefly: (1) the tremendous range and diversity in the subject matter of collective bargaining, depending on such variables as the nature and size of the firm, the structure and objectives of the union, and the economic characteristics

[7] In the 1958 negotiations, however, for the first time there appeared to be substantial evidence that Ford, General Motors, and Chrysler were working together informally in presenting a united front to the UAW.

of the industry; (2) the variety of union-management relationships appraised in terms of differing degrees and types of interinstitutional accommodation; (3) the variety of types illustrated by the structural form of bargaining and; (4) the blend of unity and diversity revealed in the development of centralized bargaining relationships and pattern bargaining.

THE SEARCH FOR COMMON PRINCIPLES OF CONSTRUCTIVE COLLECTIVE BARGAINING

Most scientists, including social scientists, are constantly preoccupied with the search for norms and common principles. In a field as protean, dynamic, and variegated as collective bargaining, can we discover any common denominators of constructive labor relations that cut across industry and union lines? Are there any general precepts that can be validly applied with confidence by union and management negotiators in any labor relations situation? Do we have ways of discovering the basic elements making for a successful union-management relationship? Conversely, can we point to common sources of disruptive relationships? An essay on variety should end with a search for unifying principles. In so doing, we shall first consider legal prerequisites for effective collective bargaining and then consider some pragmatic considerations above and beyond such prerequisites.

STATUTORY PREREQUISITES FOR EFFECTIVE BARGAINING

Since 1935, the right to bargain collectively through representatives of the workers' own choosing has been guaranteed by federal law. Since 1935 employers have been prohibited from refusing to bargain collectively with a *bona fide* labor organization representing a majority of employees in a unit appropriate for purposes of collective bargaining. Refusal to bargain with a union upon request under such circumstances constitutes an unfair labor practice. Since 1947 a corresponding obligation has been imposed upon unions to bargain collectively with employers.

Although a refusal to bargain collectively is an unfair labor practice under the law, there was no attempt in the Wagner Act to spell out in affirmative language what constitutes a fulfillment of the obligation to bargain collectively. This obligation, binding equally upon employers and unions, has been specifically set forth in Section 8(d) of the Taft-Hartley Act in these words:

> ...the performance of the mutual obligation of the employer and the representative of the employees to meet at reasonable times and confer in good faith with respect to wages, hours, and other terms and conditions of employment, or the negotiation of an agreement, or any question arising thereunder,

and the execution of a written contract incorporating any agreement reached if requested by either party, but such obligation does not compel either party to agree to a proposal or require the making of a concession....

Also specified in detail are the procedural requirements that must be fulfilled by a party desiring to terminate or to renegotiate an existing contract, including the filing of notice of intention to terminate or to renegotiate at least sixty days before the expiration of the current agreement. Severe disabilities may be incurred by workers who strike within this sixty day period.

The jurisdiction of the National Labor Relations Board under the Taft-Hartley Act is extensive. Thus the above definition may fairly be said to constitute the prevailing legal standard for assessing current practice in collective bargaining.

A large number of National Labor Relations Board decisions between 1935 and 1947 went into the final composition of the statutory definition now under discussion. Basic to all of these decisions is the "good faith" concept. If good faith is absent, the collective bargaining relationship cannot be fruitful. Since good faith is fundamentally a question of intent, no statutory prescription can insure its presence. Still, there are certain outward indices of good faith that have been incorporated into the definition. For example, the obligation to set forth an agreement upon terms and conditions of employment in a written instrument derives from an earlier NLRB ruling that refusal to do so indicates an absence of good faith and constitutes a refusal to bargain collectively within the meaning of the Wagner Act.

In recent years the National Labor Relations Board in its decisions on charges of refusal to bargain collectively has definitely attempted to determine the scope of collective bargaining. In a number of cases in which there was no question of failure to grant union recognition or absence of good faith on the employer's part, the board has nonetheless found the employer guilty of refusing to bargain collectively because of refusal to negotiate concerning particular terms of employment, such as merit increases or pension plans. This trend in board decisions raises some serious questions for the future of private bargaining relationships.

Archibald Cox and John Dunlop have pointed out some disturbing implications for private bargaining in NLRB decisions determining what is bargainable and what is not bargainable and also in the board's failure to distinguish between contract negotiation and administration in several rulings requiring continuous bargaining.[8]

In evaluating statutory requirements it is important to remember that

[8] See Archibald Cox and John T. Dunlop, "Regulation of Collective Bargaining by the NLRB," *Harvard Law Review*, LXIII (January, 1950), 389–432; and, by the same authors, "The Duty to Bargain Collectively During the Term of an Existing Agreement," *Harvard Law Review*, LXIII (May, 1950), 1097–1133.

the obligation to bargain in good faith does not compel either party to agree to a particular proposal or require the making of a concession. In recent years a number of employers and unions in their bargaining strategies appear to be coming perilously close to the type of take-it-or-leave-it bargaining that Section 8(d) seeks to avoid. In specific cases it is difficult to tell whether a refusal to agree on a particular proposal is in good faith or not.[9] A similarly critical question is posed when one party or the other breaks off negotiations with a final offer or a final demand. How much negotiation is necessary to reach a *bona fide* impasse or deadlock?

A NOTE ON "BOULWAREISM"

The importance of this problem has been underscored in recent years by the wide publicity given to a new management bargaining strategy now generally known as "Boulwareism," named after Lemuel F. Boulware, formerly vice president in charge of industrial relations for the General Electric Corporation. Boulware's approach to collective bargaining in the hands of less skillful management pattern followers could easily become bad faith bargaining. His basic idea is to develop for each contract negotiation a management package of improvements that represents the company's best judgment as to what it can agree to for the forthcoming contract period, and then to stick to that offer come hell or high water.[10]

This first-and-last offer approach undercuts the conventional bargaining pattern of compromise, proposal, and counter-proposal. It eliminates the ritualistic aspects of negotiations going down to the wire of a fixed strike deadline before a settlement is reached. Its fundamental purpose, however, seems to be to deprive the union of the privilege of claiming that it "won" any contract improvements from a reluctant management. The Boulware approach requires envisioning the union as an outside force, set apart from the employees themselves. It seeks to exclude the union from the channels of communication between management and employees. It assumes that a worker cannot have a "dual allegiance" to company and union alike.[11]

[9] For a penetrating current analysis of some of the problems and difficulties inherent in the NLRB's proctoring of the bargaining table, see Archibald Cox, "The Duty to Bargain in Good Faith," *Harvard Law Review*, LXXI (June, 1958), 1401–42.

[10] A thoughtful appraisal of the implications of the Boulware approach will be found in Monroe Berkowitz and Allan Weisenfeld, "A New Look in Collective Bargaining," *Labor Law Journal*, VI (August, 1955), 561–66.

[11] Recent research findings indicate, however, that many union members can and do maintain dual loyalties. See Lois R. Dean, "Union Activity and Dual Loyalty," *Industrial and Labor Relations Review*, VII (July, 1954), 526–36. See also a penetrating and thorough case study of Swift and UPWA in Father Theodore Purcell's *The Worker Speaks His Mind on Company and Union* (Cambridge: Harvard University Press, 1953).

Boulwareism has not been in effect long enough to permit confident generalization as to its operational impact on union-management relations over any period of time. However, it violates what this author feels is a fundamental determinant of constructive labor relations: regarding the union as an integral part of the industrial relations framework rather than as an alien, competitive force.

The popularity of Boulwareism among many employers involved in a containment-aggression type of relationship with unions cannot be denied. It is also popular among those employers who cling to the belief that unionism is a "passing phase" after which their employees will "return" to single-minded devotion to their companies.

UNIFORM PRINCIPLES OF CONSTRUCTIVE LABOR RELATIONS

In the writer's view, constructive labor relations will not be achieved by cautious adherence to statutory minima. Constructive bargaining cannot be equated with successful avoidance of a "refusal to bargain" charge. When a union is certified as bargaining representative for a specified group of employees, the union in question and the employer with whom it is empowered to negotiate enter upon a continuous relationship that can be fruitful and productive or hostile and disruptive, depending in great measure on how the respective parties approach the task of working out a viable method of getting along with one another.

The theme of this chapter has been variety. Union leaders and management representatives have proved over and over again that no one policy or pattern is suitable for all relationships. A field as complex and volatile as labor relations is peculiarly well-suited for underscoring the validity of the familiar maxim that one man's meat is another man's poison. Yet, the author believes that there are discoverable principles of constructive labor relations sufficiently generic in character to have nearly universal applicability.[12] Empirical case studies of contemporary bargaining relationships, for example, tend to support the general statement of "first principles" presented below:

1. Effective collective bargaining presupposes an intelligent understanding by both management and union of the needs, aspirations, objectives, and problems of the other party to the bargaining process. Union leaders must have full knowledge of the economics of the industry in which they operate and an intimate working acquaintance with the particular objectives and problems of the companies within that industry. Management needs to have a developed awareness of the nature of the

[12] See chapter 18. For a more detailed exposition, see Harold W. Davey, "Constructive Labor Relations," *Journal of the American Dietetic Association,* XXXIII (June, 1957), 579–82.

union as a political institution operating in an economic environment. Management needs to know and to understand why the union leader (as head of a body politic) behaves differently in certain situations from the businessman.

2. Management needs to recognize the union as an integral part of the total industrial relations picture. Collective bargaining cannot become fully effective if management continues to regard the union as an alien, outside force. Nor can it become effective if the union continues to pursue the militant, aggressive strategy that may have been necessary in the organizing stages. Such a strategy is not appropriate to the building of an enduring, stable relationship. In short, management and the union (although maintaining their institutional integrity) must work cooperatively to utilize the collective bargaining process as a method of problem-solving.

3. Both management and union must have a healthy regard for the rights and responsibilities of the other party to the contract. Management needs to regard collective bargaining as a feasible "method of management." It must accord wholehearted, rather than grudging, acceptance to the rights of the union and workers under the agreement. By the same token the union needs to recognize the rights of management under the contract. There must be a thorough acceptance of the necessity for making a profit and for retaining an effective right to act in the interests of consistent and efficient administration.

4. Both management and the union must have a basic will to agree and to make collective bargaining work. Collective bargaining is, of course, a conflict process. In a constructive relationship, however, there will be unceasing effort to reach workable compromises of conflicting basic interests. In other words, a healthy relationship involves maximum effort to achieve accommodation. It requires a joint recognition of the requirements for mutual survival.[13] An emphasis on accommodation rather than conflict is a necessity.

5. Finally, and perhaps most important, the maximum effectiveness in collective bargaining cannot be attained without maturity of leadership on both sides of the bargaining table. Selekman has underlined vividly the importance of this requirement. He defines an emotionally mature person as one who, when faced with a difficult and vexing problem, meets the problem rather than hates it.[14]

Support for the foregoing principles can be found in the case studies of "successful" union-management relationships sponsored by the Na-

[13] See E. W. Bakke, *Mutual Survival* (New Haven: Yale Labor and Management Center, 1946). Many of his points have continuing validity today.

[14] See Benjamin M. Selekman, *Labor Relations and Human Relations* (New York: McGraw-Hill Book Co. Inc., 1947), Chapters 7 and 8.

tional Planning Association. These studies were conducted in a variety of industries by responsible scholars in a search for common denominators of constructive labor relations. In its final report on these case studies nine common factors were found in all relationships, as indicated below:[15]

1. Management decides unionism is inevitable and does not attempt to fight it.
2. Management accepts the collective bargaining process and unionism as an institution.
3. The unions fully accept private ownership and operation of the industry. They recognize that the welfare of their members depends on the successful operation of the business.
4. The company stays out of the union's internal affairs. It doesn't try to alienate the workers' allegiance to their unions.
5. The unions are strong, responsible, and democratic.
6. The parties trust and have confidence in each other. They have no serious ideological differences.
7. Neither party has taken a legalistic approach to collective bargaining.
8. Negotiations are "problem centered." More time is spent on day-to-day problems than on defining abstract principles.
9. There is widespread union-management consultation and highly developed information sharing.

The close parallel between the foregoing list of common factors and the writer's own statement of principles of constructive labor relations will be readily apparent.[16]

QUALITIES OF A SUCCESSFUL UNION OR MANAGEMENT REPRESENTATIVE

A serious problem of management is the dearth of qualified personnel in the industrial relations field. We are already far removed from the day when the personnel or labor relations function was allocated to a worn-out or incompetent production man for whom management could find no other spot. Most firms today, whether large or small, are suitably impressed with the importance of the personnel and labor relations function to the total welfare of the business. There is a developing awareness of the need for trained and specialized talent.

Similarly, on the union side, there is a constant problem of a shortage of suitable leaders. Increasing centralization in union policy-making, with the attendant decline in the importance of the local union, has accentuated

[15] See Clinton S. Golden and V. D. Parker, eds., *Causes of Industrial Peace under Collective Bargaining* (New York: Harper & Brothers, 1955).

[16] Similar first principles of constructive relationships were developed by Frederick H. Harbison and John R. Coleman in *Goals and Strategy in Collective Bargaining* (New York: Harper & Brothers, 1951).

the leadership problem. Local unions are the logical training ground for the development of union career men. The demand far exceeds the supply. It is not only difficult to recruit competent international representatives, but it is increasingly difficult to develop trained stewards. In nonfactory unionism where the business agent remains the key figure, the problem of securing trained personnel is equally acute.

One reason for the shortage in suitable personnel on both the management and the union side is the increasingly exacting combination of personality and experience essential to success because of the complex, technical nature of contemporary collective bargaining. More than a good physical constitution, simple honesty, and native intelligence are needed by today's labor or management leader. The principal specifications for successful union and management negotiators and administrators under modern conditions are summarized below.

A good union or management representative must be intelligent, resourceful, and conscientious. He must be emotionally well-balanced, honest, and thoroughly informed on the plant or industry involved. He needs to be sufficiently flexible to be firm in one context and pliable in another. He must have the capacity to demonstrate righteous indignation, although maintaining at all times a sense of humor and a sense of proportion.

Perhaps most important, a good management or union representative must be able to see a problem as a whole. He must be fully aware of the compulsions under which the other person may be operating. He must have the capacity to distinguish between basically important and trivial issues. He must know when it is wise or necessary to compromise and when it may be fatal to concede.

Effective management and union representatives are at all times mature realists. They must be capable of handling rather than hating difficult or unpleasant situations. This frame of mind may be difficult to achieve in practice. Yet it is essential to the development of constructive union-management relationships.

The picture of the model union or management representative now emerges: he must be a tactician, diplomat, informed expert, and psychologist, all in one. Obviously, few, if any, such paragons are to be found. Yet the essential elements for success are readily discernible.

CONCLUSION

This chapter has been intended to illustrate the diversity in collective bargaining relationships from a number of different viewpoints. The range and differences in subject matter of bargaining were treated briefly. The wide variation in union-management relationships analyzed in terms of the degree of accommodation (or absence of accommodation) has been illustrated. The variety and complexity of structural bargaining arrangements have been explored.

In the second part of the chapter an effort was made to discover and set forth some unifying principles of constructive union-management relations (including leadership requisites) that would cut through the fundamental patterns of diversity.

SELECTED BIBLIOGRAPHY

Allen, Arthur P. and Betty V. H. Schneider, *Industrial Relations in the California Aircraft Industry*. Berkeley: Institute of Industrial Relations, University of California, 1956.

Aller, Curtis, *Labor Relations in the Hawaiian Sugar Industry*. Berkeley: Institute of Industrial Relations, University of California, 1957.

Barkin, Solomon, "Labour Relations in the United States Textile Industry," *International Labour Review*, LXXV (May, 1957), 391–411.

Bertram, Gordon W. and Sherman J. Maisel, *Industrial Relations in the Construction Industry*. Berkeley: Institute of Industrial Relations, University of California, 1955.

Carpenter, Walter H., *Case Studies in Collective Bargaining*. Englewood Cliffs, N. J.: Prentice-Hall, Inc., 1953.

Chalmers, W. E. and others, *Labor-Management Relations in Illini City*, 2 vols. Champaign: Institute of Labor and Industrial Relations, University of Illinois, 1954.

Cox, Archibald, "The Duty to Bargain in Good Faith," *Harvard Law Review*, LXXI (June, 1958), 1401–42.

Davey, Harold W., "Constructive Labor Relations," *Journal of the American Dietetic Association*, XXXIII (June, 1957), 579–82.

Dean, Lois R., "Union Activity and Dual Loyalty," *Industrial and Labor Relations Review*, VII (July, 1954), 526-36.

Derber, Milton, W. Ellison Chalmers, and Ross Stagner, "Uniformities and Differences in Local Union-Management Relationships," *Industrial and Labor Relations Review*, XI (October, 1957), 56-69.

Goldberg, Joseph P., "Constructive Employee Relations in Government," *Labor Law Journal*, VIII (August, 1957), 551–56.

Haber, William and Harold M. Levinson, *Labor Relations and Productivity in the Building Trades*. Ann Arbor: Bureau of Industrial Relations, University of Michigan, 1956.

Herzog, Donald R., "Labor Relations in the Maritime Industry," *Labor Law Journal*, VII (June, 1956), 348–52.

Jensen, Vernon, *Collective Bargaining in the Non-ferrous Metals Industry*. Berkeley: Institute of Industrial Relations, University of California, 1955.

Kaufman, Jacob J., *Collective Bargaining in the Railroad Industry*. New York: King's Crown Press, 1954.

Kennedy, Van Dusen, *Nonfactory Unionism and Labor Relations.* Berkeley: Institute of Industrial Relations, University of California, 1955.

McCaffree, Kenneth M., "Collective Bargaining in Atomic-Energy Construction," *Journal of Political Economy*, LXV (August, 1957), 322–37.

McMurry, Robert N., "War and Peace in Labor Relations," *Harvard Business Review*, XXXIII (November-December, 1955), 48–60.

Pierson, Frank C., *Collective Bargaining Systems.* Washington: American Council on Public Affairs, 1942.

Purcell, Theodore, *The Worker Speaks His Mind on Company and Union.* Cambridge: Harvard University Press, 1953.

Rosen, Hjalmar and R. A. H. Rosen, "The Union Business Agent Looks at Collective Bargaining," *Personnel*, XXXIII (May, 1957), 539–45.

Schlickman, Eugene F., "Labor Relations in the Foundry Industry," *Labor Law Journal*, VIII (July, 1957), 482–87.

Schneider, Betty V. and Abraham Siegel, *Industrial Relations in the Pacific Coast Longshore Industry*. Berkeley: Institute of Industrial Relations, University of California, 1956.

Scheuch, Richard, "Labor Policies in Residential Construction," *Industrial and Labor Relations Review*, VI (April, 1953), 378–82.

Selekman, Benjamin M., "Varieties of Labor Relations," *Harvard Business Review*, XXVII (March, 1949), 175–99.

Seligson, Harry, "Union-Management Relations," *Labor Law Journal*, VII (July, 1956), 403–13.

Strauss, George, "Business Agents in the Building Trades: A Case Study in a Community," *Industrial and Labor Relations Review*, X (January, 1957), 237–51.

Thompson, Kenneth M., "Human Relations in Collective Bargaining," *Harvard Business Review*, XXXI (March-April, 1953), 116–26.

Weisenfeld, Allan and Monroe Berkowitz, "A New Look in Collective Bargaining," *Labor Law Journal*, VI (August, 1955), 561–66.

"White-Collar Unionism" (symposium), *Journal of Business*, XXVII (October, 1954), 257–311.

The simple dichotomy between management + rank-and-file assumed in Taft-Hartley is not realistic

3

Collective bargaining and public policy

Principle concern of chapter is the examination of those provisions of the act that restrict the discretion of management and unions in collective bargaining relationships

Collective bargaining today takes place within a broad and comprehensive framework of governmental control. At many points in their relationships, unions and companies find their private discretion circumscribed, limited, and conditioned by public policy. Although the focus throughout this book is on collective bargaining at the level of the individual firm, no realistic appreciation of contemporary bargaining issues can be achieved unless some account is taken at the start of the pervasive impact of labor relations laws.

This chapter is concerned with the labor relations policy of the federal government as expressed in the Labor Management Relations Act of 1947, generally referred to as the Taft-Hartley Act. Such an emphasis should not cause the student to lose sight of the many other federal and state laws and administrative agencies whose impact upon collective bargaining policies is considerable.

Collective bargaining on the wage issue in many firms in such industries as textiles, hotel and restaurant, retail outlets, and the like is directly affected by the applicability of the $1 per hour minimum wage under the federal Wage and Hour law. Negotiation on any form of supplemental unemployment benefit plan must take account of whether payments from an SUB fund are regarded as wages within the meaning of the state's unemployment compensation law. Collective bargaining in nineteen states is conditioned and limited by so-called right to work laws. Many negotiated pension plans provide for monthly retirement benefits directly related to the amounts received by the retired employee from federal old age insurance.

Many more examples could be cited to illustrate the complex network of federal and state policies that have a direct or indirect impact upon collective bargaining policies and procedures. The focus of this chapter, however, is limited to federal public policy directly concerned with organized relationships between unions and employers.[1]

THE ROLE OF PUBLIC POLICY

In broad terms public policy toward collective bargaining can be one of suppression, toleration, encouragement, or regulation. Views as to what is the appropriate role of national labor policy depend necessarily on the assumptions made about the desirability of collective bargaining as a method of fixing the terms and conditions of employment. Strong supporters of unionism and collective bargaining will favor a public policy of encouragement with a minimum of government regulation. Opponents of unionism and collective bargaining will incline toward public policies ranging from regulation to outright suppression.

The criterion for evaluating public policy employed here will be whether the operational effect of law has been to strengthen or weaken collective bargaining institutions. This criterion derives from the expressed conviction that in a political democracy and a private enterprise economy, collective bargaining is the most equitable and appropriate method of determining the terms and conditions of employment for nonsupervisory wage earners.

Although the main test applied to federal and state policy will be the strengthening or weakening effect on collective bargaining, it should also be emphasized that public policy toward collective bargaining must necessarily be governed by the requirements of maintaining industrial peace. Ideally, in terms of the assumptions of this analysis, governmental policy should aim at maximizing the values of private collective bargaining while at the same time insuring minimum recourse to economic

[1] For a comprehensive and thoroughly documented survey of state labor legislation over the past twenty years, see Harold A. Katz, "Two Decades of State Labor Legislation: 1937–1957," *Labor Law Journal*, VIII (November, 1957), 747–58, 818. For comparison, see Katz' earlier article written with Harry A. Millis, "A Decade of State Labor Legislation: 1937–1947," *University of Chicago Law Review*, XV (1948), 282-310. Additional references to pertinent literature on the state field will be found in the bibliography at the end of the chapter.

force by employers or unions. Industrial peace as an objective of public policy becomes more important as the economy becomes more complex and more highly unionized.

Any labor relations policy of the federal government is only a stage in a continuous process of developmental change in governmental attitudes toward unions and collective bargaining. In considering labor relations, however, little can be gained by looking backward. The problems are too dynamic in nature. The pattern of public policy toward labor relations will require evolutionary change in conformity with changing circumstances in an economy that is in a state of perpetual flux. The orientation of public policy in labor relations should be forward rather than backward.

It is difficult to be confident about the future shape of national labor policy. In the event of total war the policies and procedures of collective bargaining will be subordinated to the emergency requirements of the public interest. The pattern of regulatory controls seems certain to be more complete than under the comparative voluntarism that prevailed during World War II and under the National Wage Stabilization Board during the Korean War. However, the experience gained in 1942–1945 and 1950–1952 should be relied upon in determining appropriate and feasible policies if another war should develop.

We now have more than eleven years of experience under Taft-Hartley to appraise and analyze. Neither the dire predictions of its opponents or the extravagant claims of its supporters have been borne out in experience. The Act certainly has not proved to be a "slave labor law," the principal epithet applied by its detractors. Nor has the Act eliminated many of the alleged abuses it was designed to correct. However, on one major conclusion it would be possible to secure complete agreement—the Taft-Hartley Act in its present form and as currently interpreted and administered is not the "last word" on federal labor relations policy.[2] We are still a long way from striking a satisfactory balance between the requirements of public policy and the needs of private parties in the labor relations field. Taft-Hartley continues to represent the high-water mark in the tide of increasing governmental regulation of the procedures and policies of collective bargaining. At this writing, partially as a result of

[2] No law in modern times has produced such a torrent of commentary as the Taft-Hartley Act. The reader who wishes to get the flavor of the debate might profit by reading the following: on the "liberal" side, consult Wayne L. Morse, *Perversion of the Taft-Hartley Act by the Eisenhower National Labor Relations Board*, Senate Speech, March 23, 1956 (Washington: U.S. Government Printing Office, 1956) and Mozart G. Ratner, "Policy-making by the New 'quasi-judicial' NLRB," *University of Chicago Law Review*, XXIII (Autumn, 1955), 12–35; on the "conservative" side, Sylvester Petro, *The Labor Policy of the Free Society* (New York: The Ronald Press Company, 1957) and Roscoe Pound, *Legal Immunities of Labor Unions* (Washington: American Enterprise Association, 1957).

disclosures by the McClellan Committee, there appears to be mounting pressure for still greater public regulation of private discretion. At the same time, the strength of a united labor movement that is finally taking vigorous action to put its own house in order may well combat the current pressure for more governmental controls. It is not yet certain whether the tide of regulatory policy will advance or recede.

Understanding of the significance of the Taft-Hartley Act and its operational effect requires placing the law in historical perspective.[3] We can then proceed to an analysis of the specific impact of the Act on collective bargaining policies and procedures.

PRELUDE TO TAFT-HARTLEY

As World War II drew to a close, an insistent chorus of professional opinion urged a prompt return to free collective bargaining. Many management representatives, trade union leaders, and top officials of the National War Labor Board expressed the hope that the government would be able to get out of industrial relations and stay out.

Some dubious motives may have been at work in producing this remarkable accord on the virtues of collective bargaining. Some companies and unions undoubtedly favored removing government from the bargaining table so that they could attack one another with no holds barred. Some strong unions, long restrained by wartime regulations, were anxious to capitalize at once on their tremendously increased economic power. A few "unreconstructed" employers looked upon a return to private bargaining as a basis for decimating the strength of unions. The strike statistics for 1946 in part reflect the efforts of these two groups.

But the sentiment for a return to private collective bargaining was not always dictated by selfish motives or power drives. The genuine values of private collective bargaining were appreciated by many employers and labor leaders as well as government representatives.

These groups gained much in understanding from their wartime experience with extensive public control of industrial relations. They were not hopeful about the prospects for legislating industrial peace. They

[3] Space does not permit an extensive excursion into the past here. As in so many other aspects of labor relations, however, a thorough knowledge of the past is invaluable for understanding current policies and problems. The best analysis of public policy for the period prior to 1932 is that of Edwin E. Witte, *The Government in Labor Disputes* (New York: McGraw-Hill Book Co., Inc., 1932). See also Calvert Magruder, "A Half Century of Legal Influence upon the Development of Collective Bargaining," *Harvard Law Review* L (1937), 1071–1117. A thorough account of the origins of the Wagner Act will be found in Irving Bernstein, *The New Deal Collective Bargaining Policy* (Berkeley: University of California Press, 1950). The definitive history and analysis of the Wagner Act period, 1935-1947, will be found in Harry A. Millis and Emily Clark Brown, *From the Wagner Act to Taft-Hartley* (Chicago: The University of Chicago Press, 1950).

realized that responsible relationships between labor and management are the product of extensive experience in dealing with one another.

When both management and labor are aware that the real locus of power lies outside their relationship, it is difficult to develop constructive private arrangements. Both parties are under a constant pressure to shape their tactics and policies with a view to influencing an outside party. Neither is in a position in which he must face up to the necessity for establishing a satisfactory, enduring relationship with the other party.

THE LEGACY FROM THE NWLB

The National War Labor Board during its four years of operation attempted to strengthen collective bargaining. In so far as possible, the NWLB attempted to compensate for the fact of its own existence. It frequently returned cases to the parties for additional negotiation on unresolved issues. It shunned the job of writing contracts. When forced to do so, it largely avoided innovation.

However, the NWLB could not avoid the consequences of its own position as the wartime agency for the final settlement of all labor disputes affecting the war effort. It made little difference that board members ardently preached the virtues of private negotiation. Both labor and management remained aware that an unsettled dispute would wind up eventually in the lap of the board. They shaped their strategies and policies accordingly.

Every wartime contract was negotiated or renegotiated with a steady eye on War Labor Board policy. The parties were not as interested in developing a good working relationship with one another as they were in winning their cases before the board. Such attitudes were not conducive to effective private relationships in the postwar period.

As a result of the wisdom and restraint generally manifested by the War Labor Board in its policy-making decisions, the contracts actually written by the board in wartime were frequently better contracts than those which might have been worked out by the parties without outside intervention. However, a poorly drawn, inadequate contract, privately negotiated, may prove to be a more effective instrument for actual contract administration than an agreement drafted in whole or in part by a third party. Management and unions made rapid strides toward advanced collective bargaining (as far as subject matter is concerned) under War Labor Board direction or influence. But they made less headway in the important business of learning to deal responsibly with one another.

Under NWLB influence unions and management often came to the realization for the first time of the desirability of providing adequate arbitration machinery for the final settlement of disputes arising over the application or interpretation of their contract. Many came to appreciate the effective use of rate ranges in wage administration. Some unions during the war lost much of their traditional fear of job evaluation and wage incentive systems. Such matters as paid vacations, paid holidays not worked, sick leave, and night shift differentials received a considerable impetus under wartime decisions of the National War Labor Board.

In short, recent agreements reflect a considerable legacy from the board's wartime policies. Agreements today are better agreements. They are more complete and adequate instruments for industrial relations. Unfortunately, however, the maturity of the parties does not always measure up to the contents of their contracts. Responsibility and mutual confidence do not develop out of contract clauses. They are a product of experience in living together.

APPRAISING THE 1946 STRIKE RECORD

In assessing the industrial disputes record of 1946, it is important to remember that collective bargaining was in its infancy in most of our key industries when the war came upon us. At the time of Pearl Harbor management and unions in many newly organized industries were still in the fighting stage of their relationship. The war drove them into a shotgun marriage. Frictions, resentments, and misunderstandings multiplied frequently, concealed by the emergency compulsion for uninterrupted production. After V-J Day the lid blew off.

The year 1946 was not acceptable proof that private collective bargaining had failed. It was good evidence that collective bargaining in many instances had not yet been tried, and in others was a long way from perfection. This was especially true in the newly unionized, critical mass production industries such as steel, automobile, and electrical appliance manufacturing.

1946 was abnormal in several respects. The wave of major strikes was, in part at least, the explosive result of too rapid a change of fundamental relationships in many key industries. Too much readjustment had been compressed into too short a time. The necessity for a wartime policy of self-restraint helped to conceal the fact that these adjustments had not been made.

THE NEW LABOR POLICY

Drastic reformulation of national labor policy in 1947 had been foreshadowed by the growth of restrictive labor relations legislation at the state level, particularly in 1943. Pressure for revised public policy at both federal and state levels reached a peak in 1947. In that year ten states passed legislation outlawing strikes and lockouts and requiring compulsory mediation followed by compulsory arbitration in public utility industries. A number of states passed union democracy laws. Union security clauses in collective agreements were banned in many states.

When Congress reformulated the national labor policy in 1947, it was disposed to ignore the exceptional aspects of the strike record of 1946, noted above. Influenced by the staggering total of manhours lost, Congress failed to recall that even in this, the biggest strike year in our history, the total time lost by strikes was only 1.43 per cent of manhours worked. Some 75,000 collective labor agreements were in force in 1946. The overwhelming majority of these agreements were negotiated or renegotiated peacefully without recourse to economic force. Yet the new national labor policy was geared to a fractious and troublesome minority.

The strike record of 1946 evoked a decision that collective bargaining as an institutional process (and unions specifically) must be regulated extensively in the public interest. The Labor Management Relations Act of 1947 was the result.

In essence, the Taft-Hartley Act represented a conviction that free collective bargaining had failed. It was the end product of a short-run historical judgment that collective bargaining could not be permitted to operate without substantial restriction. The Act embodies a conviction that responsible private conduct can be insured by statutory control. It puts the federal government squarely in the middle of the collective bargaining table by directly regulating the scope, procedure, and contents of collective bargaining as well as the parties to the bargaining process.

This is an age in which political power rather than economic strength frequently plays a decisive role in shaping the course of union-management relationships. Both management and labor in recent years have developed a habit of turning to the government for help against one another. As might have been anticipated, the party seeking regulation for the other has found himself in turn subjected to increasing regulation.

THE PARADOX OF TAFT-HARTLEY

After eleven years of experience under one of the most controversial laws in our history, it is mildly astonishing to discover how little sound empirical research has been done on the operational impact of the Taft-Hartley Act on collective bargaining relationships. The legal periodicals and economic journals have been continuously filled with articles on NLRB policies and decisions under the Act, but only a small part of academic writing has dealt with the operational impact of the law.[4]

[4] A challenge to scholars to undertake significant empirical work on the operational effect of Taft-Hartley was issued by Bernard Samoff, "Research on National Labor Relations Board Decisions," *Industrial and Labor Relations Review*, X (October, 1956), 108–117; reprinted under the title, "Research on the Results and

No experienced observer of the labor relations scene, however, can fail to be impressed by an outstanding apparent paradox in experience under the Act. We have witnessed in recent years two divergent trends. On the one hand, there has been a trend toward increasingly mature and stable bargaining relationships in industries formerly characterized by sharp conflict, such as automobiles and steel.[5] At the same time, there has been a trend toward increased employer resistance to new unionization in the South, particularly in textiles, combined with a stiffening of employer attitudes toward unionism in the shape of a new bargaining strategy—"Boulwareism."[6] It would be rash to attribute all the gains from the former trend or all the antagonisms generated by the second trend to the Act as such. All that can be said from a coldly objective viewpoint is that these trends have paralleled one another during the eleven years that the Act has been in effect. In particular cases it is possible to lay the development at the doors of the NLRB. The temptation to generalize further must be resisted, pending the conduct of more empirical studies.

Within the limits of the need for caution just expressed, it is possible to make some general observations about the impact of the Act. There is little doubt, for example, that the liberalized free speech privilege of employers under the Act has been directly instrumental in blunting the effectiveness of new organization drives in the southern textile industry. The freedom to make antiunion speeches so long as no direct threat or promise of benefit is involved has also been helpful to many small and medium-sized employers in small cities in successfully resisting organization.

In certain respects the Act has been of direct benefit to employers in more successful resistance to union economic pressure in particular bargaining situations. The ineligibility of economic strikers to vote in representation elections has strengthened the employer's hand considerably in conventional economic disputes where the right to strike has been invoked. The general prohibition against use of secondary

Impact of NLRB Decisions," *Labor Law Journal*, VIII (April, 1957), pp. 235–38, 283–88. In a partial response to Samoff's challenge, the writer undertook an essay in empiricism based primarily on extensive correspondence with union, management, and public representatives. For the results of this survey, see Harold W. Davey, "The Operational Impact of the Taft-Hartley Act upon Collective Bargaining Relationships," Chapter IX in Harold W. Davey, Howard S. Kaltenborn, and Stanley H. Ruttenberg, Eds., *New Dimensions in Collective Bargaining*, Industrial Relations Research Association Publication No. 21 (New York: Harper & Brothers, 1959.)

[5] The major automobile companies and the UAW deadlocked on negotiations for several months in 1958, operating without a contract. The basic relationship, however, did not seriously deteriorate.

[6] The reader is referred back to the previous brief discussion of "Boulwareism" in Chapter 2.

economic pressures by unions has also strengthened the employer in tests of economic strength.

Some of the Act's more stringent and sweeping provisions undoubtedly have had an operational impact. For example, the ban on jurisdictional strikes and the setting up of the NLRB as a court of compulsory arbitration for final and binding determination of such disputes were undoubtedly of decisive importance in causing the labor movement to develop effective internal machinery for settling such disputes peaceably. Also, the severe penalties imposed on any striking federal government employee (mandatory discharge and no re-employment for three years) have had a profound effect on the nature and functioning of unions in government employment.

On many of the problem areas treated by Taft-Hartley, however, it is hazardous to generalize in the absence of empirical data. For example, one of the most clear-cut trends is the declining percentage of representation elections won by unions in Taft-Hartley years as compared with Wagner Act years. In Wagner Act days, unions were accustomed to winning as many as 80 per cent of the elections. Under Taft-Hartley this percentage has steadily declined to an all-time low of 61 per cent won by unions in elections held in fiscal 1956.[7] Union leaders tend to blame the Act, citing the employer's freedom to say almost anything he wants prior to twenty-four hours before the election and certain revised election rules of the board, notably the new run-off rule. The latter now provides for a run-off between the two top choices, one of which may be no union. Formerly, where a majority of votes cast were for some union, the run-off was between the unions involved, since it was felt a majority had signified their desire for union representation. Under the revised rules the odds shift to favor a no-union selection.

On the other hand, a plausible explanation of the reduced percentage of elections won by unions in recent years is that organizational activity now takes place at the "frontier" where the going for unionism is inherently tougher than it was during the late '30's and the war years, when enthusiasm for unions was at its peak. Related to this would be the argument that economic conditions have been so generally favorable in recent years that many workers, rightly or wrongly, feel that they do not need a union in order to improve their economic position. The fact is that we just do not know what the true explanation is for this declining percentage of elections won by unions.

To take another illustration, the statistical picture on industrial peace has been most encouraging in virtually all the Taft-Hartley years in comparison to the Wagner Act years. Does this mean that the Taft-Hartley Act has "succeeded" in promoting industrial peace? One answer would

[7] The percentage won in fiscal 1957 was even lower.

be that the exemplary strike record in recent years is not due to the Act at all, but rather is due to increasing maturity and stability in union-management relationships formerly characterized by conflict. Another explanation, equally logical, is that the Act must be given credit for the virtual elimination of certain types of strikes (e.g., by Government employees, jurisdictional strikes, secondary pressures, etc.), and that these are the principal reasons for the improved strike record.

On these and many other questions regarding the operational impact of the Act, we can find an abundance of deductive generalizations and a paucity of empirical fact. In the balance of this chapter we shall concentrate attention on those provisions of the Act that, directly or indirectly, intentionally or unintentionally, have had a specific impact on collective bargaining policies and procedures. For convenience and for greater sharpness of focus, the discussion has been divided into: (1) provisions of the Act directly or indirectly affecting the structure and subject matter of collective bargaining; (2) provisions affecting collective bargaining procedures; and (3) ways in which the Act may be said to have strengthened or weakened collective bargaining.

PUBLIC POLICY AND THE SCOPE OF COLLECTIVE BARGAINING

In the minds of its sponsors the original National Labor Relations Act was to be concerned solely with setting the stage for collective bargaining. The 1935 law was not intended to do more than remove certain barriers to the right to organize and the right to bargain collectively, thus paving the way for employers and unions to negotiate concerning wages, rates of pay, hours of work, and other conditions of employment.

What they bargained about and what they agreed or disagreed on were to be the parties' own business. However, in the course of handling allegations of employer refusal to bargain collectively in violation of Section 8(5) of the original act, the NLRB soon found itself enmeshed in the difficult problems of determining what was bargainable and what was not. By the time the Taft-Hartley Act was under consideration, ample precedent had developed for carrying the function of the NLRB beyond the threshold of bargaining and into the conference room itself. We shall address ourselves first to the ways in which the Taft-Hartley Act directly or indirectly affects the subject matter of bargaining.

TAFT-HARTLEY AND UNION SECURITY

Clearly, the most important substantive restriction on the discretion of the parties is the ban on closed shop contracts between unions and firms whose operations affect interstate commerce, thus falling within the jurisdiction of the board. Of vital related importance is Section 14(b) of the Act, which gives priority to state legislation that may be even "tougher" on the subject of union security than the federal Act. Since 1951 the Taft-Hartley Act has contained no limitation on the negotiation of union security clauses short of closed shop agreements. However, in nineteen states with so-called right-to-work laws banning all forms of union security clauses, the state law on the subject prevails over the federal, an express exception to the normal rule of federal supremacy in case of a conflict of laws.

The stated objective of the original Taft-Hartley strictures on union security was the curbing of so-called union monopoly power and the protection of the individual worker in his right to refrain from self-organization. The thinking behind these restrictions was best indicated by the original requirement that unions seeking a union shop or maintenance of membership type of security clause could not do so without having first petitioned for and then won an "authorization" election conducted by the NLRB. As an added hurdle the framers of the Act required that such authorization to negotiate union security clauses must be given by a majority of workers eligible to vote in such elections, not a majority of those voting, as is customary in most democratic election procedures.

EXPERIENCE WITH UNION SHOP AUTHORIZATION ELECTIONS

Supporters of the union shop authorization election requirement felt that the results of such elections would confirm their belief that the union security issue was one of interest to union leaders only and that there was in fact a sharp conflict of opinion between leadership and rank-and-file on this matter. Seldom has legislative opinion been proven wrong in such convincing fashion. Between 1947 and October, 1951, when Congress adopted the Taft-Humphrey amendment repealing the union shop authorization election requirement, the unions won over ninety per cent of such elections, usually by overwhelming majorities. The experience conclusively demonstrated that the requirement was unnecessary, time-consuming, and expensive. Congress wisely chose to abandon it.

The net result of four years' experience with the union shop authorization elections was to strengthen rather than weaken unions in most cases. Although such elections were regarded initially by union leaders as an irritating procedural encumbrance, they were rapidly turned to the advantage of organized labor as a bargaining weapon. They furnished an ideal opportunity to demonstrate objectively to employers that the unions enjoyed worker support. An employer who had been resisting a demand for a union shop clause found the logic of his position completely undermined when presented with the results of a union shop authorization election indicating that the preponderant majority of his employees wished the union to negotiate just such a requirement.

REGULATION OF UNION ADMISSION AND EXPULSION

The Taft-Hartley ban on closed shop contracts continues in force and, as noted, gives priority to the laws of nineteen states that prohibit any form of union security clause in collective bargaining agreements. Another provision of the Act indirectly affects the admission and expulsion policies of unions, thus qualifying the value of valid union shop or maintenance-of-membership agreements. The Act bars the employer from discriminating against an employee for nonmembership in a union if the employer has "reasonable grounds" for believing that such membership was not available to the employee on the same terms and conditions generally applicable to other members, or if he has reasonable grounds for believing that the union denied or terminated membership for reasons other than the failure of the employee to tender the periodic dues and initiation fees uniformly required as a condition of acquiring or retaining membership. It is also an unfair practice for a union under the Act to attempt to cause an employer to violate the foregoing restrictions or for a union to require an initiation fee that the NLRB finds to be "excessive or discriminatory under all the circumstances."

The foregoing combination of restrictions and prohibitions constitutes substantial legislative interference with private discretion, the wisdom of which is certainly open to question. The issues of union security and internal union democracy continue to be serious ones on the American scene, and both partisans and allegedly impartial experts differ vigorously on appropriate solutions. The literature on this subject is endless, repetitious, and frequently intemperate. The following contribution will be as brief and meaningful as possible.

UNION SECURITY ISSUE INVOLVES A POWER STRUGGLE

First, it is important to recognize that the controversy over the need for, and propriety of, legislative restriction on union security clauses reflects an underlying struggle for power rather than an issue over principle, notwithstanding the fact that the arguments of both sides are usually couched in terms of principle. The blunt fact is that "right to work" legislation is intended to prevent unions from solidifying their position in particular plants and industries. Unions seek an end to such legislation so that they may secure such a position. Most of the solicitude for the rights of the individual worker that dominates the discussion is, realistically, beside the point. No worker has any inalienable right not to join a labor organization if he chooses to accept employment with a firm that, as part of its contract with the union, requires union membership as a condition of employment. Nor does any worker have a constitutional duty or obligation to join a labor organization if he does not wish to.

In short, the much discussed right to work is a qualified right, as are most other "rights" in this dynamic field. The right to strike and the right to lockout are qualified rights. The right to bargain collectively is a qualified right. Employer and union leader exercise of the constitutional right of free speech is a qualified right in a labor relations context.

A union security clause seems to impose one more qualification on an always qualified right to work as applied to any particular job or firm. When union membership is required by contract as a condition of employment, it becomes one more factor associated with employment by a particular firm that a prospective employee must consider and evaluate in determining whether or not to accept employment if offered.

CLOSED SHOP WITH CLOSED UNION: A SPECIAL CASE

The one serious problem that requires public regulation is the rare situation of a closed shop combined with a closed union. No economic or political case can be made for such a combination in a society that stresses individual opportunity and opposes monopoly control. The question is what is the most appropriate method of handling the problem. The answer is not to outlaw closed shop contracts as such. The employer and the union should be free to negotiate closed shop, union shop, or maintenance-of-membership agreements without legislative interference, provided the union in question is an "open" union and does not discriminate against applicants on the basis of race, creed, color, or sex, and provided the union has adequate safeguards of the rights of members to protect against arbitrary suspension or expulsion. These are important qualifications.

The policy answer to the need for effective safeguards is not an easy one. It is, however, easy to state a model situation and then to analyze the most appropriate ways of insuring it. One model situation is where employer and union are free to require (or not to require) union membership as a condition of employment, depending on the needs and bargaining strength of the parties. The union in question is an open union that has adequate judicial procedures for internal discipline cases. Meeting the test of adequacy requires an independent appellate step available to a union member who feels his suspension or expulsion has been unjust, arbitrary, or discriminatory.

SUGGESTED POLICY SOLUTIONS

Assuming the model to be desirable, is legislation necessary to insure it? Some legislation may be essential, although nonlegislative solutions are preferable. Ideally, the best cure for the closed shop-closed union problem is the maintenance of full employment. Pressure for closing the membership books generally derives from scarcity of job opportunities for union members, although the economic motive of raising the price by restricting the supply cannot be ignored. Similarly, full employment is a logical answer to the problem of discrimination on racial, religious, or political grounds. Still speaking ideally, the best safeguard of union internal democracy is an alert and informed rank-and-file. It must be recognized, however, that recent studies of internal unionism have indicated a serious problem of membership "apathy," even in some of the most democratic unions. It is perhaps also true that those unions whose members are most in need of internal procedural safeguards are the ones least likely to adopt them on a voluntary basis.

From the standpoint of desirable public policy several approaches may be suggested. One that is already followed by a number of courts is to declare contracts for the closed shop held by closed unions to be judicially unenforceable. The applicant for employment who is turned down because of a closed union or one with discriminatory admission policies could thus go to court to enforce observance of his "right to work." He would not have a right to join the union holding bargaining privileges, but he would have a method of effectively challenging the union's effort to enforce an artificially scarce labor supply or to discriminate among applicants.

It must be admitted, however, that judicial remedies are not the best medium for enforcement of individual worker rights because of the time and expense involved in litigation. A more forthright approach might be the adoption of a fair union democracy law, one that protects against arbitrary or discriminatory union admission or expulsion policies but does not unwarrantedly interfere with union internal affairs.

INADEQUACY OF TAFT-HARTLEY APPROACH

The Taft-Hartley approach to the problem is oblique and generally unsatisfactory. The Act operates only to protect the worker against the employment consequences of arbitrary restrictions on admission or undemocratic expulsions. As Benjamin Aaron and Michael Komaroff have pointed out,[8] the Act overlooks or disregards the fact that arbitrary denial of admission to membership can still work to the serious detriment of employees even if it does not cost them their jobs. Also, arbitrary expulsion from a union, even if it does not result in discharge from employment of the expelled member, can undermine the democratic structure of the union.

These provisions of the Act seriously weaken the union's legitimate interest in disciplining members for infractions other than nonpayment of dues or initiation fees. The union is apparently compelled to accept anyone to membership if he offers to pay the initiation fees and dues, but although he may be expelled from the union in terms of the union's own rules, he cannot be discharged by the employer except when the reason for lack of good standing is nonpayment of dues.

Furthermore, as Aaron and Komaroff have pointed out, the Act does not touch unions that are parties to contracts without union security clauses. The Act does contain detailed filing requirements for all labor organizations that wish to utilize the services of the NLRB. Among the many matters about which information must be furnished are union admission qualifications and the like. The only penalty for failure to file such information, however, is denial of NLRB services to noncomplying unions. This is often a serious practical handicap to unions that are experiencing difficulty in obtaining employer recognition or in combatting employer unfair labor practices, but it barely scratches the surface of the problem of undemocratic union admission or exclusion policies. Many unions with unwholesome practices in this regard do not utilize the NLRB at all, or are outside of its jurisdiction. The most flagrant examples of racial discrimination, for example, are practiced by some railroad unions, which are outside the jurisdiction of the Taft-Hartley Act.

PROPOSED UNION DEMOCRACY LAW

A more direct approach to the union democracy problem is required. One possibility is to specify through legislation a minimal code of "fair practices" for unions as to admission policies (as now required in the New York State Fair Employment Practices Act), and also a minimum code of procedural rights on union discipline cases including the right to appeal to arbitration an allegedly unfair expulsion. Proof of adherence to such a legislative code would be a requirement for utilizing the services of the NLRB in representation cases and unfair labor practice cases.

[8] See Benjamin Aaron and Michael Komaroff, "Statutory Regulation of Internal Union Affairs," *Illinois Law Review*, XLIV (September, 1949), 425–66.

The precise content of such a proposed legislative bill of rights for union members or applicants for admission to union membership will not be spelled out here. The general principles involved are clear and well-understood. No applicant for employment where union membership is required should be denied admission to the union except for failure to meet legitimate training qualifications or unwillingness to assume the financial responsibilities of union membership. Similarly, every union member should enjoy the same basic rights within the union that are available to him as a citizen in a free society, i.e., the right to free elections, the right of free speech and free press, the right to a fair hearing when charges are brought against him, and so on. The union member has a right to protection against arbitrary or discriminatory expulsion practices, whatever the effect on his employment in a particular firm.

Historically, unions have answered that there is no problem of union democracy and that legislation should not interfere with the internal affairs of private, voluntary associations. It may well be true that opponents of unionism have exaggerated the need for legislative regulation of the disciplinary powers of unions. It must be constantly borne in mind, however, that unions in contemporary society are more than purely private, fraternal groups. They are in a realistic sense quasi-public institutions, particularly in those situations where they control the supply of particular types of labor in local or regional labor markets. No union whose procedures are genuinely democratic would have anything to fear from a reasonably drawn fair practices statute. At least two unions in recent years, the UAW and the Upholsterers, have inaugurated independent appellate channels available to members who feel they have been unjustly expelled. The steps taken by these unions point the way to desirable public policy in this area.

SUMMARY ON UNION SECURITY ISSUE

The pros and cons of union security clauses from the standpoint of effective contract administration will be dealt with in Chapter 9. We can conclude our discussion here by emphasizing again that the outright ban on closed shop contracts in Taft-Hartley and the Act's encouragement of restrictive legislation on union security at the state level constitute a serious intrusion of public policy on the subject matter of collective bargaining. The union security issue should be dealt with at the bargaining table rather than through legislation. Public policy on union security should be designed to eliminate specific evils such as the closed shop-closed union combination. Blanket prohibitions are both unnecessary and unworkable. The outright ban on the closed shop has not prevented its continuance in many instances. Employers and unions satisfied with such an arrangement have continued it under one disguise or another in defiance of the law. In "right to work" states many contracts provide for the inauguration of union security clauses of one kind or another as soon as state law permits, thus testifying to joint private agreement as to the desirability of such requirements.

At this writing the union security issue continues to be highly controversial. Pressure for federal "right to work" legislation is intense and the drive for expanded state legislation is strong. At the same time approximately three out of four collective agreements now in force provide for some form of union security clause. This fact, especially when viewed in the light of the experience with the union shop authorization election requirements, should give pause to those who continue to argue that only union leaders are interested in this issue. Rank and file union members have consistently been opposed to working alongside a minority of nonunion employees ever since unionism began in this country at the end of the eighteenth century.

BARGAINING UNIT RESTRICTIONS UNDER TAFT-HARTLEY

The Taft-Hartley Act affects the discretion of the parties in determining the structural basis of their bargaining relationships in two ways: (1) the legislative preference for smaller bargaining units expressed in the limitations on the NLRB's discretion; and (2) the legislative exclusion of certain occupational classifications from conventional bargaining units.

When a union seeks a contract from an employer, one of the first issues likely to arise is definition of the group of employees that the union seeks to represent as exclusive bargaining agent. In the great majority of cases there is no dispute on the appropriate unit for purposes of collective bargaining, and only one union is involved. Not infrequently, however, disputes do arise as to what is the most appropriate unit. In such cases one of the NLRB's most important functions under the Act is to decide upon the appropriate unit or area of worker representation. The board's exercise of administrative discretion on this problem is severely restricted under Taft-Hartley, in contrast to the breadth of discretion granted it under the Wagner Act. The exercise of that discretion as conditioned by the limitations in the Act itself has a profound effect on the structure of bargaining relationships.

NLRB policy on bargaining unit matters will be discussed in greater detail in the next chapter. However, it is desirable to note here in general fashion the impact of the Act and of board decisions on this important problem area. The Taft-Hartley Act establishes a preference for craft groups and a subtle bias against large-scale bargaining units by three basic restrictions. In the first place, the Act prohibits the NLRB from deciding that any craft unit is inappropriate on the ground that a different unit had been established by a prior board determination, unless a majority of employees in the proposed craft unit have voted against separate representation. Such a restriction invites craft groups to split themselves off from "P and M" units (units of production and maintenance employees), even when the latter may have been operating effectively for some time.

Secondly, the board's discretion is limited on the matter of giving recognition to partial or incomplete self-organization when the "most appropriate" unit has not yet been fully organized. This puts an all-or-nothing requirement on most new organization campaigns.

Finally, the Act places an indirect obstacle in the way of multi-employer bargaining by making it an unfair labor practice to compel an employer to join an employers' association. This restriction invites a policy of separation on management's side of the bargaining table.

Clearly, the most important issue concerns the status of minority craft groups in relation to inclusive groupings of production and maintenance employees. Taft-Hartley places a premium on a maximum of self-determination by employee groups.

The logic of according great weight to the desires of the employees themselves is incontrovertible. The question is, however, *which employees?* The provisions of Taft-Hartley can be used to put craft unionism back in the driver's seat. The Act's provision that a craft unit may not be declared inappropriate on the ground that a different unit was established in an earlier NLRB determination, unless a majority of employees in the proposed craft unit vote against separate representation, is a constant invitation and encouragement to craft separation and rival unionism.

THE AMERICAN POTASH DOCTRINE

The board's decision in the *American Potash* case [9] lays down some sensible requirements that must be fulfilled before a severance petition will be entertained. For one thing, the separate craft or departmental unit sought must be a true craft or traditional departmental group. The board also continues to insist that the union seeking severance must be "the historical and traditional representative of the employees it seeks" to represent in the particular case. The burden of proof properly rests with the union to establish that it is the traditional representative of the type of employees it seeks to sever.

Perhaps more effective than *American Potash* in dampening any gen-

[9] 107 *NLRB* No. 290 (March, 1954).

eral breakaway of the crafts from established industrial units will be the practical impact of the AFL-CIO merger, which should reduce the problem of raiding and reorganizing the organized. Also, a number of industrial unions are developing internal answers to the dissatisfactions of their skilled members by giving them more effective representation rights in trade union government.

The writer believes that the Taft-Hartley Act should be amended to restore full administrative discretion to the NLRB in determination of appropriate bargaining units. Congress should not favor one pattern of bargaining structure over another. Legislative preference for a particular form of bargaining unit prevents full freedom of choice among employees. It introduces external control over a matter that by its very nature should be determined by the facts of particular cases, not by legislative decree. There is no justification in experience for a legislative presumption favorable to one form of union organization. In some situations a craft unit is clearly most appropriate. In others an industrial or plant unit is most feasible. In some cases multi-employer units are logical; in others they are not. The most realistic approach, therefore, is to vest full discretion in the administrative agency handling representation disputes. A return to the original language of Section 9(b) of the Wagner Act appears to be a sounder approach than to establish even an *implicit* favoritism for a particular form of bargaining unit structure.

The most feasible limitation on NLRB discretion might well be judicial rather than statutory. The NLRB's determinations of bargaining units have never been judicially reviewable, except by the rare possibility of a successful independent suit in equity, or as part of the entire record in an NLRB unfair labor practice proceeding.

The courts have held that the determination of a bargaining unit and other NLRB findings in representation cases are not final orders, as are findings of unfair labor practices. Representation cases are not adversary proceedings.

Such a conclusion, although perhaps good law, ignores the practical impact of NLRB decisions in representation cases. The losing union in a representation case can be seriously injured, without adequate remedy, by an arbitrary NLRB decision. This conclusion gains added force when a strike against an employer who is respecting an NLRB certification becomes an enjoinable unfair labor practice. Perhaps a carefully drawn provision for judicial review here is desirable. Court review should not, however, operate to stay an NLRB certification. If this were allowed collective bargaining rights might be lost in a maze of legalistic delays. The NLRB certification would have to be observed unless later amended or nullified by the courts.

IMPACT OF ACT ON SUPERVISORY AND PROFESSIONAL EMPLOYEES

Another substantial legislative infringement on employer and union discretion in collective bargaining is the way in which the Act affects the status of: (1) supervisory employees; (2) professional employees; and (3) plant guards and watchmen. Its policy toward each of these groups will be briefly considered.

Supervisory workers are excluded from the definition of "employee" in the Act. Practically, this means that any employee held by the board to be a supervisor is excluded from the protection of the Act, and that unions representing such employees are unable to utilize the board's services. Furthermore, such supervisory employees cannot be included in the same bargaining unit with nonsupervisory employees.

Foremen's unions and bargaining units of supervisory employees are not outlawed by the Taft-Hartley Act. But organized foremen are strictly on their own in dealings with employers. The facilities and protection afforded by the NLRB and the Act to other employees are specifically denied to supervisory employees.

It is not appropriate here to argue the legitimacy of foremen's unions. A strong case can be made on their behalf. An equally strong argument can be made that foremen's unions are inconsistent with the position of such employees as management's front-line representatives in dealing with production and maintenance workers.

Foremen's unions grew rapidly in basic manufacturing during the war and in the postwar period. Many foremen were convinced that they were forgotten men in the industrial relations scene. In some industries (notably maritime and printing) foremen have a long history of unionization and effective collective bargaining with management.

The Taft-Hartley Act made no distinction between established bargaining relationships and the newly developing foreman organizations in mass production industries. It thus afforded encouragement to employer groups to smash old as well as new foreman unions. By the same token, it encouraged continued employer neglect of the very problems of lack of a clearly defined status and of inadequate wage differentials which gave impetus to the union drive among foremen.

The principal concern in this chapter on public policy is examination of those provisions of the Act that restrict the discretion of management and unions in collective bargaining relationships. Taft-Hartley treatment of supervisory employees has had an observable impact on such relationships.

By excluding such employees from the protection of the Act, Congress may have promoted the following consequences:

1. If faced by employer opposition or nonrecognition, foremen's unions must either disintegrate or strike for collective bargaining rights. Neither option seems as satisfying from the standpoint of stable and constructive industrial relations as the peaceful alternative of seeking recognition through the representation machinery of the NLRB. This option is no longer available to supervisory employees.

2. Disputes continue to arise as to whether certain classifications of employees are supervisory or nonsupervisory according to the Act.

3. The Act has forced a wholesale reorganization of the policies of a number of unions, such as those in the printing trades, which for years have organized foremen and have bargained effectively with management for them on a mutually satisfactory basis.

4. The Act has encouraged shortsighted employers to continue to neglect the real problems created by the ambiguous status of foremen in many industries.

5. In terms of democratic theory, the policy of the Act may be criticized on the basis that, in effect, it labels a large and vitally important body of workers as second-class citizens. The simple dichotomy between management and rank-and-file assumed in Taft-Hartley is not realistic.

Plant guards and watchmen are neither fish nor fowl according to the Act. Such employees are granted the protection of the Act, but they may not be included in any bargaining unit with production workers. If organized, they must constitute a separate bargaining unit. This decision is based presumably on an assumption that their monitorial or custodial functions preclude the requisite community of interest with other employees. Here again the Act disturbed established bargaining relationships on a seemingly plausible but unrealistic distinction.

The case for separation of professional employees from units of production and maintenance workers rests on more solid ground. The Act's protection extends to unions of professional employees, but the NLRB is prohibited from merging professional workers with other employees in the same bargaining unit without the former's consent.

Most frequently, professional workers who have sought to organize have done so on a craft basis and have considered themselves in a class apart from unions of production workers. The chief problem under the present law is determining the dividing line between professional and nonprofessional employees in particular cases. It is sometimes difficult to decide on which side of the line a given occupational grouping falls.

As a matter of fact, in previous practice the NLRB had rarely merged *bona fide* professional groupings with plant-wide units. Such classifications as engineers, chemists, laboratory technicians, draftsmen, and the like, when organized at all, usually were represented by a different union than the one which had organized the production workers. When unorganized, such professional workers were often antagonistic to the industrial union. The latter was seldom anxious to represent them. The NLRB has determined that the present law protects the right of a small group, such as a cluster of professional workers, to decertify itself out of a broad unit.

We may expect problems to continue to arise with respect to the inclusion or exclusion of various fringe groups of employees from conventional bargaining units. For example, one problem of current interest where unions are seeking to organize clerical and secretarial personnel relates to the point at which to draw the line on employees in a "confidential" relationship with management. The board has recently stated that it will limit the term "confidential employee" only to those employees "who assist and act in a confidential capacity to persons who formulate, determine, and effectuate management policies in the field of labor relations." [10]

Acute bargaining unit issues may also arise in manufacturing industries in cases where the union representing production and maintenance employees also seeks to represent engineers or other professional employee groups.

As presently written and administered, the Taft-Hartley Act may well reflect conventional majority sentiment as to the proper status (or lack of status) of the occupational groupings discussed above. It may be held, however, that the Congress has interfered with private discretion on structural bargaining relationships without adequate basis. There is no compelling reason why employers and unions should be prevented by law from developing structural bargaining set-ups consonant with the needs and requirements of their particular situations.

RESTRICTION OF FREEDOM TO NEGOTIATE ON HEALTH AND WELFARE FUNDS

Another major restriction on the subject matter of collective bargaining in Taft-Hartley is found in the limitations and prohibitions of Section 302(c) on the types of benefit programs and pension plans that may be negotiated.

The Act limits in several ways the conditions under which employers may contribute to benefit programs and pension funds. The fund must be for the sole benefit of the employees and their families and dependents. Payments must be held in trust for paying "for medical or hospital care, pensions on retirement or death of employees, compensation for injuries

[10] See B. F. Goodrich Company, 115 *NLRB* 722.

or illness resulting from occupational activity, or insurance to provide" any of these. The same trust limitation applies to employer contributions into a fund for unemployment benefits, life insurance, disability and sickness insurance, or accident insurance. Another statutory requirement is that the basis for making payments must be incorporated in a written agreement. Funds established must be jointly administered, with equal representation of employees and employers. Neutral persons shall be agreed upon to break any deadlocks that may occur in administration, or the parties must agree on an impartial umpire for deciding disputes that may arise. If they cannot agree on an umpire within a reasonable time, the appropriate federal district court shall appoint such umpire on petition of either group. The written agreement must also provide for an annual audit of the trust fund. The results of the audit must be available for inspection "by interested persons." Finally, payments intended to provide pensions or annuities must be made to a separate trust, and the funds therein may not be used for any other purpose. Of course, the application of the foregoing restrictions was prospective rather than retroactive and did not touch union health, welfare, and pension funds in force prior to the Act.

All negotiated plans since Taft-Hartley have had to conform to the foregoing limitations and prohibitions. In short, Section 302(c) may be said to have established a national pattern for this phase of the subject matter of collective bargaining.

The Taft-Hartley provisions in question were apparently drafted with a particular case in mind, that of the United Mine Workers' welfare fund. A more thoroughgoing survey might have indicated that the subject of pension and welfare plans is so complex and technical that it does not lend itself readily to a uniform pattern established by law. The subject seems peculiarly suited to the flexibility afforded by collective bargaining.

Disclosures by Congressional and state agencies in recent years, particularly the Douglas Report,[11] and that of the New York State Commissioner of Insurance,[12] have revealed some shocking examples of corruption and abuse in administration of health and welfare funds. There is a generally recognized need for legislation beyond the present strictures of Section 302(c) of Taft-Hartley to eliminate the abuses recently disclosed. The necessity for Federal legislation is admitted by top leadership of the AFL-CIO. The latter organization has a strongly worded ethical

[11] *Final Report of the Subcommittee on Welfare and Pension Funds*, Senate Report No. 1734 (Washington: U.S. Government Printing Office, 1956).

[12] Adelbert G. Straub, Jr., *Whose Welfare? A Report on Union and Employer Welfare Plans in New York ... to ... (the) Superintendent of Insurance* (New York: New York Insurance Company, 1954).

practices code concerning health and welfare funds. No legislation was passed by Congress in 1958.[13]

RESTRICTION OF FREEDOM TO NEGOTIATE ON "WORKING RULES"

The so-called "anti-featherbedding" provision of the Taft-Hartley Act makes it a union unfair labor practice "to cause or attempt to cause an employer to pay or deliver or agree to pay or deliver any money or other thing of value in the nature of an exaction, for services which are not performed or not to be performed."

It is common knowledge that some unions, particularly certain craft unions in the construction trades but also some industrial unions, are still addicted to the "lump of labor" fallacy. They are unimpressed by the economist's arguments on the relationship of real income and productivity. They are equally unimpressed when told that in the long-run there is no such thing as technological unemployment. Unions are interested in the short-run, where there *is* technological unemployment. They make every effort to conserve dwindling job opportunities for their membership.

Featherbedding, which may be defined roughly as a practice of forcing the employer to retain more workers than the job warrants, is not outlawed by Taft-Hartley in so many words. Enforcement of such a policy would necessitate an extensive incursion of the administrative authority into the realm of managerial discretion. It is frequently a difficult task to determine objectively how many workers are actually needed on a given operation. Remembering the union movement's sad historical experience with the speed-up and the stretch-out, it is easy to see why many unions have overcompensated for these previous managerial sins once they have assumed power. As part of the strategy of controlling job opportunities, in many instances restrictive working rules and practices have been enforced by unions over employer opposition. The line between a normal work load and featherbedding is an easy one to draw in principle, but not in practical application.

Effective public policy in this area must be framed with caution. There is such an infinite variety of industrial practices and conditions in the field of workng rules that it is perhaps wise to limit public control to cases of extreme abuse. The matter should be left largely to the flexible ministrations of private bargaining. The language of Taft-Hartley seems clearly to imply no intention of disturbing ordinary working rules arrangements, since it speaks of securing money for services not performed when such moneys are *in the nature of an exaction.*

[13] In the last days of the 85th Congress, a mild version of the Douglas bill for regulation of welfare and pension funds was passed.

Realistically construed, the provision has no proper application to ordinary working rules (even when an economist might think boondoggling or excessively full crews were involved), or to such matters as paid vacations, paid holidays not worked, and severance pay (which might be construed erroneously as constituting pay for services not performed).

Section 8(b) 6 outlaws only stand-by featherbedding. The prohibition of such extreme practices has earned widespread public approval. But it is extremely unlikely that the subtler problems of make-work policy can or should be solved by legislation.[14]

NLRB DETERMINATIONS ON THE SUBJECT MATTER OF BARGAINING

We have discussed so far statutory provisions that directly or indirectly condition and limit the discretion of employers and unions in bargaining. Before turning to the Act's provisions that restrict discretion on collective bargaining procedures, it is essential to consider the important role played by the NLRB in determining the scope and nature of collective bargaining by its decisions dealing with what is and is not bargainable under Section 8(d) and by its affirmations that the parties have a *continuing duty* to negotiate during the life of an operating contract.

Archibald Cox and John Dunlop, in a pair of penetrating articles,[15] have warned of the developing gap between the needs and practices of voluntary collective bargaining and the board's interpretation of the legal obligation to bargain. Their basic criticism is that the NLRB is in error when it conceives of collective bargaining as "continual, uncanalized negotiations between management and union concerning any item of 'rates of pay, wages, hours of employment or other conditions of employment' which either party desires to change." Such a conception may be appropriate in the organizational stages of a union-management relationship, but its application to mature bargaining relationships is likely to prove disruptive. Cox and Dunlop are also properly critical of the board's conception of the duty to bargain as one "compelling equal participation and continuous and unlimited negotiation, as one encouraging disregard for established grievance procedures, and as

[14] For an illuminating analysis of the problems in governmental control of featherbedding, consult Benjamin Aaron, "Governmental Restraints on Featherbedding," *Stanford Law Review*, V (July, 1953), 680–721.

[15] Archibald Cox and John T. Dunlop, "Regulation of Collective Bargaining by the National Labor Relations Board," *Harvard Law Review*, LXIII (January, 1950), 389–432; and, by the same authors, "The Duty to Bargain Collectively During the Term of an Existing Agreement," *Harvard Law Review*, LXIII (May, 1950), 1097–1133. See also Cox, "The Duty to Bargain in Good Faith," *Harvard Law Review*, LXXI (June, 1958), 1401–42.

one of sanctioning proposals to revise conditions of employment which the parties earlier agreed to stabilize."

Over the years the board has taken a broad, elastic view of what constitutes the appropriate subject matter of collective bargaining. It has ruled, for example, that a duty to bargain upon request exists on such matters as pension plans, merit increases, subcontracting of work, stock purchase plans, and so on. It has also taken an increasingly expansive view of the employer's duty to furnish the union with various types of wage and other data in negotiation and for purposes of checking on contract administration.[16] It is not easy to quarrel with the board's determination that specific subjects are within the conventional framework of collective bargaining. The fundamental point is whether at this stage of the game the parties should not be left to their own discretion in determining what matters are bargainable and what matters are not.

It is worth recalling here that the framers of the original Wagner Act did not contemplate that the board would do more than set the stage for good faith bargaining. There was no thought that the board would be engaged in the business of determining what is and is not bargainable. Given the precondition of good faith, the employer and the union should be free to negotiate about what they please. If one party does not choose to bargain upon request on a particular demand, the party making the demand would have to decide whether the particular demand was important enough to warrant a test of economic strength. Certainly as to contract administration, the board's concept of continuous duty to bargain runs counter to established principles. Durability and stability in union-management relationships require fixed rules prohibiting the reopening of any part of the contract, except by mutual agreement, during the contract's life. Many contracts now provide rather rigid waiver articles to preserve the basic distinction between contract negotiation and contract administration.

A representative waiver article is that contained in the 1955-1958 John Deere Waterloo Tractor Works-UAW contract, which reads as follows:

The parties acknowledging that during the negotiations which resulted in this Agreement, each had the unlimited right and opportunity to make demands and proposals with respect to any subject or matter not removed by law from the area of collective bargaining, and that the understandings and agreements arrived at by the parties after the exercise of that right and opportunity are set forth in this Agreement. Therefore, the Company and the Union, for the life of this Agreement, each voluntarily and unqualifiedly

[16] See David E. Card, "Information Requests in Collective Bargaining," *Labor Law Journal*, VI (November, 1955), 777–96; Max J. Miller, "Employer's Duty to Furnish Wage and Economic Data to Unions," *Labor Law Journal*, VI (March, 1955), 151–64, 192; and David I. Shair, "A Look at the Books,' *Labor Law Journal*, VI (January, 1955), 53–57, 64.

waives the right, and each agrees that the other shall not be obligated, to bargain collectively with respect to any subject or matter referred to or covered in this Agreement, or with respect to any subject or matter not specifically referred to or covered in this Agreement, even though such subjects or matter may not have been within the knowledge or contemplation of either or both of the parties at the time that they negotiated or signed this Agreement.

The writer suspects that clauses such as the above are a direct outgrowth of the parties' joint fears as to the possibly disruptive effects of the NLRB's continuous bargaining concepts.

TAFT-HARTLEY RESTRICTIONS ON COLLECTIVE BARGAINING PROCEDURES

The framers of the Taft-Hartley Act paid considerable attention to procedures for the renegotiation or termination of existing collective agreements. The Act specifies directly certain procedural requirements that must be adhered to by management and the union.

The party wishing to terminate or make changes in an existing contract must serve notice of such intention on the other party not less than sixty days prior to the expiration date of the present contract. Negotiation as to termination or proposed changes presumably must commence forthwith. If agreement has not been reached by thirty days prior to the expiration date, the law imposes an obligation to notify the Federal Mediation and Conciliation Service of the existence of the unresolved dispute. Resort to economic force during the sixty days prior to the expiration of an agreement is virtually prohibited by making strikers subject to discharge without recourse.

The legislative intent in these procedural requirements is clear. The Congress wished to insure by law sufficient time for full bargaining over proposed contract changes. It is hard to quarrel with such an objective. The point may be urged, however, that the parties themselves are in the best position to work out suitable renegotiation procedures. The present law lays down an inflexible procedural mold into which all contract renegotiations must be cast.

Although there is nothing intrinsically unreasonable in the procedural regulations of the Taft-Hartley Act described above, certain objections may be noted:

1. The law allows no room for negotiation of suitable alternative procedures in particular situations.
2. The penalties for violation of these requirements are more severe upon the workers than upon management.
3. The law may in practice encourage evasion of fundamental responsibilities on a legal technicality. If one party fails to live up to the

precise letter of the law, the other party may contend that he is relieved from any further bargaining obligations. This will increase rather than reduce industrial strife.

Although, ideally, collective bargaining procedures should be left to the private discretion of unions and management, it must be recognized that the public will have some say in such matters. It is important, therefore, to make sure that public policy is consistent with the need for flexibility in private arrangements. Public policy might lay down a general dictum that the party intending to renegotiate or terminate a contract should give reasonable notice to the other party and should provide an adequate opportunity for conferring on its proposals prior to the contract expiration date. This would leave determination as to what is reasonable notice and adequate opportunity to confer in the hands of the National Labor Relations Board in disputed cases. Discretion here is desirable. At present the board is charged with administration of an inflexible rule, which may work serious hardships in particular cases.

The sixty-day compulsory negotiation period makes it virtually impossible for a union to resort to a surprise strike. The average layman might say "fine" to this. If the element of timing a strike is denied to a union, however, the effectiveness of its legal right to resort to the strike weapon is materially reduced. In contrast, the employer has ample time to prepare his defenses. Further, by using his liberalized rights of free speech under the Act, the employer can often use this considerable period of time before contract expiration to undermine employee support for union contract demands by arguments just short of the dividing line between free speech and coercive conduct. Of course, the union is equally free to use this sixty-day period to stir up sentiment for a strike in the event negotiations prove unsuccessful. In short, the sixty-day period is no guarantee of more responsible and mature negotiations. It can be used by either or both of the parties as a "heating-up" period rather than as an aid to constructive and thorough negotiations designed to eliminate the need for economic force.

CONTRACT ENFORCEMENT BY CIVIL SUIT

The Taft-Hartley Act permits damage suits by either party in federal courts to remedy breach of contract and to enforce contract agreements. Few would argue that a damage suit is calculated to improve union-management relationships. The lawyer's concept implied in the damage suit option under Taft-Hartley ignores certain basic distinctions between a collective agreement and an ordinary private-law contract.

A collective agreement is a kind of private statutory law setting forth the terms and conditions of the relationship involving the employer, the workers, and the union for a fixed period of future time. The parties to such an agreement have to live and work together on a daily basis during the contract's lifetime. It is thus not the type of contractual instrument that lends itself appropriately to enforcement via a specific performance type of approach implied in a damage suit remedy.

Most unions and employers have recognized the unsuitability of damage suits as a method of improving labor relations or repairing bad relations. Comparatively few suits have been filed under the permissive provisions of the Act.

Instead of promoting responsible observance of contracts, the Act may well have promoted (unintentionally, to be sure) more disputes over administration of contracts than formerly occurred. Fear of damage suits has caused many unions to insist on the dropping of no-strike, no-lockout pledges from contracts negotiated since 1947. There has been a steady increase in the number of limited liability clauses since 1947 and a corresponding reluctance to negotiate so-called union responsibility clauses after the pattern of the Ford-UAW contract of 1946. Thus a statutory provision designed to encourage greater responsibility in the observance of contract terms may actually have promoted in some instances the opposite result from that intended. Many recent contracts contain an exculpatory clause or a covenant not to sue. Such clauses are valid under the Act.

Furthermore, the strict concepts of agency applied in Taft-Hartley have caused many international unions to assume more complete control over the affairs of member local unions. Paradoxically, then, a law that is in many respects clearly antagonistic to the growing power of strong international unions has had the effect of prompting an acceleration of the trend toward increased authority in the hands of the international at the expense of local union autonomy.

FEDERAL COURTS AND ARBITRATION

One recent development is the resort to federal courts to enforce arbitration clauses in collective agreements. Experts are divided in their opinion as to the merits of such a procedure. Some argue that this development will encourage litigiousness in labor relations; others argue that use of the courts to enforce arbitration agreements will promote more responsible contract administration. Parties with a proper understanding of arbitration will not need to resort to the courts for enforcement of agreements to arbitrate. It is probably desirable, however, to have the enforcement option available in cases where one party or the other refuses to honor a contractual agreement to arbitrate. The one sobering thought here is that if the federal courts are to be a protective refuge for enforcement of arbitration clauses, they may also become a haven for those employers and unions who choose to test the arbitrability of particular questions.[17] If any such trend should develop, the consequences for stable contract administration could be disastrous.

TAFT-HARTLEY AND INDIVIDUAL GRIEVANCES

The Act impinges upon collective bargaining procedures by specifically protecting and affirming the right of individual employees to present grievances to the employer independently of the union which may be their lawful bargaining agent. The articulated premise here is that rank-and-file workers are not adequately represented by union leaders. Individual workers are thus encouraged to by-pass the union in presenting their grievances. In particular situations this could have an adverse effect on contract administration.

A combination of an unsympathetic employer with a strong nonunion minority in a plant could destroy the union's position as a bargaining agent if full advantage were taken of the right to present grievances individually. Under the Act in such cases, the union representative can observe but cannot participate in the proceedings except with the consent of the employee raising the grievance. Of course, the Act precludes individual settlement of grievances on terms inconsistent with the requirements of the contract. But this admonition is worded with sufficient elasticity to permit internal undermining of the union's position as the workers' bargaining representative.

A statutory provision should not be condemned by the device of pushing its logic to an absurd extreme. In most well-established union-management relationships, the union continues to function as the worker's representative in the processing of individual grievances. In an unstable or hostile relationship, however, the Act offers direct encouragement to nonunion workers and employers to undercut the union's authority. It may thus be productive of considerable unrest, friction, and resentment. In extreme situations indiscriminate filing of individual grievances under provision of the Act might in practice nullify the majority rule principle of representation rights. The union will technically remain the exclusive bargaining agent under the contract, but its actual authority over contract administration might well be reduced to a shadow.

Considerations of equity make it essential that the individual worker's right to press his own grievance be safeguarded. If this were not done, an iniquitous policy of favoritism in the processing of grievances might develop under exclusive union control. The union might give prompt

[17] Of fundamental importance here is the Supreme Court's decision in *Textile Workers v. Lincoln Mills*, 77 Sup. Ct. 54 (June, 1957). The probable significance of this decision is discussed in Chapter 7.

and vigorous attention to processing the grievances of union members, while ignoring or giving only lip service to the complaints of nonunion employees.

It is important to insure that the union be required to win its spurs as exclusive bargaining agent by fair-minded processing of all meritorious grievances, regardless of the status of the employee filing them. To say this, however, is not the same as to say that a federal law should by clear implication encourage affirmatively the individual worker to by-pass the union as a processor and adjuster of grievances. This approach cannot lead to stable, constructive relations between management and union. One of the first principles of effective union-management relations is the acceptance of the union by management as an integral operating force in the industrial relations framework. The adoption of this viewpoint is discouraged by a statute that impliedly considers the union as an outside force. Such a law encourages division rather than unity, conflict rather than cooperation.

TAFT-HARTLEY AND THE RIGHT TO STRIKE

The right of the union to strike and the right of the employer to lock out his employees are essential concomitants of the free collective bargaining process as it has developed in the United States. The will to agree in collective bargaining is conditioned by the presence of the ultimate sanction of resort to economic force.

The Wagner Act placed no statutory restrictions on the right to strike. The Taft-Hartley Act specifically outlaws several types of strikes, including the following:

1. Any strike by government employees.
2. Any strike to achieve an objective that is an unlawful objective under the Act, for example, a strike to secure a closed shop contract.
3. Any strike to force an employer to violate the Act (to compel him him to cease bargaining with a duly certified union).
4. Any general or sympathetic strike (outlawed by clear implication by the complete legislative ban on secondary boycotts).
5. Any jurisdictional strike.

These are the principal outright prohibitions of strike action. Severe and specific limitations of the right to strike also are provided in those sections dealing with contract renewal procedures and national emergency disputes.

A powerful limitation on the right to strike is contained in the Act's denial to striking employees the right to vote in an NLRB representation election unless they are eligible for reinstatement under the Act. This means in fact that striking employees are ineligible to vote unless the strike is clearly one against employer unfair labor practices rather tnan an economic strike.

The prohibitions and limitations on the right to strike are sufficiently extensive to make the statutory declamation that "except as provided herein nothing shall be construed as abridging the right to strike, etc." sound rather hollow.

State legislatures have also placed various prohibitions and limitations on the right to strike. At least twelve states require a majority vote by affected employees before any strike can be called. In a number of states cooling-off periods are mandatory before strike action may be taken. Strikes in violation of collective agreements, strikes by public utility employees, strikes in the nature of a secondary boycott, jurisdictional strikes, and many others are prohibited in many states.

It is difficult to appraise accurately the net impact of the federal law and the numerous state restrictions on the right to resort to economic force. The sharp decline in jurisdictional strikes is attributable in part to public policy and in part to the vigorous efforts of the labor movement itself to develop effective internal machinery for resolving this type of dispute. The record on economic strikes in recent years is most encouraging from a statistical point of view. It is problematical as to how much of this decline is due to federal and state legislation, how much to improving stability in union-management relations, and how much to economic conditions. The period since 1947 has been generally one of full employment during which the incidence of strikes is usually higher.

The Taft-Hartley Act itself appears to have had little direct effect on the more powerful unions. The various limitations and required delaying actions, however, undoubtedly have weakened the militancy of some of the more insecure unions. It seems clear that the Act may have encouraged some employers to make concerted efforts to replace striking employees instead of sitting it out, as most employers faced with a strong union have felt constrained to do.

It is probably not unfair to conclude that the net impact of the new national labor policy on the right to strike has been to reduce union propensity to strike. The effectiveness of the union's chief economic weapon has been reduced by the compulsory sixty-day negotiation period on contract renewals. At the same time the employer's ability to resist strike action effectively has been enhanced in several respects, principally through the liberalized free speech provision and the freedom to replace striking employees. The employer might freeze out the union by calling for a representation election with newly hired workers voting in place of the strikers.

The law's sweeping prohibition of all forms of secondary boycott set back the legal status of union resort to economic pressure approximately to where it stood in the 1920's. For all practical purposes, the strike weapon must be confined to disputes in which the disputants stand in the proximate relation of employer and employee. Unless this is true, there is a serious danger of running afoul of one of the numerous restrictions of Taft-Hartley.

STRIKES AND THE PUBLIC INTEREST

Preservation of the right to strike is a major part of the cost of preserving free collective bargaining. The right to bargain collectively, guaranteed in both the Wagner Act and Taft-Hartley, loses most of its significance if the strike weapon is taken away or drastically curtailed.

The American economy has become so complex and interdependent that the right to strike under contemporary conditions should only be exercised in extreme cases as a measure of last resort. But it is important that the function of the strike and its role in reference to the collective bargaining process be thoroughly understood. Strikes cannot be eliminated by legislation in a democratic society. Their use can be minimized by the development of a mature sense of self-restraint in the parties to the bargaining process. Many examples can be cited in which collective bargaining has proceeded without loss of production from strikes over extended periods of time. Paper and pulp, men's and women's clothing,[18] glass, and hosiery come easily to mind. But the right to strike (coupled with the employer's correlative right to lock out) is always present in the minds of the parties at the bargaining table. It is the knowledge of the ultimate sanction of economic force that provides the most powerful incentive to agree.

Under modern conditions, the strike must necessarily be an *in extremis* remedy. Ultimately, it is to be hoped that it will become obsolete as a tactic in union-management relations. But until more progress has been made in the process of institutional accommodation, strikes will continue to occur—legislative prohibitions notwithstanding. The chief function of a strike (or a lockout) is to produce agreement which cannot be consummated at the bargaining table.

If this method of producing agreement is no longer to be available, alternative procedures must be developed. In a free society a fundamental right should not be restricted or denied without supplying a reasonably satisfactory alternative.

If it is assumed that collective bargaining is the most logical and equitable method of determining the terms and conditions of employment, the right to strike must be preserved. The ideal situation will be attained when the parties to collective bargaining recognize that they should

[18] The 1958 garment industry strike was the first in more than twenty years. It was a fairly short and "friendly" strike, ending in a new contract running to 1961.

themselves develop machinery and customs that would make actual strikes and lockouts obsolete. This is not the same as saying that the right to strike or lockout should be made obsolete.

We shall return to the troublesome question of the appropriate role of public policy in relation to economic force in Chapter 17.

A PRELIMINARY BALANCE SHEET ON TAFT-HARTLEY

It is difficult to make a fair evaluation in a few words as to the operational impact of the Act upon collective bargaining. As noted at the outset of the chapter, the amount of reliable empirical evidence is surprisingly sparse after eleven years' experience under such a controversial statute.[19] Because of the dearth of persuasive, concrete knowledge, the danger of slipping into *post hoc ergo propter hoc* reasoning is increased. However, it is possible to generalize with caution as to several of the more significant ways in which the Act has contributed in some cases to a strengthening and in others to a weakening of the bargaining process.

FAVORABLE EFFECTS ON BARGAINING

There seems to be little doubt that the law's numerous limitations on private discretion have alerted both employers and unions to the necessity of developing mature, responsible relationships if they wish to avoid still more stringent public control. The union movement has been made painfully aware of the high cost of political dependency when the political climate changes. At the same time, many employers, aware of the extent to which their own discretion is limited by the Act, have moved slowly or not at all in utilization of what may be only temporary legislative advantages. In short, the very extent to which the Act has restricted private discretion has had the observable effect of inducing the parties to concentrate on improving their relationships with one another and to abandon the quest for governmental aid in restricting one another.

The Act has certainly contributed in a positive way to the elimination of concededly undesirable practices that had formerly interfered with stable bargaining. The ban on strikes to force an employer to bargain with a union other than the certified union is one illustration. It also seems probable that the Act deserves some credit for material reduction in the amount of take-it-or-leave-it bargaining that was formerly a characteristic approach of a number of powerful unions. No legitimate argument can be advanced for not imposing equal obligations on unions as well as

[19] For a comprehensive treatment of Taft-Hartley in perspective after ten years of operation, the reader should consult the April, 1958 issue of the *Industrial and Labor Relations Review*. The issue includes seven articles representing a variety of viewpoints and subjects.

employers to bargain in good faith. Finally, it is probable that the sixty-day requirement of intention to terminate or seek changes in the existing contract has encouraged more thorough consideration of demands for contract change in many cases and in some instances may have reduced the likelihood of strikes in connection with contract expirations.

The quality and stability of contract administration may well have been improved in particular cases by the Act's provisions for damage suits in breach of contract and for specific enforcement of contract terms, including agreements to arbitrate. In this connection the strict concept of agency may have promoted more responsible contract administration by inducing tighter control over local union discretion by the international desiring to eliminate wildcat stoppages.

The various limitations and prohibitions on the right to strike have doubtless had some salutary results. The decline of the jurisdictional strike may be attributed in great measure to the Act. Also, the employer's complete freedom to replace economic strikers has reduced the number of economic strikes. The union in each case is forced to weigh very carefully the practical consequences of resort to economic force.

Another plus value might include the inducement afforded in the Act to improve the quality of union representation in bargaining. The impetus here can come from a number of different provisions of the Act. One source is the decertification procedure, which makes it possible for employees to change representatives when they feel their interests are not being adequately served by the incumbent bargaining agent. The decertification procedure has not been used with great frequency (in fiscal 1956 there were only 129 such elections, with 89 decertifications). The threat of such a procedure, however, is one factor in keeping bargaining agents on their toes. Another beneficial stimulus flows from the Act's prohibition of coercive organizing practices and its virtual elimination of the possibility of indirect organizing through the employer (by secondary pressures). In this fashion the Act necessarily encourages a direct and democratic approach to union qualification for exclusive bargaining rights. Unions can no longer take the easy road of organizing the unorganized. Finally, the Act's encouragement of the right of individual presentation of grievances should operate to stimulate greater union interest in effective and equitable presentation of worker grievances.

ADVERSE EFFECTS ON BARGAINING

On the negative side, the Act must be held to have had an adverse effect on collective bargaining in several respects. In general, by giving equal legislative weight to the right to *refrain from* self-organization and collective bargaining, the Act signalized federal abandonment of the

Wagner Act policy of affirmatively encouraging the spread of union organization and collective bargaining. In this connection it is necessary to distinguish between the impact of the law on established bargaining relationships and new or potential bargaining relationships.

It seems beyond dispute that the Act has had a serious inhibiting effect on the success of unions in organizing nonunion territory. The Act gives the nonunion employer considerably more latitude in combatting unionism than did the Wagner Act. The net result of board decisions on the right of free speech under Section 8(c) is that the employer is privileged to say virtually anything he pleases right up to twenty-four hours before a representation election, so long as he does not obviously threaten employees or openly promise them benefits for voting against the union.

The board's recent decisions in this area seem to indicate that it has lost sight of the realities of coercion and free choice in practical labor relations. For example, the employer may now interrogate his employees individually as to their union sentiments. The success of southern employers in utilizing such freedoms to block unionization is eloquent proof of the serious disabilities under which the labor movement is now operating in its effort to extend the scope of its influence and control. Whether one approves or disapproves of the new board policies on these matters depends in large part on one's own value judgments as to the role of public policy. From the author's standpoint, the present board's policies on such matters stack the cards too heavily in favor of the employer.

The Act has not had too serious an adverse impact upon established bargaining relationships. At the same time, it would be difficult to argue the proposition that the Act has positively improved such relationships, except to the extent described in the section on plus values.

The Act may have weakened private bargaining relationships in that it has encouraged one party or the other to run to government for help. Numerous sections of the law encourage litigation, a process not ordinarily conducive to improved private relationships.

The numerous direct restrictions upon the subject matter and procedures of collective bargaining have inevitably introduced a greater amount of legalism into bargaining relationships. This has probably not contributed to a strengthening of constructive private bargains.

At a number of points the Act encourages self-determination and minority rights to the point at which the stability of existing relationships may be unnecessarily threatened. Rival unionism is encouraged by the amended Section 9(b). On the other hand, raiding is discouraged by making it an unfair labor practice to strike an employer bargaining with a duly certified union. Perhaps these two cancel each other to some extent.

The philosophical premise of the Act, that there is a distinction between the union and its members, is reflected in a number of provisions. The net effect of these provisions has been to encourage some employers to drive a wedge between union leadership and rank-and-file. When this has been done, collective bargaining has suffered. Employers who accept collective bargaining have not taken advantage of the Act's invitation in this respect. They have continued to regard the union as an integral component of the total industrial relations picture.

The equalizing amendments appear to bear more heavily on unions than on employers. Unions have been disarmed of some of their most potent economic weapons. This has made union organization campaigns more hazardous and has made the conduct of an effective economic strike more difficult. The Act appears to encourage conflict rather than to reduce the conflict potential that inheres in collective bargaining as an institutional process.

CONCLUSION

The analysis in this chapter has been limited to those sections of the Taft-Hartley Act that have a substantial direct or indirect effect upon collective bargaining as a method of governing union-management relationships. Although the Act constitutes the high water mark of government regulation of collective bargaining in peacetime, there are strong indications that further government intervention may be anticipated. There seems little likelihood that a counter trend toward decreasing regulatory control will develop. These considerations make it desirable to precede the substantive discussion of contemporary collective bargaining with a description of the public policy within which it operates. In Chapter 17 we shall return again to public policy, in consideration of criteria for the formulation of a durable and equitable national labor policy.

SELECTED BIBLIOGRAPHY

Bernstein, Irving, *The New Deal Collective Bargaining Policy*. Berkeley: University of California Press, 1950.

Brown, Emily Clark, "Needed—a New Start on National Labor Relations Law," *Labor Law Journal*, IV (February, 1953), 71–77.

Cohen, Samuel Harris, "Labor, Taft-Hartley and the Proposed Amendments," *Labor Law Journal*, V (June, 1954), 391–438.

Cohen, Sanford, "The Impasse in Collective Bargaining Law," *Labor Law Journal*, V (May, 1954), 307–10, 379–84.

Cox, Archibald, "The Duty to Bargain in Good Faith," *Harvard Law Review*, LXXI (June, 1958), 1401–42.

——— and John T. Dunlop, "Regulation of Collective Bargaining by the

National Labor Relations Board," *Harvard Law Review*, LXIII (January, 1950), 389–432.

——— and John T. Dunlop, "The Duty to Bargain Collectively During the Term of an Existing Agreement," *Harvard Law Review*, LXIII (May, 1950), 1097–1133.

Ezrine, Ivan A., "Nadir of the No-Strike Clause," *Labor Law Journal*, VIII (November, 1957), 769–816.

Gregory, Charles O., *Labor and the Law*, 2nd ed. New York: W .W. Norton & Co., Inc., 1958.

Jacobs, Arthur T., "Impact of Government Regulation upon Collective Bargaining Negotiations," *Labor Law Journal*, III (May, 1952), 311–24.

Jones, Dallas L., "The Implications of the 'Right-to-Work' Laws," *Michigan Business Review*, IX (November, 1957), 1–8.

Katz, Harold A., "Two Decades of State Labor Legislation: 1937–1957," *Labor Law Journal*, VIII (November, 1957), 747–58, 818.

Krislov, Joseph, "Union Decertification," *Industrial and Labor Relations Review*, IX (July, 1956), 589–94.

Kuhlman, John M., "Right-to-Work Laws: The Virginia Experience," *Labor Law Journal*, VI (July, 1955), 453–61, 494.

Meyers, Frederic, "Effects of 'Right to Work' Laws: A Study of the Texas Act," *Industrial and Labor Relations Review*, IX (October, 1955), 77–84.

Millis, Harry A. and Emily Clark Brown, *From the Wagner Act to Taft-Hartley*. Chicago: The University of Chicago Press, 1950.

Mittenthal, Richard, "Employer Speech—A Life Cycle," *Labor Law Journal*, V (February, 1954), 101–10.

Morse, Wayne L., *Perversion of the Taft-Hartley Act by the Eisenhower National Labor Relations Board*. Washington: U. S. Government Printing Office, 1956.

Petro, Sylvester, *The Labor Policy of the Free Society*. New York: The Ronald Press Co., 1957.

Phelps, Orme W., *Union Security*. Los Angeles: Institute of Industrial Relations, University of California, 1953.

Pound, Roscoe, *Legal Immunities of Labor Unions*. Washington: American Enterprise Association, Inc., 1957.

Ratner, Mozart G., "Policy-making by the New 'Quasi-judical' NLRB," *University of Chicago Law Review, XXIII* (Autumn, 1955), 12–35.

Roberts, Harold S., *The Doctrine of Preemption, Federal-State Jurisdiction*. Honolulu: Industrial Relations Center, University of Hawaii, 1957.

Samoff, Bernard, "Research on the Results and Impact of NLRB Decisions," *Labor Law Journal*, VIII (April, 1957), 235–38, 283–88.

——— and Harold X. Summers, "The Effect of Collective Bargaining Provisions on NLRB Action," *Labor Law Journal*, VIII (October, 1957), 676–99.

Slichter, Sumner H., "The Taft-Hartley Act," *Quarterly Journal of Economics*, LXIII (February, 1949), 1–31.

———, "Revision of the Taft-Hartley Act," *Quarterly Journal of Economics*, LXVII (May, 1953), 149–80.

Spielmans, John V., "Bargaining Fee Versus Union Shop," *Industrial and Labor Relations Review*, XLVII (July, 1957), 609–19.

———, "Measuring the Results of Organizational Union Representation Elections," *Industrial and Labor Relations Review*, IX (January, 1956), 280–85.

Taylor, George W., *Government Regulation of Industrial Relations*. Englewood Cliffs, N. J.: Prentice-Hall, Inc., 1948.

University of Michigan Law School 1950 Summer Institute, *The Law and Labor-Management Relations*. Ann Arbor: University of Michigan Law School, 1951.

Witney, Fred, "Changing NLRB policies: 1953-1954," *Southern Economic Journal*, XXII (July, 1955), 89–103.

Wyle, Benjamin and William H. Englander, "Free Speech or Lawful Coercion?" *Labor Law Journal*, V (April, 1954), 270–83.

4

The structure of bargaining relationships

A bargaining unit is an area of worker representation for purposes of collective bargaining. The scope of the bargaining unit determines the coverage of the collective labor agreement. Decisions on the shaping of the appropriate bargaining unit will frequently determine whether or not Union *X* is entitled to sole bargaining rights.

VARIETY IN BARGAINING UNIT STRUCTURES

A *bona fide* labor organization is legally entitled to certification by the National Labor Relations Board as sole bargaining agent for all employees in the bargaining unit upon proof of majority representation, assuming the unit is deemed appropriate for purposes of collective bargaining.

The appropriate unit is always one of the first matters discussed when a union requests recognition as bargaining agent. The employer's first question would naturally be, "Which workers do you claim to represent?" In most instances there is no disagreement as to the appropriate unit. In not a few, however, particularly when rival unions are involved, there may be a fundamental difference of opinion as to what is the most appropriate unit for purposes of collective bargaining. Even when only one union is involved, there may be sharp conflict over the propriety of including or excluding certain employee groups from the bargaining unit.

A survey of contemporary agreements reveals an astonishing variety in the shape and scope of structural patterns for collective bargaining. In basic manufacturing the most typical bargaining unit is the so-called "P and M," consisting of all production and maintenance employees, excluding only clerical and supervisory personnel. Such an industrial unit includes all categories of labor—skilled, semiskilled, and unskilled. Frequently an industrial employer will be confronted with bargaining obligations toward multiple units of employees rather than a single union. For example, an industrial union such as the UAW may have exclusive bargaining rights for all production and maintenance employees, exclusive of clerical and supervisory and machine shop employees. The International Association of Machinists may have bargaining rights for all employees in the machine shop and toolroom. In other industrial situations there may be two or more craft unions in the picture who have succeeded in splitting off well-defined skilled groups from the inclusive, plant-wide unit. A modern metropolitan newspaper may have collective bargaining contracts with a dozen or more unions, including the International Typographical Union, the American Newspaper Guild, the Photoengravers, the Machinists, the Mailers, and so on. In the building trades an association of contractors may negotiate jointly or separately with a large assortment of unions representing various crafts whose skills are essential to the completion of any construction project. In some industries such as coal mining, only one union is in the picture. In others, one union may be dominant but other unions may enjoy bargaining rights in certain plants or certain segments of the industry. The automobile industry illustrates this latter situation: the UAW is clearly the dominant union, but must yield its bargaining hegemony to a number of craft unions in particular plants. In short, the structure of bargaining relationships in the American economy reflects a pattern of variety and diversity.

No complete census of bargaining unit structures exists. Its compilation would be a monumental and expensive undertaking, for there are probably upwards of 100,000 collective agreements in force today. We have available, however, two informative samplings on unit structures that yield a reasonably accurate and similar picture of the bargaining "universe" in this country. The Bureau of Labor Statistics has published analyses based on approximately 12,000 contracts filed with it for 1947, 1950, and 1951.[1] More recently, Neil Chamberlain has published the

[1] See Nelson M. Bortz and Alexander Moros, "Characteristics of 12,000 Labor-Management Contracts," *Monthly Labor Review*, LXXIII (July, 1951); and Laura C. Chase and Ernestine M. Moore, "Characteristics of Major Union Contracts," *Monthly Labor Review*, LXXIX (July, 1956), 805–11.

findings of a unit structure study based on reports from Federal Commissioners of Conciliation covering some 18,000 bargaining units serviced by the commissioners in 1953.[2]

CRITERIA OF APPROPRIATENESS IN BARGAINING UNITS

It is important at the outset to consider carefully the considerations that determine in particular situations the most appropriate basis on which collective bargaining should take place. In other words, what are the relevant criteria for determining the coverage of collective bargaining contracts in particular situations?

Since unions are presumably functioning to promote the best interests of the workers they represent in collective bargaining, it is logical to assume that the most important criterion for determining the most appropriate structure of bargaining is the *desires of the employees themselves.* The NLRB has always accorded great recognition to this criterion in representation cases under Section 9 of the Act. In cases involving a dispute between an employer and a union on what is the appropriate unit for bargaining, the employer's arguments are normally not given great weight (no matter how logical they may be) if the pattern of self-organization by his employees has taken a different course. In cases where the employer and the union agree or stipulate as to the structure of the bargaining unit, however, the unit agreed upon by the parties will normally be adopted by the board.

While the desires of the employees themselves should be fundamental in any determination of appropriate units, there are other significant criteria that have a bearing on the decision as to appropriateness. Among the more important may be listed: (1) bargaining history in the plant or industry; (2) the membership eligibility requirements of the union or unions involved; (3) the presence of a "community of interest" among the employees in the unit sought as appropriate; (4) the similarity of wage scales, hours, and working conditions among employees in the unit sought as appropriate; (5) the form or extent of present self-organization among employees; (6) the presence of a "functional coherence and interdependence" among the work operations covered in the unit sought as appropriate; (7) the organization of the employer's business and its relationship to the proposed bargaining unit, including geographical considerations if more than one plant is involved.

TYPES OF UNIT STRUCTURE CONTROVERSIES

While many bargaining unit cases are relatively uncomplicated, critical issues do arise as to which unit structure is most appropriate. The most

[2] See Neil W. Chamberlain, "The Structure of Bargaining Units in the United States," *Industrial and Labor Relations Review,* X (October, 1956), 3–25.

serious controversy involves the situation in which an industrial union seeks a plant-wide "P and M" unit, while one or more craft unions in the picture contend that separate units should be established covering workers in the crafts involved. Another common dispute concerns whether the bargaining unit in a multi-plant company should be company-wide or whether each plant should constitute a separate unit. Still a third type of important controversy arises where the union or unions in question seek a bargaining unit embracing the employees of more than one employer and the employers in question prefer to bargain on a single- rather than multi-employer basis. Finally, in many cases today, disputes arise with respect to the inclusion or exclusion of borderline categories of employees where the general shape of the basic unit is not disputed.

Of course, the craft unit versus industrial unit controversy has been, over the years, the most bitterly fought. In the years following the original AFL-CIO split in 1935 the NLRB constantly found itself on the horns of an unenviable dilemma in rival union disputes of this type. The author's study of the board's unit determinations in the critical period 1935-1939 when the AFL-CIO feud was at its height led to the conclusion that there was no convincing evidence of bias or arbitrary action by the NLRB.[3] The board stuck to an individual case approach instead of laying down broad policies consistently favoring either craft or industrial unit claims. This commendable failure to line up decisively with one side or the other drew the critical fire of both union federations.

In appraising competing claims as to the appropriateness of different bargaining structures it is important to remember that there is no scientifically correct answer as to what is the most appropriate basis for bargaining. As far as basic manufacturing is concerned, the trend over the past twenty years or more has clearly been in favor of industrial bargaining units. In recent years, however, a reverse trend toward craft separatism has set in, stimulated in part by a shift in governmental policy and in part by practical dissatisfaction of skilled minorities with their economic status in industrial bargaining units.

THE GLOBE DOCTRINE

In 1937 the Wagner Act NLRB finally hit upon a formula for settling craft-industrial controversies known as the *Globe doctrine*.[4] The policy was to allow the votes of employees in minority craft groups to determine the nature of the appropriate unit or units. When the considerations appeared to the board to be evenly balanced, the board allowed the wishes of the employees in the contested minority group(s) to determine its decision in fact. The ballots of the employees in the disputed group(s)

[3] Harold W. Davey, *Administrative Discretion under the National Labor Relations Act*, Cambridge: 1939, unpublished doctoral dissertation.

[4] See *In Re Globe Machine and Stamping Co.*, 3 NLRB 294 (1937).

were segregated. If a majority voted for the union urging the inclusive plant-wide unit, this was held by the board as decisive in favor of their inclusion in the confines of the industrial unit, and vice versa.

PRESENT NLRB POLICY

It is important to note, however, that as originally formulated, the Globe doctrine was to be employed only where the board felt that the record indicated the considerations were *evenly balanced*. Under the Taft-Hartley Act, the policy is now presumptively favorable to self-determination by minority craft groups. The amended Section 9(b) of the Act limits the discretion of the board by providing that it may not decide that any craft unit is inappropriate on the ground that a different unit has been established by a prior board determination, unless a majority of employees in the proposed craft unit vote against separate representation. This legislative proviso has stimulated movements toward craft separatism in many industries where industrial bargaining units had been long established.

Of course, it would be contrary to the best interests of free collective bargaining to freeze minority groups within an industrial unit against their will. At the same time, it is questionable whether the national policy should be geared in favor of one type of bargaining unit structure. The NLRB emphasizes that under the Act it retains sufficient flexibility of discretion to decide under what conditions craft workers may or may not be permitted to vote on separate representation. Although the board has retained some minimum hurdles that a craft union seeking separate representation must jump, the present policy leans strongly in the direction of encouraging severance.

The leading case on the subject for some time has been the *American Potash* case. As noted in Chapter 3, this case lays down the basic requirements that the employees in the unit sought as appropriate must constitute a "true" craft grouping and that the union which seeks to represent these employees must prove that it historically has represented employees in this craft. In other words, all that *American Potash* does is distinguish between what might be termed legitimate and illegitimate raiding of established bargaining units. The board has moved a long way from the former leading case on craft separation, where it refused to permit a separate election for bricklayers in a steel mill on the basis that their work was closely integrated with the production of steel.[5]

IMPACT OF AFL-CIO MERGER ON UNIT QUESTIONS

One of the more important practical consequences of the AFL-CIO merger may well be to reduce considerably the incidence of bargaining

[5] See *In Re National Tube Company*, 76 *NLRB* 1199 (1948).

unit disputes among rival unions. Even when rival unionism was at its height, the great majority of disputes concerned rival claims to the allegiance of the same group of employees, with no dispute as to the structure of the unit. In a considerable number of cases, however, the key issue has involved bitter dispute over the appropriate basis for bargaining.

The architects of the merger anticipate coordination rather than conflict in future organizational efforts and an abandonment of efforts to switch the allegiance of already organized employees.[6] To the degree that the new federation is successful in achieving these goals, the board's discretionary duty of determining the most appropriate bargaining unit in representation disputes will be greatly simplified. Parenthetically, it may be observed that the free choice of the workers involved will be proportionately narrowed to the degree that interunion rivalry is eliminated. In many industries workers seeking to unionize will be limited to one union and one type of bargaining unit structure.

EMERGING PATTERNS IN THE STRUCTURE OF BARGAINING

Future developments in bargaining unit structures will be conditioned by such factors as: (1) the way in which self-organization proceeds among unorganized workers; (2) strategy of union organizing committees, influenced by changes in the structure of unions themselves in response to dynamic shifts in the structure of industry, employer bargaining strategy, or the threat of rival unionism; and (3) NLRB policies.

Although in recent years there has been a resurgence of separate craft units in manufacturing, it is logical to anticipate that the bulk of new bargaining units in this area will continue to be predominantly on a plant-wide or employer basis rather than on a multiple craft approach. The way in which unsolicited self-organization proceeds in presently nonunion areas will normally prevail and will probably occur along industrial rather than occupational lines in most manufacturing establishments. There are few important factors (other than governmental policy predisposed in favor of craft groupings) that run counter to the trend toward bargaining unit structures of an industrial or plant-wide type.

At the same time, it must be noted that the major area for future union expansion is in "nonfactory unionism," where the bargaining in organized establishments is frequently along craft lines. Among the more important

[6] For an informed analysis of the history and prospects of the merger, see Arthur J. Goldberg, *AFL-CIO; Labor United* (New York: McGraw-Hill Book Co., Inc., 1956.) For a more current account of developments since the merger, see Mark L. Kahn, "Recent Jurisdictional Developments in Organized Labor," Ch. 1 in Harold W. Davey, Howard S. Kaltenborn, and Stanley H. Ruttenberg, eds., *New Dimensions in Collective Bargaining*, Industrial Relations Research Association Publication No. 21 (New York: Harper & Brothers, 1959).

nonmanufacturing industries in which craft unionism remains dominant we may list construction, railroads, airlines, printing and publishing, and the entertainment industry. Futhermore, self-organization among such professional worker groupings as engineers, time study men, draftsmen, chemical technicians, college and public school teachers, nurses, and insurance agents will logically follow a craft pattern. In such areas as food service, retail stores, and distribution, however, such organization as takes place is likely to be on broad and inclusive lines rather than in terms of well-defined occupational groups. It should also be observed that the largest area of union growth potential includes industries in which multi-employer bargaining is widely prevalent in the presently organized sectors, notably the hotel and restaurant industry and retail trades and services.

Within manufacturing the more important forces working in favor of industrial bargaining units are: (1) the composition of the work force which includes a high percentage of semiskilled workers and low percentages of skilled and unskilled; (2) the structure and eligibility requirements of unions organizing in manufacturing industries; and (3) the preference of employers themselves for negotiations with a single union rather than multi-unit bargaining.

One of the probable consequences of extensive automation in manufacturing industries, discussed in detail in Chapter 13, is the increasing numerical and qualitative importance of skilled employees in the labor force "mix." While automation may be expected to increase considerably the percentage of skilled employees in an automated plant's work force, it is unlikely that this will have any appreciable impact on bargaining unit structures. In the main, the single, plant-wide unit will continue to be the dominant one in manufacturing.

AFL-CIO POLICY ON CRAFT CONSTRUCTION WORK IN INDUSTRY

Under the merged federation, one of the critical jurisdictional difficulties relates to construction work in manufacturing plants. Should such work be done by the building trades craft unions or by craftsman members of the industrial union with "P and M" bargaining rights in the industry in question? The AFL-CIO announced in July, 1957, a policy and procedure that it hoped would resolve most work jurisdictional disputes of this type. Under this policy, construction of new buildings would be done by workers represented by the building trades craft unions, whereas production and running maintenance work would be assigned to workers represented by the industrial unions. Disputes over work assignments in doubtful areas such as "alterations, major repairs and relocation of existing facilities, changeovers, and other types of maintenance work" were to be handled in terms of "established past practices on a plant, area or industry basis." Three teams of two men each—one from the federation's Building Trades Department and one from its Industrial Union Department—would resolve any disputes on the spot. Appellate procedures were provided, falling short of "terminal arbitration" as a final step for settlement of such disputes.[7]

TREND TOWARD CENTRALIZED BARGAINING STRUCTURES

The structural relationships for bargaining now being developed by both management and organized labor are influenced greatly by the increasing centralization of authority over policy determination. There is a steady compulsion to match organizational strength with coextensive organizational strength wherever possible.

This trend toward centralization in structural arrangements for bargaining has been in evidence for some time. Centralization is a frequent corollary of increasing size of business and labor organizations. As a corporation or a labor organization expands, the possibility of effective local determination of basic policies (let alone conduct of actual negotiations in collective bargaining) has diminished accordingly.

Illustrations of this basic shift in the locus of actual power in bargaining relationships may be easily multiplied. In many unions, particularly in manufacturing, there has been a steady accretion of power in the hands of the international union at the expense of its member locals. On the management side the pattern of centralization is most clearly visible in the rapid development of employer associations for labor relations, chiefly when the labor organization is more powerful than individual employers in the industry affected.

Another vital aspect of centralization is found in the carry-over of leadership patterns from the field of business policy into labor policy. For example, the United States Steel Corporation has for many years been an acknowledged leader in price decisions and other business policies in basic steel. More recently, its negotiations with the United Steelworkers of America have set the pattern for wage policy and often for other conditions of employment in the steel industry. This remains true even though, technically, negotiations are carried on individually with all the companies in basic steel.

The rise of multi-employer bargaining, particularly on a local area

[7] At this writing (October, 1958) the foregoing procedure, devised by George Meany, had not yet been accepted by the craft groups and certain of the industrial unions were becoming increasingly irritated with the situation. Thus, the prospects do not appear bright for reaching a permanent accord on this ticklish question.

basis, is the most dramatic illustration of the trend toward centralization for bargaining purposes. As Frank Pierson has noted,[8] however, the phenomenon of pattern following may hold greater significance for the future of collective bargaining. In either procedure centralization in the determination of labor relations policies is the dominant theme.

Throughout manufacturing the typical collective labor agreement is coming to be one negotiated by a business corporation with the officers of a single international union covering all the production and maintenance employees in all of the company's plants for which the union claims representation now or in the future. This is often referred to as "corporation-wide bargaining." In such cases the international union negotiates a single master agreement on behalf of all the locals involved. Provision may be made for local negotiation on local issues, but there has been a perceptible narrowing in the range of subject matter at this level.

These corporation-wide contracts may exercise an influence far beyond the confines of the particular business empire to which they apply. If the corporation in question is dominant in its field (the General Electric Co., the United States Steel Corporation, or the General Motors Corporation), a similar bargain is usually made with other firms in the industry.

Statistically, the number and influence of industries that actually engage in industry-wide bargaining are not yet impressive. If a realistic view is taken of actual influence, however, the negotiation of pattern or leadership agreements frequently brings results similar to those achieved by formal, industry-wide agreements.

THE LOGIC OF LARGE-SCALE BARGAINING UNITS

It is logical to anticipate a continued trend toward large-scale structural bargaining units, since pressures in this direction come from both sides of the bargaining table. As industries become more fully unionized, the principal union or unions in the picture will seek a structural basis to obtain and then to guarantee uniformity of standards. On the contract administration level similar pressures will be exerted in the interest of uniformity in interpretation and application of contract terms. Standardization of policy and procedure in both contract negotiation and administration can best be accomplished in many cases through industry-wide or multi-employer agreements on a regional basis. Where this is not feasible, the dominant union is often strong enough to accomplish a similar result by forcing the leadership pattern on other firms in the industry or area.

[8] See Frank C. Pierson, "Prospects for Industry-Wide Bargaining," *Industrial and Labor Relations Review,* III (April, 1950), 341–61.

By the same token, when single employers face a union representing all or nearly all the workers in a particular industry and whose economic strength is far superior to that of any one firm in the industry, the logic of pooled management strength and know-how through multi-employer organization for labor relations purposes is coming to be keenly appreciated. As might be expected, the centralizing of policy determination in employer associations has developed first in such highly competitive, small-firm industries as men's and women's clothing, trucking, baking, etc., rather than in essentially oligopolistic industries such as automobiles, steel, and meat packing. In the latter situation the more powerful firms in the industry are generally reluctant to surrender any portion of their existing sovereignty to a central labor relations policy committee. They feel that their individual economic strength is sufficient to conduct effective separate negotiations with the chief labor organization involved.

Although the formal structure of bargaining on a single-employer basis may prevail for some time to come in oligopolistic industries, one suspects that in a number of industries there is an increasing amount of informal consultation and information-sharing going on among major companies for their common welfare.[9]

The principal pressures favoring the growth of multi-employer bargaining derive from management and union needs for greater institutional security. Although the main incidence of multi-employer bargaining lies in nonfactory industries, there are strong economic and institutional forces working in favor of such bargaining structures in many areas of manufacturing as well.

An important pressure from the union side in recent years has been the drive for greater security by many of the industrial unions. The economic power of an industrial union rests not on control of labor supply but on control of the employer. Most of the members of an industrial union are unskilled and semiskilled workers. It is not feasible for an industrial union to attempt control of the employer's hiring policies or to restrict entrance to the trade in the manner of a craft union.

The industrial union must consolidate its position by organizing at least a majority of employers in the industry or industries with which it is concerned. The logic of organizing in steel, automobile, rubber, meat packing, and other industries with a high percentage of semiskilled and unskilled workmen compels the union to organize all firms in the industry as rapidly as it possibly can. If it has only partially organized an industry, the unorganized portion stands as a constant threat to whatever wage and other employment standards the union has been able to achieve. A case in point is the difficulties of the Textile Workers' union in maintain-

[9] The 1958 automobile negotiations support this conclusion.

ing standards in northern mills in the face of competition from unorganized southern mills.

For such reasons there is logic in a powerful drive toward complete unionization of an industry to accomplish the major purposes of taking wages out of competition and insuring effective uniformity in basic employment conditions. Once this has been done, the institutional security of the union is usually assured. Union leaders are then in a position to become more "statesmanlike." Until a union has fully organized the territory it has staked out for itself, the nonunion portion of the industry may still call the tune from time to time.

Multi-employer bargaining appeals to the union from another security standpoint. Associational bargaining reduces the possibilities for successful rival unionism.

In the mass production industries, as already noted, formalized multi-employer bargaining arrangements are still comparatively rare. The economic pattern is frequently oligopolistic. Many employers are large enough and powerful enough to deal individually with the union. The self-protection motivation characteristic of many local associational employer groupings is not present.

In these situations the union emphasis has been on pattern bargaining. Again, its motivation is primarily that of institutional security and the desire to achieve and then to protect uniform standards.

A comparable logic often lies behind management support for multi-employer bargaining arrangements. Under an associational union agreement, an employer may very well be paying higher wages and benefits than under single-company bargaining. If he knows that his principal competitors are to be subject to approximately the same conditions, however, he need no longer be concerned about being "whipsawed" by the union or undermined by destructive wage competition from a marginal employer.

The multi-employer agreement, by taking wages out of competition, removes an important unknown factor in the employer's advance calculations. It reduces risk and uncertainty and promotes stability. In spite of the constant homage to the competitive ideal in our economy, most employers seek to avoid the risks of competition whenever possible. Management support for multi-employer bargaining arrangements is frequently a product of this urge to avoid the hazards of competition.

The necessity for equalizing bargaining strength has been a powerful stimulus to multi-employer bargaining. A union organizing an industry with strong central employer control has to unionize the entire industry before it can achieve a power position equal to the employers' united front. Employers in an industry controlled by a single union have a similar incentive to combination. Each employer individually is comparatively helpless in dealing with a labor organization whose power is coextensive with the industry as a whole. It is in the self-interest of individual employers to combine into a labor relations association under such circumstances. This may be observed in local group bargaining arrangements in the garment industry, building trades, bakeries, hotel and restaurant trade, and other industries in which the typical business unit is small. Similar considerations may ultimately prevail among employers in oligopolistic, mass production industries as well.

Since multi-employer bargaining is likely to become more important in future years, it is desirable to outline some of the principal arguments that have been advanced for and against this structural form. When these arguments have been reviewed and analyzed, it will be be readily apparent that multi-employer bargaining as a structural phenomenon cannot be viewed realistically as either an unmixed blessing or an unmitigated curse.

THE CASE FOR MULTI-EMPLOYER BARGAINING

The principal arguments in favor of multi-employer bargaining arrangements may be summarized as follows:

1. Determination of wage policy on a multi-employer basis (particularly when the bargaining is genuinely industry-wide or area-wide) will effectively remove wages as a competitive element in cost. Such a stabilization through application of uniform standards enables employers to know where they stand on the vital element of labor cost in comparison with their competitors in the industry or in the area.

2. Removal of labor cost as a competitive item will intensify product and market competition in other areas such as managerial efficiency, worker productivity, quality of product, and distributive efficiency. The consumer is held to be the chief beneficiary of such intensified nonwage competition.

3. Multi-employer bargaining is held to be more mature and responsible than individual plant negotiations. The employers and the union may be expected to have a better informed and more far-sighted approach to the wage bargain.

4. Multi-employer bargaining is advantageous from the standpoint of industrial peace. Fewer strikes will occur under multi-employer bargaining. The parties are able to appreciate and to reckon with the external impact of a strike and the possible adverse effect upon public opinion. Two common strike situations under individual plant bargaining are eliminated in centralized bargaining. One is the strike wherein a particular employer is picked as the target for gaining new objectives. Another is the strike to bring an erring employer into line.

5. Multi-employer bargaining makes possible more unified and more

effective joint efforts to withstand the ruinous competition from non-union sectors of the same industry or from low-paying producers of substitutable products. As multi-employer bargaining expands toward genuine industry-wide arrangements, the sub-marginal firm is either brought into line or frozen out.

6. The individual employer has more of a voice under multi-employer bargaining than is likely to be the case under pattern bargaining. Contrary to popular belief, it is argued, multi-employer bargaining is sufficiently flexible to permit special departures from the industry norm when this is necessary. Under pattern bargaining, the individual firm faced by a very powerful union may be compelled to swallow the whole pattern on a take-it-or-else basis.

7. Only through multi-employer bargaining can desirable standards of practice be achieved on a joint basis. Centralized bargaining permits constructive joint attention to such vital matters as wage uniformity, standardization of job titles and job classifications, interplant wage rationalization (elimination of interplant inequities), and raising productivity levels.

8. Multi-employer bargaining is more likely to have beneficial effects from the standpoint of general economic stability than bargaining on an individual plant basis, for at least two reasons:

a) Under centralized bargaining, the parties can give serious consideration to the relationship between increases or decreases in wage rates and the volume of employment opportunities. This is not possible under a fractionalized bargaining structure.

b) Experience warrants a conclusion that general wage movements are slower and less extreme in industries under multi-employer bargaining arrangements than is frequently the case under individual plant bargaining. Thus the growth of multi-employer bargaining may operate as a restraining influence in inflationary periods and serve as a cushioning or stabilizing force during deflationary periods.

9. Multi-employer bargaining arrangements permit the development of a workable reconciliation of the need for uniformity and the need for diversity. The interdependent structure of our economy increasingly requires central determination of major policy issues in the interest of uniformity. This can best be done through multi-employer bargaining. At the same time, the values of democratic labor relations can be insured by providing for a maximum of decentralization in the administration and implementation of centrally negotiated collective agreements.

This, in summary fashion, is the case for multi-employer bargaining. It will be noted that some of the arguments are oriented toward employer interests, some toward union interests, and some toward the interests of the consumer and the economy at large. It is essential in weighing conflicting arguments over the merits of an institutional phenomenon such as multi-employer bargaining that the origin and direction of the arguments be kept clearly in mind. In the realm of controversy positions shift frequently and rapidly, depending on whose ox is being gored.

THE CASE AGAINST MULTI-EMPLOYER BARGAINING

The principal arguments raised against multi-employer bargaining arrangements may be summarized as follows:

1. Multi-employer bargaining on wages and other income issues will result in a stultifying uniformity rather than equitable stabilization of labor costs and will inevitably end in collusion against the consumer.
2. Instead of raising the level of nonwage competition, multi-employer bargaining will result in a cost structure so high that new firms will be unable to enter the industry. Thus undesirable economic concentration will be promoted at the consumer's expense.
3. Under multi-employer bargaining, strikes may be fewer in number but their destructive potential, when they occur, is far greater than under individual plant bargaining. Strikes that involve all or a large number of firms in an industry may exert paralyzing effects on other sectors of the economy dependent on the struck industry.
4. Multi-employer bargaining will intensify wage rigidities in a declining market. This will increase unemployment, reduce purchasing power, and otherwise assist the deflationary spiral.
5. Under multi-employer arrangements, individual firms will be powerless to achieve policies suited to their own needs. They will be bound by the terms of a master agreement in the negotiation of which they may have had little chance to secure recognition of their particular problems.
6. On the union side, multi-employer bargaining involves the loss of decision-making authority by the local union. This is incompatible with the concept of the union as an instrument for the democratization of industrial relations. Multi-employer bargaining involves the complete subjection of local unions to the power of the international union not only in negotiation of major policy issues but in contract administration as well.
7. Finally, centralized bargaining structures, especially when industry-wide in scope, are antagonistic to the principles of the competitive, free-enterprise system. Multi-employer bargaining strengthens and solidifies monopoly power on both sides of the bargaining table. It is completely unrealistic to assume that two giants under organized bilateral monopoly will become more responsible and more sensitive to consumer interests. As consumer frustration and anger increases, the demand for increased public intervention will lead eventually to wage-price-investment controls and the destruction of the private enterprise economy.

EMPIRICAL EVIDENCE ON MULTI-EMPLOYER BARGAINING

Careful analysis of the arguments for and against multi-employer bargaining will indicate that many of them are couched in terms of what *may* happen under such structural bargaining arrangements. As is true with most man-made institutions, multi-employer bargaining clearly has potential for constructive accomplishment and also potential for development in ways that would be regarded as uneconomical from the consumer standpoint and undemocratic from the standpoint of the individual firms and local unions involved. It is therefore desirable to survey briefly the empirical evidence that we have available on multi-employer bargaining in practice.

Since the first edition of this book, several case studies of collective bargaining in particular industries and areas have been completed.[10] In general, the findings of these studies support the main conclusions of two earlier studies[11] that were favorable to multi-employer arrangements. Of course, how one evaluates experience will depend on one's basic assumptions and position. For example, there is little doubt that multi-employer bargaining increases stability in the relationship at the expense of some loss of discretion and flexibility in local plant-local union relationships. Whether this is counted as a plus or a minus depends on the importance attached to stability on the one hand and local management or union autonomy on the other. Again, multi-employer bargaining clearly has promoted wage uniformity for particular types of labor and for changes in wage levels throughout the unit covered. In fact, the primary motivation of multi-employer arrangements is frequently that of taking wages out of competition. Most employers and unions that are parties to such arrangements view the achievement of wage uniformity as a positive accomplishment. On the other hand, those who as a matter of principle favor single-employer bargaining or who believe that the level of consumer costs will be less when wages are "competitively" determined will regard such a development as a negative item.

Similarly, multi-employer bargaining tends to divorce wage policy from local labor demand-supply market forces. Whether one regards this

[10] Worthy of special mention here are several monographs in the West Coast Collective Bargaining Systems series, edited by Clark Kerr and Curtis Aller, and published by the Institute of Industrial Relations, University of California at Berkeley, since 1955. See particularly Gordon W. Bertram and Sherman J. Maisel, *Industrial Relations in the Construction Industry: The Northern California Experience;* Betty V. H. Schneider and Abraham Siegel, *Industrial Relations in the Pacific Coast Longshore Industry;* and J. B. Gillingham, *The Teamsters Union on the West Coast.*

[11] See Richard A. Lester and Edward A. Robie, *Wages under National and Regional Collective Bargaining* (Princeton: Industrial Relations Section, Princeton University, 1946); and Clark Kerr and Lloyd H. Fisher, "Multiple-Employer Bargaining: The San Francisco Experience," in Richard A. Lester and Joseph Shister, eds., *Insights into Labor Issues* (New York: The Macmillan Company, 1948.)

as a favorable or unfavorable consequence depends on one's assumptions.

The writer's own assumptions cause him to view the growth and development of multi-employer bargaining arrangements in a generally favorable light. Such structural arrangements have developed in response to felt needs by both employer and union forces, and there has been no disposition to revert to single-employer bargaining in most situations. The real advantages of greater stability, more informed bargaining, and incentives to competition among employers on a nonwage basis tend to outweigh the disadvantages of reduced local autonomy, somewhat greater rigidity in wage movements, and higher labor costs and ultimate product costs (in some cases) that may result from such arrangements.

In the last analysis the academic arguments pro and con do not alter the fact that multi-employer bargaining structures have proved to be durable and generally satisfactory to the participants. There is no logical basis for concluding that the importance of multi-employer bargaining will diminish. Since the potential for monopolistic collusion and excessive centralization of authority is always present, there is a continuing need for watchful observation of such bargaining structures. There is also a continuing problem in determining in particular cases the proper blend of central policy determination and local discretion. As Frank Pierson has pointed out,[12] there is a need for a "judicious mixture" of various bargaining types so that the broader issues that lend themselves to uniform treatment can be handled on a multi-employer basis while issues better adapted to local discretion may continue to be handled on a narrower base. This aspect of the problem is treated in more detail in Chapter 16.

SUMMARY AND CONCLUSIONS

Certain basic observations in this brief survey of bargaining unit structures and problems may now be restated briefly. First, although single-employer bargaining remains the most common form of unit structure, there is an increasing development of multi-employer bargaining. Multi-employer units are characteristically found in such industries as construction, printing, bakery, hotel and restaurant, and men's and women's clothing rather than in the basic mass production industries. No further growth of pure industry-wide bargaining structures may be anticipated. Within basic manufacturing the dominant basis of representation will continue to be industrial rather than craft, with the typical unit embracing the production and maintenance employees of a single employer, exclusive of clerical and supervisory. NLRB policies favoring craft severance, however, have produced more multiple units in manufacturing establishments than were common a few years ago.

The AFL-CIO merger will doubtless reduce the incidence of rival

[12] Frank C. Pierson, *op. cit.*, p. 361.

unionism and conflicts over appropriate units. This may limit the freedom of choice of unions among workers, but it will sharply reduce the conflicts attributable to raiding of established units by rival unions.

The growth of multi-employer bargaining has necessarily contributed to increasing the concentration of policy-making authority in the hands of international unions at the expense of local unions and has similarly reduced the discretion of the individual firm in exchange for enhanced group strength through an employer labor relations association.

Increasing institutionalization and centralization of bargaining structures appear to have contributed to greater uniformity in wage level changes and occupational rate structures, and to less flexibility in wage movements than was characteristic of single-employer bargaining. While there is evidence in some cases of higher costs to the ultimate consumer as a consequence of multi-employer bargaining arrangements, there seems little doubt that the fears of opponents of such unit structures have been considerably exaggerated.

SELECTED BIBLIOGRAPHY

Albers, Henry H., "Union Jurisdiction," *Labor Law Journal*, IV (March, 1953), 183–95.

Bureau of Labor Statistics, United States Department of Labor, *Collective Bargaining with Associations and Groups of Employers*, Bulletin No. 897. Washington: U.S. Government Printing Office, 1947.

Carpenter, Jesse T., *Employers' Associations and Collective Bargaining in New York City*. Ithaca: Cornell University Press, 1950.

Chamberlain, Neil W., "The Structure of Bargaining Units in the United States," *Industrial and Labor Relations Review*, X (October, 1956), 3–25.

Garrett, Sylvester and L. Reed Tripp, *Management Problems Implicit in Multi-Employer Collective Bargaining*. Philadelphia: University of Pennsylvania Press, 1948.

Jones, Dallas L., "The NLRB and the Multiemployer Unit," *Labor Law Journal*, V (January, 1954), 34–46.

Kerr, Clark and Lloyd H. Fisher, "Multiple-Employer Bargaining: The San Francisco Experience," in R. A. Lester and J. Shister, eds., *Insights into Labor Issues*. New York: The Macmillan Company, 1948.

Krislov, Joseph, "NLRB on Craft Severance: One Year of American Potash," *Labor Law Journal*, VI (May, 1955), 275–78, 334–35.

Law Note, "Multi-Employer Bargaining and the National Labor Relations Board," *Harvard Law Review*, LXVI (March, 1953), 886–98.

McCabe, David A., "Union Policies as to the Area of Collective Bargaining," in *Interpreting the Labor Movement*, Industrial Relations Research Association Publication No. 9. Champaign: IRRA, 1952, pp. 110–29.

McCaffree, Kenneth M., "Regional Labor Agreements in the Construction Industry," *Industrial and Labor Relations Review*, IX (July, 1956), 596–609.

Naumoff, Benjamin B., "NLRB Handling of Unit Problems in Representation Cases," *Labor Law Journal*, V (February, 1954), 119-27.

Pierson, Frank C., *Multi-Employer Bargaining: Nature and Scope*. Philadelphia: University of Pennsylvania Press, 1948.

———, "Prospects for Industry-Wide Bargaining," *Industrial and Labor Relations Review*, III (April, 1950), 341-61.

Slate, Daniel M., "Trade Union Behavior and the Local Employers' Association," *Industrial and Labor Relations Review*, XI (October, 1957), 42–55.

Snavely, Tipton R., "The Impact of Multi-unit Bargaining on the Economy," *Southern Economic Journal*, XIX (April, 1953), 445–57.

Somers, Gerald G., "Multiemployer Proposals and the Coal Operators," *Labor Law Journal*, VI (May, 1956), 296–310.

———, "Pressures on an Employers' Association in Collective Bargaining," *Industrial and Labor Relations Review*, VI (July, 1953), 557–69.

Steele, Ellsworth H., "The Impact of Multi-Unit Bargaining on Industrial Relations," *Southern Economic Journal*, XX (October, 1953), 130–44.

Stephansky, Ben, "The Structure of the American Labor Movement," in *Interpreting the Labor Movement*, Industrial Relations Research Association Publication No. 9. Champaign: IRRA, 1952, pp. 39–69.

Taylor, Milton C., "Representation Proceedings and the New Long-term Contracts," *Labor Law Journal*, III (June, 1952), 464–74.

5

Preparation for bargaining and contract negotiations

Most experienced union and management negotiators would agree that the time to begin preparing for the next contract negotiation is immediately after the current agreement has been signed and put into effect. In a constructive relationship both parties will be constantly looking ahead rather than taking pride in recent accomplishments or licking their wounds after a real or fancied defeat in the negotiations just concluded.

The degree and kind of advance preparation for negotiations will vary considerably depending on the size and importance of the bargaining relationship. If the company and local union in question are part of a multi-employer bargaining set-up, their roles may be somewhat limited. Or, if it is customary in the relationship to use a pattern set by an industry leader as the point of departure for negotiations, a great deal of advance preparation may not be necessary. Many bargaining relationships today are not essentially different from what they were fifteen or twenty years ago and involve comparatively uncomplicated bargaining issues.

As a general proposition, however, it is now customary for companies and unions to do a great deal of factual spade-work and opinion-seeking in preparation for actual negotiations. The larger industrial unions generally have a rather elaborate apparatus for obtaining accurate information as to rank-and-file sentiments and pressures. They are also becoming rather adept in the use of modern public relations techniques for "creating" membership enthusiasm for future contract demands regarded as critical by the leadership. The UAW's long advance campaign for the Guaranteed Annual Wage prior to 1955 negotiations is a prime illustration of this technique. Its publicity first on the thirty-hour week and later on profit-sharing as a key demand for 1958 followed a similar vein.

On its part, too, management is becoming increasingly aware of the need to anticipate future negotiations. Most companies will schedule regular conferences between line supervision and industrial relations personnel to find out what contractual changes may be desirable from a managerial standpoint. The ink is scarcely dry on a new contract before it is examined for flaws, "bugs," or unnoticed ambiguities that may require clarification at the next negotiations if they are not so serious as to require adjustment by mutual consent before then.

Careful analysis of the nature and sources of grievances arising under a contract is, of course, an indispensable tool of both management and union in preparing for the next contract negotiation. The incidence of grievances will usually reveal unworkable or ambiguous clauses in short order. Daily contract administration thus provides much of the raw material for future bargaining demands and counterproposals.

The increasingly complex and technical nature of many issues in collective bargaining also demands thorough preparation for contract negotiation. Among the issues commonly found on negotiation agenda today that require extensive advance professional preparation, the following may be listed: (1) revision of a negotiated pension plan; (2) revision and expansion of a negotiated group life insurance and hospitalization plan; (3) revision and extension of an SUB plan; (4) proposal to change from an hourly method of wage payment to some form of incentive system of wage payment; (5) introduction of joint job evaluation; (6) drafting appropriate contract language to cover policies governing the manner and rate of "automating" a plant where substantial curtailment of employment will result; (7) proposed shortening of the work week from a basic forty hours to a basic thirty-two or thirty hours.

The more conventional issues in bargaining today also demand more thoroughgoing technical preparation than formerly. As the number and quality of sources of wage data continue to improve, the parties are inclined to rely increasingly on such data to support their respective positions on the basic wage issue. Most major unions and most large companies today have their own economic research units whose task is to supply their principals with factual ammunition on wages and other collective bargaining issues. Frequently, exhibits are tailored for particular negotiations utilizing data prepared by staff economists. The substantial improvement in "official" data in recent years, however, has reduced somewhat the need for self-help in this area. More objective bargaining is likely to ensue when both parties are agreeable to arguing their cases in terms of the same body of data, gathered by the Bureau of Labor Statistics, the Federal Reserve Board, or a state agency whose information is jointly regarded as reliable.

MANAGEMENT PREPARATION FOR BARGAINING

It is easy to generalize on the importance of careful preparation for bargaining but somewhat more difficult to lay down a meaningful prescription as to how to do it. The extent of preparation will depend in part on the bargaining requirements of the parties and their economic resources. Obviously, there will be a great difference between the kind of preparations by General Motors and the UAW on the one hand and a small machine shop and a local lodge of the IAM on the other. Summarized below are some of the principal preparation techniques or procedures now in use by major companies. The small firm may utilize some of these, but will not have the resources or, in most cases, the need to use others.

1. Thorough study of the present contract with a view to discovering sections that require modification.
2. Close analysis of grievances in order to discover defective or unworkable contract language, and to indicate future union demands.
3. Frequent conferences with line supervision for the dual purpose of better training of supervision in contract administration and receipt of intelligence as to how the contract is working out in practice.
4. Conferences with other employers in the same industry or area who have contracts with the same union for the purpose of exchanging viewpoints and anticipating future union demands.
5. Use of attitude surveys to test the reactions of employees to various sections of the contract that management may feel require change or modification.
6. Informal conferences with local union leaders (stewards, shop committeemen, or business agents, as the case may be) to discuss the operational effectiveness of the contract and to send up trial balloons on management ideas for change at the next negotiations.
7. Study of a commercial reporting service on labor relations matters for the purpose of keeping abreast of recent developments that may affect future contract negotiations.
8. Collection and analysis of economic data on issues likely to be of importance in the next negotiations.

9. Study and analysis of arbitration decisions under the current contract with a view to formulating proposals for changed contract language at the next negotiations.

10. Use of the prenegotiation conference, to be discussed presently.

UNION PREPARATION FOR BARGAINING

Unions vary considerably in the manner and degree of their advance preparation for negotiations. A building trades craft union business agent will discuss future demands with his executive board and may sound out craftsmen informally as he makes his rounds of various construction projects. He may confer with other business agents servicing related crafts and attend meetings of the joint bodies in his area. From such a combination of meetings and interviews the business agent will develop an idea of what to shoot for at the next negotiations, but from then on will be largely on his own.[1]

In a large industrial union, however, where major negotiation objectives are determined by the top international officers, a lengthy and complex procedure of opinion gathering and sifting precedes the reopening of any major contract. Each local union affected will hold meetings to bring out matters that the rank-and-file feel require action. The various demands emerging from such local meetings will be discussed, and then separated into local demands and issues relating to international union policy. District or regional meetings attended by local union officers follow a similar procedure. There is normally free interchange of views between local union officers and international representatives at such conferences. If the top international officers have decided upon a particular contract demand as a "must" in the next negotiations and no substantial grass roots sentiment for such a demand has emerged, an elaborate effort is then made to build support for such a demand through the union newspaper and international representatives, as well as public media of communication. The larger unions, as noted, have full-time economic research units whose basic task is to provide the statistical and factual underpinnings for whatever demands are decided upon by the policy-making officers.

In all unions, large or small, regardless of the structure and degree of internal democracy, there is considerable "communication" between membership and leadership. The United Mineworkers, for example, is not noted for its internal democracy. Nevertheless, few would deny that John L. Lewis for years has accurately felt the pulse of the great majority of miners as to their economic goals and requirements. As collective bargaining has become more technical and complex, the function of policy determination in many unions has become more centralized. The fact

[1] The literature is surprisingly sparse on the functioning of the union business agent. See Wilma Rule Krauss and Van Dusen Kennedy, *The Business Agent and his Union* (Berkeley: Institute of Industrial Relations, University of California, 1955).

remains that union leadership must maintain rapport and good communication with membership as a condition of success in maintaining that leadership.

Keeping in mind the extraordinary variety in the structure and size of American unions, it is possible to summarize briefly some techniques and procedures that contemporary unions employ in preparation for negotiations. In many cases it will be noted that the technique or procedure parallels the management listing. Many unions today use some, if not all, of the following techniques or procedures:

1. Careful analysis of the current contract to note any flaws from the union's standpoint that may form the basis for new demands.
2. Careful analysis of the nature and source of grievances as a guide for future negotiation proposals and as a means of discovering imperfections in the current instrument.
3. Use of the grievance procedure as a means of testing new contract language to see whether it is satisfactory or may require further modification in future contracts to accomplish the union's objective.
4. Close analysis of arbitration decisions under the existing contract as a basis for formulating demands for changed language, new contract sections, or contract deletions.
5. Periodic conferences with shop stewards or committeemen for the dual purpose of improved contract administration and receiving ideas from those in the front lines of the grievance process as to how the contract is working out on a day to day basis.
6. Careful comparison of the current contract with other agreements in the industry or area held by rival unions or other locals of the same union as a source of ideas for improvement.
7. Informal conferences with management as a device for sounding out potential management reactions to various proposals that may be in the union's future expectations.
8. Holding of one or more local union membership meetings considerably in advance of contract negotiation time for the specific purpose of receiving rank and file suggestions for union demands.
9. Collection and analysis of economic data on wages and other issues likely to be important.
10. Obtaining membership authorization of a strike if necessary as a means of adding power to union negotiators.
11. Educating the membership in advance as to the basic content and rationale of the union's principal bargaining demands to insure united support.
12. Use of the prenegotiation conference to be discussed shortly.

Negotiation of contracts today is a job for professionals, not amateurs. It is a job for specialists and not something to be handled by anyone as a portion of a multi-functional assignment. Most professionals and specialists in collective bargaining would agree, we think, that their effectiveness in negotiations is in direct relationship to the thoroughness and far-sightedness of their preparation. There is no danger in being completely prepared both as to your own case and as to the probable case of the other party. There are serious dangers in entering negotiations with an experienced and knowledgeable party on the other side of the table when you yourself are only partially prepared for the task.

THE PRENEGOTIATION CONFERENCE

The need for a rational and informed approach at bargaining tables today affords strong support for use of the prenegotiation conference. Such a conference may serve the useful purpose of preventing extreme demands. In many instances at the present time, such demands are widely publicized long before the actual contract negotiations begin, even though there may be no realistic possibility of their being achieved. Negotiations may thus fail because one party or the other is so far out on a limb that it cannot later withdraw or compromise effectively without losing face. A prenegotiation conference enables management and union to take stock of their respective positions in a general way before final demands are formulated and before actual negotiations begin. It facilitates the possibility of reaching agreement on basic factual data essential to a determination of some of the points of conflict.

George W. Taylor, who pioneered in the use of the prenegotiation conference when he was impartial chairman of the full-fashioned hosiery industry, reports to the writer that the basic idea of such a conference seems to have caught on very well on an informal basis. Taylor states that he has observed a "great deal of informal discussion between representatives of unions and companies of a prenegotiation nature." Taylor, however, indicates that the step has probably remained an informal one in most cases for fear of misinterpretation or misunderstanding by constituents.[2]

Of course, effective, formal use of a prenegotiation conference would presuppose a mature union-management relationship in which the parties have dealt with one another on a good faith basis over a considerable period of time. If the parties are in the hostile stage, neither will be disposed favorably toward a procedural technique designed to narrow the base of disagreement prior to negotiations. It is apparent, however, that today's bargaining problems are often complex and technical in nature. A wealth of factual information and expert knowledge is essential to intelligent bargaining. As an appreciation of the need for factualized

[2] Personal Communication, George W. Taylor to Harold W. Davey, June 18, 1957.

bargaining develops, the prenegotiation conference should come into more widespread favor as an accepted procedural device. Its advantages may be summarized as follows:

1. Such a conference enables management and the union to explore jointly in informal fashion the relevant economic facts about the plant or industry in question before either party crystallizes its negotiation demands in final form.

2. Such an advance exploration of the facts will serve to prevent extremism in formulating demands. It will minimize the present tendency to publicize insupportable demands in advance of negotiations.

3. Holding of a prenegotiation conference may result in advance agreement on a body of pertinent factual data. Such an agreement may in itself eliminate or narrow the subsequent area of conflict in the actual negotiations.

Whether or not a prenegotiation conference is used, the aim of management and the union in any contacts or announcements prior to the commencement of actual negotiations should be to act in such a way as to maximize the possibilities for ultimate agreement. This involves a moratorium on name-calling, exchange of threats via the newspapers, and heating-up sessions of either rank-and-file or supervisors. It involves a willingness to forego the expensive luxury of announcing extreme demands that the leadership knows are impractical of accomplishment.

Perhaps the foregoing suggestions involve too much sweetness and light to be realistically capable of attainment. Collective bargaining is a conflict relationship. At any contract negotiation or renegotiation, there will be one or more basic issues on which compromise and agreement will be extremely difficult. Yet collective bargaining is also a process of accommodation whereby essentially conflicting interests are compromised effectively to achieve continuous production and workable human relationships. The fundamental necessity of living together means that a rational effort must be made to strengthen the agreement-making potential of collective bargaining rather than to emphasize its disruptive potential. In short, a problem-solving approach is called for, with recognition of the existence of essential disagreements arising out of the competing political or economic requirements of management and the union.

CONTRACT NEGOTIATION PROCEDURES

Success in bargaining requires a blending of several variables, including: (1) thorough preparation for bargaining; (2) sound contract proposals; (3) negotiation from a position of economic bargaining strength as well as equity; (4) skilled, experienced negotiators; and (5) a positive approach toward collective bargaining involving good faith and a will to reach agreement.

Assuming the foregoing requisites, there is a wide variety of managerial and union approaches to the strategy and tactics of contract negotiation. Successful negotiation is an art and not a science, for no universally valid formula for effective negotiation can be set forth. It is possible, however, to explore certain fundamental questions that arise as to bargaining procedure and to describe briefly some of the more common approaches now in use.

The mutual purpose of negotiation should be achievement of a collective agreement that will work. The attitude of the parties in negotiation and the procedures they employ should be governed by a continuing joint awareness of this fundamental objective. Workability is the test of a good agreement.

The goal of negotiation is an instrument that will serve as the basic statutory law governing the parties' relationships over a period of usually one or two years. The contract will be good private law only if it permits smooth administration of its provisions for its duration. A contract that avoids or straddles fundamental conflicts of interest will produce, at best, an armed truce. A contract that attempts to conceal or gloss over an actual difference of intent will be productive of continuing friction and disagreement in subsequent attempts at application. These are contingencies which the able negotiator will keep constantly in mind during the contract negotiations.

What negotiation procedures are best adapted to the achievement of a good, workable collective agreement? It is generally recognized by experienced negotiators that sound procedures can be of great value in facilitating agreement on substantive issues. Advance agreement on negotiation procedures can be an excellent medium for establishing a constructive relationship between the parties. The bitterness on such explosive substantive issues as union security, wages, seniority, and management rights can frequently be alleviated by intelligent initial attention to desirable and efficient negotiation procedure.

The actual procedures employed will vary considerably from one case to another. Much depends on whether the bargaining is between one company and a local union, between one company and the international union, or between a multi-employer group and a local or international union.

In multi-employer bargaining, even in first contract experience, the parties have developed a degree of sophistication through individual plant negotiations that should minimize difficulties over bargaining procedures. But when single employers are bargaining with a local union or with the union's international representatives, a basic prior agreement on procedures to be followed in negotiation is particularly helpful.

A central procedural problem in negotiation is whether to dispose of the disputed issues one by one or to defer final settlement on any one issue until all have been bargained out successfully. Especially in bargaining over issues involving money outlays, it is important to decide whether it is preferable to take up each demand separately on its merits or to apply the "basket" approach.

BARGAINING ON MONEY ISSUES

The consensus among practitioners would probably favor deferring formal agreement on all key disputed issues until a tentative understanding on all points in conflict has been reached. Such an approach may lengthen negotiations somewhat and, in some cases, add to the tension and bitterness. However, it is one sure way for each party ultimately to determine which of a variety of issues the other party is most fundamentally concerned about and what its minimum requirements for settlement are likely to be.

Where several key union demands would involve substantial money outlays by the employer, the parties frequently endeavor to reach tentative agreement on how much additional labor cost the employer is willing to absorb for the coming contract period and then do hard bargaining on the allocation of this lump sum among competing demands. Among the more familiar choices that have to be made in this respect in current negotiations may be listed one between a general increase in wages versus an expanded pension plan, or improved vacation schedules versus introduction of a sick leave plan, and so on. Frequently there is also the possibility of trading off an economic demand for a noneconomic improvement in employment conditions, or the other way around. Many unions push vigorously at successive negotiations for a union shop as a "stalking horse" to get the employer to raise his initial wage proposal. In somewhat different circumstances a union might be willing to forego a wage increase entirely as a concession to obtain a union shop or an improved layoff and recall provision.

FACTORS AFFECTING THE ATMOSPHERE OF NEGOTIATIONS

The pattern and atmosphere of contract negotiations will vary greatly from one situation to another depending on such factors as: (1) history of prior relations between the parties; (2) the basic attitude of the company toward unionism; (3) the economic circumstances of the company; and (4) the compulsions that may be operating upon union leadership which may or may not be related to the company with which the union is negotiating. Each of these factors deserves brief attention. If the parties have a past history of bitter conflict, or if tensions have built up in administration of the contract about to expire, the bargaining is likely to be tough, long drawn out, and perhaps unsuccessful. On the other hand, many companies and unions renegotiate contracts with a bare minimum of conflict and dispute year after year.

If past relationships have been unsatisfactory, negotiations will probably have to proceed on a "goldfish bowl" basis, with a maximum of partisan speech-making designed to impress the ears of constituents. If past relations have been stable and peaceful, contract negotiations may be limited to the principals directly concerned (the firm's industrial relations director and the union's business agent or international representative), with subsequent membership ratification a mere formality.

The pattern of negotiations will vary also in terms of the economic circumstances of the company. The union must always seek "improvements" over the previous contract. A company that accepts the union will not begrudge such political compulsions operating upon union leadership. In a situation where the company in question cannot grant any contract changes involving added labor cost (or may even require a decrease in labor costs), however, a realistic union will recognize these compulsions on a hard-pressed firm.[3] In one such case, when asked what he obtained from the negotiations, the union representative replied cryptically, "We couldn't get any money, but we got a lot of language." Implied in this statement is a recognition of the company's straitened economic condition, with the "gains" to the membership that year coming from a firming-up of contract language on various noneconomic issues.

The pattern and atmosphere of negotiations may also be affected by conditions external to the company or union. The company in question may be under pressure from other employers to resist a particular union demand. Conversely, the union in question may be obligated by international union policy to press hard for certain demands (e.g., an SUB plan) about which the local union membership as such is not particularly concerned. In such cases the external pressures on one or both participants may be strong enough to convert the negotiations into an endurance contest that is foreign to the desires of the participants themselves.

The lay observer of contract negotiations is frequently puzzled by the apparent ferocity with which negotiators attack one another during the early stages of bargaining. He is also disturbed by the extremity of the union's initial demands and the niggardliness of the employer's original counter offers. Such attitudes ignore the fact that collective bargaining has the attributes of any other type of bargaining in human society. To abstain entirely from a certain amount of melodramatic build-up

[3] For an illuminating and perceptive treatment of bargaining problems in four different situations involving "marginal" firms, see A. Howard Myers, *Crisis Bargaining: Management-Union Relations in Marginal Situations* (Boston: Bureau of Business and Economic Research, Northeastern University, 1957.)

by approaching the matter coldly and logically would "take all the fun" out of bargaining. It would also destroy the maneuverability and flexibility that each party desires to maintain until he is reasonably sure in his estimate of the relative strength or weakness of the other party's position and of what the other party's real minimum demands or real offers are likely to be.

This is not to say that the parties to bargaining should not continue to rely increasingly on facts in support of their negotiation positions. Neither must all contract negotiations proceed until the participants are physically and emotionally exhausted with a strike deadline staring them in the face before agreement should be reached. No harm is done, however, by judicious respect for the dramatic unities in the negotiation process. Considerable harm to union-management relationships may be done by an approach such as "Boulwareism" that undercuts all bargaining conventions by its emphasis on a "first and last offer."

Contract negotiation is certainly the most dramatic phase of the collective bargaining process. There is a constant awareness that if agreement is not reached, a strike or a lockout will result. *The possibility of economic force is the chief sanction that keeps the parties at the table in search of an agreement*. Each party has his minimum position from which he will not retreat. In the overwhelming majority of cases the possibility of successful accommodation of conflicting demands is found through negotiation, and resort to economic force is thereby avoided. In most cases the union's minimum requirements and the employer's final ability to grant improvements will overlap or coincide in a way to make agreement possible. In the minority of cases where this is not possible, collective bargaining is continued by other methods—a strike or a lockout, much harsher methods of producing agreement.

THE ART OF NEGOTIATION

Since negotiation is an art rather than a science, it is difficult—in fact somewhat presumptuous—for an outsider to attempt to set down in objective fashion those personal qualities or techniques that make for successful negotiation. There is no universal prototype of the successful union or management negotiator. However, a few general observations can be made with some confidence.

First, no matter how adept in human relations an individual negotiator may be, he is unlikely to be successful unless he has the facts and a basic economic strength working with him. Second, there is no substitute for personal integrity and courage. A successful negotiator must have these attributes in abundance. Third, success in negotiation as in other aspects of union-management relationships involves an informed awareness and understanding of the compulsions that are operating upon the other party.

A knowledgeable management negotiator, for example, will not become disturbed when his union opposite number begins negotiations with a flaming speech about the callous, hard-hearted, stingy company whose profits are enormous but whose offers are meager. Nor will an adept union leader become exercised when the management negotiator launches into a prolonged dissertation on the inviolability of certain managerial prerogatives. In each case, other things being equal, there is an awareness of the need for a certain amount of speech-making for the benefit of constituents. Such conduct in negotiations is not deliberately deceitful or harmful, provided it is not carried to extremes. No poised negotiator will be thrown off balance by such tactics.

Fourth and finally, a successful negotiator (management or union) must believe in the collective bargaining process as a viable method of joint decision-making and as a method of accommodating conflicts of interest. A negotiator with a cynical or a "take-it-or-leave-it" approach, no matter how personally intelligent or experienced he may be, cannot be successful in achieving constructive union-management relationships.

SUGGESTED NEGOTIATION PROCEDURES

1. Both the union and management negotiating committees should be kept reasonably small. If the union or company committee is too large and everyone insists on participating, much time will be consumed, tempers will become frayed, and much irrelevant material may be introduced.
2. One person should be in charge of conducting the negotiations for each side. Division of authority in negotiation is fatal to orderly procedure and usually impedes the agreement-making process.
3. The parties should agree in advance on the time of day and desired length for bargaining sessions. Each side can then make its plans accordingly.
4. Careful advance preparation for negotiations should be made. If possible, the parties should exchange demands or proposals for study before the actual bargaining sessions begin. A frequent source of trouble is the springing of a complicated new proposal during negotiations.
5. Advance agreement should be secured on the procedures to be followed in bargaining sessions. This eliminates many unnecessary arguments over correct procedure, such as whether subject *X* is "in order at this time." Advance agreement on procedures provides a healthy common basis for accord on substantive issues at the bargaining table.

6. Company and union negotiators should have authority to make decisive commitments in the course of negotiations. Company negotiators should have the power to bind their principals. In most unions the negotiated terms are subject to ratification or rejection by the membership. In the vast majority of cases, however, the rank-and-file do not exercise their veto power. Realistically, therefore, it is possible for union negotiators to make binding commitments. Company negotiators must have similar power.

7. Negotiations should begin with a well-planned agenda that includes a complete statement of all disputed issues together with a listing of proposals and counterproposals on the disputed points.

8. There should be, if possible, an agreed statement as to relevant factual information. Agreement on such a statement will be easier if the parties have already made effective use of the prenegotiation conference.

9. The negotiators should first eliminate the least controversial issues and reduce agreement on these to writing before proceeding to negotiation of the tougher issues.

10. The difficult issues may be divided into those that involve money outlays and those that are noneconomic demands.

11. Noneconomic issues may be taken up individually and decided in each case on their intrinsic merits, instead of allowing the cruder measure of the economic strength of the principals to determine whether a particular demand will be accepted or rejected.

12. Use of the basket approach on economic issues is recommended. If the prenegotiation conference has produced agreement on relevant factual information as to the economic state of the industry and the financial condition of the plant, it may be possible to reach agreement on a lump sum available for disposition of income demands (wage increase, paid holidays not worked, call-in pay). The negotiations can then proceed on the basis of allocation of this over-all total in terms of the relative urgency of the competing demands for economic benefits.

The procedures suggested above may not be suitable in all situations. For example, many experienced negotiators do not agree on the merits of the basket approach to the negotiation of economic issues. Nor is the prenegotiation conference prevalent enough to warrant an assumption that the parties will arrive at the bargaining able with a common core of factual information. Nevertheless, most of the foregoing suggestions have considerable practical validity regardless of the industry or the particular type of union-management relationship involved.

NEGOTIATING THE FIRST CONTRACT

Most of the foregoing suggestions are based on the assumption that the company and union have been bargaining with one another for some time.

One of the most difficult negotiation situations is obviously that of a newly certified union bargaining for a first contract.

The negotiation of the first contract between a company and a union usually takes place in an atmosphere ranging from uncertainty to outright hostility. The negotiations may be proceeding under the imminent threat of a strike or a lockout. They may be held after a strike or lockout has already occurred, or is still in progress. Frequently the negotiations may be held following certification of the union as exclusive bargaining agent by the National Labor Relations Board.

Most first contract cases have some or all of the following features:

1. The union has to make a good showing. This is a political necessity for the union in dealing with a recently unionized company.

2. The company usually feels a compulsion to give as little as possible in the first contract.

3. Company and union negotiators may not be well-acquainted with each other's strengths and weaknesses. An atmosphere of suspicion, if not outright lack of faith in the other party, is usually prevalent.

4. One or both parties to a first contract may be inexperienced in negotiation. This lack of maturity or knowledge is frequently a serious handicap.

5. The local union shop committee may wish to convert the negotiation of the basic agreement into a general complaint session over a large backlog of grievances. Although this is frequently understandable, the timing is unfortunate for the successful negotiation of the contract itself.

6. If the company happens to be one of the last to be organized in its industry, the pressure to adopt a contract incorporating at one stroke the advantages accrued in years of bargaining with other firms may complicate matters.

These are some of the basic difficulties common to first contract negotiations. No sensible person would contend that such problems can be overcome by a perfect set of negotiation procedures. Applied knowledge of generally acceptable modes of procedure, however, can assist the parties over some of the hurdles. With the exception of the prenegotiation conference, most of the procedural suggestions outlined earlier for contract negotiations can be applied profitably to first contract cases. The use of the prenegotiation conference, as pointed out previously, depends for its effectiveness on some stability and mutual understanding in the relationship. Such an understanding is unlikely to be present in first contract negotiations.

PUBLIC POLICY AND CONTRACT RENEGOTIATION

As noted in Chapter 3, the framers of Taft-Hartley paid considerable attention to the procedures for renegotiation of expiring contracts or the reopening of continuous contracts. The Act lays down definite requirements that must be adhered to in all such cases. As indicated in Chapter 3, it is somewhat questionable whether the discretion of the parties should be so rigidly circumscribed as to bargaining procedure.

LONG-TERM CONTRACTS AS "LIVING DOCUMENTS"

When long-term contracts came into vogue some years ago, one of the key questions raised by the skeptics was whether an agreement of three to five years' duration would be sufficiently flexible to meet dynamic change. What would happen when it was found that a particular section was unworkable or had become outdated? Most long-term contracts contained rather tightly worded waiver articles, the net effect of which was to enable either party to stick grimly to the language of the instrument for the full length of the contract if he chose to do so.

Sensing that they might have paid too high a price for stability, many union leaders began speaking of the need for such contracts to be regarded as "living documents." A crisis arose fairly early in the pioneering GM-UAW five-year pact when the Bureau of Labor Statistics changed its base for computing the Consumers Price Index, thus affecting the contract's escalator clause. The agreement was reopened to accommodate this new development by mutual consent and was reopened on several other occasions for various purposes. Unions now operating in industries subject to technological change of the "automation" type are skeptical of long-term agreements because of the extraordinary shifts in employment conditions that may occur in a short span of years.

It seems probable that long-term contracts are here to stay in most of the industries that have adopted them. Many current contracts are being negotiated for periods of three years or longer in industries that formerly operated on the conventional one-year basis. One reason for mentioning this development in a chapter on negotiation procedures is that when one is considering an instrument that is going to be jointly binding for such long periods of time, the need for careful preparation and negotiation is obvious.

A FOOTNOTE ON MANAGEMENT NEGOTIATION STRATEGY

The writer cannot close a chapter on negotiation without commenting on a basic problem of management strategy as to proposals for contract change. The conventional management approach to bargaining has always been to wait in tight-lipped silence until it receives union demands for the coming contract, and then formulate counter-proposals. It is difficult to understand why most companies in collective bargaining do not take a more positive approach to the submission of demands in negotiation. Why should not management submit to the union its own set of demands for change in the coming contract? If it is a good faith relationship and management has found by experience that certain changes or modifications in the contract are necessary, it would seem that such proposals would have a better chance for union acceptance if they were advanced affirmatively at the start of negotiations rather than brought in by the back door as counter-proposals.

It is for this reason that it was suggested earlier in the section on preparation for bargaining that management do a thorough job of contract and grievance analysis as a foundation for proposals for change. There are still many companies whose approach to collective bargaining is that of the confirmed counter-puncher in boxing. While counter-punching occasionally works in boxing against an inexperienced opponent, it does not seem to be the most fruitful way for management to exploit its position at the bargaining table. The psychology of such an approach is necessarily negative and defensive. While the other extreme of "Boulwareism," making one offer and one only, may be inadvisable, there is no reason in logic or experience why management should not come to the bargaining table with concrete proposals for change instead of waiting to see what the union demands.

CONCLUSION

In preparation for bargaining and actual negotiation the rules of the game and the most acceptable techniques and strategies must necessarily be determined by the parties themselves in terms of their own experience and economic conditions. No one can lay down a blueprint that will work in any and all situations. This chapter has traced a variety of techniques and procedures used by management and union representatives in preparing for bargaining and in the actual negotiations themselves. No technique or procedure, however, can ever be a substitute for good faith, intelligence, integrity, courage, and experience in the bargaining process. Bargaining remains an art rather than a science.

SELECTED BIBLIOGRAPHY

Bambrick, James J., Jr. and Marie P. Dorbandt, "Role of Foremen in Collective Bargaining," *Management Record*, XIX (January, 1957), 3-5, 21-22.

———, "The Use of Bargaining Books in Negotiations," *Management Record*, XIX (April, 1957), 118-21, 143-45.

———, "Who Bargains for Management," *Management Record*, XIX (June, 1957), 198–201, 220–24.

Barkin, Solomon, "Financial Statements in Collective Bargaining," *Labor Law Journal*, IV (November, 1953), 753–58.

Card, David E., "Information Requests in Collective Bargaining," *Labor Law Journal*, VI (November, 1955), 777–96 .

Gardiner, Glen, *When Foreman and Steward Bargain.* New York: McGraw-Hill Book Co., Inc., 1945.

Krauss, Wilma Rule and Van Dusen Kennedy, *The Business Agent and His Union.* Berkeley: Institute of Industrial Relations, University of California, 1955.

Layman, Allen E., "Games Bargaining: A Proposed Application of the Theory of Games to Collective Bargaining," *Yale Law Journa*l, LXV (April, 1956), 660–93.

Lind, John H., "How to Handle Crisis Bargaining," *Personnel*, XXXI (September, 1954), 151–57.

McPherson, William H., "Grievance Mediation under Collective Bargaining," *Industrial and Labor Relations Review*, IX (January, 1956), 200–12.

Miller, Max J., "Employers' Duty to Furnish Wage and Economic Data to Unions," *Labor Law Journal*, VI (March, 1955), 151–64.

Peters, Edward, *Strategy and Tactics in Labor Negotiations.* New London: National Foremen's Institute, 1955.

Rosen, Hjalmar and R. A. H. Rosen, "The Union Business Agent Looks at Collective Bargaining," *Personnel*, XXXIII (May, 1957), 539-45.

Taylor, George W., "Ground Rules for the Use of Statistics in Collective Bargaining," *Proceedings of the Fifth Annual Meeting, Industrial Relations Research Association.* Madison: IRRA, 1953, 10–20.

Witney, Fred, *What You Should Know About Collective Bargaining Negotiations.* Bloomington: Bureau of Business Research, Business Information Bulletin No. 17, Indiana University, 1953.

6

Contract administration: principles and procedures

Contract negotiation is that part of the union-management iceberg that shows above the surface. The larger and more important part of the iceberg that is seldom seen is the significant process of administration of collective agreements. *A contract is no better than its administration.* The test of the soundness of a union-management relationship lies in how effectively the parties implement their contract in the troublesome process of living together under the agreement.

Just as contracts vary in subject matter, so also does experience vary in the matter of contract administration, making generalization a hazardous enterprise. In some hostile and undisciplined relationships, the union enforces (or ignores) the contract through slowdowns, wildcats, or chronic absenteeism. In other similarly unsatisfactory relationships, management enforces (or ignores) the contract in an arbitrary and inequitable manner, knowing that the union with whom it is dealing is too weak to challenge effectively the managerial approach to contract administration. We are not concerned, however, with undesirable extremes, but with the great majority of management-union relationships where the parties have a sincere desire to administer their joint agreement equitably according to their understanding of the terms of that agreement.

The primary responsibility for administration of the terms of the employment relationship usually rests with management. American experience with joint administration of contractual provisions is comparatively limited. In most cases these are management's jobs: to recruit and hire employees; to train employees; to schedule the work; to assign workers to jobs; to transfer employees; to promote employees; to determine merit increases; to institute technological changes; to set temporary rates on new or changed jobs; to lay off workers when a reduction in force becomes necessary; to recall workers when business picks up.

In the performance of most of these functions management is operating subject to one or more provisions of a collective agreement setting forth the terms and conditions of employment. The mechanism for insuring responsible observance of the terms of the agreement is established in the agreement itself: the grievance and arbitration machinery. The right of the individual worker, the union, or the management to present and to process a grievance is the procedural device for insuring adherence to contractual provisions.

Jack Barbash, one of the most knowledgeable observers of trade unionism, states flatly in his recent book that the "handling of workers' grievances on the job is perhaps the single most important function of modern unionism." [1]

The grievance procedure (capped and supplemented in most cases by arbitration) is the mechanism for breathing life into the bare language of the contract. Individual cases of alleged contract violation as they are compromised, adjusted, and settled give substantive content and significance to such familiar contract phrases as "good and just cause" in discipline cases, "equal pay for equal work" in job classification cases, equitable sharing of overtime, and so on. Grievance adjustment is just as important to management as it is to the union since it affords a medium for management to check on both the troublesome or unworkable contract provisions and also the effectiveness and skill of line supervision in handling their human relations responsibilities under the contract. With a smoothly functioning grievance procedure management can be alerted to problems before they reach critical proportions, and thereby cement its reputation for fair dealing by the way in which it meets and answers grievances.

In large bargaining units covering thousands of employees the formation of a body of shop law or industrial jurisprudence through the grievance procedure becomes rather formalized. In others grievances are rarely reduced to writing and are handled in a most informal fashion.

[1] Jack Barbash, *The Practice of Unionism* (New York: Harper & Brothers, 1956), p. 191.

In some situations departmental foremen and shop stewards play key roles. In a highly centralized relationship these men are by-passed in recognition that real discretion for grievance adjustment lies higher up on the chain of command.

In the realm of nonfactory unionism grievance adjustment is one of numerous functions performed by a jack-of-all-trades business agent as he moves from job to job and from shop to shop. In some relationships few grievances are settled in the lower steps of the procedure, since the parties prefer to make extensive use of arbitration for final resolution of disputes under an existing contract. In other cases, although their contracts provide for arbitration, the parties pride themselves on settling the overwhelming majority of grievances at the foreman-steward level and rarely, if ever, resort to arbitration. The structure of the grievance and arbitration procedure itself varies greatly in the degree of complexity and formality. There is also considerable difference in practice as to the types of grievances entertained.

Notwithstanding these patterns of variety, there are certain basic principles of, and hindrances to, effective grievance adjustment that can be enumerated. The ensuing discussion is framed in terms of the writer's experience as arbitrator in a variety of manufacturing industries with industrial bargaining units. The illustrations are from actual cases and will be identified wherever appropriate or necessary.

WHAT IS A GRIEVANCE?

Management is interested in running an efficient and orderly enterprise with a minimum of friction and resentment on the part of employees. As such, management is interested (or should be) in settling any individual or group dissatisfaction that may threaten the achievement of these objectives. Similarly, the union's principal role in contract administration is to function as an agent or representative of employees in handling individual or group complaints that may arise, and to check independently on the way in which management is exercising administrative initiative in effectuating contract terms and conditions.

In this broadest sense of their respective functions any company and any union must subscribe to the fundamental psychological proposition that *a grievance exists whenever an employee feels aggrieved*, whether or not the source of his grievance is contractual.

If an employee or some employees feel, rightly or wrongly, that they are being unjustly treated, a human relations problem exists that merits the attention of both management and the union.

At the same time, the interest of intelligent and orderly administration of contracts requires that a distinction be made and clearly understood by all parties between those grievances which raise a question of contract interpretation or application and those grievances which, no matter how intrinsically sincere or meritorious they may be, are outside the scope of the collective agreement. Some highly prerogative-conscious managements will refuse to discuss with union representatives any grievance that does not relate directly to the contract. Such an approach of uncompromising legalism may succeed in "putting the union in its place," but it is not conducive to constructive labor relations. From a realistic standpoint, a grievance procedure should be designed to carry all grievances.

Now, obviously, in any concrete situation a line has to be drawn somewhere. If a collective labor agreement is to mean anything, its provisions must be adhered to by both parties for its duration. It would be inviting chaos to say that all grievances must be entertained whether or not they bear any relationship to a contractual provision. At the same time, genuine grievances will arise over problems not covered or contemplated by the contract. These grievances are no less real because the contract may happen to be silent on the matter. Some procedural outlet must be provided.

In attempting to draw an equitable line between a strict legalistic approach to grievance administration and an excessively liberal definition of "what is a grievance?" the most feasible approach would appear to be one that precludes resort to arbitration as a final step except when the unsettled grievance involves a question of contract interpretation or application.

This would permit the worker to raise a complaint on any subject in the early steps of the grievance machinery, but would limit his avenues of appeal when the subject of his grievance is not arbitrable under the contract. Of course, one of the first questions in many arbitrations is the arbitrability of the disputed issue.[2] Some test cases might go all the way in the interests of avoiding resort to economic force. One may agree that wide-open arbitration clauses are dangerous and may lead to practical nullification of collective agreements, without subscribing to the notion that grievances must be defined and a rigid line drawn between acceptable and nonacceptable grievances. A genuine grievance requires an airing, even if it is not strictly in order under the existing contract.

Perhaps the best exposition of this realistic attitude toward grievance adjustment is the clinical approach advocated by Benjamin M. Selekman.[3]

[2] For a scholarly analysis of arbitrability issues by an experienced arbitrator, see Jules J. Justin, "Arbitrability and the Arbitrator's Jurisdiction," Chapter I in Jean T. McKelvey, ed., *Management Rights and the Arbitration Process*, Proceedings of the Ninth Annual Meeting of the National Academy of Arbitrators (Washington: Bureau of National Affairs, Inc., 1956), pp. 1–34.

[3] See Benjamin M. Selekman, *Labor Relations and Human Relations* (New York: McGraw-Hill Book Co., Inc., 1947), pp. 75–110.

Such an approach involves seeking out the fundamental determinants of a grievance rather than accepting its surface rationale, which may not touch the heart of the matter at all. Many grievances are filed in such a way as to obscure the real basis for the antagonism or sense of injury. The surface explanation is not the real motivating force behind the grievance. Intelligent, sympathetic digging is required to probe into the actual causation of many grievances.

Selekman concedes the necessity for some legalism in the grievance machinery of large plants and in cases of multi-employer or company-wide bargaining. His clinical approach is designed to supplement, strengthen, and broaden the legalistic approach rather than to supplant it entirely.

As Selekman points out, the clinical or realistic approach to grievance adjustment places the emphasis on treating the problems found to underlie the grievances rather on the mechanics of accepting or dismissing grievances in terms of whether or not they are within the contract.

Management may not be the only party to suffer by an overly legalistic approach to contract administration. The union also must frequently make choices between enforcing the letter of the contract and a more "flexible" attitude rooted in the realities of the particular circumstances. If a union insists on strict adherence by management in all situations, it invites a management policy of refusing to budge in other cases except as the contract requires.

To take one illustration, suppose the contract contains a flat prohibition against supervisors doing any production work except as instructors or in starting new jobs. The main reason behind such a policy is the conservation of job opportunities for employees in the bargaining unit. Not infrequently, however, in the course of daily business it makes sense occasionally for the foreman to lend a hand in a particular job. Should the union always grieve in such situations, or should it look the other way? A policy of always grieving, regardless of the realities of the situation, might well provoke management into an extremely strict view in borderline situations when, for instance, an incentive worker is entitled to his average hourly incentive earnings rather than just his guaranteed occupational rate.

THE POLITICS OF GRIEVANCE ADJUSTMENT

Industrial unions in particular are not homogeneous institutions whose members all have common interests and common problems. It is important to keep in mind that there are sharp interest differences among various groups within an industrial union that complicate the task of union leadership in contract administration. The interests of senior workers and junior employees frequently are in conflict. In problems on sharing of available overtime work, for instance, when the overtime is assigned to one classification, another group may feel aggrieved. Frequent differences arise between hourly paid and incentive employees.

The balancing and accommodation of these conflicting interests are difficult tasks of union leadership in grievance handling. This political burden is not always well-understood by management. A company that is interested in building durable relationships with a responsible union is usually sensitive to the manifold conflicting pressures operating upon local union leaders. It will try to avoid actions or policies that embarrass or undercut such leadership. Much of the formalism and legalism that is characteristic of contract administration in manufacturing today is due not so much to management's initiative as it is to the union leadership's need to insulate itself from rank-and-file pressures.

Sayles and Strauss, in their pioneering empirical study of local unions,[4] list five ways in which local leaders can maintain their freedom to choose the grievances they want to push while at the same time avoiding identification with defeats: (1) requiring members to sign grievances; (2) careful screening of grievances before negotiating with management; (3) never negotiating without another officer being present; (4) relying on precedents and legalistic interpretations; and (5) "passing the buck" to the arbitrator.[5]

PRINCIPLES OF GRIEVANCE ADJUSTMENT

Certain general principles should govern the handling and adjustment of grievances.[6] One principle universally endorsed is that grievances should be adjusted *promptly*, preferably at the first step in the grievance procedure, and that the adjustment of grievances should be *on their merits.* Although few practitioners take exception to this principle, there are not a few cases in which the principle is ignored. Many observers, including Sayles and Strauss, have noted the increasing tendency in many relationships to by-pass the departmental foreman and the steward in grievance adjustment. In a smoothly functioning relationship, however, the overwhelming majority of grievances can and should be informally adjusted and disposed of at the foreman-steward level. Where discretion to adjust is denied to the foreman, the authority of the steward correspondingly declines, since he is the foreman's opposite number. Many companies and unions are apparently more interested in uniformity and

[4] Leonard R. Sayles and George Strauss, *The Local Union: Its Place in the Industrial Plant* (New York: Harper & Brothers, 1953).

[5] *Ibid.*, p. 74.

[6] For a thoughtful analysis, see Van D. Kennedy, "Grievance Negotiation," Chapter 21 in Arthur Kornhauser, Robert Dubin, and Arthur M. Ross, eds., *Industrial Conflict* (New York: McGraw-Hill Book Co., Inc., 1954).

more fearful of possible embarrassing precedents than they are in democratic decision-making at the shop level.

The answer to these fears is not to take away discretion from the foremen and stewards but to do a thorough and effective job of foreman and steward training in contract administration. Preferably, this training should be jointly conducted in informal groups of fifteen or twenty foremen and stewards right after a contract is negotiated. Such a training program is admittedly difficult to plan and administer. However, the dividends from the time and effort spent should be well worth the trouble. Properly trained foremen and stewards could be encouraged to adjust grievances in the initial stages instead of passing them up the line.

The very essence of contract administration requires that grievances be adjusted in an equitable, nondiscriminatory, and reasonably uniform manner. Of course, there should be some room for flexibility in the solution of problems raised by grievances. The basic pattern of adjustment on the merits in accordance with contract principles, however, must be adhered to if the grievance process is to perform its fundamental function.

A second basic principle is that the machinery for submission of a grievance must be easy to utilize and well-understood both by the worker and his supervisor. The functional relationship among the worker, his steward, and the foreman must be clearly established.

Third, regardless of the particular mechanical details or number of steps in the procedure, it is essential that the need for a direct avenue of appeal from the rulings of line supervision be recognized.

Finally, effective grievance adjustment requires establishment of voluntary arbitration by a disinterested party as the terminal step in the contract's grievance machinery. Discussion of the proper uses of arbitration in contract administration is reserved for the next chapter.

PROBLEMS IN GRIEVANCE ADJUSTMENT PROCEDURE

Even where there is general agreement on the basic principles of effective grievance adjustment, problems frequently arise as to the best procedural mechanisms to facilitate contract administration. The most common questions relate to such matters as: the number of steps in the grievance and arbitration procedure; reducing grievances to writing; time limits and their enforcement; distinction between contract grievances and matters outside the contract; use of grievance procedure by management as well as by the worker or the union; penalties for failure to utilize the grievance procedure; and filing of grievances by individual employees independently of the union. Satisfactory mutual agreement must be reached on such matters if the grievance machinery is to operate efficiently and equitably.

The task of contract administrators is greatly simplified in those cases where the parties have given careful thought to the need for clear and unambiguous contract language detailing the grievance and arbitration procedure. A little extra time spent in negotiations can save a great many headaches in contract administration.

MODEL CONTRACT LANGUAGE

The John Deere-UAW contracts are fairly representative and models of clarity as to intent and purpose. As a basis for discussion of a number of points in connection with the mechanics of grievance processing, the grievance and arbitration article of the 1955-1958 Deere-UAW contract (Waterloo, Iowa plant) is reproduced in full below:

ARTICLE XII

Grievance Procedure

Section I. Should any employee or the Union desire to present a grievance to the Company concerning any matter involving rates of pay, wages, hours of employment, or any other condition of employment such grievance shall be handled under the following Grievance Procedure:

Step A—Between the aggrieved employee with his departmental steward and his foreman. The foregoing shall not be construed to mean that an employee cannot discuss conditions and circumstances involving his work with his foreman without the presence of his steward.

1. The grievance shall be reduced to writing and signed by the aggrieved employee and the departmental steward. All handling of the grievance by either party shall thereafter be in writing. Such written grievance shall be presented to the employee's foreman within five (5) working days from the date on which the act or condition complained of last occurred. The foreman shall give his answer in writing to the departmental steward and the aggrieved employee, within one working day from receipt of the written grievance.
2. Any grievance which is not carried to Step B within three (3) working days after the foreman's written answer in Step A, shall be deemed settled on the basis of said written answer.

Step B—Between the Divisional Steward and the Director of Industrial Relations.

1. Any grievance which remains unsettled after completion of Step A shall, if carried to Step B, be presented to the Director of Industrial Relations by the Divisional Steward.
2. The Director of Industrial Relations shall give his answer in writing to the Divisional Steward and the aggrieved employee as soon as possible after his receipt of the written grievance from the Divisional Steward, and in any event, within four (4) working days.

3. Grievances which involve cases of disciplinary action shall enter the Grievance Procedure at Step C, provided that:
   a. Such grievances must be presented to the Director of Industrial Relations by the Divisional Steward within three (3) working days after the disciplinary action took place.
   b. Such grievances shall be in writing.
4. Grievances of a general character, i.e., those affecting all employees in the bargaining unit, or those involving matters which are outside the jurisdiction of the department foreman, shall enter the Grievance Procedure at Step B. Such grievances shall be written by the Divisional Steward and presented to the Director of Industrial Relations.
5. Any grievance which is not carried to Step C by the second regular weekly meeting of the Shop Committee and the Company following the date of the Director of Industrial Relations' answer in Step B, shall be deemed settled on the basis of said answer.

Step C—Between the Shop Committee of the Union and the Plant Manager or other Company representatives who may be designated by him.

1. Grievances which remain unsettled after completion of Steps A and B and only such grievances shall be discussed at the second regular meeting of the Shop Committee and the Company following the date of the Director of Industrial Relations' answer in Step B provided that the Shop Committee shall submit to the Director of Industrial Relations, in writing, at least one (1) working day before the regular weekly meeting, a list of all grievances to be discussed at said meeting, which list shall contain the number of each grievance and a brief statement of the position of the Union Shop Committee in regard to said grievance. No grievance shall be discussed at a regular weekly meeting which has not been presented to the Director of Industrial Relations in writing, as above provided, at least one (1) working day prior to the time of the meeting.
2. The Director of Industrial Relations shall give the Shop Committee and the aggrieved employee the Company's written answer to any grievance in Step C not later than three (3) working days after the regular weekly meeting at which the discussion of the grievance is concluded.
3. Should the Company desire to present a grievance to the Union, such grievance shall enter the Grievance Procedure at Step C.

Step D—Between the Shop Committee of the Union and an International Representative of the Union and the Plant Manager or representative who may be designated by him.

1. Should the Union desire to submit a grievance to Step D, it may request a special meeting for such purpose within ten (10) working days as provided in Paragraph 4 of Step C, and shall state in writing to the Director of Industrial Relations at least five (5) working days prior to the date of the special meeting, the grievance to be discussed.

In the written appeal to Step D the Union shall set out the alleged contract violation, if any, the Section or Sections of the Contract violated, and the specific relief sought thereunder. Should there be any dispute as to whether the Step D appeal conforms to these requirements, the Union may amend its appeal in the Step D hearing so to conform to the requirements of this provision.

Should the Union refuse to amend and the Company still considers that the Step D appeal does not meet the requirements of this provision and the grievance is later appealed to Step E, then either party may submit this dispute directly to the arbitrator who shall determine whether or not the written appeal conforms with the requirements of this provision.

2. Any grievance, which is submitted to Step D, shall be answered, in writing, to the Chairman of the Shop Committee and the aggrieved employee not later than ten (10) working days after the meeting in which the discussion of the grievance is concluded and, if the grievance is denied or remains unsettled, the Company in its answer shall state that the contract provisions cited by the Union are not violated or that other contract provisions govern the subject matter of the grievance or that no contract provision is involved in the grievance or any combination of these positions.
3. Any grievance which is not carried to Step E within fifteen (15) working days from the date of the Company's written answer in Step D shall be deemed settled on the basis of said answer.

Step E—Grievances involving interpretation and application of the provisions of this Agreement, except for grievances involving (1) changes in existing incentive standards other than those grievances specifically referred to in Article XVII, Section 11-B, (2) the establishment of new incentive standards, (3) the rate range for new hourly paid job classifications introduced into the plant, or (4) the occupational rate for new incentive work job classifications introduced into the plant, which had been processed through the grievance procedure, and only such grievances, may be submitted to arbitration as provided below:

1. Should the Union desire to submit such a grievance to Step E, it shall give written notice to the Company within fifteen (15) working days from the date of the Company's written answer in Step D and may at this time, if it wishes, amend the language of its Step D appeal to cite additional or substitute contract provisions allegedly violated and to amend the relief sought. In such event, the Company shall have an additional five (5) days to amend its Step D answer in the same fashion as set out above.

Such appeal and answer in Step D, or as amended in Step E, shall constitute the issue for determination by the Arbitrator, provided, however, that either party may in the arbitration proceeding cite any other contract language only in the same manner that it might submit any other type of evidence or argument in support of its position.

2. Within five (5) days following the date of notice as outlined in Paragraph 1 above (or ten (10) days if the Union elects to amend as provided above), either the Company or the Union shall submit a request to the Arbitrator that he set a date for a hearing on the disputed issue. A copy of this request shall be given to the other party at the same time as it is submitted to the Arbitrator.

3. Either party shall be entitled to present its claims to the Arbitrator in such manner as the party may desire, provided that the Arbitrator may determine the relevancy of the evidence presented. The decision of the Arbitrator shall be final and binding, shall be reduced to writing, and each party shall be furnished with a signed copy thereof.
4. The Arbitrator shall have no power to alter, change, detract from or add to the provisions of this Agreement, but shall have power only to apply and interpret the provisions of this Agreement to the settlement of grievances arising hereunder.
5. Not more than three (3) grievances covering different subject matters may be arbitrated at one arbitration hearing.
6. Each party shall bear its own costs, and the expense of the arbitration proceedings shall be shared equally by the Company and the Union.
7. a. The Arbitrator shall be selected as follows:

    The parties agree to the selection of Harold W. Davey as the Permanent Arbitrator referred to herein, subject to all the conditions contained herein. In the event of his removal for any of the reasons listed below, the provisions of Paragraph (b) and (c) shall be effective and shall be effective upon the removal of any Arbitrator subsequently selected. The Arbitrator so selected shall serve during the life of this contract, subject, however, to his removal by death, resignation or his removal by either party as herein provided.

   b. In the event either party desires to remove the Arbitrator, that party shall notify the other party and the Arbitrator, in writing, of its decision and the reason or reasons therefor, whereupon each party shall within 10 days submit to the other party a list of five (5) names of arbitrators whom it would be willing to accept as a new Permanent Arbitrator. If no agreement is reached within five (5) days after the expiration of the aforestated ten (10) day time limit, then during the period between the removal of the Permanent Arbitrator and the selection of a new Permanent Arbitrator an arbitrator shall be selected in the following manner:

    The parties shall make joint application to the Federal Mediation and Conciliation Service for a list of five (5) names of arbitrators not included on the prior exchange of lists. Said joint application shall specify that the list of five (5) names is to be forwarded to the parties promptly by registered mail, return receipt requested. In the event the parties are unable to agree upon one of the five (5) named arbitrators within ten (10) days of receipt, each party may strike two (2) names from the list and shall then return it to the Federal Mediation and Conciliation Service by putting it in the U.S. Mails no later than the 11th day from receipt and that upon receiving the list from each party, the Federal Mediation and Conciliation Service shall immediately appoint the arbitrator from the remaining name or names, who shall serve until removed by either party or until a permanent arbitrator is selected.

The Arbitrator so selected shall serve during the life of this contract, subject, however, to his removal by death, resignation or his removal by either party as herein provided.

The Arbitrator so appointed shall be compensated on a case-by-case basis. The compensation shall include a daily fee for time spent in hearing the case and preparing the award. Additional compensation for travel, stenographic assistance, etc., shall also be allowed. Should the parties desire some other or more continuing basis of compensation, then by mutual agreement between the Union, the Company and the Arbitrator an agreement may be prepared covering such items as tenure, retention fee, hearing costs, incidental expenses and other related matters.

c. If the Arbitrator is no longer available because of any of the reasons set out above, then each party shall within ten (10) days submit to the other a list of five (5) names as provided in (b) above and thereafter proceed as provided in (b) above.

Section 2. All grievances and answers thereto which are required to be reduced to writing under the provisions of the foregoing Section of this Article, shall be recorded on a mutually acceptable grievance form, and when a grievance is reduced to writing in the first instance, it shall be signed by the aggrieved employee whose presence may be required by either party in any step of the Grievance Procedure.

Section 3. Minutes of all meetings in Step C and D shall be prepared by the Company and a copy of such minutes shall be handed to the Shop Committee of the Union within five (5) working days following the date of such meeting.

These minutes shall be typed and shall conform essentially to the following outline:

A. Date and place of meeting.
B. Names and Positions of those present.
C. Identifying number and description of each grievance discussed.
D. Brief statement of Union's Position.
E. Brief statement of Company's Position.
F. Abstract of important aspects of the discussion.

Section 4. All agreements concluded between the Union and the Company in Steps C and D of the Grievance Procedure shall be final and binding upon the employees concerned.

The foregoing treatment is more detailed than might be necessary in most contracts. The reader will note, however, the careful distinction drawn between an open grievance procedure in the early steps and a tightly restricted arbitration step. Only grievances relating to contract interpretation and application may be admitted to arbitration. Certain types of contract grievances relating to essentially "political" rather than "judicial" issues are excluded from the arbitrator's jurisdiction and are therefore subject to strike action under the contract.

The reader will also note that the Deere-UAW contract carefully spells out time limits at the various levels of the grievance procedure hierarchy. This precision on time limits is not regarded as desirable by some authorities. To facilitate orderly administration in a plant of large size, however, such limitations seem to be essential. A grievance is settled on the basis of the company's answer at the previous step unless appealed within the time limit specified. Few grievances are "lost" without consideration on the merits in this fashion. The time limits serve to insure against undue delays in the processing of grievances. In another relationship in which the writer has served as arbitrator no such time limits were imposed, and frequently the grievances being arbitrated were as much as two years old.

The Deere-UAW contract requires that the grievance be reduced to writing at the first step. This is in accord with the weight of experience that grievances not settled informally on the spot should be put in writing to protect against frivolous use of the grievance procedure for harassing purposes and also to begin a factual record to facilitate investigation at later steps in the procedure.

MANAGEMENT USE OF GRIEVANCE PROCEDURE

It will be noted that the Deere-UAW contract specifically provides for the filing of management grievances against the union in Step *C*. In this particular relationship management has not availed itself of this option to any great extent. However, it seems wise to provide for the use of the grievance procedure by management.

Historically, in collective bargaining grievance machinery has been a one-way street for prosecution of complaints by individual workers or by the union against management. Yet there appears to be no logical reason why the processing of grievances cannot be a two-way proposition. Since management has the primary responsibility and initiative in administration of contract provisions, the preponderance of filed grievances will be by individual employees or groups of employees. Management is constantly taking affirmative action, subject to challenge. Nevertheless, in a mature relationship, management should have the right under the contract to initiate grievances when it feels union or employee actions are taken in contravention of some provision in the agreement.

Management would be likely to initiate complaints through the grievance machinery against individual workers or the union in only a limited number of situations. Examples would be those involving alleged violations of union responsibility clauses or claims that the union was attempting to discredit management in the eyes of the workers.

In contracts containing union responsibility clauses the union undertakes to police its membership in the interests of responsible observance of the contract. The objective is usually to curb absenteeism, to eliminate wildcat stoppages, or to stop solicitation of dues on company time.

When management feels that such commitments have not been fulfilled, it has three principal options:

1. To take the initiative by disciplinary action against individual workers, thus allowing the issue of contract violation to be argued, if at all, through union challenge of such disciplinary action.
2. To file a grievance against workers or the union for contract violation and to impose disciplinary penalties (if justified) pursuant to the final disposition of management's grievance.
3. To file a civil damage suit alleging breach of contract, under provisions of the Taft-Hartley Act.

Employers have not availed themselves of the third option to any appreciable extent. The employer interested in developing constructive union-management relationships knows that a damage suit approach is the wrong way to proceed, no matter how clear his legal justification might be. The common law approach encouraged by the civil damage suit option under Taft-Hartley has been severely criticized by industrial relations experts.

Option 1 is the orthodox approach to disciplinary problems and the one most commonly employed today. There are situations, however, in which resort to the grievance machinery by management may have highly salutary effects. One advantage flowing from Option 2 is the necessary assumption by the union of a share in responsibility for any disciplinary measures that may ensue. If management initiates a complaint against a worker or a group of workers, usually in the higher levels of the grievance machinery, the union shares responsibility when the complaint is settled by an agreement to discipline or discharge the offending employee(s).

In practice Option 2 may never assume major significance in most union-management relationships. Intelligent management may be expected to avail itself increasingly of this option, however, particularly in potential disciplinary cases, as a preventive technique. Utilization of the grievance procedure by management as a means of registering complaints to the union about worker conduct that appears to call for disciplinary measures can often produce more constructive results than the orthodox approach. The grievance machinery may also be useful to management as a means of securing corrective action on undesirable union practices (such as solicitation of dues on company time) without the necessity of disciplining individual workers.

In some instances the union may object to management's utilization of the grievance machinery. It thus forces management into the conventional approach of taking affirmative action, subject to union challenge. The union may not wish to assume the responsibility for taking corrective action, which it impliedly undertakes if the grievance procedure is designed to carry management as well as union complaints.

If the union is weak, insecure, or immature, such a reluctance to assume responsibility may be understandable if not excusable. In stabilized and mature union-management relationships, however, the grievance machinery should be designed to carry complaints by both parties.

PENALTIES FOR FAILURE TO USE CONTRACT MACHINERY

The foregoing discussion of management-initiated grievances raises the question as to whether the contract should specifically provide penalties for failure to follow the grievance procedure in adjustment of disputes arising during the life of the agreement. There should be no need for special clauses to this effect. A resort to "direct action" rather than the grievance procedure is a valid basis for discipline under a proper interpretation of the key phrase "good and just cause." No employee or group of employees should take the law into their own hands by walkout, slowdown, or other direct action methods during the life of a contract, no matter how meritorious their grievances may appear to be. The proper course of action is always to process a grievance and, if necessary, to carry it to arbitration. If the complaint is valid, relief will eventually be forthcoming. Of course, in many situations employees become restless under the restraints and delays of the grievance procedure. In the long run, however, the employees themselves are the ones who stand to benefit the most from scrupulous adherence to the prescribed contract method for adjustment of complaints.

Perhaps the most understandable situation arising in daily plant life where a worker is tempted to take direct action is when he is given a job assignment by supervision that he feels is improper under the contract or dangerous to his health and safety. Except in the most unusual circumstances, such orders should be obeyed and promptly grieved rather than flouted. In the rare situation where an employee might genuinely feel concern for his personal safety in carrying out an order of supervision a walkout or a refusal is still not the answer. He should, however, go to his steward immediately and, through the steward, over the foreman's head.

The writer has heard a number of arbitration disputes over the years that came as discipline issues where the defense against the discipline was that the workers had an excuse for not following the grievance procedure because of the intrinsic contractual merit of their case against the foreman's order. In every such case discipline for short-circuiting the grievance procedure was sustained, even where the foreman's order was contractually in error. In labor relations, as in other phases of interpersonal relations, *two wrongs do not make a right.*

In a case where the contract does not provide for arbitration as the terminal step in the grievance procedure, the decision might be different, for in such cases management has the last word unless the union resorts to direct action. In a contract with a clear channel of grievance adjustment steps culminating in arbitration, however, there is no excuse for direct self-help.

Most contracts today make the scope of the arbitrator's authority congruent with the coverage of the contract's no strike-no lockout clause. If under the contract a grievance is arbitrable, the union is estopped from strike action during the life of the agreement. In some contracts such as the Deere-UAW contract quoted earlier, certain issues are reserved for strike action during the life of the contract by excluding them from the scope of the arbitrator's authority. However, the majority of contracts provide that any grievance relating to contract interpretation and application may go to arbitration, thus insuring against the possibility of any lawful strike during the life of the agreement.

INDIVIDUAL GRIEVANCE SETTLEMENTS INDEPENDENT OF THE UNION

As a matter of law, a union that represents a majority of employees in a unit appropriate for purposes of collective bargaining may be certified as exclusive bargaining agent for all employees in the unit and is placed under obligation to represent all employees, members or not. The Taft-Hartley Act, however, specifically safeguards the right of individual employees to file and present their grievances independently of the union if they so desire. But the union's interest in uniform contract enforcement is protected by the requirements that an individual grievance settlement may not be inconsistent with the contract and that a union representative must be given an opportunity to be present when grievances are individually adjusted.

It is probable that in actual practice the legislative privilege of individual settlement is seldom used. In a union shop, of course, all employees are members of the unit. In cases where the union does not have the security of a closed or union shop clause and a minority in the unit are not members, the politics of the situation would normally preclude discrimination against nonunion workers in grievance handling. The union presumably is interested in securing these holdouts as members by proving to them how valuable its services are. In other situations, however, it is likely that a nonunion member would have a very difficult time obtaining service from the union whose attitude might understandably be, "If you want our services, join up."

PROBLEMS IN ADMINISTRATIVE APPLICATION OF CONTRACT PROVISIONS

Many contract provisions are largely self-administering, evoking little or no controversy in application. These include such now familiar items as: (1) provision of union bulletin boards; (2) posting of seniority lists at regular intervals; (3) checkoff of dues, initiation fees, and the like.

On the other hand, many contract provisions may be controversial in application. These require carefully established procedures for administration during the life of the agreement. Application of clauses dealing with seniority, promotions, transfers, demotions, work scheduling, shift changes, layoffs, discharges, fixing rates on new or revised jobs—all these and many others are not self-administrable.

The logic of industrial jurisprudence requires the development of acceptable procedures for administration of such contract provisions. Contracts today are increasingly specific as to the procedures to be followed in the implementation of contractual provisions on such subjects. Two examples will have to suffice:

1. When promotions are contemplated, should vacancies be posted? Should provisions be made for a trial on the job before a final decision is made? Or should management discretion be completely unfettered on this matter? There is a great diversity among current collective bargaining approaches to this problem. Some contracts are silent on the matter, leaving promotional procedure and policy completely in management's hands. Others require union consent before a promotion can be effectuated. Between these extremes there are many variants. Ordinarily, the right to promote is vested in management, subject to challenge through the grievance machinery. Management has the right of administrative initiative. Frequently, however, contracts make provision for posting of vacancies, filing of applications by interested workers, and so on. Whatever the policy in the individual situation, it is of vital importance that the procedure for implementation of that policy be clearly understood and workable.

2. In the setting of rates on new jobs there is also wide diversity as to procedures. Some contracts provide for joint time study and joint negotiation of the rate during the life of the agreement. But the majority of agreements leave the setting of rates on new jobs to management, subject to challenge by the union within certain time limits.

When a contract is negotiated, one of the more important problems is the working out of effective procedures for administration of negotiated policies that are not inherently self-administrable. Sound administrative theory might accord to management the right of administrative initiative on most matters. If mutual consent were to be required, operating efficiency would be virtually impossible. On the other hand, there are some problems that can be handled feasibly under joint administration—such as safety programs, job evaluation, and time study. The procedures to be used must be suitable to the relationship between the parties. The importance of a careful spelling-out of such procedures must always be recognized.

Many cases can be found where exclusive discretion has been delegated to management, via collective agreements, on matters normally subject to collective bargaining. For example, pension plans, merit increases, and subcontracting arrangements, although jointly considered in many industries, have by contractual arrangements in many cases been assigned exclusively to management.

CONCLUSION

Most employers and union leaders agree that the real heart of collective bargaining is in the administration of collective agreements. This conclusion points up the crucial importance of developing smoothly functioning, equitable machinery for the adjustment of grievances.

Orderly and efficient operation of the enterprise and the logic of industrial democracy require that a mechanism be developed for prompt, fair disposition of all cases where employees feel aggrieved, rightly or wrongly, and that this machinery also be available to management for registering complaints about union or employee violation of contract.

If procedures and principles of grievance adjustment are clear-cut, simple, and well-understood both by line supervision and by stewards and employees, the great majority of problems in contract administration can be solved in the early steps of the machinery. Much needless friction can thereby be completely avoided. *Perhaps most important, an effective grievance and arbitration procedure eliminates any necessity for interruption of production during the life of a contract.*

SELECTED BIBLIOGRAPHY

Chamberlain, Neil W., *Collective Bargaining Procedures.* Washington: American Council on Public Affairs, 1944.

Cox, Archibald, "Rights under a Labor Agreement," *Harvard Law Review,* LXIX (February, 1956), 601–57.

Dunau, Bernard, "Employee Participation in the Grievance Aspect of Collective Bargaining," *Columbia Law Review,* L (June, 1950), 731–60.

Kovner, Joseph and Herbert J. Lahne, "Shop Society and the Union," *Industrial and Labor Relations Review*, VII (October, 1953), 3–14.

Lapp, John A., *How to Handle Labor Grievances*. Deep River: National Foremen's Institute, 1945.

Michigan State University, Labor and Industrial Relations Center, *The Grievance Process* (Symposium). East Lansing: 1957.

Miller, Glenn W. and Ned Rosen, "Members' Attitudes Toward the Shop Steward," *Industrial and Labor Relations Review*, X (July, 1957), 516–31.

Rose, George, "The Nature of a Grievance in Labor Relations," *Labor Law Journal*, III (September, 1952), 599–612.

Ryder, M. S., "Some Concepts Concerning Grievance Procedure," *Labor Law Journal*, VII (January, 1956), 15–18.

Seidman, Joel and others, "Management Views the Local Union," *Journal of Business of University of Chicago*, XXVI (April, 1953), 91–102.

Teele, John W., "The Continuous Contract," *Harvard Business Review*, XXXI (March-April, 1953), 103–12.

7

Grievance arbitration: principles and procedures*

The term "voluntary arbitration," as used here, refers to submission of labor disputes to a third party for final and binding decision, through the voluntary action of the parties themselves, either by contractual agreement or as a result of an *ad hoc* stipulation. Perhaps the most fully descriptive term is one coined by the Bureau of Labor Statistics, "voluntarily adopted compulsory arbitration." This emphasizes the key feature of private arbitration wherein the parties voluntarily commit themselves in advance to accept the arbitration award as final and binding.

Approximately 90 per cent of collective bargaining contracts today provide for arbitration as the terminal step in grievance procedure. This

* The present chapter relies heavily on three general articles on the arbitration process by the writer published in 1948, 1955, and 1958 and on a special treatment of the Deere-UAW arbitration system, published in 1957: "Hazards in Labor Arbitration," *Industrial and Labor Relations Review,* I (April, 1948), 386–405; "Labor Arbitration: A Current Appraisal," *Industrial and Labor Relations Review,* IX (October, 1955), 85–94; "The Proper Uses of Arbitration," *Labor Law Journal,* IX (February, 1958), 119–26; and "The John Deere-UAW Permanent Arbitration System" in Jean T. McKelvey, ed., *Critical Issues in Labor Arbitration* (Washington: The Bureau of National Affairs, Inc., 1957). 161–92.

simple statement of fact underlines perhaps the most constructive development in labor relations since the end of World War II. Arbitration as an instrument for improved contract administration is so generally accepted today that it is difficult to remember that prior to World War II this procedure for final settlement of grievances under existing contracts was utilized in only a few industries.

Dissenting voices may still be heard. Arbitration clauses in many contracts have never been used. In others arbitration is resorted to so rarely as to suggest that it has not become an integral element in the parties' machinery for maintaining constructive, stable relationships.[1] There can be little argument today, however, that arbitration is better understood and more widely and intelligently used than at any previous time.

AN ARBITRATION BALANCE SHEET

This chapter is concerned solely with *grievance arbitration,* i.e., arbitration as a device for final and binding settlement of disputes over the interpretation and application of the terms of existing collective agreements. The use of arbitration as an alternative to economic force in settling disputes over the terms of future contracts is reserved for consideration in Chapter 17.

In appraising recent developments in grievance arbitration the writer is generalizing primarily from personal observation and experience.

Among the more noteworthy developments in grievance arbitration in recent years the following deserve to be included:

1. Marked improvement in understanding of the proper uses of arbitration.
2. An increasing professionalization of the arbitration function.
3. A perceptible increase in the number of "permanent" arbitration relationships.
4. Definite improvement in contract clauses defining the grievance and arbitration procedure and the limits of arbitral discretion.
5. Increased research interest in arbitration.
6. Recent development of new uses for arbitration as a method of determining interunion jurisdictional disputes and pension rights problems, and also as an appellate procedure in union discipline cases.
7. Decline of the tripartite board in grievance disputes.

Most of the foregoing developments are logical concomitants of increasing acceptance and growth. They can be listed safely on the asset side of the arbitration balance sheet.

[1] For example, a survey of arbitration in Wisconsin firms showed surprising infrequency in resort to arbitration. See Daniel H. Kruger, "Arbitration and its Uses in 36 Firms in Wisconsin," *Labor Law Journal,* VI (March, 1955), 165–81.

Certain attitudes and practices, however, should give pause to those who envisage a bright future for arbitration as a tool for improved contract administration and industrial peace. These questionable trends or conditions include the following:

1. An observable tendency to exaggerate the precedential value of awards and to overlegalize the arbitration process.
2. Continued excessive use of arbitration in some relationships as a substitute for mature collective bargaining.
3. Inadequate use of arbitration decisions as instruments for training foremen and stewards in better contract administration.
4. Continued cynicism in some quarters, as shown by inequitable use of the blacklist and the decision box-score.
5. Continued deficiencies in the preparation and presentation of cases.
6. Inadequate screening procedures prior to arbitration.

The arbitrator is the employee of the company and the union jointly.

THE PROPER USES OF ARBITRATION

Before companies and unions can make the most effective use of arbitration as an instrument for improved contract administration they must agree on the type of arbitration they want. In many cases the potential value in arbitration has not been realized because the parties do not have the same expectations from arbitration or the same conception of its proper function. In typical cases the company will be seeking a judicial approach to arbitration and the union a "split the difference" approach. Obviously, if one party expects the arbitrator to be strictly judicial and the other party wants the arbitrator to function as a mediator wherever possible or to compromise with the merits in his decisions, no constructive progress can be expected.

If the parties prefer an arbitrator to function as a "mutual friend," as a labor relations psychiatrist, or as a father-confessor, they are privileged to seek out an arbitrator who can fulfill such a role. If they prefer an arbitrator to adhere strictly to the traditional quasi-judicial approach, this can be made clear. It is important to the success of the relationship that the parties understand and agree upon the type of arbitration they want and that they make this clear to the arbitrator.

The writer holds the view that in grievance arbitration the arbitrator's function is properly a quasi-judicial one. The great majority of grievance arbitrations are still handled on an *ad hoc* basis, notwithstanding the rapid growth in permanent umpire machinery. It seems evident that in *ad hoc* arbitration the quasi-judicial approach is the more suitable. Even in a permanent arbitration relationship the arbitrator should consider his function to be quasi-judicial, unless the parties indicate explicitly that they wish him to function otherwise.

Only a gifted minority of arbitrators can handle the delicate dual assignment of mediator-arbitrator. Nor are there many companies and unions that wish the arbitrator to depart from straight adjudication. It must be emphasized that the arbitrator is the employee of the company and the union jointly. If the parties wish to utilize the arbitrator in a consultative capacity during negotiations, or if they wish him to initiate proposals for settling grievances that have been formally submitted to arbitration, the customers are always right. Yet, the writer's experience and observation lead him to conclude that there are very few arbitrators who can function effectively in the George Taylor manner. It seems probable that the majority of arbitrators sincerely believe that better results can be achieved in general by the arbitrator's adhering strictly to a quasi-judicial approach.

As one example, a major factor in the successful use of grievance arbitration as an instrument of contract administration in the John Deere-UAW relationship has been the joint agreement through the years on a preference for judicial arbitration. Deere and UAW do not want an arbitrator to try to bring them into agreement, nor do they want an arbitrator to tell them how they *should* have done something. In this relationship the arbitrator always assumes that the parties have agreed to disagree and makes his decisions strictly in terms of the contract rather than in terms of his personal value judgments as to what may be fair and equitable. When, as sometimes happens, contract and equity call for different conclusions, the contract always governs.

With Deere and UAW, the company feels somewhat more strongly on this point than does the union. The latter has been critical of several decisions for being overly strict in contract construction to the point of being allegedly unrealistic and inequitable. However, at no time has the union ever sought to invoke the arbitrator's offices as a mediator of a case actually in arbitration. Nor has the union ever used a straight box-score approach as a method for evaluating the arbitrator's services. As a matter of fact, had the Union been so disposed, the arbitrator's tenure would have ended long before it did in fact, since the quantitative box-score was substantially in management's favor.[2]

It is obvious that in some situations the parties do not expect the arbitrator to function in a judicial capacity. For example, when several grievances are carried to arbitration at one time, there are union representatives who expect the arbitrator to decide some in favor of the union and some for the company, regardless of the merits of the individual grievances. This expectation that an arbitrator will split the difference

[2] The writer served as Deere-UAW permanent arbitrator from August 1, 1952 to June 12, 1958. The termination was by the UAW local unions concerned because of "general dissatisfaction and disagreement with many" decisions.

in multiple grievance cases or that he will compromise in a particular case calling for a clear-cut answer one way or the other is an attitude that menaces the integrity of the entire arbitration process. It should not be tolerated. Although an arbitrator should not conduct himself so stiffly as to make a settlement between the parties impossible, he should be properly cautious about taking the initiative in efforts to settle the dispute informally. At the decision stage there should be no question at all about the proper procedure. The arbitrator must make his decision in each case on the merits in terms of the contract, notwithstanding any direct or tacit pressure for political, compromise decisions.

The writer abruptly lost his status as "permanent" arbitrator in one midwestern union-management relationship when the union brought seven grievances to arbitration in one batch and lost six out of seven. Four of these grievances were "dogs" that the union had no business carrying to arbitration. Only three involved *bona fide* questions of contract interpretation and application. It is possible that the union expected to win only one of those three that it did win. It brought in a batch of seven, however, in the hope that the arbitrator would be reluctant to rule against the union in such a large number of grievances.

To recapitulate, the first principle in effective use of arbitration in contract administration is joint agreement on the type of arbitration wanted. Arbitration is the private creation of the parties. They can structure it as they see fit, but they must be in basic agreement in their expectations of the process. It is also important to spend enough time on contract language dealing with grievance and arbitration machinery to insure that the contract spells out clearly the joint agreement as to what arbitration is designed to do and what it is not intended to do. Careful drafting will save many subsequent headaches over arbitrability issues and related problems. For an excellent illustration of contract language that meets these requirements the reader may wish to turn back to the quoted sections from the Deere-UAW contract in the previous chapter.

SELECTION OF AN ARBITRATOR

When a company and a union agree in advance to be bound conclusively by the determination of an outsider on a dispute that they have themselves been unable to resolve, the importance of the selection of an arbitrator cannot be overstated. Assuming that the parties are agreed on the judicial approach to arbitration, their first consideration in selecting an arbitrator will be personal integrity. They will seek an arbitrator who has demonstrated his capacity for deciding cases as he sees them under the contract without regard to his "expendability." All the expertise in the world will be of little value if the expert cannot be depended upon to decide cases impartially in terms of the contract under which he is operating. A good arbitrator must always maintain the ability to divorce his personal feelings and value judgments from the case at hand. If the contract requires it, he must be prepared to rule against his heart and even, in some cases, against his own industrial relations common sense.

A great deal of progress has been made in recent years in raising the ethics and standards of the arbitration profession to an exemplary level. The National Academy of Arbitrators, founded in 1947, and the American Arbitration Association, have played a major role in this process. In 1950 the first edition of this book reported that:[3]

> There is no longer a dearth of qualified arbitrators, but there seems to be some poverty of confidence in the integrity of the arbitration process. This has produced a cynical minority of arbitrators who have turned an essentially judicial calling into what amounts to a racket, who privately boast of following politics rather than merits, and who consider it high strategy to follow variants of the split-the-difference technique whenever possible.

It is encouraging to report in 1958 that the arbitrators themselves have raised the ethics and standards of this comparatively new profession to the point where there are now only a few unscrupulous individuals still operating. There has been a marked improvement also in the understanding of the arbitration function by management and union representatives that has reduced the amount of indiscriminate "blackballing" so common a few years ago.

The blacklist and the box-score method of analysis still continue to be troublesome. It should be obvious that indiscriminate blacklisting is a two-edged and, ultimately, a self-defeating weapon. Perhaps the various appointing agencies could be somewhat tougher and more inquisitive than they appear to be before complying with notifications that certain arbitrators are regarded as "not acceptable." Of course, individual companies and local unions should be entirely free to reject arbitrators as not acceptable, although simple fairness would appear to dictate the propriety of informing the arbitrator that he is no longer acceptable to Company *X* or Union *Y*. The propriety of an industry-wide, area-wide, or union-wide blacklist seems more questionable.

Box-score analysis *as such* is clearly an inaccurate and questionable guide to an arbitrator's integrity and ability. Each decision should be evaluated independently, since that is the way arbitrators must decide cases. If management or the union "loses" a consecutive string of cases, this may or may not be indicative of the arbitrator's bias or incompetence. The only fair way to evaluate an arbitrator's performance is to study

[3] Harold W. Davey, *Contemporary Collective Bargaining*, 1st ed. (Englewood Cliffs, N. J.: Prentice-Hall, Inc., 1951), p. 304.

The only fair way to evaluate an arbitrator's performance is to study each of his decisions thoroughly and then judge his work as a whole.

each of his decisions thoroughly and then judge his work as a whole.

Of course, once an arbitrator ceases to be acceptable to one party or the other his usefulness in the relationship is at an end. Whether he is on an *ad hoc* basis or a permanent basis, an arbitrator serves at the pleasure of the parties. As union and company representatives gain experience and insight into the true nature of the arbitration function, it is to be anticipated that their criteria for selection of arbitrators will be confined to qualities of integrity, competence, and courage. Eventually, there will be an end to the business of discarding arbitrators because of the "loss" of a particular case.

SINGLE ARBITRATOR OR THREE-MAN BOARD?

Most grievance arbitration in the United States is handled by single arbitrators. This is consistent with the judicial approach to grievance arbitration. If, however, the parties have a preference for a mediatory approach to grievance arbitration, the use of tripartite boards is understandable.

Although the use of tripartite boards in grievance arbitration appears to be steadily declining, many companies and unions remain wedded to this device. In a 1955 article the writer predicted that the tripartite board would become "completely vestigial" as far as grievance arbitration was concerned.[4] A number of critical comments about this premature announcement of the death of three-man boards were received. It is worth noting, however, that in many situations where the contract still provides for tripartite machinery, the first act of the parties at a hearing is to stipulate that the impartial third man shall act as if he were in fact the sole arbitrator. The writer has not sat on a board since 1951 where the board actually functioned as such at the decision level. Although the logic of tripartite boards in grievance arbitration of the judicial type is doubtful, there are definite advantages in tripartitism for arbitration of disputes over future contract terms or in grievance arbitration where the parties expect a mediatory rather than a quasi-judicial approach to the resolution of grievances.

AD HOC OR PERMANENT ARBITRATION MACHINERY?

For companies and unions with a considerable amount of arbitration there would appear to be many values to be derived from adopting permanent arbitration machinery rather than *ad hoc*. Many parties that retain *ad hoc* selection procedures in their contracts nevertheless achieve what amounts to permanent arbitration, for the same individual is

[4] Harold W. Davey, "Labor Arbitration: A Current Appraisal," *Industrial and Labor Relations Review*, IX (October, 1955), 87.

selected in case after case. This may be a satisfactory arrangement if only one or two cases a year are involved. If the case load is fairly heavy and predictable, however, it would seem desirable to consider formalizing a permanent arbitrator relationship.

Ad hoc arbitration is still far more common than permanent arbitration, although the latter seems to be difinitely on the increase. There are comparatively few situations where a company and union have returned to an *ad hoc* set-up after having adopted permanent arbitration machinery.

The permanent arbitrator system has several important advantages. The arbitrator is the mutually chosen employee of both parties. He can be carefully selected for his impartiality and knowledge of industrial relations. He serves the parties over a sufficient period of time to develop an informed understanding of the problems and difficulties of the particular industry and the particular labor-management relationship. Furthermore, the relative stability of such an arbitration relationship is perhaps the best procedural insurance of decisions on the merits. This is admittedly a debatable conclusion. The contrary view would hold that an arbitrator appointed on an *ad hoc* basis is freer and in a better position to decide impartially on the merits.

It is significant perhaps that permanent arbitration machinery has proved conspicuously successful in those industries in which unions and management over the years have achieved maturity and stability in their collective bargaining relationships. The men's and women's clothing industries and the full-fashioned hosiery industry are two outstanding examples. It is also worth noting that the automobile and steel industries have made considerable progress in improved contract administration through the device of a permanent, impartial umpire machinery.

In some permanent arbitration relationships the arbitrator is expected to be a "statesman" or a mediator and must be sensitive to the political nuances of the disputes reaching him for decision.[5] In most cases, however, the judicial type of arbitration appears to be preferred.

IMPORTANCE OF THE RIGHT TO ARBITRATE

In most situations with which the writer is familiar, as the company and union deal with one another over a period of time, the incidence of arbitration will normally decrease. However, the acceptance of the arbitration process as an integral part of contract administration becomes firmer than ever.

The presence of arbitration machinery in the contract and the right of either party to resort to it when necessary are much more important than

[5] Some arbitrators report the necessity for being adept at catching "signals" from the parties. Where such a requirement exists, it is not proper arbitration.

As the co. + union deal with one another over a period of time, the incidence of arbitration will normally decrease. Also, the acceptance of the arbitration process as an integral part of contract adm. becomes more firm.

its actual use. *The right to arbitrate bears the same critical relationship to successful contract administration as does the right to strike and lockout to effective, successful contract negotiation.* Arbitration should always be regarded, however, as a supplement or adjunct to collective bargaining, never as a substitute for it.

It would be rash to suggest a mathematical border between judicious and excessive resort to arbitration. For example, in recent years UAW relations with both Ford and General Motors appear to have been generally stable and constructive. Yet the Ford set-up requires the services of four arbitrators to handle the large case load, whereas in General Motors a single umpire has had comparatively few cases, considering the much larger number of affected employees.

Arbitration is most effective when used sparingly. Implementing this principle involves unremitting effort to settle as many grievances as possible short of arbitration; it involves better screening procedures to wash out duplicatory or weak grievances; it involves reducing to a minimum the political or face-saving type of grievance. In short, it involves a joint determination to see to it that only *bona fide* disputes over contract interpretation and application are submitted to arbitration.

In recent years an increasing number of companies and unions have avoided excessive arbitration in an intelligent and discriminating fashion. In some situations, however, there is ground for suspicion that the remarkably reduced case loads are due not to growing maturity but to cynicism about the utility of the arbitration process. The arbitration mechanism is maintained and used occasionally, but the arbitrator's case load consists largely of "dogs" because the parties are unwilling or afraid to trust arbitration on vitally important issues. This is an unfortunate state of affairs and one that cannot be documented. An arbitrator who finds himself involved in such a relationship would do well to depart therefrom as quickly as possible. Although an arbitrator is the employee of the parties, he has a professional obligation not to serve in a relationship where one (or both) of his "employers" has demonstrated a lack of faith in the integrity and the validity of the arbitration function.

WHAT ISSUES ARE BEST SUITED TO ARBITRATION?

An inspection of the index to any labor arbitration reporting service will show that nearly every conceivable issue that might arise in day to day labor relations has been the subject of arbitration at one time or another. Yet experienced practitioners concede that certain types of issues are well-suited to arbitration while others are not. Broadly speaking, disputed issues arising out of an existing contract are adaptable to arbitration *because the contract itself provides guidance and limits for the arbitrator's judgment.* Interpretation of contract clauses on seniority, vacations, holiday pay, job classifications, discharge, and the like are frequently the subject of intelligent, effective arbitration. On the other hand, such issues as the degree of union security or the granting or withholding of a general wage increase are more difficult to be judicial about, involving as they do the fundamental interests or principles of the parties.

Taking grievance arbitration for the country as a whole, approximately one out of three cases involves a discipline issue. One reason for this is that discipline cases furnish an ideal illustration of the best use of the judicial approach in arbitration. The arbitrator is asked to weigh the evidence presented to him in a judicial manner to see whether the company has sustained the burden of showing "good and just cause" for the discipline. The contract in question lays down the basic principle governing the administration of discipline, but reasonable men can reasonably differ on the adequacy of proof of cause for discipline in particular situations. Protection of the individual worker on the job against arbitrary, inequitable, or discriminatory discipline is one of the principal functions of collective bargaining in democratizing the industral relations process.

In the construction industry, where closed shop contracts are customary, the union rarely attempts to condition or limit the employer's power to discipline. Employees usually work only a short time for any one employer and the union is confident of being able to place discharged employees on another job. In manufacturing, however, it is customary for the employer's discipline prerogative to be limited to those cases involving discipline for "good and just cause" or a similar phrase. The burden of proof in all such cases rests with the employer. About the only exception to this proposition is the recent development in connection with discharging employees who have been proven to be members of the Communist party or who have refused to testify as to their membership in the Communist party. In this type of case the burden of proof has been shifted from the employer to the employee. Where the discharge is for membership in the Communist party or refusal before appropriate authorities to discuss membership in the Communist party, arbitrators have held that the employee is properly subject to discharge. A recent case in point is *Westinghouse Airbrake Company*, 27 *LA* 265.

In the ordinary discipline case it is entirely proper for the employer to assume the burden of proving good and just cause for discipline. The employee charged with an offense should be regarded as innocent until proven guilty as far as the grievance procedure and ultimate arbitration is concerned. Only a minority of highly prerogative-conscious employers would dissent from the foregoing proposition.

A much more debatable point is the discretion an arbitrator should enjoy in reviewing disciplinary action by management. Many contracts restrict the arbitrator's discretion solely to the determination of whether cause for discipline existed in a particular case. Such contracts deny the arbitrator discretion to modify penalties. The great majority of contracts, however, do not limit the arbitrator's authority to modify penalties.

In those cases where an arbitrator has no discretion to modify penalties, the unlooked-for consequence is frequently a verdict of innocence in cases where the arbitrator feels that the employee was properly subject to discipline but feels also that the penalty imposed was far too severe for the offense in question. If an arbitrator is restricted to ruling simply on whether cause for discipline was shown, there is a strong temptation to hold that the company did not sustain the burden of proof in borderline situations.

On balance, it would seem preferable to leave the modification of penalty discretionary with the arbitrator. Most experienced arbitrators will not substitute their judgment for that of management as to the penalty to be imposed. A penalty should only be modified by the arbitrator where in his judgment the penalty in relation to the offense in question was clearly arbitrary, capricious, or discriminatory. The arbitrator has no right to substitute his judgment for that of management as to the proper penalty merely because as a matter of personal judgment he feels that he would have administered a lesser penalty.

To understand fully the foregoing principle, the reader may be interested in evaluating the facts in a discipline case heard by the writer. Two foundry laborers were engaged one morning in cleaning up sand. Each of them had a shovel. Laborer *X* left the work area to dump a load of sand. While *X* was gone, Laborer *Y* took *X*'s shovel and placed it against a wall about fifteen feet away from the pile of sand which both were cleaning up. Before *X* returned, *Y* left to dump a load of sand. When *X* returned, he picked up *Y*'s shovel and began to load more sand. *Y*, upon his return, told *X*, "You have my shovel." "No, it's my shovel." *Y* repeated that it was his shovel and *X*, becoming angry, insisted that it was his shovel. After a few exchanges of "that's my shovel—no it's my shovel," *Y* reached down as though to take the shovel away from *X*. At this point *X* directed a blow at *Y*'s arm.

The foreman, who had been observing the two laborers engaged in this altercation, immediately jumped in and restrained *X* by placing his arms around him. *X* broke away from the foreman's grasp and said "I'll fight anybody in the joint." As soon as he saw that it was the foreman who had restrained him, *X* immediately calmed down. The foreman called both employees into his office and also called his general foreman to hear about the incident. *X*, upon the advice of another employee, brought his steward into the office with him. After a few moments the foreman told

Y to return to his job. This was the last that *Y* heard about the situation as far as management was concerned. After a disciplinary action hearing required by the contract, the management's decision was to give X a one-week suspension for fighting on the job and for using threatening language to his foreman.

At the arbitration hearing which protested the discipline given to X the parties involved told sharply conflicting views of the incident. The arbitrator credited the foreman's testimony as to the facts of the incident rather than the testimony of X and *Y*. However, the arbitrator ruled that under the circumstances the disciplinary penalty against X should be modified to a written warning. The reader is asked to draw his own conclusions as to why the arbitrator felt that equity demanded modification of the penalty.[6]

INTERPRETATION OF CONTRACT LANGUAGE

Each discipline case is in a real sense unique, involving different individuals and different sets of factual circumstances, although similar issues and situations frequently arise. In a discipline case the arbitrator's judicial function is to impartially weigh the facts in the light of an accepted contract principle.

The judicial approach can also be used in grievance arbitration on any case involving differences in opinion as to the proper meaning of particular contract language. Such issues frequently arise in daily contract administration. Language that was thought to be clear in its meaning when negotiated often turns out in application to be susceptible to two or more different interpretations.

An excellent issue of this type is raised in the case reported below as to the proper construction of a "spell-out time" clause in a meat packing plant contract. The agreed facts, the contract clause, and the contentions of the parties are reproduced from the writer's opinion in that case.

Preliminary Recital

This case involves construction of Paragraph 13(b) of the contract, dealing with spell-out time, as applied to an agreed set of facts. Paragraph 13(b) reads as follows:

"(b) 15 minutes spell-out or relief time for personal needs will be allowed with pay in each half day of over three hours."

The agreed facts (as summarized by counsel for the Company and subscribed to by the Union representative) are as follows:

COMPANY: "It is stipulated and agreed between the parties that the following are the facts in connection with Grievance No. 28:

[6] See In Re John Deere Malleable Works and Local 81, UAW, Decision No. 1956–18, September 18, 1956, reported at 27 *LA* 279.

"Five and one-half hours were scheduled for the afternoon shift starting at one o'clock p.m. A mechanical break-down occurred about one hour and forty minutes after the start and the employees were sent on break at that time. Since normally they would have gone on break about two and one-half hours after starting, they had their spell-out about 40 minutes early, resulting in their working about three hours and twenty-three minutes after coming back from the break; whereas, in the normal case they would have worked only three hours. Repairs were completed during the break period."

UNION: "Yes, those are the facts." (See Transcript, p. 147)

The above-described incident occurred on the hog-kill chain on March 15, 1952."

The Issue

The issue for determination is whether working the employees three hours and 23 minutes consecutively without a spell-out on March 15, 1952 constituted a violation of Section 13(b).

Contentions of Parties

The Union maintains that Section 13(b) prohibits the Company from working employees more than three hours at a stretch in any half day of over three hours. In support of its contention, the Union stressed past practice in the plant as shedding light on proper interpretation of 13(b). According to the Union, the incident that produced this grievance is the only time that management has ever worked employees more than three hours at a stretch in any half day.

The Company maintains that the Union's construction of 13(b) is totally unwarranted. In order to hold for the Union, says the Company, the arbitrator would have to substitute or add some words to the language written into the contract. All that Paragraph 13(b) requires is that the Company must give a spell-out in any half day of over three hours. The contract contains no stated or implied restriction on the management's discretion as to when the spell-out should be given. The contract simply states that in each half day of over three hours a spell-out will be allowed. This obligation was met by the Company in the instant case. Therefore, in the Company's view, the grievance should be dismissed.

The reader is asked to make up his own mind as to how he thinks the parties intended this contract language to be interpreted and applied. The decision is found in the Appendix.[7]

Some brief comments are now in order on preparation and presentation of cases in arbitration.

First; a thourough + tough-minded screening procedure for both parties

PREPARATION AND PRESENTATION OF ARBITRATION CASES

The first requisite in the preparation of cases for arbitration is a thorough and tough-minded screening procedure for both parties. Before

[7] See p. 367.

Before going into arbitration, the company and union should have explored fully the possibilities of informal adjustment and settlement going into arbitration, the company and the union should have explored fully the possibilities of informal adjustment and settlement. Failing a settlement, it is then incumbent upon each of the principals to determine whether the best interests of constructive contract administration require going ahead. In most relationships where the parties are experienced in arbitration, each has a screening step wherein the final decision is made as to whether to arbitrate, even after grievances have actually been referred to the arbitration step. Any experienced arbitrator can recall numerous cases where it was fairly obvious that more effective screening would have washed out grievances that should have been dropped by the union or adjusted by the company.

An orderly, informative, and complete hearing is best assured by careful preparation of cases. This principle is often honored more in the breach than in the observance. Unions are frequently at some operational disadvantage in case preparation. The international representative who presents the cases is frequently obliged to service more locals than he can handle effectively. His first contact with the case may come the day before the actual hearing. If the local union has done a poor or incomplete job of case preparation, the international representative may have to "play it by ear" during the hearing.

Such disadvantages can be minimized by more complete staffing, by closer working relationships between the international and the local at the screening stage, and by better training of local officials in the task of case preparation. Companies ordinarily do not suffer from manpower deficiencies in the same manner as do unions. However, there are not a few situations in which sins of inadequate preparation can properly be charged against management.

As to the actual presentation of cases there is little of an original nature that can be said. Each party should certainly have the right to present his case in the manner he sees fit. Some prefer to use a great many stipulations. Others prefer to bring in their case through direct testimony of witnesses. Some employ an elaborate panoply of prehearing briefs, written stipulations, posthearing briefs, and reply briefs. It is hard to generalize on what techniques or methods are most effective, but it is well to remember that the arbitrator is a professional and is interested in finding out the true facts of any situation. Whatever method is best suited to conveying to him a full, accurate picture of the facts and contentions is the method that should be used.

PRECEDENTS AND EXCESSIVE LEGALISM

Twin tendencies toward undue reliance on precedents and toward excessive legalism in grievance arbitration require comment. Within a particular arbitration relationship it is desirable to utilize prior decisions as a basis for policy. A sequence of decisions on basic substantive issues of contract interpretation and application will result over a period of time in the development of a body of principles that can be concretely and meaningfully applied by the parties. Such private case law *within* a particular relationship can serve to prevent grievances, settle grievances informally, eliminate duplicatory arbitrations, and head off flanking operations designed to escape the consequences of an unpalatable earlier award.

However, there are fundamental reasons for avoiding the excessive citation of *outside* decisions. The citation practice leads inexorably to improper emphasis on the precedential value of such awards. It fosters a dangerous misconception as to the nature of the arbitration process itself. It encourages false optimism about the possibility of evolving substantive principles of universal applicability, while ignoring the basic fact that arbitration is intended for final determination of specific disputes on specific sets of facts under a particular contract.

Several recent research investigations have taken the raw material of published decisions in particular subject matter areas and attempted to derive therefrom principles of universal validity and applicability. It is natural and desirable to search for "first principles," but arbitration is a specialized tool for settlement of particular disputes in a specific focus. As Manson points out, an arbitrator must not become a middleman for the transmission of another's views. "Where the arbitrator accepts principles as precedent in place of proof, he is abdicating his function, and yielding to absentee arbitration." [8]

This is not to indicate opposition to the practice of publishing arbitration decisions. Such publication has provided a valuable educational medium for both students and practitioners of industrial relations. The availability of such materials, however, offers a continuing temptation to depart from the proper use of precedent in labor arbitration.

In applying the phrase "excessive legalism" to some of the current arbitration systems, the following practices are contemplated: (1) overtechnical presentation, principally in such matters as strict adherence to the rules of evidence and rigid formality in the examination of witnesses; and (2) insistence upon prehearing and/or posthearing briefs.

Arbitration hearings are designed to establish truth. They are conducted by individuals who may be presumed to have a degree of expertise. The arbitrator does not need to be "protected" by procedural formalism. At the same time, most witnesses are untutored laymen who tend to "freeze" under highly formal conditions. The straight legal method of examining witnesses is out of place in the average arbitration case. Perhaps

[8] Julius J. Manson, "Substantive Principles Emerging from Grievance Arbitration: Some Observations," *Proceedings*, Industrial Relations Research Association, December, 1953, pp. 136–49, at p. 148.

. "Outside" decisions are disadvantageous for a basis of policy. The basic fact is that arbitration is intended for final determination of specific disputes on specific sets of facts under a particular contract.

the arbitrators themselves are to blame for an unduly legalistic atmosphere in many current arbitrations. Where this is true the "customers" are at liberty to correct the situation.

Briefs take time to prepare and time to study. Their use always involves delay in decision making. Furthermore, their necessity in the average case has never been demonstrated to the writer's satisfaction. In six years' arbitration for Deere and UAW briefs were filed in only one case. In the great majority of arbitrations an oral argument following presentation of the direct case should suffice.

Use of briefs and undue preoccupation with precedent appear to go hand in hand.

Arbitrators must decide cases on the record made before them. The delays incident to the filing of posthearing briefs overbalance any benefits of clarification that the briefs might bestow. Only in situations where complex legal issues may be involved are briefs essential. Fairness requires noting, however, that briefs are often helpful in *ad hoc* arbitration.

As noted, there are ominous portents for the future of arbitration in current tendencies toward a more litigious approach and toward a misguided emphasis on the allegedly binding force of outside decisions as precedents. There appear also to be some indications of an overprofessionalization in arbitration. In some of the larger companies, for example, one suspects (perhaps wrongly) the existence of considerable featherbedding of the industrial relations function.

Arbitrators are not inculpable in such matters. Attorneys probably hear the lion's share of arbitration cases in the United States. Their background and experience may be in part responsible for this trend toward greater legalism in arbitration. The other chief source of supply consists of professors who are not notoriously well-paid for their academic services and therefore may not resist developments that make hearings more protracted and decisions longer, thus adding to the arbitrator's income.

The blunt fact remains that the sole beneficiary of the litigious approach to arbitration is the arbitrator himself. Arbitrators have a clear professional obligation to resist the trend toward excessive legalism in arbitration.

ARBITRATION AND THE COURTS

The foregoing remarks require notice of the possibly fundamental impact of the Supreme Court's recent decision (June, 1957) in the *Lincoln Mills* case.[9] The net effect of this decision is to convert the federal courts into a protective haven for those seeking enforcement of contractual

[9] 77 *Sup. Ct.* 54. For an early commentary on this case consult Alexander M. Bickel and Harry H. Wellington, "Legislative Purpose and the Judicial Process: The Lincoln Mills Case," *Harvard Law Review*, LXXI (November, 1957), 1–39.

agreements to arbitrate under the aegis of Section 301 of the Taft-Hartley Act. If one feels that arbitration is a desirable instrument of contract administration, it is difficult to argue against the idea that agreements to arbitrate should be enforceable. However, the Court's decision may open a veritable Pandora's box of litigiousness by parties seeking motions to stay arbitration or to contest arbitrators' awards. It is too early to say with precision what the net impact of the Court's important ruling will be.[10] As a general proposition, most students of industrial relations would agree that the courts are not a proper forum for resolving disputes over collective bargaining rights.

SUGGESTIONS FOR UTILIZING ARBITRATION DECISIONS

There are many postdecisional uses of arbitration decisions that could lead to improved contract administration. Many companies and unions do not get their money's worth from the arbitration process by failing to use arbitration decisions as training tools for foremen and stewards. Although some arbitration decisions are so poorly written and confused that their educational utility would be minimal, there are literate arbitrators who will prepare thorough and clear opinions if encouraged to do so by the parties. If the arbitrator in his opinion carefully states the issue, the contentions of the parties, and the reasoning by which he arrived at his award, his decisions can be of great value to both management and union in improving the understanding of foremen and stewards as to the implications of the contract.

Industrial training to be effective must deal with real-life problem situations that will be meaningful to the people being trained. If this hypothesis is correct, then certainly actual arbitration cases provide a readily available source of raw materials for a realistic management or union training program. Such a program would require a great deal of time, thought, and resourcefulness. It would not be desirable in most cases to use the decisions as written. They would probably have to be abstracted and translated by some knowledgeable individual with a flair for living prose. In order to avoid prejudging, the arbitrator's reasoning and decision should be withheld until after the trainees have discussed the problem among themselves.

ARBITRATION AND NEGOTIATION

Another obvious use of arbitration decisions after the fact is in preparation for the next contract negotiation. Arbitration decisions over the

[10] One interesting question is whether the impact of the decision will accelerate or blunt the recent drive for a federal uniform labor arbitration act. For a review of the arguments on this issue prior to the *Lincoln Mills* decision see Robert L. Howard, "Labor-Management Arbitration: 'There Ought to be a Law'—Or Ought There?" *Labor Law Journal*, VIII (March, 1957), 171–92, 212.

years have been a very effective means of improving contract language and are widely utilized for this purpose. Grievance arbitration shows up "bugs" in a contract with amazing rapidity and clarity, and the subsequent contract can frequently be improved to eliminate the ambiguity or confusion.

OPERATIONAL EFFECT OF AWARDS

Another facet of the relationship of arbitration to contract administration that is particularly interesting is the operational impact of specific decisions. This is a matter on which most arbitrators are usually kept in the dark and it is probable that few companies and unions give systematic attention to it. Some interesting and rewarding results might follow from postoperative studies of the impact of key decisions on subsequent contract administration. What happens when the arbitrator reinstates a discharged employee on the basis that the company failed to prove good and just cause? What happens when an arbitrator rules that an employee was arbitrarily denied a merit increase or a promotion? What happens when an arbitrator rules that certain duties should be slotted as Engine Lathe Operator "A" rather than Engine Lathe Operator "B"? Some formal follow-up in such cases might provide some useful insights for both management and union leadership entirely apart from any intrinsic human interest that might be present.

How many companies and unions make a systematic analysis and inventory of the source and kind of grievances that arise during a contract year and the manner of their disposition? Such studies might prove invaluable as a guide to improved foreman and steward performance in a plant of any considerable size.

RESEARCH IN ARBITRATION

Perhaps the most encouraging development in terms of the future of arbitration is the substantial amount of research activity already completed, in progress, and contemplated. A bibliography compiled by the American Arbitration Association lists no fewer than 344 books and articles dealing wholly or in part with some aspect of voluntary labor arbitration.[11]

The National Academy of Arbitrators is stimulating interest in empirical research. The Academy's 1955, 1956, 1957, and 1958 Proceedings, which include some excellent research papers, have been published by the

[11] American Arbitration Association, *Arbitration Bibliography*, (New York: American Arbitration Association, 1954.) See also Vernon H. Jensen and Harold G. Ross, *Bibliography of Dispute Settlement by Third Parties* (Ithaca: New York State School of Industrial and Labor Relations, Cornell University, 1955). The Cornell bibliography is being revised and brought up to date for publication in 1959.

Bureau of National Affairs.[12] The academy is also planning a special volume of research studies of permanent umpire systems in several mass production industries.[13] The volume will be edited by William H. Davis.

Among the research areas that appear to be most challenging, the following should be listed:

1. Research on the operational impact of arbitration decisions in contract administration and their effect on subsequent negotiations.[14]
2. Comparative analyses of both substantive and procedural issues in a variety of systems.
3. Research designed to develop standards for improving the preparation and presentation of cases.

The arbitration field would benefit greatly by the publication of some frank, introspective analyses by leading arbitrators. Perhaps this latter enterprise can only be undertaken with safety by *emeritus* arbitrators.

CONCLUSION

Intelligent and sparing use of arbitration under an existing contract is the *sine qua non* of effective administration of collective labor agreements. The evidence on grievance arbitration over the past ten years warrants an optimistic prognosis as to its continued growth and acceptance.

We still have much to learn about how to use arbitration more effectively as an instrument for improved contract administration. Certain unfavorable attitudes and practices constitute something of a problem. Yet it is clear that when grievance arbitration is properly understood and properly utilized, it can contribute substantially to the achievement of the following four objectives sought by mature management and union representatives:

1. Establishment of a mutually acceptable alternative to strikes during the life of a contract.
2. Effective training of foremen and stewards in improved understanding of the contract, thus leading to a more equitable and efficient adjustment of grievances at lower steps in the grievance procedure.

[12] All four volumes were edited by Jean T. McKelvey of Cornell University. Complete citations will be found in the bibliography at the end of this chapter.

[13] The first two of the umpire studies have been completed and others are reportedly under way. The study of the Deere-UAW system was published in the 1957 NAA *Proceedings* volume (see introductory chapter footnote, *supra*). David Wolff's study of the Chrysler-UAW system appears in the 1958 NAA *Proceedings* volume, *The Arbitrator and the Parties*, 111–141.

[14] See, for example, James J. Healy, "The Factor of Ability in Labor Relations," in Jean T. McKelvey, ed., *Arbitration Today* (Washington: The Bureau of National Affairs, Inc., 1955), pp. 45–54; and Arthur M. Ross, "The Arbitration of Discharge Cases: What Happens after Reinstatement" in Jean T. McKelvey, ed., *Critical Issues in Labor Arbitration* (Washington: The Bureau of National Affairs, Inc., 1957), pp. 21–56.

3. Achievement of more clear-cut, intelligible contract language.

4. Improvement of personnel policies by postoperational studies of arbitration decisions and intelligent application of this knowledge in policy formation.

SELECTED BIBLIOGRAPHY

American Arbitration Association, *Arbitration Bibliography*. New York: American Arbitration Association, 1954.

———, *Labor Arbitration: Procedures and Techniques*. New York: American Arbitration Association, 1957.

———, *Procedural and Substantive Aspects of Labor-Management Arbitration: An AAA Research Report*. (Braden Memorial Pamphlet, No. 1). New York: American Arbitration Association, 1957.

Bickel, Alexander M. and Harry H. Wellington, "Legislative Purpose and the Judicial Process: The Lincoln Mills Case," *Harvard Law Review*, LXXI (November, 1957), 1–39.

Cole, David L., "Arbitration—Whose Responsibility?" *Proceedings of the Fourth Annual Meeting, Industrial Relations Research Association*. Madison: IRRA, 1952, pp. 151–56.

Cox, Archibald, "Rights under a Labor Agreement," *Harvard Law Review*, LXIX (February, 1956), 601–57.

Davey, Harold W., "Hazards in Labor Arbitration," *Industrial and Labor Relations Review*, I (April, 1948), 386–405.

———, "Labor Arbitration: A Current Appraisal," *Industrial and Labor Relations Review*, IX (October, 1955), 85–94.

———, "The John Deere-UAW Permanent Arbitration System," in Jean T. McKelvey, ed., *Critical Issues in Labor Arbitration*. Washington: Bureau of National Affairs, Inc., 1957, pp. 161–92.

———, "The Proper Uses of Arbitration," *Labor Law Journal*, IX (February, 1958), 119–26.

Elkouri, Frank, *How Arbitration Works*. Washington: Bureau of National Affairs, Inc., 1952.

Frey, Alexander, "The Logic of Collective Bargaining and Arbitration," *Law and Contemporary Problems*, XII (Spring, 1947), 264–80.

Howard, Robert L., "Labor-Management Arbitration: 'There Ought to be a Law'—Or Ought There?" *Labor Law Journal*, VIII (March, 1957), 171–92, 212.

Isaacson, William J., "A Partial Defense of the Uniform Arbitration Act," *Labor Law Journal*, VII (June, 1956), 329–34.

Jensen, Vernon H. and Harold G. Ross, *Bibliography of Dispute Settlement by Third Parties*. Ithaca: New York State School of Industrial and Labor Relations, Cornell University, 1955.

Kennedy, Thomas, *Effective Labor Arbitration*. Philadelphia: University of Pennsylvania Press, 1948.

Kruger, Daniel H., "Arbitration and its Uses in 36 Firms in Wisconsin," *Labor Law Journal*, VI (March, 1955), 165–81.

Law Note, "Rights of Individual Workers in Union-Management Arbitration Proceedings," *Yale Law Journal*, LXVI (May, 1957), 946–54.

National Academy of Arbitrators, *Arbitration Today*. Jean T. McKelvey, ed. Washington: Bureau of National Affairs, Inc., 1955.

———, *Critical Issues in Labor Arbitration*. Jean T. McKelvey, ed. Washington: Bureau of National Affairs, Inc., 1957.

———, *Management Rights and the Arbitration Process*. Jean T. McKelvey, ed. Washington: Bureau of National Affairs, Inc., 1956.

———, *The Profession of Arbitration*. Washington: Bureau of National Affairs, Inc., 1957.

———, *The Arbitrator and the Parties*, Jean T. McKelvey, ed. Washington: Bureau of National Affairs, Inc., 1958.

Roberts, Benjamin C., "Precedent and Procedure in Arbitration Cases," *Proceedings, Sixth Annual New York University Conference on Labor*. Albany: Matthew Bender & Co., 1953, pp. 149–60.

Roberts, Harold S., *Essentials of Labor Arbitration*. Honolulu: University of Hawaii, 1956.

Shulman, Harry and Neil W. Chamberlain, *Cases on Labor Relations*. Brooklyn: The Foundation Press, 1949.

Singer, Morton, "Labor Arbitration: Should it be Formal or Informal?" *Labor Law Journal*, II (February, 1951), 89–94.

Summers, Harold X. and Bernard Samoff, "A New Look at the NLRA and Arbitration," *Labor Law Journal*, V (August, 1954), 535–42, 590.

Warren, Edgar L. and Irving Bernstein, "The Arbitration Process," *Southern Economic Journal*, XVII (July, 1950), 16–33.

Witte, Edwin E., *Historical Survey of Labor Arbitration*. Philadelphia: University of Pennsylvania Press, 1952.

Young, Stanley, "Fifty Years of Grievance Arbitration: The Anthracite Experience," *Labor Law Journal*, VIII (October, 1957), 705–13.

8

Managerial authority and the scope of collective bargaining

One of the perennial issues in many union-management relationships is the conflict over the relationship between managerial authority and the scope of collective bargaining. Disputes continue to arise over what matters are bargainable and what matters are within the exclusive domain of managerial control. The growth of the economic power and influence of unions has been reflected in the expanding subject matter of collective bargaining. Viewing this trend toward enlarging the scope of collective bargaining, many management representatives have become increasingly concerned about contractual impairment or deterioration of management functions that they maintain should be immune from negotiation.

The first level of this dispute over managerial authority and collective bargaining takes place at the negotiation table, finding its expression in management refusal to consider certain union demands or insisting on a "strong" management rights clause. The second level of the dispute arises in contract administration where, in the opinion of some management representatives, the arbitration process is being skillfully used by unions to persuade arbitrators to chip away at basic management rights.

The dispute over what is bargainable and what is not bargainable in some cases reflects genuine disagreement in principle as to which matters should be subject to joint decision-making. In other cases the dispute is merely a reflection of a latent power conflict where the ultimate outcome mirrors the comparative economic strength of the parties. In some cases both issues of principle and of bargaining power are involved.

In the typical situation management representatives will seek to define and limit the scope of collective bargaining in concrete terms. They wish to draw a clear line between management functions not subject to contractual rule-making and matters properly amenable to joint decision-making. Union representatives, on the other hand, typically argue that collective bargaining must remain a fluid, dynamic process. They contend that it is not only unwise but in fact impossible to limit the scope of collective bargaining. Management and union representatives may agree perfectly in principle that collective bargaining is properly concerned with *all matters directly relating to wages, hours, and other conditions of employment.* In specific situations, however, the parties may differ sharply in their views as to what subjects are *directly related* to wages, hours, and working conditions.[1]

When management and union are in basic disagreement over the scope of collective bargaining, the developing of constructive relationships is virtually impossible. Adding to the bitterness is the disposition of some managements and some unions to view issues over the scope of collective bargaining as a suitable arena for an uncompromising struggle for ultimate supremacy. The sovereign status of competing institutional entities is held to be at stake. When the issue is defined in terms of management prerogatives versus union rights, the basic will to agree, so essential to constructive relationships, dissolves completely in a struggle for power.

FACTORS TENDING TO EXPAND THE SCOPE OF COLLECTIVE BARGAINING

Unquestionably, the trend is toward expansion in the scope of collective bargaining. As the economy becomes more interdependent and as the influence of trade unionism increases, the content of matters directly

[1] The literature on the prerogative controversy is considerable, but much of it is of an emotional or polemical nature. Neil Chamberlain's study remains the most searching treatment of the nature of managerial authority in relation to collective bargaining and the union's impact thereon. See Neil W. Chamberlain, *The Union Challenge to Management Control* (New York: Harper & Brothers, 1948). For an illuminating comparison of viewpoints expressed by informed partisans, see the papers by James C. Phelps, speaking for management, and Arthur J. Goldberg, speaking for labor, in Jean T. McKelvey, ed., *Management Rights and the Arbitration Process* (Washington: The Bureau of National Affairs, Inc., 1956), pp. 102–29. Comments on these two papers by Sidney A. Wolff, New York attorney and arbitrator, and Neil W. Chamberlain are also of great value. *Ibid.*, pp. 129–48.

affecting the employment relationship becomes more inclusive. This is not to say that trade unionism is in the process of taking over management functions. Rather, the expanding scope of collective bargaining is an expression of a broadening view of what matters actually affect directly the employment relationship.

Looked at unemotionally, the increasing scope of collective bargaining is a logical reflection of the growing complexity of the industrial system as well as a function of the enhanced bargaining power of trade unions. The American economy is a dynamic one. Collective bargaining is a dynamic process. It is entirely natural that the scope of matters directly affecting the employment relationship is broader and more inclusive today than it was in 1900, or in 1940.

This trend may be expected to continue. But the basic nature of the management-union relationship will not be changed necessarily. There is no reason to anticipate an inevitable socialization of industry or any preemption of managerial functions by unions. Management will still manage.

Occasionally, some employers in mock or real despair have begged unions to "take my business and see what you can do with it." Most unions turn down such offers. They do not want the responsibility of running the business. They recognize that this is properly a management responsibility. But unions insist on having a say in the formulation of any policies that, in their view, directly affect the employment relationship.

ALTERNATIVE APPROACHES TO MANAGERIAL AUTHORITY

Broadly speaking, there are two main schools of thought concerning the nature of managerial authority in labor relations. They may be termed the *residual theory* and the *trusteeship theory*. Each of these views of managerial authority deserves full exposition because the approach of management is conditioned fundamentally by the theory it holds as to the nature of its authority in the collective bargaining relationship. In general, the residualists seek to draw a strict line of demarcation between what is bargainable and what is not—and then hold that line as firmly as possible. Such an emphasis on prerogatives is frequently productive of conflict in the union-management relationship whenever the union may seek to use its economic power to shift that line of demarcation. Acceptance of the trusteeship theory involves regarding collective bargaining as a *method of management* rather than as a series of concessions or retreats.

THE RESIDUAL THEORY OF MANAGERIAL AUTHORITY

The residual theory assumes that all rights, functions, and prerogatives belonged to management in the preunion days of unilateral responsibility,

The introduction of unionism and collective bargaining was thus a progressive encroachment on a formerly exclusive domain. The collective agreement is viewed as a specific infringement upon, or restriction of, managerial authority. The familiar distinction between delegated and reserved powers is employed. If something has not been delegated otherwise by the contract, it is reserved to management.

From an historical viewpoint much can be said for this theory of managerial authority. Certainly, in preunion days management was in sole command of the terms and conditions of employment. Many companies, prior to unionization, gave their employees excellent wages and working conditions. They voluntarily gave up some of their "rights" as a means of raising worker morale. But even under the best of circumstances such rights and privileges as employees may have enjoyed stemmed from unilateral managerial decision rather than joint policy-making. No reciprocal relationships of an enduring nature were established, certainly not in any institutionalized form.

Both paternalistic and antiunion employers see collective bargaining as an intrusion on provinces assigned by natural law to management. When compelled to surrender a portion of their previously unlimited sovereignty (either through legislation or union economic pressure), it is perhaps natural for them to assume a defensive and negative approach to collective bargaining. Collective bargaining is looked upon as a vehicle for restricting the scope of management's essential activities. One who holds these convictions cannot appreciate, even intellectually, the affirmative possibilities for improving industrial relations through collective bargaining.

In its highest form the residualist school affirms belief in collective bargaining and advocates meeting all legal requirements with reference to procedure and substance. However, one may doubt whether meeting minimum statutory standards of required performance in collective bargaining is sufficient to produce constructive relationships.

The residualist school assumptions may be summarized as follows:

1. Prior to unionism, management possessed full power over all phases of employee relations.

2. Collective bargaining introduces certain specific restrictions on managerial authority and discretion.

3. Management retains all powers, rights, and privileges not specifically given away or restricted by the collective agreement. Any subject not covered by the agreement is still under exclusive, unilateral management control.

4. Management has an obligation to contain unionism to the extent necessary to preserve intact the essential functions of management. The content of "essential" varies considerably among particular supporters of the prerogative approach.

5. Collective agreements are viewed largely as treaties of peace rather than as instrumentalities for mutual protection, benefit, and advancement.

THE TRUSTEESHIP THEORY OF MANAGERIAL AUTHORITY

This theory emphasizes the multiple obligations of management.[2] It notes that management has a primary responsibility to the stockholders which requires promotion of the economic welfare of the company. It also recognizes that management has responsibilities to employees, to the community, and to the consumers of the product.

Awareness of multiple obligations is not a monopoly of the trusteeship school. Many proponents of the residual theory are fully aware of their multiple responsibilities. But the residualists are distinctly favorable to that method of exercising managerial responsibility which stresses the retention of a maximum of unilateral authority in the hands of management.

The trusteeship school recognizes that the welfare of the various interested groups may be promoted through alternative methods, one of which is collective bargaining. According to this view, management has no divine or inalienable rights. There is an awareness that unilateral management control may well have been the best method of running the business a generation ago and may still be the best method in certain situations today. But there is also a willingness to experiment with collective bargaining as a potentially useful method of management and as a basis for providing a more equitable allocation of the industrial product among the various interested groups.

The trusteeship theory of management sees the manager as a highly skilled employee who is hired for certain specific purposes: (1) to make a profit, to satisfy stockholders; (2) to sell a quality product at a just price, to satisfy customers; and (3) to ensure sound industrial relations policies, to satisfy employees.

Such an approach looks toward a rational allocation of functions rather than a defense of absolute rights or prerogatives. It does not view the expanding scope of collective bargaining as a barrier to constructive relationships.

Management cannot consider a sharing or an allocation of functions until it becomes convinced of the practical usefulness of collective relationships with a union. A labor organization cannot adopt a cooperative

[2] An excellent contrast between what I have termed the residual and trusteeship theories of managerial authority is provided by Florence Peterson in "Management Efficiency and Collective Bargaining," *Industrial and Labor Relations Review*, I (October, 1947), 29–49.

approach until its institutional requirements of survival are thoroughly satisfied.

The trusteeship theory of managerial authority appears to represent a more realistic approach to contemporary developments in industrial relations. It is, therefore, the more likely to survive. In contrast, the negativism of the management prerogative or residualist school precludes attaining the degree of flexibility necessary in a highly dynamic economy.

A rejection of residualist assumptions does not imply the surrender of certain functions that should be primarily, or even exclusively, assigned to management. Management must always retain the right to manage if operational efficiency is to be maintained. The vital area for the exercise of managerial authority is in the field of administration, not policy-making. There is no logical basis for permanently vesting policy-making on certain subjects exclusively and irrevocably in management (or in the union).

A practical approach requires determining for each specific labor-manangement relationship which subjects shall be open to joint policy-formulation and which subjects shall not. The precise limits of policy-making will vary appreciably over a period of time. It is virtually impossible to draw in general terms a satisfactory line between subjects appropriate to negotiation and subjects rightly outside negotiation.

UNLIMITED VERSUS LIMITED SOVEREIGNTY

One of the basic differences between the residualist school and the trusteeship school is their respective definitions of sovereignty. The former tends to define sovereignty as absolute, unlimited, and indivisible. The latter tends to view sovereignty as compatible with a concept of limited government, of authority limited by reciprocal institutional obligations.

In those union-management relationships that are built upon a pattern of containment-aggression political scientists can find many concrete illustrations of unlimited sovereignty concepts at work. In such relationships collective bargaining is almost always of the armed truce variety.

In labor relations, as in political theory, there are sharp differences of opinion as to whether sovereignty is by its very nature not limitable. If the analogy is not pushed too far, significant parallels can be drawn between the diplomatic involvements of rival nation-states in the international sphere and the clashes over prerogatives and inherent rights in the labor relations area.

In the realm of political theory concepts of sovereignty are formulated in an effort to discover and explain the true nature and source of governmental authority. As Hyman Cohen has pointed out, there is considerable variance among the theorists' concepts of sovereignty: [3]

[3] Hyman E. Cohen, *Recent Theories of Sovereignty* (Chicago: The University of Chicago Press, 1937), p. 3.

Theories of sovereignty are theories of politics, theories of power. Sovereignty resides in one. Sovereignty resides in the many. Sovereignty is fragmentary. Sovereignty is supramundane. These are the patterns of the concept as it appears in history.

When applied to international relations, the view of domestic sovereignty as supreme, illimitable power requires considerable adaptation and reformulation. Cohen writes: [4]

> ... owing to the exigencies of an international situation in which the possession of sovereignty was the index to internal government supremacy, sovereignty externally was limited in meaning to the recognition that the government was supreme domestically and that it could enforce what it would on its own domain. Externally, it claimed no supremacy; it claimed only a freedom from external control—independence. It claimed, in other words, the right to make such obligations for itself and its nation as it pleased, of its own free will.

When the foregoing is thoughtfully translated into such terms as management prerogatives, union prerogatives, exclusive functions, and subjects not open to collective bargaining, the meaningfulness of the analogy becomes clear.

The political phenomena of nation-states and balance of power strategy in international relations have been familiar since the sixteenth century. It can hardly be said that the nation-state (with its associated doctrine of sovereignty) has produced harmonious international relations. It is difficult to see how a similar philosophy can be successfully applied in labor relations. Whether the problem is relations among nations or among institutional groups within industry, most pragmatic proposals for improvement rely on a basic recognition of the need for a doctrine of *limited sovereignty*.

Of course, many political philosophers hold that limited sovereignty is a contradiction in terms. For example, Jacques Maritain, after a careful review of the principal writings of the main theorists on sovereignty (Jean Bodin, Thomas Hobbes, and Jean-Jacques Rousseau), states that "the concept of Sovereignty ... is but one with the concept of Absolutism." [5]

According to Maritain, one of the most eminent of contemporary political theorists, sovereignty means "independence and power which are *separately* or *transcendently* supreme"; it means possession of a supreme power "which is exercised *without accountability*." From his analysis Maritain concludes that "The two concepts of Sovereignty and Absolutism have been forged together on the same anvil. They must be scrapped together." [6]

[4] *Ibid.*, p. 2.

[5] Jacques Maritain, "The Concept of Sovereignty," *American Political Science Review*, XLIV (June, 1950), 343–58, at 355.

[6] Ibid., 355–56 and 357. The emphasis is Maritain's.

It must be agreed that equating the term sovereignty with absolute, unlimited authority is a useful device for making a sophisticated apology for despotism. As so defined, the sovereignty concept is intrinsically wrong and capable of serious misuse when applied to questions about the nature of governmental authority. It is equally wrong in the sphere of labor relations. Many of the power struggles in labor relations today are traceable to private adherence to concepts of unlimited sovereignty—for sovereignty read exclusive and unlimited management or union prerogatives—borrowed consciously or unconsciously from a political theory that has now been largely discredited.

GOVERNMENT BY CONSENT IN LABOR RELATIONS

An imperative requirement for constructive labor relations is a workable concept of limited government based on consent and reciprocal obligations. In short, the approach called for is one of *constitutionalism.*

In political theory the constitutionalist distinguishes between fundamental law and statutory law. Our fundamental law, the United States Constitution, places definite limits on the authority of both federal and state governments. Within these limits the powers of government are plenary. However, there is a complete rejection of the notion that any powers or authority are inherent or inalienable or illimitable. Furthermore, in the constitutionalist's view, the concept of governmental accountability is of critical importance. The emphasis on accountability is based on a deep-seated faith in the principle of government by consent.

The principles of limited constitutional government, of rule by consent, of a "government of laws and not of men," and of governmental accountability are all basic to the American concept of the nature and source of political authority. If their validity in political affairs is conceded it is difficult to deny their proper application in problems of industrial government.

There can be a direct and practical carry-over of these principles to the realm of union-management relationships. Collective bargaining has emerged in recent years as a dominant force in industrial government. Its constructive utilization as a method of industrial government or as a method of management precludes a continuing adherence to concepts of either managerial or union authority as illimitable, sovereign power.

Most writers on administrative management (either private or governmental management) agree that the essence of authority lies not in the power to give orders but in the degree to which orders are accepted and carried out. In other words, consent is the basis of sound administration in labor relations even as it is in constitutional government.

Notions of unlimited sovereign authority cannot be made consistent with the foregoing view of administrative policy. Democratic industrial relations can develop only when both employers and unions think in terms of limited government, in terms of authority obtained by consent rather than by administrative fiat or from claims of inherent, inalienable rights.

Returning to the main theme of managerial authority in relation to the scope of collective bargaining, what is the precise significance of the concept of limited government applied to the prerogative controversy? One fundamental conclusion emerges. *The scope of collective bargaining must itself remain subject to bargaining.* The basic difference between the residualist view of managerial authority and the trusteeship view is that the former cannot accept this proposition whereas the latter takes a calm, pragmatic view of the implications in such a statement. The residualist is inclined to believe that a permanent line must be drawn somehow between matters that are bargainable and matters that are not bargainable because they are, or should be, exclusively under management's sovereign authority.

The employer who looks upon collective bargaining as a method of management bases his thinking about the scope of collective bargaining not upon immutable principles but upon a pragmatic view of what should be bargainable at a particular time in the light of particular circumstances. He recognizes that the line may be drawn at a certain point at one time and at a different point when the contract comes up for renegotiation. He is not concerned about the protection of management or union prerogatives *as such.* He is concerned only with a rational allocation of functions based on a realistic appraisal of the requirements of the particular union-management relationship.

WHAT IS BARGAINABLE

The scope of collective bargaining at any one period will depend upon: (1) the policies and attitudes of management and the union; (2) the power relationships between the parties; (3) economic conditions in the industry; and (4) the general economic milieu. The scope of bargaining cannot be made contingent realistically upon a generalized formula of allegedly sovereign management (or union) prerogatives.

In almost any union-management relationship at contract renewal periods a difference is likely to develop between the parties as to whether a certain union (or management) demand is properly bargainable. The decision should be based on a pragmatic evaluation of the circumstances rather than in terms of abstract principles. As a general proposition, it can be stated that the decisive consideration should be whether Demand *X* relates directly to the employer-employee or employer-union relationship.

The dividing line as to what is bargainable and what is not bargainable has real meaning only in terms of specific cases and circumstances. As a preface to an illustrative discussion, however, certain general principles may be useful. It is probable that the following four principles will be basically valid for most union-management relationships over a considerable period of time:

1. All matters *directly* affecting the employment relationship should be subject to joint negotiation.

2. In general, the administration of policies affecting the employment relationship should be vested exclusively in management, subject to challenge through the contract's grievance machinery.

3. Policy formation and execution on matters not directly affecting the employment relationship should be vested exclusively in management (or the union) and not subject to challenge.

4. The scope of collective bargaining must, of course, itself remain negotiable in order that collective bargaining may continue to perform its dual function of stabilization and adaptation to dynamic change.

It is essential in application of the foregoing principles to emphasize the importance of the distinction drawn between management (or union) functions calling for exclusive, unchallengeable control and those functions requiring only administrative initiative. Still thinking in general terms, this distinction can be clarified by the following reformulation:

1. Management should have exclusive, unchallengeable authority in the exercise of functions that have no direct impact on human relationships. Management should have only the right of administrative initiative when the exercise of a managerial function has a direct impact on employees and the latter's relationships with management.

2. By the same token, unions should have exclusive, unchallengeable authority over their own internal affairs, except when the execution of internal union functions has a direct impact on industrial production and worker relationships with management.

EXCLUSIVE MANAGEMENT FUNCTIONS

It is essential now to consider some practical applications of these general principles. The above analysis suggests a norm that is not always easy to apply. The infinite variety in union-management relationships today and the diversity of conditions among industries require adaptation of general principles to particular circumstances.

Many employers today would still find themselves in complete agreement with a comprehensive list of *proposed exclusive management functions* developed by the management members of the Committee on Management's Right to Manage at the President's Labor Management Conference in November, 1945. This list follows: [7]

[7] U.S. Department of Labor, Division of Labor Standards, Bulletin No. 77, *The President's National Labor-Management Conference*, November 5–30, 1945, Summary and Committee Reports. (Washington: 1946), p. 58.

The determination of products to be manufactured or services to be rendered to customers by the enterprise; and the location of the business, including the establishment of new units and the relocation or closing of old units. (When it becomes necessary to relocate a unit, or close an old unit, or transfer major operations between plants, management should give careful consideration to the impact of such moves on the employees involved, and discuss with them or their accredited representatives possible solutions for the resulting problems.)

The determination of the lay-out and equipment to be used in the business; the processes, techniques, methods, and means of manufacture and distribution; the materials to be used (subject to proper health and safety measures where dangerous materials are utilized) and the size and character of inventories.

The determination of financial policies; general accounting procedures—particularly the internal accounting necessary to make reports to the owners of the business and to government bodies requiring financial reports; prices of goods sold or services rendered to customers; and customer relations.

The determination of the management organization of each producing or distributing unit; and the selection of employees for promotion to supervisory and other managerial positions.

The determination of job content (this refers to establishing the duties required in the performance of any given job and not to wages); the determination of the size of the work force; the allocation and assignment of work to workers; determination of policies affecting the selection of employees; establishment of quality standards and judgment of workmanship required; and the maintenance of discipline and control and use of the plant property; the scheduling of operations and the number of shifts.

The determination of safety, health, and property protection measures, where legal responsibility of the employer is involved.

These functions are clearly appropriate for managerial action. The critical question becomes whether or not they should be removed from consideration at the bargaining table or labeled "off limits" for grievance action during the life of a collective agreement.

The labor members of this Committee on Management's Right to Manage did not take issue directly with this list of management functions. They did, however, affirm that it would be unwise to build a fence around any specific set of management functions. An inflexible list of management functions would not be workable in practice in view of the rapid change in industrial relations, according to the labor viewpoint.

Management spokesmen felt that the refusal of union representatives to go along on specifying any set of management functions was indicative of a real desire to take over or, at least, to restrict or impair essential managerial authority. The union representatives denied that this was true.

The writer's own experience leads him to conclude that management's fears as to unions' ultimate intentions are frequently grounded in a confusion between extending the scope of collective bargaining and actual union participation in, or assumption of, managerial decision-making authority. Virtually all union leaders are interested in the former; virtually none of them in the latter. Contracting about more items does leave to management fewer matters about which it can decide independently. As Father Brown has pointed out,[8] however, the essential quality of management's freedom remains unimpaired and the ultimate decisions rest with management. It is worth noting that formal union participation in management has been and continues to be exceedingly rare.

NEGOTIATION VERSUS CONSULTATION

Of course, a theoretical case could be made for the extreme proposition that almost any function of management today has a direct bearing on the wages, hours, and working conditions of employees. The concern here, however, is with a workable, realistic allocation of functions and responsibilities rather than with tenuous, theoretical considerations.

Almost all of the functions listed by management representatives as ones that should be excluded from the bargaining table have been subject to joint policy formation in particular union-management relationships in one industry or another. For example, in the garment industry there is an extensive sharing or even a taking over by the union of many functions and responsibilities that are generally considered unchallengeable management functions. The needle trades experience is, however, exceptional. It has evolved from the peculiar power relationship between the International Ladies Garment Workers' Union and the large number of small concerns making up the industry. In this case the union is the stabilizing force in the industry and makes many decisions about "business policy" that would normally be managerial responsibilities.

In industry generally, most of the functions in the list remain exclusively in the hands of management. They are not subject to consideration at the bargaining table, but in many cases management utilizes the consultative process in the exercise of such functions. Recognizing the necessity for consent as the soundest basis for efficient operation, many managements take their workers and union representatives into their confidence by advance consultation about many moves that they would never negotiate. There appear to be few subjects in the foregoing list in which consultation, as contrasted with negotiation, would not occasionally make good administrative sense. Of course, even the use of the consultative process is contingent upon a previously established, sound relationship between management and union. Unless management feels institutionally secure it will not expose its prerogatives even to consultation for fear that

[8] Leo C. Brown, S. J., "The Shifting Distribution of the Rights to Manage," *Proceedings*, First Annual Meeting of the Industrial Relations Research Association. (Champaign: IRRA, 1949), pp. 132–45.

the union may use such overtures as the opening wedge for an invasion of exclusive managerial spheres.

When a sound relationship exists, consultation can be an extremely useful device. The fear of poaching on prerogatives is rarely present in such cases. For example, management frequently consults unions on such functions as:

1. Establishment of a new plant or relocation of an existing plant.
2. Determination of layout and equipment to be used.
3. Processes, techniques, and especially methods of manufacture.
4. Services rendered to customers and customer relations.
5. Selection of employees for promotion to supervisory positions.
6. Determination of job content.
7. Allocation and assignment of work.
8. Selection of new employees.
9. Establishment of quality and performance standards.
10. Discipline.
11. Scheduling of operations and number of shifts.

It may also be noted that in some cases these functions are subject to collective bargaining. Companies and unions with well-established union-management cooperation plans regularly confer about items 2, 3, and 6. Craft unions frequently bargain with management on items 5, 7, 8, and 9. In short, the nature of the labor-management relationship in particular cases determines the subject matter or scope of collective bargaining.

MANAGEMENT STRATEGY ON EXCLUSIVE FUNCTIONS

Price policy is frequently cited as illustrative of the type of management function that should be solely and exclusively within the employer's domain. The famous "battle of prerogatives" between General Motors and the UAW over the issue of tying a company's price policy into the union's wage demands resulted in a 113-day strike in 1945–46. The UAW's major demand was for a thirty per cent increase in basic wage rates. The proposed increase was designed to maintain the same take-home pay with the changeover from a wartime work week of forty-eight hours to a peacetime forty hours.

The prerogative issue arose over the UAW's offer to reduce its wage demands if General Motors could demonstrate that it could not afford such an increase without an accompanying increase in the price of cars. The UAW brief directly coupled its wage demands with the corporation's price policy. In effect, it announced that it was fighting the battle of consumers generally as well as the battle of the auto workers.

General Motors stood firmly on the principle of managerial prerogatives with respect to price policy. It refused to negotiate as long as the union's wage demands were linked to the corporation's price policy. GM said that its ability to pay was none of the union's business, and denied the union's demand to "take a look at the books."

A long, costly, bitter, but notably peaceful strike ensued. Although it received strong financial and moral support from other unions, the UAW was unable to enforce its demands. It ultimately had to settle for a pattern increase of eighteen and one-half cents per hour. This pattern had been developed by General Motors' signing with the United Electrical, Radio and Machine Workers while the auto workers were still on strike.

Since the UAW lost this conflict over price policy prerogative, no major union has again essayed to link its wage demands formally to an agreement on no price increases.[9] Price policy, then, is clearly one area of managerial authority that is still far from being subject to joint formulation or even consultation.

It should be added that GM's refusal to discuss its ability to pay without increasing prices stressed only the tie-in to price policy. Economic circumstances frequently condition the choice of criteria in formulation of both management and union wage policies. Unions stress the importance of an increase in the cost of living as a basis for wage demands during an economic upswing, but will minimize increased real wages from lowering prices during a downswing. Employers will generally disclaim the validity of ability to pay as a criterion during a period of high profits, but they have no objection to arguing inability to pay when profits are low.

When management and a union have instituted profit-sharing programs through collective bargaining, the prerogative issue seldom arises.[10] Experience has indicated that "a sense of participation and partnership is the fundamental prerequisite" for the success of a profit-sharing plan. In one markedly satisfactory case reported by the late Joseph Scanlon [11] management insisted on including the following clause in the profit-sharing agreement:

> The United Steelworkers of America, C.I.O., shall have access to the books of the company at any time in order to verify the operating statements.

In the main, however, price policy and related decisions constitute an area that is exclusively in the hands of management. Other functions in

[9] The UAW's 1957 suggestion that the auto industry reduce the prices on 1958 models by $100 each is not an exception to the foregoing generalization. It was not linked formally to the wage demands that were actually made in the spring of 1958.

[10] The 1958 automobile industry negotiations *do* constitute an exception to this generalization since automobile management clearly regarded the UAW's profit-sharing proposal as an opening wedge for invasion of exclusive managerial domains.

[11] See Joseph N. Scanlon, "Profit Sharing under Collective Bargaining," *Industrial and Labor Relations Review*, II (October, 1948), 58-75, at 70. For a current account of some problems in Scanlon Plan relationships, see George Strauss and Leonard R. Sayles, "The Scanlon Plan: Some Organizational Problems," *Human Organization,* XVI (Summer, 1957), 15–22.

this category include such matters as the determination of products to be manufactured, marketing and distribution methods, manufacturing processes and methods, product design, location and relocation of plants. Decisions on plant relocation, however, afford an example of a management function where consultation with employees and the union is clearly desirable.

Management policies differ widely as to which functions they regard as indispensably exclusive in particular cases. Some companies insist on retaining complete control over time study and the setting of production standards. Others are amenable to joint time study and joint standard-setting. Some companies refuse to negotiate a contract policy governing promotions within the bargaining unit. Others do not guard this normal management function jealously, and are agreeable to contractual provisions on posting of vacancies, job bidding, and assignment to senior qualified applicants. Some companies insist on the prerogative of granting merit increases within rate ranges. Others are not opposed to granting automatic progression at regular time intervals. And so it goes.

A firm that intends to refuse a union demand on an issue that management regards as being within its exclusive control should be prepared for the consequences of such refusal if the issue is within the area of bargainable subjects as determined by the National Labor Relations Board. If the union demand is strongly enough felt to be backed by economic pressure (i.e. a strike), the firm must weigh the cost of sticking to its principle. It must also consider the possibility of facing a "refusal to bargain" charge under Taft-Hartley.

In relation to the good faith bargaining issue it is important to keep in mind that neither the company nor the union is compelled to agree to the other's proposals. They must negotiate in good faith, but neither is compelled to agree to a particular demand simply because the subject matter of the demand is within the broad framework of bargainable issues. However, he who contemplates holding out indefinitely on an issue that he knows to be a bargainable one as a matter of law should be prepared to back his convictions by resort to economic pressure and, if charged with bad faith, to defend his position. The best defense would appear to be the development of arguments showing that retention of exclusive managerial authority is rational and logical under the conditions prevailing in the particular situation. Stubborn reliance on prerogatives for their own sake will not be very convincing if the issue lies within the framework of collective bargaining.

MANAGEMENT FUNCTIONS REQUIRING ADMINISTRATIVE INITIATIVE

How can a line be drawn between management functions that are exclusive and unchallengeable and those calling for administrative initiative, subject to challenge through the grievance machinery? One possible answer is to distinguish between management functions affecting *things* and those affecting *people*.

In the conduct of any business enterprise there are many functions performed daily that logically and rationally belong to management, but whose exercise has a direct impact on the employees in the bargaining unit. The right to discipline by discharge, suspension without pay, or written reprimand is properly vested in management. The impact is so direct upon the employee, however, that management's right of administrative initiative in discipline cases may clearly be subjected to challenge by the employee affected or by the union through the grievance and arbitration procedure of the contract.

Promotion, layoff, and rehiring policies are other good illustrations of functions requiring administrative initiative by management, subject to check through the grievance procedure. The principles of sound administration require that authority and primary responsibility for action rest with management. Yet, in practical operation, the performance of such functions usually affects important contractual rights of the workers. If management's authority to discharge, promote, transfer, layoff, and rehire were completely unfettered, the collective agreement would have little real significance for the worker. His job security and right to equality of treatment would be at the mercy of the employer. Hence, it is a prime aim of unionism to obtain limitations and checks upon management's exercise of such functions, which have a direct impact upon the worker, at the same time conceding that performance of such functions is primarily a responsibility of management.

On some matters there is very little disagreement between employers and unions about the nature and scope of management's authority. For example, the management right to discharge in almost all contracts is conditional upon the implied or stated assumption that the discharge must be for just cause. Many contracts require prior consultation with the union. In almost every case the exercise of the discharge prerogative may be made the subject of a grievance.

Management's right to promote, however, is another matter. A survey of contemporary contracts reveals a considerable variety in practice here as to the degree to which managerial discretion is limited. In some situations management retains virtually unfettered freedom to promote the employee of its choice, subject only to general contract strictures against discrimination. At the other extreme, as in many railroading occupations, promotion follows length of service with management retaining little if any discretion. Many industrial union contracts afford a variety of compromises between undiluted seniority and straight managerial control.

An effective compromise between the union's interest in length of service and the managerial interest in rewarding efficiency and ability is to provide for the posting of vacancies and receipt of bids, with the vacancy going to the "senior qualified applicant." Under such an arrangement management determines the qualifications for the vacant position and screens the applicants to determine which of them are qualified and which are not. At that point managerial discretion ends, and the vacancy must go to the senior qualified applicant.

On such functions as promotion it is difficult to say where the line should be drawn. It is clear, however, that at a minimum management should have an unquestioned right of administrative initiative. What conditions may or may not be attached to this right will usually depend on the nature of the relationship between the parties or the custom of the industry in question. When the union has confidence in managerial good faith, it may not attempt to enforce any limitations on management discretion beyond a general safeguard against discriminatory treatment. On the other hand, if suspicion or lack of faith prevails, there may be a concerted effort to restrict or even to remove discretion. If this is true, the contract clause will reflect the naked bargaining power of the parties rather than a mature decision as to which policy may be most feasible administratively.

Leaving special cases aside, it seems clear that management must have administrative initiative to discharge, to promote, and to lay off workers as a primary function. Since the exercise of such functions affects the worker's equity in his job, however, the contract should provide a mechanism for obtaining redress and protection against arbitrary action.

When a high degree of mutual confidence prevails and the parties have been bargaining over a long enough period of time to achieve the requisite maturity and flexibility in their day to day dealings with one another, few discharge cases are carried to arbitration. Nor is it usual in such cases to find basic disagreement on promotion policy. In newly developing relationships, however, discharge and promotional policy are a frequent source of irritation, misunderstanding, and even open conflict. Many wildcat strikes have their origin in a protest against managerial disciplinary action. The rank-and-file are unwilling to observe contractual procedures for handling grievances as a means of obtaining redress for a fancied or real injustice.

SETTING OR CHANGING PIECE RATES

Another illustration of a management function requiring administrative initiative, subject to challenge in its exercise, may be found in plants with an incentive method of wage payment, where job content changes rapidly and piece rates have to be reset or rates on new jobs established. Clearly, such matters have a direct bearing on the worker's wages, and are, therefore, a proper matter for collective negotiation. But, in terms of administrative practice, which is the more logical method of handling such changes? Few union leaders or rank-and-file workers are skilled in the mysteries of time study and incentive rate setting. There is a tendency to fear the unknown, colored by memories of past abuses of incentive plans under speed-up or sweating techniques. What is the best answer?

It seems logical to assign to management primary responsibility for setting piece rates and for changing existing rates. It is a management function, pure and simple. Nevertheless, in a relationship that depends upon consent for its effectiveness, there must be an avenue for protest against improper rates. Again the grievance machinery of the contract provides the answer.

Normally, management should and must have the responsibility for setting and changing piece rates, with its actions subject to challenge through the grievance procedure of the contract. Most management representatives appreciate the need for worker understanding and acceptance of incentive systems. Some employers encourage the training of union representatives in time study, so that the union can appraise the operation of management time study experts in an intelligent, informed manner.

The reader can supply still other illustrations of functions that are rationally allocable to management, but that require a check on arbitrariness if industrial relations are to develop in democratic fashion. In all such cases the major conclusion points to the basic wisdom of concepts of limited government (government by consent) in labor relations.

There are many functions that management cannot effectively share if plant efficiency is to be maintained. There are, however, few functions of management today which do not have a real bearing on the wages, hours, and working conditions of the employee. It is difficult, perhaps impossible, to arrive at unchanging limitations on the scope of collective bargaining. It should remain flexible. Prerogatives jealously guarded in an unending battle over institutional status will enhance elements of conflict and reduce the possibilities for effective cooperative action.

IS THE PREROGATIVE CONTROVERSY DIMINISHING?

The intensity of the prerogative controversy seems to be diminishing. In union-management relationships that have become fairly well stabilized in recent years the parties have been able to work out a mutually satisfactory *modus vivendi*, and the prerogative issue seldom arises during negotiations. This appears to be true in the automobile [12] and steel indus-

[12] The 1958 negotiations in the automobile industry were an exception to this generalization because of the UAW's profit-sharing proposal and management's vigorous resistance thereto, largely on prerogative grounds. The ultimate settlement reflected no change in the present content of managerial prerogatives in the automobile industry.

tries at the present time. No serious prerogative controversies can be noted in industries with long collective bargaining histories such as building and construction, printing, and the garment trades. The pattern of accommodation varies widely from one industry to another, but workable and durable arrangements have lasted over long periods of years.

The fires of controversy continue to burn steadily in new bargaining relationships and in the small firm category. The small employer, newly organized, is likely to smart under collective bargaining restrictions for some time. The new method of handling employment relationships represents a sharp change and appears to be a substantial encroachment on previous unilateral authority. Substitution of uniform policies and rules, an inevitable concomitant of collective bargaining in any industry, does not have the same shock effect on a large firm with many employees. A sizable labor force requires general principles and rules, whether the firm is union or nonunion. The smaller firm, frequently owner-managed, may have operated on a basis of personalized discretion. The change to uniform rules is frequently a traumatic experience for the employer in such cases, no matter how well-disposed he may have been toward his employees.

It is reasonable to anticipate that the scope of collective bargaining will continue to expand in the years ahead. It is unlikely, however that there will be any substantial movement in the direction of the union's taking over, or jointly participating in, functions now controlled exclusively by managment. Those who fear such a development ignore the basic nature of American unionism as a protest institution within the private enterprise framework. If a protest organization assumes joint or sole responsibility for the exercise of functions that it has previously been free to challenge or criticize, it necessarily reduces its effectiveness as a protest force. The British trade union leaders learned this hard fact when as officials of the party in power they attempted to restrain the wage demands of the rank-and-file. It is difficult for anyone to play two inconsistent roles simultaneously. If a union leader shares responsibility with management in the performance of a managerial function, he must defend the exercise of that function.

The overwhelming majority of American union leaders prefer to let management do the managing and to remain free-wheeling, critical agents of managerial performance. Such union leaders recognize that they are not equipped or trained to share in the exercise of most functions now performed by management. There are no straws in the wind that would indicate the advent of codetermination on the German pattern, industry councils, or any other substantial departure from the conventional allocation of functions.

A standard allocation of functions is likely to prevail in most cases for any one or a combination of the following reasons:

1. Management's refusal to bargain on certain functions or responsibilities as a matter of principle, backed up by the requisite bargaining strength to maintain this position.

2. Disinclination on the union's part to assume the responsibilities that accrue from joint participation in either policy formation or administration.

3. As a function of point 2, a contractual agreement to delegate to management exclusive authority over certain subjects, such as granting of merit increases or pension fund administration, that might normally be handled by joint negotiation or joint administration.

A NOTE ON PUBLIC POLICY AND THE SCOPE OF COLLECTIVE BARGAINING

In connection with the third point just noted it is essential to keep in mind that the legal scope of bargainable issues as defined by the National Labor Relations Board is considerably broader than many unions and companies prefer to make it in their own contractual arrangements. The NLRB has consistently taken an expansive view of subjects coming within the bare legislative phrase "rates of pay, wages, hours, or other conditions of employment." It has held that employers are under a legal duty to bargain in good faith upon request on such matters as stock purchase plans, merit increases, pension plans, and many other items. It has also taken a sweeping view of the employer's duty to furnish wage data and other information upon request in connection with negotiations or in contract administration.

Most of the board's decisions in these areas have been a logical by-product of deciding on the merits in particular cases where a refusal to bargain in good faith has been alleged. It is difficult to see how the board could have avoided a determination as to what was bargainable or not in such cases. Also, it is a little late in the game to attempt to challenge successfully its practice of doing so. The most casual survey of collective bargaining practices, however, would reveal a great variety of company-union arrangements in drawing private dividing lines between functions exclusive with management and matters subject to joint decision-making. Public policy certainly should be sufficiently flexible to permit the parties to work out their own arrangements for assigning admittedly bargainable issues (e.g., merit increases) to management's exclusive control if they so desire.

UNION PREROGATIVES

Controversies as to the proper scope of collective bargaining usually develop over managerial prerogatives. It is important to note, however, that a corresponding question sometimes develops over allegedly exclusive union functions and responsibilities.

For example, unions maintain vigorously that their criteria of membership in good standing are none of management's concern.

Although the Taft-Hartley Act has narrowed the employer's obligation to discharge under union security clauses to those cases where the reason for bad standing is nonpayment of dues or initiation fees, the unions, with considerable justification, continue to maintain that they are entitled to the right of exclusive control over whether union members are in good or poor standing. They protest that the Taft-Hartley limitation on discharge under union security clauses hampers legitimate union efforts at proper internal discipline and furnishes a valuable weapon to the antiunion employer. Such an employer might hire confirmed antiunion workers who would join the union under the terms of the union security clause, keep paid up in their dues, etc., and at the same time serve as a disrupting or antagonistic minority within the union. The union could expel them under such circumstances, but under the Taft-Hartley Act cannot compel their discharge.

Since a union's policies of admission or exclusion are likely to affect directly the composition of the employer's work force, it is entirely natural for management to take an interest in a matter that is concededly within the union's exclusive territory. Here again, the practical accommodation of rights to circumstances can best be worked out by the parties themselves in negotiation.

Leaving the Taft-Hartley limitation aside, it is entirely natural for management to be interested in finding out why it is being asked by the union to discharge some one who might have been a thoroughly satisfactory employee. A refusal on the union's part to disclose the reasons for the worker's bad standing in the union would normally illustrate the lack of wisdom in relying arbitrarily on prerogatives. Clearly, it is a union prerogative to determine qualifications for membership and to set criteria for maintaining such membership. Technically, management has no more concern with such a matter than the union might have with the criteria for admission of managerial representatives to their industry's trade association. In practice, however, where administration of such a right has a direct impact on the other party, industrial relations are not improved by a legalistic stand for exclusive privilege. If the union has nothing to hide, there is no reason why it should not disclose to management, upon request, its specific reasons for demanding the discharge of a worker under such circumstances.

Union insistence on its prerogatives in such cases was doubtless an important contributing factor in producing the Taft-Hartley restriction on the employer's obligation to discharge.

Unions are also alert to insure against any contract interpretation that might interfere with such matters as selection of shop stewards and other union officers. The writer recalls a recent arbitration case in which the issue concerned the company's obligation to recall a laid-off employee out of line with his natural seniority because of his election as departmental steward during a major layoff period. The company argued that the contract required stewards to be "full-time employees" of the company and that a worker in layoff status was not a full-time employee under the contract. The contract also provided for top seniority for stewards. The writer sustained the grievance and ruled that the employee-elected steward, even while on layoff, should be construed as a "full-time employee" within the meaning of the eligibility clause in the contract. A contrary ruling would require viewing the contract as having imposed a limitation on internal union affairs. The contract language afforded no support for a conclusion that the parties had intended such a limitation.

RESIDUAL RIGHTS OF LABOR

In discussion of union prerogatives it is pertinent to note the union version of the residualist theory discussed earlier with reference to managerial authority. As stated by Arthur Goldberg, it is historically inaccurate and misleading to conceive of management as the only party giving up rights when a collective bargaining relationship with a union is undertaken. In Goldberg's view, the resultant contract does not represent labor's imposition on management's reserved rights, but rather a basis on which both parties agree to go forward. Citing as "inherent" labor rights the right to strike, the right to organize, the right to a fair share of the company's income, and the right to safe, healthful working conditions, Goldberg affirms that it is inaccurate to think that prior to bargaining management's reserved rights were all-embracing to the exclusion of any labor right.[13]

Goldberg makes a persuasive case for his thesis against the more conventional view of the nature of managerial authority. Starting from Goldberg's assumptions, unions can be viewed as having imposed limitations on their pre-existing rights when they contract not to strike during the life of an agreement, when they forego the right to raise inequity grievances on existing job classifications spelled out in a contract for the duration of the contract, and when they agree to discipline members engaging in wildcat strikes, restriction of output, or slowdowns.

PREROGATIVE ARGUMENTS AT THE CONTRACT ADMINISTRATION LEVEL

Most of our discussion so far has centered on the scope of collective bargaining and the prerogative issue in terms of contract negotiation, i. e.,

[13] See Arthur J. Goldberg, *op. cit.*, footnote 1 *supra.*

determining a rational dividing line between what is bargainable and what is not bargainable. The Goldberg thesis leads us logically to a second stage of the prerogative controversy at the contract administration level. Issues frequently arise in arbitration of contract grievances today over arbitrability and also over the extent of the arbitrator's authority in reviewing a challenged exercise of managerial discretion. Each of these will be treated briefly.

A typical situation is one in which the union takes an inclusive view as to what grievances are arbitrable under the contract and management urges a restricted version of what the contract provides. The end product of such pulling and hauling is generally a considerable number of arbitration cases where the issue is whether the arbitrator has any business hearing the case at all, under a clause that limits his authority to hearing and deciding grievances concerning only contract interpretation and application.

The literature on arbitrability has been extensive in recent years, reflecting the shift in the scene of prerogative battles from the picket line to the arbitration hearing room. Management is typically fearful that in particular disputes the arbitrator will be tempted to go beyond the contract and chip away at managerial authority which the company had thought to be adequately safeguarded. The union, on the other hand, is typically fearful that under the pervasive impact of the residual theory of managerial authority the arbitrator will give greater weight to the directing force (management) than to the objecting force (union).

Viewing the vast body of private jurisprudence built up by thousands of arbitration decisions since World War II, it could scarcely be argued that arbitrators have always been consistent in their approach to these matters. The writer prefers to speak solely from his own experience, most of which has involved companies that are prerogative-conscious and unions that are militant in extracting from the contract all that is there. Yet there were only one or two cases involving an arbitrability issue in all that time.[14] This leads to the suggestion that there are no insoluble difficulties in the way of a workable solution to prerogative questions in contract administration any more than there are in contract negotiation. The secret of a successful relationship lies in agreement on the judicial type of arbitration and a clearly written contractual statement on the nature and limits of the arbitrator's authority.

Two special facets of the prerogative controversy in relation to contract administration are of more than passing current interest. One is the intriguing question as to whether or not it is preferable to include a management rights clause in the contract. The residualist school of managerial authority is split sharply on this point, although a survey of current

[14] A survey of the literature on arbitrability compels the conclusion that this limited contact with arbitrability issues may well be atypical.

contracts shows that those favoring inclusion of such a clause are in the great majority. The second question relates to whether an arbitrator has any authority to substitute his judgment for that of management in reviewing the latter's discretionary acts.

THE PROS AND CONS OF INCLUDING A MANAGEMENT RIGHTS CLAUSE IN THE CONTRACT

Those who favor inclusion of a management rights clause will admit readily that from the residualist standpoint such a clause adds nothing to managerial power under the contract, since by definition management has all power not specifically limited by contract. However, they believe that such a clause serves a valuable educational purpose in reminding union leaders and employees that certain subjects are taboo at the bargaining table and that managerial authority is supreme in many areas, even where the exercise of authority is subject to challenge through the grievance procedure. Advocates of including a rights clause will also urge that such clauses settle more issues over the arbitrability of a borderline grievance than they are likely to raise. Finally, it is felt that such clauses constitute a firm and well-defined line of defense against further encroachment by unions in subsequent bargaining.

Some who favor management rights clauses have a preference for what might be called the short-form clause, as in Article IV, Section 1, of the 1955-1958 Ford-UAW contract:

> The Company retains the sole right to manage its business, including the rights to decide the number and location of plants, the machine and tool equipment, the products to be manufactured, the method of manufacturing, the schedules of production, the processes of manufacturing or assembling, together with all designing, engineering, and the control of raw materials, semi-manufactured and finished parts which may be incorporated into the products manufactured; to maintain order and efficiency in its plants and operations; to hire, lay off, assign, transfer and promote employees, and to determine the starting and quitting time and the number of hours to be worked; subject only to such regulations and restrictions governing the exercise of these rights as are expressly provided in this Agreement.

Others prefer the long form that spells out the nature and scope of managerial authority in greater detail. Typical of such clauses is Article III of the 1957–1959 contract between the Coleman Company of Wichita, Kansas and the UAW:

> Section 1. Exclusive Management Rights. The Union recognizes the Company's right to manage the plant, including the right to hire, the number of shifts, the right to adopt and put into effect rules and regulations not inconsistent with the provisions of this Agreement, the right to determine

parts, services, and products to be manufactured or purchased, the number and location of plants, the plant layout and equipment to be used, the schedules of production, the methods, processes and means of manufacturing, the sources of materials and supplies, the disposition of products and the frequency and standards of inspection, the size and character of inventory, the determination of financial policies including all accounting procedures, prices of goods sold and customer relations and the determination of the Management organization. The exercise of such rights by the Company is not subject to the grievance procedure or arbitration. The above rights are not all inclusive but enumerate by way of illustration the type of rights which belong to Management and any other rights, powers, or authority Management had prior to the signing of this Agreement are retained by Management except those which have been specifically abridged, delegated or modified by this Agreement or any supplementary agreements that may hereafter be made between the Company and the Union.

Section 2. Limited Management Rights. Subject to all the provisions of this Agreement, including the grievance procedure, the Company shall have the right to direct its working forces, promote, demote, transfer, classify, or reclassify, layoff, recall, transfer from one shift to another, discipline or discharge for cause, maintain discipline and efficiency of employees and to establish standards of production.

The Coleman clause is a classic example of the residual theory of managerial rights. Do such clauses help or hinder management in accomplishing its objective of drawing a clear line between exclusive functions and those subject to collective bargaining? Many staunch residualists would answer in the negative. Their premise is a simple one: in the beginning there was management, and any contract represents specific limitations or conditions upon management's former plenary authority. By this reasoning, if a matter is not touched upon in the contract it is automatically still within management's exclusive control. Including a management rights clause is unnecessary and in fact dangerous. It may lead to erosion of managerial rights by interpretation in contract administration. If there is no management rights clause, there can be no limitation of authority by shortsighted grievance settlements or misguided arbitration decisions.

Opponents of a management rights clause would also argue that its omission from the contract removes a potent source of friction between the parties where management is firm about its prerogatives and is dealing with a militant, aggressive union. A management clause is as subject to interpretation as any other section of the contract. If it is in the contract as a target for the union to shoot at, there is the constant possibility of a gradual circumscribing of managerial authority through interpretation.

Most of the writer's recent arbitration experience has been with John Deere and UAW, a prerogative-conscious company and a militant union. Deere-UAW contracts have contained no management rights clause, but the parties have had a clear understanding as to what were arbitrable grievances under these contracts. Disputes on arbitrability rarely arose.

Given the residualist assumption, there is greater logic to omitting a management clause than to including it. But logic does not always triumph over experience. The majority of employers evidently have preferred to include such a clause in union contracts, even though it may be tautological in terms of their assumptions.

PRINCIPLES GOVERNING REVIEW OF MANAGERIAL DISCRETION

Let us turn now to contract administration experience in those areas where management has the right of administrative initiative subject to challenge through the grievance procedure. The Goldberg thesis is that a reviewing arbitrator should give equal weight to both the objecting force and the directing force. It is difficult to agree with this bald statement of equality. It is the writer's feeling that an arbitrator reviewing a challenged act of managerial discretion should not reverse that exercise of discretion unless it has been clearly shown to be arbitrary, capricious, or discriminatory. In a typical discipline case where the contract permits the arbitrator to modify penalties, what should the arbitrator do if he finds that management has proved that discipline was for good and just cause, but where he feels the punishment does not fit the crime? It is the writer's belief that he should modify the penalty only where he thinks that it was clearly arbitrary in relation to the offense. An arbitrator should not modify the penalty on the basis that if he had been administering discipline in the case in question, he would have given a lesser penalty. Similarly, in deciding disputes on employee qualifications in promotion cases the arbitrator should not substitute his judgment for that of management unless the managerial exercise of discretion is clearly shown to have been arbitrary, capricious, or discriminatory.

The basic principle here is one of orderly, efficient, and responsible direction of an enterprise. An arbitrator is a judicial watchdog of the contract. When his services are invoked, there is a charge that the contract has been violated. The arbitrator's touchstone is the contract. He is not employed as an omniscient solver of day-to-day industrial relations problems. He is not employed to tell the parties how *he* would have handled a situation. He is asked only to determine, on the facts of particular cases, whether the contract has been violated, or to decide the meaning of particular sections of the agreement.

Such restraint on the arbitrator's part cannot be properly criticized as giving greater weight to the directing force than to the objecting force. On the contrary, sound principles of contract administration preclude an arbitrator from substituting his judgment for that of management in cases where the contract gives management the right of administrative initiative subject to challenge.

A FINAL NOTE ON PREROGATIVES AND CONTRACT ADMINISTRATION

The attitude of the parties toward grievance machinery frequently provides an excellent index to the true character of their relationship. There are times when it is wise for a prerogative-conscious management to "bend" a little in contract administration. Of course, there must be a clear and realistic limitation on grievances going to arbitration. A completely open grievance machinery would virtually destroy the meaning and value of the contract and would be productive of chaos in contract administration. It would certainly seem advisable, however, to keep the grievance procedure open in the earlier steps, confining the arbitration step solely to grievances raising a question of contract interpretation or application. Circumstances might even arise when it would make sense from a human relations standpoint for management to permit a technically nonarbitrable grievance to go to arbitration and argue it on the merits rather than on the arbitrability issue.

As an illustration, what should be done when a union requests the discharge of a foreman? In such a case management well might claim that supervisory employees are under its exclusive jurisdiction and that the union has no right to question the conduct of its foremen. Management justifiably can insist on its exclusive authority here. However, if a union or an employee has a strong enough grievance against a foreman to demand his discharge, it would pay management to look into the reasons for this animosity, rather than to fall back on a technically strong contractual position, refusing to deal with the union on the matter.

A real opportunity is present in such a case for a common-sense approach by management. Under most contracts management could resist arbitration, arguing that the union's demand was not arbitrable. In such a case the arbitrator undoubtedly would refuse to rule on the union's demand for disciplining of the foreman. Such a decision, although technically correct, would solve nothing. In fact, it might increase whatever bad feeling already existed.

In an unreported case heard by the writer involving a union demand for the discharge of a foreman accused of using foul and obscene language in the presence of female employees, management did not argue arbitrability. It argued on the merits as to what disciplinary action, if any, should be taken against the offending foreman. By following such a policy management gained stature in the eyes of its employees. It is doubtful whether it lost face or showed weakness by not relying on a strong contractual position. The ultimate decision penalizing the foreman for his offensive acts by a four-week disciplinary layoff removed the pent-up resentment of employees in his department.

SUMMARY AND CONCLUSIONS

The scope of collective bargaining is expanding and will doubtless continue to do so. That is, the number of subjects bargained about will increase. The bulk of the change, however, will occur within the broad framework of "conventional" bargaining subjects, i.e., wages, rates of pay, hours of work, and other conditions of employment. There appears to be little evidence of union desire to share or take over basic managerial functions.

Practically speaking, it is difficult if not impossible to draw any permanent general lines separating exclusive management functions, joint functions, and exclusive union functions. Most union-management relationships today, however, appear to be fairly well-stabilized and to have a fundamental working understanding as to what is bargainable. A few relationships on the conflict fringe, principally in small businesses or newly organized firms, continue the battle of prerogatives with undiminished vigor. The larger and more sophisticated relationships have transferred the conflict to the contract administration phase or have resolved the problem in a mutually satisfactory manner.

Most management representatives appear to subscribe to the residualist theory of managerial authority in one form or another. In practice, however, many of these same representatives follow the trusteeship theory in regarding collective bargaining as a viable method of management. No general rules can be laid down for correct allocation of functions. The scope of collective bargaining should remain flexible, tailored to the particular needs and compulsions of the parties. What is suitable and satisfactory as a division of functions in one context may be completely unworkable in another.

The writer's built-in bias against the residualist view of managerial authority may be observed in the preceding pages. The trusteeship approach seems more conducive to constructive and positive joint relationships. The residualist theory is basically one of containment and is thus inevitably negative in its focus.

At the same time, some of the best union-management relationships from the standpoint of stability and intelligent contract administration have been those in which the management was prerogative-conscious in the residualist sense and where the union was content to work militantly within the framework of the residualist assumptions.

The prerogative controversy appears to be diminishing in intensity. This trend should continue, provided that unions do not shift their emphasis fundamentally in the direction of joint management of enterprise. The most enduringly fruitful approach to the problem is that which stresses a division between bargainable and nonbargainable items based on a rational allocation of functions rather than on legalistic reliance upon prerogatives. Such an approach recognizes that concepts of unlimited management or union sovereignty are barriers to constructive progress in union-management relationships.

SELECTED BIBLIOGRAPHY

Brown, Douglas V., "Management Rights and the Collective Agreement," *Industrial Relations Research Association First Annual Meeting Proceedings*. Champaign: IRRA, 1949, pp. 145-55.

Brown, Leo C., S. J., "The Shifting Distribution of the Rights to Manage," *Industrial Relations Research Association First Annual Meeting Proceedings*. Champaign: IRRA, 1949, pp. 132-44.

Chamberlain, Neil W., *The Union Challenge to Management Control*. New York: Harper & Brothers, 1948.

Coleman, John, "Research on Union Challenge and Management Response," *Proceedings of the Ninth Annual Meeting, Industrial Relations Research Association*. Madison: IRRA, 1957, pp. 306-17.

Conway, Jack, "Union Influence on Management Decisions—A Union Point of View," *Proceedings of the Seventh Annual Meeting, Industrial Relations Research Association*. Madison: IRRA, 1955, pp. 18-28.

Cook, A. Samuel, "The Right to Manage," *Labor Law Journal*. IX (March, 1958), 187-217.

Derber, Milton, W. Ellison Chalmers, and Ross Stagner, "Collective Bargaining and Management Functions: An Empirical Study," *Journal of Business*, XXXI (April, 1958), 107-20.

Lipstreau, Otis, "Management Rights: Conflict or Cooperation?" *Labor Law Journal*, VII (September, 1956), 558-63.

Morton, James F., "Limitations upon the Scope of Collective Bargaining," *Labor Law Journal*, VII (October, 1956), 603-606, 652-56.

Peterson, Florence, "Management Efficiency and Collective Bargaining," *Industrial and Labor Relations Review*. I (October, 1947), 29-49.

Petshek, Kirk R., "Scope and Extent of Collective Bargaining," *Proceedings of the Fifth Annual Meeting, Industrial Relations Research Association*. Madison: IRRA, 1953, pp. 220-31.

Ryder, M. S., "The Collective Bargaining Impact on Management Rights," *Michigan Business Review*, IX (November, 1957), 26-31.

Tripp, L. Reed, "The Union Role in Industry—Its Extent and Limits," in *Interpreting the Labor Movement*, Industrial Relations Research Association Publication No. 9. Champaign: IRRA, 1952, pp. 89-109.

Turnbull, John G., "The Small Business Enterprise and the Management Prerogative Issue," *Industrial and Labor Relations Review*, II (October, 1948), 33-49.

Twentieth Century Fund Labor Committee, *Partners in Production: A Basis for Labor-Management Understanding*. New York: Twentieth Century Fund, Inc., 1949.

9

Collective bargaining and industrial jurisprudence

Workers do not live by bread alone. There are many vital issues in collective bargaining that cannot be given a price tag. The most useful phrase yet developed to cover the principal nonincome issues in collective bargaining is "industrial jurisprudence."

As this term is defined by Sumner Slichter, it refers to the utilization of collective bargaining as a mechanism for introducing civil rights into industry—of requiring that management be conducted by rule rather than by arbitrary decision.[1]

The subject matter of industrial jurisprudence includes many problems of vital significance in contemporary collective bargaining: control of entrance to the trade, control of employers' hiring policies, control of layoffs, control of output and work assignments ("make-work" policies), adjustment to technological change, and methods of wage payment (as distinguished from the price of labor as such).

The specific policies of different unions on these matters vary greatly.

[1] Sumner H. Slichter, *Union Policies and Industrial Management* (Washington: The Brookings Institution, 1941), p. 1.

Some of the differences are explainable by differences in union leadership or by differences in the stage of union development. In the main, however, they are based on differences of conditions in particular industries.

In all cases the fundamental objective is to establish through collective bargaining a system of industrial rights and duties that will effectively implement the desire of the workers for protection against arbitrary and uncontrolled discretion of management.

The various specific rights and obligations of the union, the employer, and the worker are set forth in considerable detail in most modern collective agreements. The grievance and arbitration machinery of the contract provides the medium for enforcement of contractual rights in the event of a disagreement between the parties.

JOB SECURITY AND FAIR TREATMENT

The worker's interest in industrial jurisprudence may be summed up in two potent phrases: (1) job security; and (2) protection against arbitrary treatment. In the minds of many workers the greatest benefit they have derived from union membership has been the achievement of these dual objectives. In some instances the gains from collective bargaining in these areas are more important than advancement in money wage rates. The desire to achieve a system of industrial jurisprudence may explain the successful unionization of many benevolently paternalistic companies whose wages were higher than union scale, but who did not give their workers two important privileges: a say in setting basic working conditions; and a set of uniform rules arrived at by a process of joint decision-making rather than by unilateral whim.

In this chapter attention will be given primarily to such matters as management and union security; contract provisions relating to control of hiring, layoffs, recalls, and promotions; control of output and work assignments; working rules; work sharing and equal distribution of overtime; methods of wage payment; and, finally, administration of discipline. Collective bargaining practice in relation to fundamental technological change is treated in Chapter 13, and recent developments in negotiated employment and income security plans in Chapter 14.

MANAGEMENT SECURITY AND UNION SECURITY

The phrase "industrial jurisprudence" is normally associated with protection of job rights of individual workers. It is important to note, however, that a very important aspect of industrial jurisprudence through collective bargaining relates to the use of the contract for formalizing the rights and responsibilities of the company and the union as institutional entities. What the contract has to say about these matters has a direct bearing on those sections of the agreement outlining the rights and responsibilities of the individual worker.

Under the broad heading of management security the most controversial issue relates to the contractual statement regarding the rights of management with respect to the conduct of the enterprise and the direction of the working force. As noted in Chapter 8, the great majority of employers today prefer to spell out those areas of exclusive managerial authority in a so-called management rights clause. Whether or not such a clause is included in the contract itself, most employers are careful in negotiations to avoid contract commitments on any matter that involves giving up or sharing any function that they regard as rationally allocable to management.

Related to the management rights phase of management security are the clauses in contemporary contracts concerning mutuality of purpose and union responsibility. Many management representatives (and union leaders too) take mutuality of purpose clauses seriously and regard them as more than just glittering generalizations for public relations value. A clause such as the one quoted below from a current agreement expresses the joint interest of the parties in maintaining a sound productive enterprise. It may have considerable educational value for line supervision and rank-and-file employees if properly stressed in training programs.[2]

ARTICLE I—INTENT AND PURPOSE

Section 1. It is the intent and purpose of the parties that this Agreement shall serve to establish and promote better understanding, harmony and cooperation between the Union, the Company and its employees; to improve and stabilize employment and the efficiency of production; to eliminate the causes of friction and misunderstanding; to provide an orderly collective bargaining procedure for the prompt and fair disposition of complaints and grievances that may arise; and to set forth the Agreement between the Company and the Union covering rates of pay, wages, hours of employment and other conditions of employment.

Section 2. Proper acceptance and understanding of the respective rights, responsibilities and functions of both the Company and the Union are essential considerations if sound and stable relations are to be developed between the parties. The Management fully accepts the process of collective bargaining and unionism as an institution and it believes a sound, responsible and

[2] This is taken from the 1957-1959 contract between The Coleman Company, Inc., of Wichita, Kansas and Local No. 570, UAW. It is identical with the same article in the 1955-1957 contract except that each of the three sections in the article carry headings in bold face type to emphasize further the intent and purpose of the article. Section 1 is headed "To Promote Better Understanding and Cooperation." Section 2 is headed "To Develop Sound and Stable Relations." Section 3 is headed "To Advance Best Interests of Company, Employees and Union." The reader will note that this is the same contract from which the extensive management rights clause was quoted in Chapter 8, *supra.*

democratic union to be an asset to the Company, all of its employees and the community. Likewise, the Union accepts the proposition of private ownership and the operation of industry for fair and reasonable profit and further recognizes that the economic welfare of its members, along with other segments of the Company is dependent upon the successful, efficient operation and management of the business.

Section 3. It is the mutual desire of both the Company and the Union that at all times their respective representatives, at all levels, seek to develop and maintain a spirit of good faith and friendly cooperative relations which will serve to advance the best interests of the Company, all of its employees, and the Union as the designated collective bargaining agency.

Contracts today frequently contain what is generally referred to as a union responsibility clause that further enhances management's security in the relationship. Such a union responsibility clause is the opposite number of the familiar management pledge not to discriminate against or coerce employees in any way. The Taft-Hartley Act's encouragement of civil damage suits for breach of contract, coupled with the Act's strict concept of agency, has made many unions somewhat chary about negotiating union responsibility clauses. However, most union negotiators will go along with including a clause expressing their condemnation of wildcats, slowdowns, and other forms of unauthorized resort to economic pressure, provided that the contract protects the international union and the local union as institutional entities from suits in such cases. Where such protection is forthcoming, the union in question will usually agree to take positive action to end the unauthorized strike or slowdown and will support company discipline of the offending individuals.

In addition to such specific contractual recognition of the need for management security as may be contained in management rights and union responsibility clauses, most employers are careful to protect the integrity of various managerial functions in substantive contract language dealing with employee rights under the contract. For example, the contract may contain substantial limitations on managerial discretion on such matters as discipline, layoffs, and promotions. An alert management, however, will always protect and safeguard its right of administrative initiative in all such cases and will not be lured into accepting clauses requiring union consent before action can be taken. Since the various approaches to safeguarding managerial functions have been treated in Chapter 8, we will say no more on the subject of management security here.

UNION SECURITY CLAUSES AND CONTRACT ADMINISTRATION

Unions as well as employers are interested in obtaining contract language that will protect and safeguard their positions as institutional entities. A primary objective of most unions is to secure a closed shop or union shop arrangement that will solidify the union's position in the particular enterprise. The union security issue has been treated extensively in Chapter 3. Brief attention is given here to the arguments for and against union security clauses from the standpoint of employer-union relations in day-to-day contract administration, a phase of the topic not treated in Chapter 3.

One of the most respected of union security defenders is Sumner H. Slichter, who argues that an assured status for the union in the shop is an essential prerequisite of successful union-employer relations. Granting the necessity for the union to serve the employee's keen interest in job security, the union must necessarily seek to control either the hiring or the layoff end of the employment process. If the union cannot assure its status in the shop by requiring membership in the union as a condition of employment, it must seek through contract to restrict management discretion at every point where union members may be discriminated against in favor of nonmembers. Conversely, in closed shop situations, contracts will rarely restrict the employer's discretion on discipline or layoff.

It also may be argued that contract administration is smoother where the union's status in the shop is secure. In such cases the union leadership no longer has to press any and all grievances, regardless of their merit, for fear of alienating some sectional support. The leadership is free to do a responsible job of contract administration by distinguishing at an early stage between meritorious and groundless grievances. Where the union's status is not secure, management will frequently find the union challenging every disciplinary action. If the union is secure, it can join with management in enforcing reasonable standards of discipline.

On the other side, strong arguments have been advanced to refute the proposition that union security will lead to better contract administration. Perhaps the most frequently heard argument is that with union membership guaranteed, the leadership will become smug and sluggish about the job of contract administration to the consequent neglect of the employees. Another argument is that union security provides no guarantee of mature and responsible union leadership. On the contrary, it is suggested that the employer is likely to have less freedom of action and less cooperation from the union in cases where union status is assured. Opponents of union security arrangements frequently cite lack of initiative and responsibility on the part of union leaders as a likely result of an assured position.

In evaluating these competing arguments, the objective scholar must conclude that the answer depends on the particular relationship. The writer can think of several situations in which a union shop or closed shop arrangement has brought stable contract administration. On the other hand, the acquisition of union security in some situations has contributed to a deterioration in union responsibility for effective and equitable contract administration. In short, as is true with most man-made institutional arrangements, the success or failure of the device depends on the parties involved. To reiterate what was stated in Chapter 3, it should be discretionary with employers and unions as to whether they include union security arrangements in their contract. The cold, statistical evidence is that the great majority of employers and unions have negotiated some form of union security clause.[3] The closed shop continues to be the common form in the building and construction field, according to Haber and Levinson,[4] notwithstanding the Taft-Hartley Act. The union shop is now standard in mining and much of manufacturing.

Craft unions rely essentially on the closed shop and their inherent economic strength to maintain union institutional security. Industrial unions frequently seek additional security for the union as such by insisting that the contract guarantee super-seniority or top seniority for local union officers and shop stewards. In an industry where layoffs are frequent the seniority perquisites of local union officialdom are a real attraction. They also contribute to continuity and stability in the union's contract administration team from one election to the next. Such minor matters as the furnishing of bulletin boards in the plants for union use and the privilege of plant visitation by international union representatives also add to the institutional security of the union. Union recognition clauses and provisions dealing with grievance adjustment on company time also come in this category.

In summary, both the company and the union at various places in the collective labor agreement seek to define and protect their respective status as institutional entities. An appraisal of most contracts will reveal that each party usually has been careful to define its own rights and to protect itself further by defining carefully the responsibilities of the other party under the contract. In other words, the individual worker is not the sole beneficiary of the system of industrial jurisprudence. As with individual worker complaints, the management and the union also resort to the grievance and arbitration machinery of the contract to safeguard their own rights and to enforce responsibility from the other party.

[3] The last comprehensive survey to come to the writer's attention was a BLS study covering 1,716 major agreements and 7.4 million workers. In this extensive sampling, 79 per cent provided for some form of union security (8 per cent for closed shop, 57 per cent for union shop, and 14 per cent for maintenance of membership). See "Union-Security Provisions in Agreements, 1954," *Monthly Labor Review*, LXXVII (June, 1955), 649-58. A conservative estimate of the prevalence of union security clauses today would be four out of five contracts.

[4] See William Haber and Harold M. Levinson, *Labor Relations and Productivity in the Building Trades* (Ann Arbor: Bureau of Industrial Relations, University of Michigan), 1956, p. 71 *et seq.*

CONTROL OF JOB OPPORTUNITIES THROUGH COLLECTIVE BARGAINING

Thirty years ago, in his pioneering theory of the labor movement,[5] Selig Perlman stressed the job-consciousness of American unions. In Perlman's view union policy was dictated by an underlying assumption of job scarcity and a desire to conserve limited job opportunities for the membership. Perlman was writing at a time when craft unionism was the dominant form, but his thesis of the primacy of job control in union thinking retains its essential validity today, even though industrial unionism has proved itself a viable and durable structural form. The evidence conclusively indicates that industrial unions in their own way are just as job-conscious as craft unions ever were. Any union interested in conservation of job opportunities must generally make a choice, as has been pointed out, between controlling one end of the employment process or the other. It is ordinarily neither necessary nor feasible to attempt to condition or limit the employer's discretion at both ends.

CONTROL OF HIRING

The craft union approach to control of hiring is well-known. The union makes every effort to secure closed shop arrangements with all employers in a particular labor market area and to induce employers to hire through the union. In many relationships employers are thoroughly satisfied with this arrangement of using the union as their employment agency. The *quid pro quo* for hiring through the union is the employer's relatively complete freedom to reject workers referred by the union or, alternatively, to dismiss unsatisfactory workers without challenge by the union. If a particular craft union is successful in controlling the supply of labor in its labor market area, it is in a position to conserve and allocate existing job opportunities much as it sees fit. One aspect of the craft union's devotion to the closed shop is the motive of job control. The other equally important aspect is the ability to raise the price of that labor by restricting the supply. The closed shop-closed union problem has been dealt with in Chapter 3.

The majority of industrial unions make no direct effort to control the employer's hiring policies. Conspicuous exceptions to this general policy are the hiring halls of maritime workers and longshoremen.[6]

The employer's freedom to hire is usually left unrestricted because the union has no practical way of controlling the supply of labor when the

[5] Selig Perlman, *A Theory of the Labor Movement,* (1928). (reprinted New York: Augustus Kelley, 1949).

[6] For a fascinating empirical account of the old "shape-up" method and the hiring hall in New York and Seattle respectively, see Charles P. Larrowe, *Shape-up and Hiring Hall* (Berkeley and Los Angeles: University of California Press, 1955).

vast majority of workers are unskilled and semiskilled. In such situations the union will endeavor to negotiate a union shop clause requiring that the new employee join the union at the end of his probationary or trial period. In other situations the union may have to settle for maintenance-of-membership, under which no employee is compelled to join but those who do join must maintain their membership in good standing.

Most contracts in manufacturing and other industries in which industrial unions dominate collective bargaining specify a trial or probationary period, usually from thirty days in some to ninety days in others. Perhaps the most common trial period is thirty days, the minimum specified under Taft-Hartley.

During a probationary period, a new employee usually has no seniority or other rights, except that he may not be discharged for union activity. He may be discharged by the employer at any time for any reason or for no reason, so long as it is not a discriminatory discharge within the meaning of the contract or the Taft-Hartley Act. At the end of the probationary period the employee becomes a full industrial citizen; his seniority is usually dated back to the day of his hiring.

CONTROL OF LAYOFFS THROUGH SENIORITY CLAUSES

Seniority is normally not an issue in bargaining relationships where the union has a measure of control over the supply of labor and the employer's hiring policies. Almost all industrial unions, however, continue to place a heavy emphasis on seniority restrictions on the employer's freedom to lay off, transfer, promote, and recall workers from layoff. Such contractual restrictions relating to length of service are the industrial union's most effective answer to the worker's desire for a maximum of job security. The great majority of an industrial union's constituents have no individual economic power by virtue of possessing a special skill. They are easily trained and easily replaced in a loose labor market. In many cases they work at jobs where the organization of production operations or the pace of the machines determines the limits of performance rather than differences in individual effort. Thus, length of service as a means of retaining employment or securing occupational advancement has a strong appeal to the individual worker.

Seniority (length of service) in principle is a clear-cut, impersonally objective method of determining which employees shall be laid off and in what order when employment opportunities decline. As such, it has value as a yardstick for decision-making to both employers and unions in large bargaining units. It satisfies the basic requirement of effective industrial jurisprudence—substitution of a uniform policy for arbitrary discretion.

This is not to say that there is not a great deal of controversy within industry as to the merits of length of service as the primary, if not sole, criterion for layoffs and recalls. Many employers still resent such contractual limitations on their discretion. When the union seeks to extend the principle to promotions, employer resistance frequently stiffens considerably.

THE CASE FOR AND AGAINST SENIORITY

The principal arguments raised against seniority (length of service) as a basis for layoffs and recalls are that it places a premium on mediocrity; that it discourages individual initiative by ignoring differences in ability and zeal; and, finally, that it impairs management's ability to discipline and reward in terms of performance. In terms of these arguments it is held that seniority as a criterion contributes to lower employee productivity and consequent higher labor costs.

On the other hand, it is argued in behalf of seniority that it may increase managerial efficiency by compelling employers to be more selective in hiring and more thorough in training; that it reduces costs by reducing labor turnover; and that employee morale (and thus productivity) is raised by enhanced job security. An additional consideration favoring seniority is that where it is not observed, grievances and resentment are likely to develop in proportions that will more than offset any alleged gains the employer may feel he is achieving in recognition of superior abilities. When it is recalled that differences in individual abilities are not of paramount significance on most semiskilled and unskilled operations in basic manufacturing, the strength of this latter argument may be persuasive.

Notwithstanding continued employer resistance in some cases, seniority has come to be the principal contractual determinant governing layoffs and recalls in the great majority of unionized establishments. Assuming that the basic principle of seniority is accepted, a number of vitally important practical problems have to be resolved in developing a satisfactory contract policy. Chief among these are deciding upon the seniority units within which layoffs and recalls take place and deciding whether straight or qualified seniority will prevail. Another important problem area is determining what, if any, exceptions to the seniority principle will be made.

TYPES OF SENIORITY UNITS

In most manufacturing plants the common form of seniority arrangement involves a combination of plant-wide seniority with a narrower base of either departmental or occupational seniority. Seniority arrangements must necessarily be tailored to the needs of the particular enterprise. The nature of the company's organization and the types of jobs involved will frequently be decisive. In some cases seniority follows departmental lines. In others the basic seniority will be occupational, or related departments or occupations may be grouped into specially constructed "seniority units." Whatever the arrangement, the employee first exercises his seniority within the narrower grouping, and those faced with layoff from the departmental or occupational seniority unit frequently have the option of "going plant-wide"—using their plant seniority to displace an employee junior to them on a plant-wide basis.

As a general proposition management appears to favor narrow seniority units and a policy that will involve as little bumping as possible in any layoff. Unions generally prefer broadly based seniority units. In some cases, however, the union will join management in a preference for narrow seniority districts to minimize internal union political pressures.

COMPANY-WIDE SENIORITY

One of the most controversial seniority developments in recent years has been the effort on the part of some industrial unions, notably the UAW, to extend seniority beyond the boundaries of individual plants. This drive for company-wide seniority in multi-plant companies has generally produced vigorous employer opposition and mixed reactions from the rank-and-file. The basic idea is to permit workers in one plant to bump those in another plant who have less seniority on a company-wide basis. The proposal is related to the impact of automation, the negotiation of supplemental unemployment benefit plans, and the joint interest of the employer and the union in minimizing the incidence of unemployment in a multi-plant company. It is argued that company-wide seniority might facilitate employment stabilization in the chain as a whole even though the company in question is unable to regularize the operations of each individual plant.

For example, John Deere operates eight farm equipment manufacturing plants in the Iowa-Illinois area in which the UAW is the principal or sole bargaining agent. An SUB plan was negotiated in 1955 for all eight plants. Would it be feasible to stabilize employment on a company-wide basis in this situation? The management answer probably would be resoundingly negative, even though there are many job operations common to the various plants and the most widely separated of the eight plants are less than 200 miles apart. For one thing, even though the eight contracts closely approached a master agreement on many major issues such as wage policy, there were significant differences in local plant seniority arrangements and groupings. These would have to be drastically revised to accommodate a company-wide seniority system. Furthermore, the actual interchange of workers from one plant to another would be costly and disruptive of family relationships. The average worker might not be enthusiastic about moving from one town to another and back again to maintain full wages, when he could draw approximately two-thirds of his normal wages from a combination of SUB fund payments and state unemployment insurance.

The foregoing considerations apply to what might be termed short-run employment stabilization operations in a multi-plant company with several plants in the same geographical area.

A somewhat more plausible argument can be made for company-wide employment rights for workers displaced in one plant as a consequence of the permanent discontinuance of certain operations. In such situations a stronger case can be made for giving employees permanently displaced in one plant an opportunity to bump workers junior to them in other plants of the same company.

STRAIGHT SENIORITY, OR LENGTH OF SERVICE QUALIFIED BY ABILITY?

Perhaps the thorniest issue on the role of seniority in layoffs and recalls is the degree to which worker merit and ability should be considered. The typical management position has been that length of service should govern only where merit and ability are equal. The typical union position has been that straight length of service should be the sole criterion, subject perhaps to the bare qualification that the remaining workers must be able to perform the work in question. Every seniority clause reflects how the parties have decided this vital question.

The most effective clauses in practice are those that articulate a workable compromise between the union's interest in straight seniority and the employer's interest in maintaining an efficient, capable work force. Straight seniority clauses seem to be more prevalent in industry generally, gradually replacing the management-preferred principle that length of service will govern only where merit and ability to perform the work are relatively equal. However, few industrial contracts go to the extreme of undiluted straight seniority. Although length of service is the yardstick for determining who shall be laid off, there is normally a requirement that the worker remaining must be able to perform the job he is assigned. Similarly, on recalls to employment the employee must be able to do the work to which he is recalled.

Furthermore, many contracts today are designed to avoid the chain bumping which might otherwise accompany a straight seniority method of layoff. Limited bumping is insured by a contract provision stating that a senior worker whose work has run out during a reduction in force bumps the youngest man in his seniority grouping or unit whose work he is qualified to perform, rather than the man immediately junior to him. Such a provision avoids the chain reaction and multiple displacements that might otherwise occur.

Perhaps in no other phase of industrial relations is there a greater potential for constructive cooperation or destructive friction and antagonism than in administration of contractual seniority provisions. When the relationship between management and union is on a positive, mature basis, it is unlikely that the union will be militantly insistent on an undiluted straight seniority rule. On the other hand, if the union is institutionally insecure, or if it questions the fairness of management, it will push hard for straight seniority.

EXCEPTIONS TO SENIORITY ON LAYOFFS AND RECALLS

The two most frequent specific exceptions to seniority as a basis for layoffs are: (1) super-seniority or top seniority for local union officers and stewards; and (2) establishment of a list of special employees (usually highly skilled workers) who by agreement may be exempted from the contract's layoff provisions.

Clauses illustrating each type of exemption may be of interest.

The union's interest in super-seniority for local union officials and stewards has been noted earlier in this chapter. The following section quoted from the 1955-1958 contract between the John Deere Waterloo Tractor Works and Local No. 838 of the UAW is representative of such clauses in manufacturing generally:

Section 16

A. Officers of the local Union (not to exceed 9), all members of the Shop Committee, and Union Time Study Representatives during their term of office shall, in connection with layoff from and recall to employment, head the seniority list in which they are employed in the order set out above, provided that they have a minimum of three (3) months' employment with the Company. At the termination of their services as Officers of the local Union (not to exceed 9), all members of the Shop Committee, and Union Time Study Representatives, they shall be returned to the proper place on the seniority list of their unit.

B. All Divisional Stewards during their term of office shall, in connection with layoff from and recall to employment, head the seniority list, except for Shop Committee Members, Union Time Study Representatives, and Officers of the local Union (not to exceed 9), of the unit in which they are employed to the extent which that unit is contained in the geographical portion of the plant which they serve as Divisional Steward, provided, however, that all such Divisional Stewards shall have a minimum of three (3) months' employment with the Company. Upon termination of their duties as stewards, they shall be returned to their proper seniority standing.

C. All Departmental Stewards, during their term of office shall, in connection with layoff from and recall to employment, head the seniority list, except for Shop Committeemen, Union Time Board Members (not to exceed 9), of the local Union, and Divisional Stewards, of that group of employees in which they are employed and serve as steward to the extent which that unit is contained in the geographical portion of the plant which they serve as Departmental Steward, provided, however, that all such Departmental Stewards shall have a minimum of three (3) months' employment with the Company. Upon termination of their duties as Departmental Stewards, they shall be returned to their proper seniority standing.

D. In connection with all the foregoing paragraphs of this Section, it is understood and agreed that no member of the Shop Committee, Union Time Study Representatives, Executive Board of the local Union (not to exceed 9), or any steward shall exercise this special seniority status unless he is qualified to perform the work of the employee he replaces.

It will be noted that the employer's interest is protected under the foregoing provision by the requirement that qualification to perform the work is a prerequisite to use of this special seniority status.

The same contract contains a clause that safeguards the employer's right to retain the services of designated employees without regard to their natural seniority:

B. At each layoff or recall following layoff, the Company may designate certain individual employees whose services are required under the special circumstances then existing. Such employees may be retained or recalled to service regardless of their seniority. The fact that an employee has been so designated shall not affect his regular seniority standing and he shall resume the same as soon as the special reasons in his case cease to exist. It is agreed that at no time will the total number of employees designated under this section exceed five (5) per cent of the total plant-wide list.

SENIORITY POLICY AND PROCEDURE PROBLEMS BRIEFLY NOTED

Seniority provisions in most modern collective agreements tend to be lengthy and exceptionally detailed. The governing principle may be clearly stated in a paragraph or so, but the procedure for its application may necessitate several pages of fine print.

Among the many problems that must be anticipated in writing a complete seniority clause, only a few can be noted here. For the sake of brevity, they have been phrased in question-and-answer form.

1. What is the usual status of probationary or part-time employees when layoffs are necessary? (In most cases the contract calls for such employees to be laid off before any other layoffs are made.)

2. Should the employer be required to prepare seniority lists at regular intervals and to post such lists? (Provisions to this effect are common in contracts today.)

3. How shall seniority be figured when employees are transferred? If an employee transfers from one seniority unit to another, does he carry his seniority with him, or does he retain it in the old unit and start building new seniority in the new unit? (The answer here often depends on whether the transfer is required by the company or requested by the employee. Industrial practice varies markedly. A generally equitable solution would appear to be one that requires the employee's seniority in the new unit to begin as of the date of his transfer, but which permits him to retain plant seniority as a protection against layoffs in the new unit. In the event of a layoff in the new seniority unit he might still have enough seniority on a plant basis to return to his former unit.)

4. Do laid-off employees accumulate seniority? (Most contracts provide that laid-off employees continue to accumulate seniority, except in the case of protracted layoffs of twelve to eighteen months, or more.)

5. Under what circumstances do employees lose their seniority rights? (Most contracts are specific about the factors causing loss of seniority. The more common bases are: (a) discharge; (b) voluntary quit; (c) layoffs exceeding a specified period of time, usually one to two years; (d) failure to report for work after proper notice.)

6. What seniority, if any, shall be given to rehired employees who have lost their seniority? (They usually have to start again from scratch.)

7. What groups of employees, if any, shall be given special seniority rights over all other employees? (As noted previously, in some contracts super-seniority is provided for local union officers and stewards, or for exceptionally qualified skilled personnel.)

8. Shall the company have the right to disregard seniority during emergency or temporary periods? (Practice varies here. Some contracts attempt to distinguish between clearly temporary layoffs and permanent or indefinite layoffs, giving the company the option of ignoring seniority in the case of temporary layoffs.)

9. Shall the grievance and arbitration machinery of the contract apply to disputes under the seniority provisions? (Almost all contracts so provide.)

WORK-SHARING

Conflicts within the union's membership frequently create serious problems in the application of seniority clauses. The basic clash is between older and younger members of the union. Understandably, the former are interested in absolute seniority whereas the latter are reluctant to bear the full weight of necessary layoffs. Some compromise between these conflicting interests is often necessary. This usually takes the form of a combination of work-sharing and seniority when reduction of forces is required.

The principal objection to work-sharing is that it may evolve into a sharing of the misery. To avoid this, most combination agreements in industry call for a sharing of work within departments of a plant to the point at which the employees are down to an average of, say, thirty-two hours per week. If it becomes necessary to curtail production still further, then layoffs are begun on the basis of seniority.

A few unions, notably those in the garment industry, have utilized work-sharing almost exclusively when business is slack. The needle trades are highly seasonal, and the workers frequently are employed by several companies during the year. Seniority as a basis for layoffs would operate inequitably in such a situation. Many capable workers with long experience in the industry might be the first to be laid off if they happened to be hired last by a firm whose business declined thereafter.

As a general rule today, union leadership prefers layoffs to work-sharing, and so do most workers. Wherever supplemental unemployment benefit plans and other approaches to employment or income stabilization have begun to safeguard the job security claims of the great majority of workers with sufficient effectiveness, senior employees are disinclined to share the burden of a layoff with juniors.

SENIORITY AS A FACTOR IN PROMOTIONS

Many employers now accept the principle that length of service, even undiluted, should govern layoffs and rehiring. At the same time, they will vigorously resist any effort to introduce length of service as a governing factor in promotions. Here, they insist, ability should be the determinative factor. Only when ability is equal should length of service govern. Some employers resist efforts to include any type of clause dealing with promotions in a collective agreement on the ground that the right to promote should be an exclusive, unchallengeable management prerogative.

Unions place first emphasis on the control of layoffs and rehiring. Many are willing to leave promotion policy entirely in management's hands, though stressing the right to challenge through the grievance machinery when evidence of alleged discrimination exists. Other unions have successfully negotiated clauses requiring that promotions, as well as layoffs and rehiring, be based on length of service. The railroads are, of course, the best-known industry in which promotion is conditional entirely on length of service, subject to ability to perform the better job.

It is difficult to quarrel with management's judgment that ability should be the prime criterion governing promotions and that management should be the deciding agent on ability. At the same time, promotional opportunities are of vital concern to employees. Precautions should be taken to insure against arbitrary or discriminatory action on the part of management.

The right to promote may be taken as illustrative of a managerial function or prerogative of the limited type. That is, management should have the right of administrative initiative, subject to check through the grievance procedure. Many contracts so provide. The practice of posting notice of vacancies and encouraging employees' applications appears to be increasing. Many companies consult local union officials before making promotions even when the contract does not so require. This use of the consultative technique undoubtedly prevents many grievances.

On promotions, an effective compromise between management's interest in ability and the union's interest in seniority can be worked out in a number of different ways. One workable approach is to provide for posting of vacancies with the vacancy going to the *senior qualified applicant.* Under such an arrangement management determines the qualifications for the vacancy and appraises the applicants for the vacancy to determine which of them are qualified. However, management has no discretion to choose the more qualified or most qualified if there are several qualified applicants. In such cases the vacancy must go to the senior qualified applicant. Another arrangement now widely used is to give the senior applicant for any vacancy a brief trial on the higher-rated job. If he proves to be qualified, he is assigned the vacancy. If not, he returns to his former position with no loss of status.

Certainly, promotion from within is universally regarded as a sound principle of personnel administration. In industry generally, when one considers that the overwhelming number of jobs are semiskilled, involving only slight differences in skill and responsibility and usually involving a clear line of progression, objections to promotions by length of service lose much of their force, particularly if the contract safeguards management's right to make sure that the employee promoted will be qualified and able to handle the duties of the vacant position. Management, however, must retain administrative discretion to determine which applicants are qualified. If, in a particular case, management determines that a senior worker is not qualified, such a discretionary determination should not be liable to successful challenge through the grievance procedure unless it can be shown that the determination in question was arbitrary, capricious, or discriminatory.

CONTROL OF OUTPUT AND WORK ASSIGNMENTS

Another union approach to controlling job opportunities and insuring uniform standards lies in the direction of contract rule-making on the setting of production standards, changes in job content and job duties, working rules, preventing foremen from doing production work, and so on. The variety of contract practices in this area is virtually endless. The specific policies in force in any one situation will depend on the nature of the work in question and the economic position and power of the union. A few basic illustrations here will suffice.

In manufacturing, union opposition to technological change is comparatively rare, although most industrial unions maintain an alert watch against what they regard as unwarranted extension of the worker's daily task by management. Unions take a keen interest in the question of what constitutes a "fair day's work," and will normally resist management efforts to enlarge the concept of normal task beyond what the union regards as "fair." In plants where the method of payment is hourly the scope of the worker's responsibility will be roughly defined by job description and sometimes by standards of performance in terms of "measured day work." In most cases management retains administrative initiative subject to challenge through the grievance procedure. In others joint job evaluation is used. Where operations are paid for on some type of incentive method, management will normally set the production standards on various operations, subject to union challenge through the grievance machinery. Elsewhere, production standards may be arrived at by joint union-management committees.

Whatever the organization or set-up, a perennial source of conflict between union and management arises from differing views as to what should properly constitute the average normal worker's daily task. In short, work speeds and work assignments are essentially subjective questions productive of controversy and constantly requiring change and revision as job content and work organization change under a dynamic technology.

Cases of direct limitation of output, requiring the employment of clearly unnecessary men, and similar "make work" restrictions are comparatively rare in manufacturing, although still found occasionally in the construction trades. The average worker has a fairly good intuitive idea of what constitutes a normal day's work. He is likely to resist directly or indirectly any effort by management to increase or stretch his task.

Industrial workers also appear to be developing a parochial and possessive attitude toward particular tasks and particular machines, resisting managerial efforts at job interchangeability. The craft worker's idea of property rights in his job has its counterpart in the industrial worker's attachment to a particular machine or particular work location. In some plants, for example, vacancies are posted and bid in terms of individual machines and work locations, rather than in terms of occupational classifications.

The industrial unionist has taken another leaf from the craft unionist's book in providing contractual restrictions against supervisory employees doing production work except under emergency conditions. Such limitations are fairly common in industrial union contracts today.

EQUITABLE DISTRIBUTION OF OVERTIME

An excellent illustration of the basic function of a system of industrial jurisprudence in developing a uniform policy or principle as a substitute for discretion is found in contract regulations governing the distribution of overtime. When overtime is found to be necessary in a particular department, what policy shall be used to decide which employees will have the opportunity to earn the premium pay? The most common answer is to provide for a sharing of overtime opportunities on a round-robin basis among employees in the classification that normally or customarily does the work on which overtime is needed. In the absence of a general policy the opportunities for favoritism and discrimination are obvious. To insure against arbitrary allocation many contracts contain a clause similar to the following from a 1955-58 John Deere-UAW contract:

> F. When overtime work is required in a department and is assigned to a particular classification of labor, or a group, then the overtime work shall be divided on a round robin basis between all employees in the classification or group or department provided the employees are qualified and customarily do the work required, subject to any local agreements on groups or classifications.

Grievances not infrequently arise concerning the proper interpretation and application of a clause such as the one quoted. The most common dispute arises from a difference of opinion as to whether the employees to whom management gave the overtime opportunity were the ones who customarily did the work required.

METHODS OF WAGE PAYMENT

Most contemporary contracts are specific and detailed in their statements of policy and procedure on how jobs are to be paid and when rates on existing jobs may be changed during the life of the contract. A related question of great importance is the policy and procedure for setting rates on new jobs that may be introduced during the life of the contract. In all such cases the principal objective is to formulate and enforce uniform policies and procedures as a substitute for unilateral discretion. Although these matters are an important aspect of industrial jurisprudence, they are better discussed in Chapter 11.

THE DISCIPLINE FUNCTION AND INDUSTRIAL JURISPRUDENCE

The classic illustration of industrial jurisprudence in action concerns the exercise of the managerial right to discipline employees in accordance with principles and procedures spelled out in the contract. Guarantees of fair treatment by supervision and protection against arbitrary managerial action are basic to the concept of democratized industrial relations. The right to fire (or to administer lesser penalties in the form of a disciplinary layoff or written warning) is traditionally a management prerogative and should remain so. Most collective agreements recognize this, although there are some that require union consent to disciplinary action. Yet the exercise of the disciplinary prerogative is manifestly one that should be subject to check and challenge if the concept of worker citizenship in industry is to have any real meaning. Prior to unionization, discharged workers had no effective recourse from the arbitrary action of foremen or top supervision. The desire to insure against such arbitrary or discriminatory exercise of the discipline function has been in many instances a more compelling motive for unionization than purely economic factors.

Most collective agreements contain some limitation on management's right to discipline. A common requirement is that the discipline must be only for "cause" or for "good and just cause." In some cases an effort is made to spell out the various offenses calling for discipline and to distinguish between the more serious offenses calling for discharge and the lesser offenses calling for disciplinary layoff or warning. The great majority of contracts, however, contain a clear general statement of principle governing all discipline matters and leave the application to cases as they arise.

This latter approach is preferable because it recognizes the fact that no two disciplinary cases are alike. No two sets of facts are likely to be precisely identical any more than any two individuals are likely to be identical or to behave in identical fashion. Furthermore, the severity of a particular offense will vary depending on the circumstances.

For example, smoking on the job might properly be grounds for immediate discharge in a chemical plant or an oil refinery and only a minor offense in a plant where there is no appreciable danger from fire or explosion. Certain offenses, when proved, are regarded as proper grounds for discharge in almost all situations. These include such breaches of conduct as fighting on the job, reporting drunk on the job, stealing company property, malicious destruction of company property, direct insubordination to supervision, instigating a wildcat strike, and so on. On the other hand, discharge for such offenses as chronic absenteeism, unsatisfactory work performance, or persistent inability to meet accepted production norms should be preceded by adequate notice that discharge will be the consequence of failure to improve performance.

Fair treatment by supervision is one factor that shows up high on any worker's listing of the requisites of a "good job." Since it seems to be an integral element of human nature to blame others for one's own shortcomings, a great percentage of management disciplinary actions are likely to be challenged by workers who feel that they are "not guilty" of the offense with which they are charged or who feel the penalty imposed to be excessively harsh. Furthermore, no worker likes to have a disciplinary penalty on his record. It will jeopardize his chances for advancement and, if he is discharged, may make it extremely difficult for him to find other employment even in a fairly tight labor market. Thus, in a typical enterprise, discipline grievances are likely to form a substantial part of the case load.

Although discipline grievances are inherently troublesome and in some cases explosive, there is no valid reason why a company and a union cannot work out a satisfactory relationship that will safeguard management's essential interest in maintaining an efficient and orderly establishment and the union's interest in insuring that no worker is disciplined arbitrarily or without cause.

Some employers complain that union restrictions have shorn them of their power to discipline workers. Some even state that they are afraid to fire a man because of union reprisals. Where such conditions exist, the fault probably lies with management. No company operating in good faith needs to surrender its right to discipline employees fairly and in a nondiscriminatory manner. Most union leaders are not willing to defend an employee on a disciplinary matter if they know the employee has committed the offense for which he has been disciplined. They will be properly insistent, however, that the burden of proving good and just cause for the discipline rests upon management in every case.

The most difficult discharge cases are usually those in which management feels the employee's performance on the job to be so unsatisfactory as to warrant firing. This type of discharge is resisted strenuously by many unions, particularly if alternative employment opportunities are not plentiful. The union often argues that management had an opportunity to gauge the worker during his trial or probationary period. Once past this trial period, according to this viewpoint, the worker has developed an equity in his job of which he should not be deprived except under extreme circumstances after failure to heed repeated warnings.

Since discharge is the ultimate disciplinary sanction, it should be resorted to only when no alternative remedy seems capable of producing the desired results. If management is to maintain discipline and insure efficient operation, however, its right of administrative initiative in matters of discipline and discharge must be clearly established.

Subject to reasonable standards sufficient to protect workers who are doing a conscientious but uninspired job, management should have the right to discharge chronically inefficient, lazy, or indifferent employees. When the reason for unsatisfactory performance is the difficulty of the job for the employee's abilities, he should be transferred to a less taxing assignment. Such an alternative is vastly preferable to discharge. Discharge is always an admission of failure. The remedy is to seek whenever possible the causes of the situation leading to the necessity for discharge.

If the unsatisfactory performance of the employee is based on poor mental attitude, personal troubles outside the shop, or physical or mental deficiencies, an effort should be made through counseling to correct the condition before applying the discharge sanction. To discharge a man under such circumstances merely passes the burden on to some other employer or to the community.

In any contested discipline case two fundamental issues usually arise. First, did the company prove cause for the discipline? Second, did the punishment imposed fit the crime? A union will invariably challenge management discipline if it feels that the answer to either of these questions is negative.

The problem of burden of proof is well-illustrated by the two discipline arbitration cases summarized below for the reader's consideration. For the answers of the arbitrator in these cases, see the Appendix.

Case 1 SLEEPING ON THE JOB

Preliminary Recital:

Employee *A* protests a disciplinary suspension for "sleeping on the job." The Union and Employee *A* deny that he was sleeping on the job and contend that the discipline was not for good and just cause. The Company maintains that Employee *A* was sleeping on the job on the day in question, as proved by the testimony of four eye witnesses, and therefore maintains that his suspension was for good and just cause.

The matter was heard by the undersigned at the offices of the Company on October 9, 19—.

Issue and Contract Clause Involved:

The issue for determination is whether the disciplinary suspension of Employee *A* from June 29, 19—, to July 12, 19— was for good and just cause within the meaning of Article IV, Section 1 of the contract which reads as follows:

> "The Company shall not exercise its right to discipline by reprimand, suspension, or discharge, any employee except for good and just cause."

Essential Facts:

Employees *A* and *B*, both Electricians "A," were assigned by their foreman, Mr. *X*, to grind joints on the rails of a 7½ ton overhead crane in the Company's steel shed. They received this assignment about 11 A.M. on Thursday, June 28, 19—. It was determined that *B* would do the grinding and *A* would sit in the cab of the crane with his foot on the mechanical brake to prevent any possible chance of the crane moving or rolling while *B* was doing the grinding. It was approximately 11:20 when *A* moved the crane into position and dropped the magnet.

The critical time period involved is between 11:20 A.M. when *A* and *B* began their assignment and 11:30 A.M. when X arrived on the scene in response to a phone call from Mr. *Y*, general foreman of the primary departments, to Mr. *Z*, general foreman of the maintenance department, to report his opinion that Employee *A* was sleeping in the cab.

The record shows no dispute on the facts prior to 11:20 A.M. and after 11:30 A.M. It is not alleged that *A* was asleep prior to 11:20 A.M. Foreman *X*'s testimony that *A* was awake when he arrived on the scene at approximately 11:30 A.M. is not disputed.

Foreman *Y* and three other witnesses for the Company testified in substance that they observed *A* in the cab and concluded that he was sleeping or dozing in a sitting position. *Y* stated that he observed *A* with his arms on the control levers in the cab, his eyes closed, and his head nodding. *Y* stated that *A*'s "head kept nodding and as it did he'd open his eyes—he'd lock his fingers and then when he nodded again he'd hit his fingers—we watched him five minutes or so."

Y called *A* to the attention of Mr. *M* of the Personnel department who was in the area on a regular plant tour. *M* testified that he walked directly under the cab of the crane and looked up at *A*. *A*'s eyes were closed, says *M*. "A little later he fell forward, jerked up, and gazed around—then the nodding began again," stated *M*.

Mr. *V*, foreman of the steel stores, said that he observed *Y* and *M* watching *A* so he came over and looked at *A* and said to *Y* and *M*, "That guy's asleep." According to *V*, *A*'s forearms were across the control boxes, his head was down, and his eyes closed. *V* further stated that he heard a Material Handler named *C* shout at *A*, "Hey, don't go to sleep and fall out of there."

Mr. *W* of the Methods department also testified. He was in the area to route and set up a job on a new screw machine that had not been working properly. *Y* called *W*'s attention to *A* and *W* looked up at *A* and stated "he looks like he's dozing." *W* stated that *A* "looked that way for the two or three minutes I saw him." He further stated that he could not tell whether *A*'s eyes were closed or not.

Mr. *X*, foreman of electrical maintenance who had assigned *A* and *B* to the job in question, testified that when he arrived and looked up at the crane, "I saw *A* raise his hand and look at me in recognition." *X* first spoke to *Y* and then talked first to *B* and then to *A*. He said that he talked to *B* regarding the grinding job. *B* told *X* he had called out to *A* on several occasions and he had answered him. *X* stated that when he spoke first to *A* he said "you're not supposed to be sleeping on the job" and that *A* did not reply so far as *X* could recall. *X* was emphatic in testifying that at no time did he see *A* asleep. When he talked to *A* again after lunch, *X* stated that *A* denied that he was sleeping. According to *X*, *A* told him that "he was drowsy but he had full control."

A worked on other jobs the rest of the day. He was not suspended until about 10:30 A.M. the next day (Friday).

Mr. *O*, director of industrial relations, testified concerning prior cases of two-week suspensions for sleeping on the job.

The Union called *B* and *A* as witnesses. *B* testified that it was about 11:20 A.M. when he started grinding. He said that "at one time I shouted to him (*A*) that I was going to put one foot on the ladder and one on the scaffold—he answered OK." He further stated that *A* answered him "another time" before *X* arrived at about 11:30 A.M. *B* did not hear *C* make his remark to *A*. *B* could not see *A* in the cab from where *B* was grinding. *B* stated that in his opinion "*A* was awake and doing his assigned job."

A denied that he was asleep during the period in question. He stated that he observed *Y* and *M* watching him and "wondered what the attraction was—all I could figure was that *Y* was peeved that I was sitting there doing nothing." He also stated that he observed *V* look at him twice. He further stated that he saw *W* "looking at me casually." *A* stated that *C* "did holler up and say 'don't be too comfortable and go to sleep' and I think I thumbed my nose at him."

A stated that "none of these foremen spoke to me, nor I to them." *A* quoted *X* as saying later regarding the discipline that "This wouldn't have happened if I hadn't shot off my mouth at *Y*." A stated that "I denied being asleep—nobody could sit up there an hour and not get sleepy." *A* admits he had his eyes closed part of the time, contending that his eyes were smarting because there was a lot of brake fluid and oil on the floor of the cab. He said his eyes were also "granulated and rough from welding flash." On cross examination, *A* admitted that "it's possible that I had my head in my hands and my elbows sticking out." He further stated that in order to keep one's foot on the brake it is necessary to sit leaning slightly forward in the cab. He stated that he remembered the various foremen looking at him because it "was a little unusual for so many people to be looking at you" and also because he was "very bitter" at the discipline and "that's why I remember."

A has over nine-years' seniority with no prior disciplinary record.

Contentions of the Company:

The Company contends that the record clearly proves that *A* was sleeping on the job on the morning in question. Four independent witnesses testified that they personally observed *A* sleeping or dozing in a sitting position in the cab. His actions as observed by them are those that we all associate with sleeping, i.e., eyes closed, head nodding downward and then jerking up and then nodding downward again. These four witnesses came to be witnesses under normal, natural circumstances. All observed *A* and all saw the same thing.

The record shows no reason to doubt the good faith or credibility of the testimony of the Company's witnesses. Against their testimony is the self-serving declaration of *A* and *B*'s testimony. *B* could not see *A* from his grinding position.

The testimony of the four witnesses to *A*'s conduct is conclusive proof of the charge that he was asleep and thus not capable of taking responsibility for his job. The penalty for the offense in question is clearly reasonable and the Company therefore asks that the grievance be denied.

Contentions of the Union:

The Union maintains that the Company has failed to prove its charge that *A* was "sleeping on the job." While not questioning the good faith of the Company's witnesses, the Union maintains that they were unable to tell whether or not *A* was in fact asleep. They did not apply any of the normal tests to determine this fact, says the Union. None of them spoke to *A* nor touched him. They could not hear him breathe. They saw *A* from a considerable distance with his eyes closed part of the time and with his body hunched forward in a sitting position and "assumed" that he was asleep.

The fact remains that these supervisors saw what they expected to see and jumped to a faulty conclusion, says the Union. The only one who knew whether he was asleep or not was *A* and he has testified that he was fully conscious at all times. The Union stresses the very short time interval of ten minutes during which all this is alleged to have taken place. During this short time, *A* responded at least twice to calls from *B* and observed the various foremen watching him. He could not possibly have done this and been asleep at the same time. He also replied to *C*'s joking remark. His own foreman testified without contradiction that *A* was awake when he arrived at 11:30 A.M.

In summary, the Union maintains that the Company has failed to prove even that *A* was "in a deep revery," let alone asleep. Under the circumstances, says the Union, the discipline of *A* was clearly not for good and just cause. *A* should be made whole for lost pay, including July 4th, and the discipline should be stricken from his record.

Case 2. THE CARELESS TRUCK DRIVER

Preliminary Recital:

Employee *D*, Industrial Truck Operator, protests a three-day disciplinary layoff. *D* was disciplined by the Company in connection with an accident at the plant on July 9, 19—. The charge against *D* is failure to have his jeep under control and reckless driving. The Union contends that the Company has failed to prove its case against *D*. Therefore, the Union maintains he was disciplined without good and just cause. The Company maintains that the evidence in the case admits only of one conclusion, namely, that *D* did not have his jeep under control at the time of the accident.

The matter was heard by the undersigned at the offices of the Company on September 28, 19—.

The Issue:

The sole issue is whether Employee *D* was disciplined for good and just cause within the meaning of Article IV, Section 1 of the contract which reads as follows:

> The Company shall not exercise its right to discipline by reprimand, suspension, or discharge, any employee except for good and just cause.

Essential Facts:

The accident occurred at approximately 3:15 P.M. on July 9th. *D*'s shift ended at 3:30. The jeep in question was larger than those *D* was accustomed to driving and this was the first day he had been driving this particular jeep. *D* has about one and one-half years' experience as an industrial truck operator. He had been driving the jeep all day without incident, including several trips over the route where the accident took place.

According to *D*'s testimony, after crossing some railroad tracks, for which he had slowed down, "the whole vehicle turned on me." Before he could bring the jeep under control, it hit a car parked near the concrete road on which the jeep had been traveling. Damage to the parked car amounted to around $300. According to the Company, *D*'s jeep made a ninety-degree turn off the road. This statement remains uncontradicted in the record.

The jeep in question was driven away from the accident and test-driven by Employee *E*, mechanic. *E*, testifying for the Union at the hearing, stated that he had heard that the jeep was hard to drive and that he "couldn't operate it." However, he found nothing mechanically wrong with the steering mechanism or brakes in test-driving the jeep after the accident. *E* further testified that a new steering axle had been put on this particular jeep in December of two years ago "to improve its steering" and that he hadn't heard much about that jeep in quite awhile. *E* could not recall the jeep having been in for repair since December, 19— and stated that no repair work was done on it since the accident. It appears from the record that the July 9th incident was the only occasion on which this jeep has been involved in an accident.

Another Union witness, Employee *G*, testified that he had driven the jeep in question on several occasions. He testified that the jeep was hard to steer going frontwards and that "if you drove it up to where you bump the governor, you can't handle it." *G* stated that he found this out from experience in two or three trips.

Contentions of the Company:

The Company maintains that the record clearly establishes that *D* did not have the jeep under control at the time of the accident. The record permits no other reasonable inference, says the Company. Therefore, the discipline was for good and just cause and should be sustained. In support of its argument, the Company stressed the following considerations:

1. *D*'s testimony is "highly remarkable". Although he maintains that he had the jeep under control, the fact is that the jeep suddenly made a 90-degree turn off a concrete road and smashed into a parked car, ten to fifteen feet off

the road in a parking area. The Company maintains that in the normal course of driving *any* vehicle, this could not have occurred if the driver had the jeep under control and was driving it in a prudent manner.

2. *D*'s testimony that the steering mechanism and brakes were not working properly is refuted by the testimony of *E*, who found nothing mechanically faulty with the jeep immediately after the accident. Since the proof establishes that the jeep was functioning properly, it is not reasonable to assume that *D* was operating at a reasonable speed or in a prudent manner.

3. The time of the accident is highly significant. The record warrants a permissible inference that, fifteen minutes before the end of his shift, *D* was in a hurry to get through with his last load and did not have full regard for prudent operation.

4. *D*'s testimony is inconsistent. In one breath he states that he does not know what caused the jeep to swerve, and then states his belief that the steering mechanism and brakes were faulty.

5. This jeep has never been involved in an accident before or since. No repairs have been found necessary on it since December two years ago. *D* himself had driven it nearly a full shift without incident or without discovering any defect that would cause him to report it to his foreman or to the repair department. The only possible explanation for the accident is that *D* did not have the jeep under control at the time.

For these reasons, the Company urges that the grievance be denied.

Contentions of the Union:

In the Union's view, the Company has failed completely to satisfy the burden of proof required in discipline cases. All that the Company has done, says the Union, is prove that an accident took place. The rest of the Company's case is pure assumption. On the other hand, the Union has established through witnesses that this jeep was hard to handle, that it had a tendency to veer or swerve and that the brakes were not adequate for the weight of the vehicle. When these considerations are coupled with the fact that this was *D*'s *first day* operating the jeep, no picture of reckless driving or failure to maintain proper control emerges.

Thus, the Union maintains that the Company has made no proper showing in support of its allegations against *D*. At the most, all the record shows is that on his first day of driving this hard-to-handle vehicle, *D* had an unfortunate accident traceable to his unfamiliarity with the jeep's steering eccentricities. The fact that he did not catch on to the jeep's peculiarities as fast as *G* did is no proof that he was reckless or careless. The fact remains that there is not a shred of direct proof that *D* did not have the jeep under control or that he was driving recklessly. For these reasons, in line with established policy as to the Company's obligation to sustain burden of proof in discipline cases, the grievance should be sustained. The discipline should be stricken from *D*'s record and he should be made whole for the three days' lost earnings.

A second fundamental question frequently arising in discipline cases concerns the propriety of the penalty for the offense involved. Where the penalty is challenged as excessive, should the arbitrator modify the penalty if he agrees that it is excessive? This issue is highly controversial today. It is discussed at some length in Chapter 7, where it was noted that the arbitrator should have the right to modify penalties where he finds them to have been arbitrary, capricious, or discriminatory. However, the arbitrator should never substitute his judgment for that of management.

DISCIPLINARY PROCEDURES

In concluding this discussion of discipline matters it is desirable to stress the importance of developing sound procedures to be applied in all cases where management feels that discipline may be essential. In John Deere plants the use of a uniform procedure in all cases has contributed substantially to reducing friction and has been directly responsible for an unusually small percentage of discipline cases reaching arbitration. The procedure in all eight plants is the same. Before an employee is sent out of the plant as a result of an incident calling for disciplinary action, the contracts provide that the employee's divisional steward, if in the plant, or another union representative, must be notified and have an opportunity to hear the employee's statement. Within a "reasonable time" after the employee has been sent out of the plant a so-called disciplinary action hearing is held at which the employee is entitled to be present and to be represented by his divisional steward. Both parties may call witnesses and introduce evidence at this hearing before the actual decision on discipline is made. Written minutes of the disciplinary action hearing must be furnished to the chairman of the shop committee.

This uniform procedure for handling discipline cases, supplemented by certain principles established in a number of key arbitrations, has reduced the number going to arbitration. Among the more important of these principles are: (1) the burden of proving "good and just cause" for discipline rests on management; (2) if cause has been proved, a penalty imposed will not be modified unless shown to have been clearly arbitrary, excessive, capricious, or discriminatory in relation to the offense; (3) discipline for going outside the grievance procedure will be sustained, notwithstanding the substantive merits of the employee's complaint.

CONCLUSION

Establishment of a system of industrial jurisprudence represents one of the most constructive accomplishments of collective bargaining. The essence of industrial democracy lies in the negotiation and administration of these nonincome provisions. Underlying each such provision is the contractual assurance that workers in the bargaining unit, whether union or nonunion, will receive even-handed treatment. The application of uniform rules in impartial, nondiscriminatory fashion is the crux of democratic relationships in industry.

In some aspects of industrial jurisprudence (for exmaple, the requirement that discharge be only for good and sufficient cause) the same rule applies uniformly to all workers. In other situations (for example, the application of policies on layoffs, promotions, and transfers) industrial jurisprudence is concerned with the relative rights of individual workers in particular jobs.

In *all* situations the common denominator of a system of industrial jurisprudence is the substitution of rule for arbitrary discretion in the day-to-day conduct of employer-employee relationships.

The rights and responsibilities of management, the rights and responsibilities of unions, and the rights and responsibilities of individual workers would have little practical significance if the contract did not provide a mechanism for the implementation of those rights and responsibilities. The mechanism whereby the parties can secure redress against failure to observe contractual requirements is the contract's grievance and arbitration machinery, discussed previously in Chapters 6 and 7.

SELECTED BIBLIOGRAPHY

Baumback, Clifford M., *Merit and Seniority as Factors in Promotion and In-Grade Progression.* Iowa City: Bureau of Labor and Management Research Series No. 11, 1956.

Brooks, George W. and Sara Gamm, "The Practice of Seniority in Southern Pulp Mills," *Monthly Labor Review*, LXXVIII (July, 1955), 757–65.

Brown, Richard P., "A New Technique in Seniority Administration," *Industrial and Labor Relations Review*, IX (October, 1955), 32–40.

Craig, Paul G. and W. E. Schlender, "Some Relationships Between GAW and Seniority," *Journal of Business*, XXX (January, 1957), 1–11.

Fairweather, Owen, "Seniority Provisions in Labor Contracts: Social and Economic Consequences," *DePaul Law Review*, I (Spring-Summer, 1952), 191–215.

Justin, Jules J., "Arbitrator's Authority in Disciplinary Cases," *Labor Law Journal*, IV (November, 1953), 759–65.

Kaufman, Jacob J., "Working Rules in the Railroad Industry," *Labor Law Journal*, V (December, 1954), 819–30.

Kahn, Mark L., "Seniority Problems in Business Mergers," *Industrial and Labor Relations Review*, VIII (April, 1955), 361–78.

Lester, Richard A., *Hiring Practices and Labor Competition*, (Research Report Series No. 88). Princeton: Industrial Relations Section, 1954.

——— and Robert L. Aronson, *Job Modifications under Collective Bargaining*. Princeton, N. J.: Industrial Relations Section, 1950.

Lewis, H. Gregg, "Hours of Work and Hours of Leisure," *Proceedings of the Ninth Annual Meeting, Industrial Relations Research Association.* Madison: IRRA, 1957, pp. 196–206.

Mullady, Philomena M., "Seniority—A Changing Concept?" *Personnel*, XXXIII (July, 1956), 78–81.

Myers, A. Howard, "Arbitrating Industrial Efficiency," *Harvard Business Review*, XXXI (July-August, 1953), 60–68.

Reder, Melvin, "The Cost of a Shorter Work Week," *Proceedings of the Ninth Annual Meeting, Industrial Relations Research Association.* Madison: IRRA, 1957, pp. 207–21.

Reighard, Edward, *The Long Term Contract in Labor-Management Relations.* Stanford: Graduate School of Business, Stanford University, 1954.

Slichter, Sumner H., *Union Policies and Industrial Management.* Washington: Brookings Institution, 1941.

Taylor, George W., "Seniority Concepts," in *Arbitration Today*, Jean T. McKelvey, ed. Washington: Bureau of National Affairs, Inc., 1955, pp. 127–38.

U. S. Bureau of Labor Statistics, *Analysis of Layoff, Recall, and Work-Sharing Procedures in Union Contracts.* Bulletin No. 1209. Washington: U.S. Government Printing Office, 1957.

Wood, Richard H. and Jack Chernick, *The Joint Safety Program of the Forstmann Woolen Company and Local 656, Textile Workers Union of America, AFL–CIO, 1948–1956* (Case Studies of Co-operation between Labor and Management, No. 3). New Brunswick: Institute of Management and Labor Relations, Rutgers University, 1957.

10

Wage determination under collective bargaining

Each year thousands of contracts come up for renegotiation. Then too, many employers whose employees have recently been unionized embark upon their first negotiations with a trade union. In virtually every first contract negotiation and the great majority of contract renewal negotiations a demand for an across-the-board wage increase and some demands relating to the correction of alleged occupational rate inequities are high on the list of the union's negotiation priorities. In a word, the wage bargain is still the paramount issue in most collective negotiations.

The principal aim of American unions is to improve the economic status of the employees they represent through negotiated increases in the price of labor. The main objective of management in negotiation of the wage issue is usually to make certain that the wage bargain will be consistent with its total cost picture as related to anticipated demand and level of profit.

In this chapter and the following two chapters we consider various aspects of the economics of wage determination under collective bargaining. The present chapter describes in broad terms the basic characteristics of the wage bargaining process and the determinants of employer and union policy in decisions as to changing the general level of wages in the individual firm and the individual industry. The institutionalized process of bargained wage changes will be contrasted and compared with unilateral employer determination. In Chapter 11 we will analyze collective bargaining as a method of dealing with structural wage problems within a particular firm, within an industry, and, finally, on an inter-industry basis. The third chapter in this section treats the macro-economic impact of bargained wages on the economy as a whole. An effort will be made in conclusion to summarize the present state of our knowledge as to the economic effects of collective bargaining on wage levels and the structure of occupational rates.

LABOR AS A COMMODITY

When a company and a union negotiate a demand for a wage increase or a revision in the plant's structure of occupational rates, they are engaged in a decision-making operation concerning one of the factors of production. As Kenneth Boulding has pointed out, labor *is* a commodity, "in spite of the Clayton Act, the I.L.O. and the Federal Council of Churches."[1] There is, consequently, room for supply and demand analysis in labor economics. It is essential to realistic understanding of the collective bargaining process, however, to keep in mind that labor as a commodity has certain distinguishing properties or characteristics that set it apart from other commodities studied by enonomists. Labor is a service and is performed by human beings. Labor as a commodity is: (1) perishable; (2) relatively immobile; (3) imperfectly substitutable; and (4) inseparable from the laborer himself. This combination of characteristics necessarily makes the determination of the price of labor something of a special case in value theory.

DISTINGUISHING CHARACTERISTICS OF INSTITUTIONAL WAGE DETERMINATION

As an institutionalized process, wage determination under collective bargaining has certain distinguishing characteristics that require emphasis in the interests of more realistic appraisal and understanding. While the economic calculus may be of paramount importance to most employers and to many union leaders, bargained wages usually involve a complex of variables and motivating considerations that render hazardous any generalizations or conclusions based solely on conventional economic calculations.

[1] Kenneth E. Boulding, "Collective Bargaining and Fiscal Policy," *Proceedings of Second Annual Meeting, Industrial Relations Research Association* (Champaign: IRRA, 1950), pp. 52-68, at p. 53.

Perhaps of greatest importance is the fact that trade union leaders are not sellers of commodities in the usual sense. Trade unions represent workers in negotiation with employers over the price of the workers' services. Union leaders are therefore agents. As agents, they cannot act always as "economic men" if to do so involves going against the desires of their constituency, the rank-and-file.

It is this essentially political basis of trade union authority that makes it difficult for union leaders to be as "businesslike" as the employer might prefer, or as "responsible" as the economist might prefer. Over any period of time, union leaders must cater to rank-and-file demands—or lose power.

The wage objectives of the rank-and-file may or may not be consistent with the cold economics of the situation. The workers' goal in one instance may be consistent with maximizing the total wage bill for the membership. In another instance the goal set may involve appreciable unemployment among the membership. The membership may not associate a given set of wage demands with the volume of employment opportunities. They may not be concerned about the nexus between wage rates and productivity. They are likely to have unbounded faith in a company's ability to absorb successive wage increments. Their perception of the external impact of a particular wage bargain is likely to be lacking.

The prime determinant of rank-and-file views on wages is what Arthur Ross has termed the "standard of equitable comparison."[2] The importance of this criterion explains why union leaders are so intensely concerned about matching the gains made by rival unions and why the percentage amount of the adjustment is frequently of greater importance than the absolute amount.

An informed trade union leader is naturally concerned about the anticipated economic consequences of wage demands. Nevertheless, he is operating on a political basis of authority. In the last analysis, he must deliver to the satisfaction of the membership (or at least to the satisfaction of the employed portion of the membership) if he expects to remain in office. He also has to give careful regard to the survival and growth requirements of the union as an institution, beyond the specific demands of the membership.

This latter factor helps to explain why some strikes occur when the employer and the union are only, say, two cents apart in the amount of wage increase demanded and the amount offered. When a strike is deemed necessary to maintain the integrity and standing of the union as an institution, the figures as to how many years it will take the workers

[2] Arthur Ross, *Trade Union Wage Policy* (Berkeley and Los Angeles: University of California Press, 1948), pp. 45-74 and *passim*. The presentation on union wage policy, in this chapter as in the first edition of this book, has been deeply influenced by Ross' penetrating analysis.

to make up the paychecks lost while they were striking are almost meaningless or irrelevant to the union leader and to the membership. If the alternative to striking is thought to be the destruction or the emasculation of the union, then the strike is "worth it" in their eyes.

By the same token, the institutionalization of wage determination on the employer side has introduced certain noneconomic variables not present in ordinary buyer-seller relationships. The modern corporation is a political as well as an economic institution. The corporation too has its survival and growth requirements. The owner-manager or the corporate manager, as the case may be, cannot act as a pure economic man any more than can the union leader. Considerations of personal power and prestige often induce behavior that is not dictated entirely, or even primarily, by the economic calculus.

Economic models based on an assumption that the employer is always out to maximize profits may be misleadingly unrealistic.[3] Assumptions that employers are interested in maximizing profits and that unions are interested in maximizing total membership income are useful devices for theoretical analysis, but in particular cases such assumptions contribute little to a real understanding of the underlying determinants of employer and union behavior. It may be difficult if not impossible to measure the importance of the "social-psychological penumbra" in institutionalized wage determination, but it would be fatal to accurate understanding if such factors were omitted from the analysis.

THE DOMINANCE OF THE "INSTITUTIONAL MARKET"

Analysis of wage determination under collective bargaining must take account of at least four important and interrelated factual developments in recent years. These include: (1) the increasing importance of centralized bargaining structures, as discussed in Chapter 4; (2) the continued prevalence of pattern bargaining in a number of significant industries; (3) increased control of policy formation in the hands of international union officers; and (4) the impact of the united labor movement on the policies of individual member unions. Each of these factors deserves some consideration.

A perceptive appraisal of the nature and significance of the "institutional market" was provided some years ago by Clark Kerr,[4] and has

[3] See, for example, Leland Hazard, "Wage Theory: A Management View," in George W. Taylor and Frank C. Pierson, eds., *New Concepts in Wage Determination* (New York: McGraw-Hill Book Company, Inc., 1957), pp. 32–50.

[4] Clark Kerr, "Labor Markets: Their Character and Consequences," *Proceedings of Second Annual Meeting, Industrial Relations Research Association* (Champaign: IRRA, 1950), pp. 69–84.

been brought up to date by him in a more recent paper.[5] Kerr's thesis, briefly, is that traditional market forces have been largely replaced by institutional controls on both sides of the bargaining table. A major result has been that job markets and wage markets can and sometimes do go their separate ways. In highly organized relationships supply and demand adjust to the wage rate rather than the other way around, as pictured in more conventional analysis.

The growing importance of institutional markets is attested to by many recent developments, notably the prevalance of multi-employer bargaining in many industries and the increasing centralization in policy formation that has occurred within many international unions and in many multi-plant companies. Even where local unions retain considerable discretion in wage policy, as in the construction trades, the bargaining is more often than not conducted in highly institutionalized fashion between a contractors' association on the one hand and a joint union council on the other. Among industrial unions the local with any considerable amount of discretion is the exception rather than the rule as far as changes in the general level of plant wages are concerned. Local unions frequently retain considerable discretion in bargaining to correct inequities in occupational rates, but general wage policy considerations are usually structured by the policy laid down by the international union. Departures from such policy are the exception and require substantial justification if international sanction is to be secured. Only a drastic employment effect is likely to permit local union deviation from an international union pattern calling for a wage increase.

THE INFLUENCE OF PATTERN BARGAINING

Pattern bargaining, formally or informally, continues to reinforce tendencies toward increased institutionalization and centralization of bargaining structures on wage determination. We are still a long way from what could accurately be described as national collective bargaining in the sense of an agreed-upon, over-all wage policy determined by a council of top union and industry representatives. However, a consistent thread runs through the course of many key wage negotiations in any one year.

A change in fashion on wage policy pioneered in a key relationship is quickly reflected in the negotiations of other parties. When General Motors and the UAW first negotiated a five-year pact with the wage formula of an annual improvement factor coupled with escalation, many unions announced that they would not fall in line. They intended to stick

[5] See Clark Kerr, "Wage Relationships—the Comparative Impact of Market and Power Forces," in John T. Dunlop, ed., *The Theory of Wage Determination* (New York: St. Martin's Press, 1957), pp. 173-93.

to more "orthodox" bargaining, i.e., extracting whatever the traffic would bear in annual negotiations. Yet, within a few years long-term agreements of three to five years were appearing in many industries outside the orbit of the UAW. For example, the meat packing industry in its 1956-1959 contracts approximated the long-term pattern without the wage formula. Instead of using the annual improvement factor approach the contracts provided for definite cents-per-hour increases on anniversary dates in 1957 and 1958. Other unions, of course, stick to annual negotiations or to longer term agreements with reopeners on wages every year or every six months.

Multi-industrial unions have pattern problems of their own with the various segments of their membership owing to the strong interest of the rank-and-file in "equitable comparison." The UAW, for example, finds that whatever it gets in key negotiations with the auto industry in Detroit must be approximated or exceeded in farm equipment. When the automobile contracts called for annual improvement factor increases combined with escalation in 1955, the farm equipment negotiations followed a similar pattern. The AIF in farm equipment, however, was pegged at 3 per cent a year rather than 2½ per cent as in automobiles. When SUB plans were negotiated with Ford, General Motors, and other automobile firms, similar plans were a must on collective bargaining agenda in farm equipment, an industry with perhaps even more serious stabilization problems than automobiles. The Ford plan was subsequently adopted in most of the farm equipment industry contracts and "improved upon" in the Allis Chalmers-UAW contract.

International union control over negotiations by local unions appears to have increased markedly in recent years. This development has obvious significance for wage policy. It tends to promote wage standardization and elimination of industry and geographic differentials. It also has a significant impact on parallelism in wage demands among international unions that compete directly or indirectly with one another in the same or related fields.

IMPACT OF THE AFL-CIO MERGER ON WAGE DETERMINATION

The impact of the AFL-CIO merger may also be considerable on wage negotiations in future years. Although one of the principal architects of the merger, Arthur Goldberg, denies that the merger will affect collective bargaining relationships in any marked degree,[6] critics of "labor monopoly" have become increasingly vocal in asserting that the United States

[6] See Arthur J. Goldberg, *AFL-CIO: Labor United* (New York: McGraw-Hill Book Company, Inc., 1956), at p. 219.

is entering an era of completely centralized and monopolistically determined wages and other employment conditions.[7]

Goldberg's argument rests on the familiar principle of the autonomy of the international union in relation to the federation with which it is affiliated. Examination of the constitution of the merged federation certainly would not lead to alarm over any change in the basic collective bargaining relationships with which we are familiar. The impact of the merger on bargaining as such will be primarily indirect, in terms of new organization drives and intensified political action. There appear to be no plans on the part of the federation's leadership to effectuate any control over the member unions as to their particular economic policies in dealings with employers. Nevertheless, it is reasonable to anticipate that one of the fruits of merger should be a closer coordination of policies on the part of the major pace-setting unions in the federation.[8] Or, to put it another way, it is unlikely that merger will result in greater variety in union goals in collective bargaining. On the contrary, it seems logical to assume that the trend will be toward more single-minded concentration on certain broad economic goals such as shorter work weeks, greater protection against the impact of technological change, and improved labor relations legislation.

In summary, the mirror of the future on the collective bargaining front reflects an increasing institutionalization of markets. In the writer's opinion such an alternative is far more palatable than either the compulsory atomization of markets advocated by the late Henry Simons or wage-fixing by governmental bodies. The discussion of the economics of wage determination in this and the following two chapters is framed in terms of an explicit assumption that wage markets will become increasingly institutionalized.

Of course, the wages of many workers will continue to be set unilaterally by employers under nonunion conditions. However, collective bargaining is clearly the most influential method of wage determination in our society—so influential, in fact, that in most cases the economic policies set by collective bargaining are of persuasive significance in determining the policies of nonunion employers. In measuring the economic significance of collective bargaining this important consideration must be kept constantly in mind.

The most effective way for a nonunion employer to stay that way is to make sure that his employees understand that he is paying them as well as, or better than, unionized employers in the same industry or area,

[7] See, for example, Edward H. Chamberlin, *The Economic Analysis of Labor Union Power* (Washington: American Enterprise Association, Inc., 1958.)

[8] Some unions affiliated with the newly created Industrial Union Department of the merged federation have already taken advantage of this opportunity.

thus supporting his argument that they do not need a union in order to protect and advance their economic welfare.

WAGES AS COST VERSUS WAGES AS INCOME

Few contracts are negotiated without a basic disagreement on the wage issue. If economic conditions in the firm, the industry, and the economy are generally favorable, the union will be pushing for a general upward adjustment in wages and the employer will be resisting such a demand with greater or lesser intensity.[9] We shall discuss below the actual factors that determine the amount of wage increase demanded by the union and the considerations that influence the employer in reaching his decision as to how much of a wage increase, if any, he is prepared to negotiate. At the outset, however, a basis for conflict on the wage issue is inherent in the different viewpoints from which employers and employees regard wages. Management must always regard wages (and other collective bargaining issues that involve money outlays) as a cost of doing business. The union and the workers it represents, however, tend to view wages (and other economic benefits such as paid vacations) as income to the worker.

Thus, management's basic incentives will normally cause it to keep the unit cost of labor, as distinguished from the price of labor, as low as possible. The workers' aspirations will normally cause them to seek the highest possible price per hour for their labor. The political compulsions upon union leaders oblige them to seek to deliver what can be described as economic gains each time a contract comes up for renegotiation.

These opposing ways of looking at wages furnish a basis for more or less intense conflict at the bargaining table, even in the most stable and constructive union-management relationships. Yet in every relationship there also exists a fundamental basis for accommodation and compromise. Ultimate reconciliation of conflicting demands is essential, since both profits and adequate labor income are indispensable to the health of any business enterprise.

WAGES AND PRODUCTIVITY

The general economic prosperity of recent years has given both management and union leadership an opportunity to learn and apply some

[9] Most unions with contracts expiring in 1957 and 1958 sought wage increases, notwithstanding the unfavorable employment outlook in many lines. Although employer resistance may generally be said to have been stiffer than in 1956 and earlier years, it is interesting to note that fairly substantial increases were negotiated nevertheless, the most common increase being between nine and eleven cents per hour. See BLS *Current Wage Developments Series*, No. 122, February 1, 1958.

basic economics whose importance was often obscured or unappreciated in times of severe unemployment. There is a growing joint awareness that *the real common denominator of management and labor on the wage issue is increased physical productivity per man-hour.* Both business and union leaders have repeatedly expressed their common devotion to the cause of raising the standard of living and the level of business activity by increasing physical productivity. In a relatively full employment economy both parties have shown evidence of appreciating the basic truth that there can be little improvement in the real wage position of the labor force unless gains in productivity are encouraged and forthcoming. Union restrictions on work loads and technological change are not so prevalent today as they were when the chief spectre of the laboring man was involuntary unemployment.

We shall have more to say on this in ensuing pages. Suffice it to note here that management and organized labor have an underlying mutuality of interest arising from the stake of labor in maintaining a dynamic and increasingly prosperous capitalist economy. We have already noted that the overwhelming majority of American union leaders and the rank-and-file do not seek any fundamental revision of our economic and political system. American unions still function and will continue to function as agencies to check on management in its allocation of the fruits of production. No appreciable support can be found for economic socialism in the ranks of organized labor, nor for codetermination, industry councils, or other schemes involving joint operation of industry. In this sense American unionism is basically a *conservative* institution. It seeks to preserve our present economic system while attempting to protect and improve the economic position of the worker under that system.

WAGE THEORY AND COLLECTIVE BARGAINING

Wage determination under collective bargaining has always posed perplexing and frustrating problems in economic theory. Virtually everyone who has written on the subject has expressed complete or partial dissatisfaction with the present state of theory on bargained wages. Part of the confusion and frustration has arisen from efforts to fit bargained wages into simplified economic models of price determination similar to those employed in conventional price analysis. Collective bargaining is a complex, highly institutionalized process. It exhibits an amazing variety of strategies, patterns, and approaches that defy unitary analysis. Those theorists who have attempted to explain union wage policy in purely economic terms have found that their models and predictions do not bear much relationship to reality. Others have gone to the opposite extreme in stressing the political nature of the trade union as an institution and virtually abandoned any effort to explain collective wage determination in terms of a unified theory. Most of the reasoning from all sources has been deductive. A great many empirical studies of wage determination in particular firms and particular industries now exist, but to date no one has had the requisite courage, breadth of vision, and stamina to attempt to weld this growing body of knowledge into a systematic theory of collective wage determination.

We will not review here the principal theories of wages that have occupied the attention of economists over the years. That task has been ably performed by others.[10] The analysis here starts from the same central proposition that motivated Arthur Ross in his provocative *Trade Union Wage Policy*,[11] namely, that "a trade union is a political agency operating in an economic environment." Implicit in this proposition is the conclusion that unions' motivations in collective bargaining are complex and mixed. It would be absurd to argue that union leaders ignore the economics of a situation in framing collective bargaining demands. It would be equally unrealistic to assume that union leaders frame their policies and demands in terms of solely economic criteria, or to develop full-blown theoretical models on the assumption that union leaders must necessarily be maximizing something in the economic sense.

Even on the management side of the bargaining table a model built on strictly economic lines would probably prove inaccurate and misleading. Most theoretical models assume that management, in making decisions on wage policy, is influenced primarily if not exclusively by the goal of profit maximization. Yet, a contemporary business leader writing on wage theory from a management standpoint places profits third in a list of influential determinants of managerial decision-making on wages. Leland Hazard suggests that the compulsion to maintain production and the need to maintain a feasible price rank ahead of profits in such a listing.[12] Corporations, as well as unions, have institutional survival requirements that may not jibe with the formal rationale of business enterprise to which we are accustomed.

NEED FOR A MULTIPLE MODEL THEORY

We are better informed today about wage behavior in unionized and unorganized markets than ever before. Many valuable empirical studies have appeared in recent years. A survey of this expanding literature suggests that no one is likely to emerge with a satisfactory unitary explanation of collective wage determination. Collective bargaining is conducted by

[10] See, for example, John T. Dunlop, "The Task of Contemporary Wage Theory," in John T. Dunlop, ed., *The Theory of Wage Determination* (New York: St. Martin's Press, 1957), pp. 3-27.

[11] Arthur Ross, *op. cit.*, p. 12.

[12] Leland Hazard, *op. cit.*, p. 32.

highly practical men on both sides. Their decisions are made in terms of the exigencies of particular situations. The end product is variety, not unity. Consequently, an adequate theory of bargained wages, when developed, will necessarily be a multiple model theory.

We will need one model for explaining and predicting management and trade union wage policy in industries that involve oligopolistic "competition among the few." We will need a different model to explain and predict union and management decision-making in highly competitive industries with large numbers of small firms. A third model will be needed to explain wage behavior in industries that are partially organized and partially nonunion.

The nature of the product market, the organization of the industry, the presence or absence of strong competitive market forces, the structure of the union(s) in question—these and many other variables have a significant impact on wage decision-making. It is extremely unlikely that any one model can encompass such a variety of relationships.

Can we develop a single satisfactory model that will explain why Union *X* is happy with contracts running from three to five years in duration, while Union *Y* adamantly refuses to change from its set policy of annual negotiations? Can any one construct explain why some unions rather clearly consider the employment effect of their wage demands and other unions do not? Can one model explain why a particular union with a variety of bargaining relationships will accept incentive methods of wage payment in some contracts and hold out for hourly rates in others? Can one model explain why a particular union will insist on wage uniformity throughout the industry in which it is the sole important factor on the employee side of the table, while another union, equally powerful in terms of its industrial coverage, permits wide variation in rates for comparable jobs in the same industry?

The foregoing questions indicate in some degree the difficulties in formulating a comprehensive theory of collective wage determination. Without any pretense at offering a theory of wages under collective bargaining, the concluding pages of this three-chapter section on the economics of wage determination will be devoted to summarizing our present state of knowledge in this complex area and will offer some suggestions for further research.

DO UNION LEADERS CONSIDER THE EMPLOYMENT EFFECT?

At this point, by way of illustrating the difficulties involved, it will be useful to summarize a recent academic controversy as to whether employers and union leaders do or should consider the employment effect of their wage bargains. Many economists feel that employers and union leaders should demonstrate their "responsibility" by showing concern over the relationship between wage rates and volume of employment opportunities. Arthur Ross is the most quoted exponent of the view that it is difficult if not impossible to estimate accurately the wage rate-employment ratio. Ross concludes that the volume of employment associated with a given wage rate is unpredictable before the fact and that the effect of a given rate upon employment is not decipherable after the fact.[13]

In support of this dictum Ross sets forth four links by which the wage rate may be connected to the demand for labor: (1) wage rate to labor costs; (2) labor cost to total cost; (3) total cost to price; and (4) price to volume of sales and production. In Ross' view, there is such a great deal of free play at each of these four links in the chain of the wage-employment bargain that "as a result, the initial and final links are so loosely connected that for practical purposes they must be regarded as largely independent." [14]

Ross has been charged with underestimating the extent to which unions take into consideration the employment effect of wage decisions. G. P. Shultz and C. A. Myers take issue with Ross' conclusion that instances in which wage-cost-price-employment relationships are clear and predictable (and therefore taken into account) are the exceptional cases.[15] Shultz and Myers contend that employment opportunities vitally affect wage decisions in many areas, particularly in job shops as distinguished from continuous production plants, in industries where there is strong competition in the product market, and in industries that are only partially organized.

Instead of emphasizing general wage settlements as does Ross, Shultz and Myers stress the many other wage decisions that union leaders must make, and contend that employment effects are often of basic importance in determining these decisions. In his study of the shoe industry in Brockton, Massachusetts, Shultz emphasizes the preoccupation of union leaders in that industry with the employment effect of changing piece prices, changing product lines, and the impact of technological change.[16]

The informed reader will recognize that both Ross and Shultz and Myers are "right" in terms of the industries they are taking as analytical subjects and models. The difference in opinion as to the consideration given in wage policy to the employment effect reflects fundamental differences in the nature of the industries and product markets involved. Ross is talking largely in terms of oligopolistic industries with administered

[13] Arthur Ross, *op. cit.*, p. 80.

[14] *Ibid.*, p. 90.

[15] G. P. Shultz and C. A. Myers, "Union Wage Decisions and Employment," *American Economic Review*, XL (June, 1950), 362–80.

[16] George P. Shultz, *Pressures on Wage Decisions* (New York: John Wiley & Sons, Inc., 1951.)

prices such as automobiles and steel. Shultz and Myers are focusing their attention on highly competitive industries where labor cost is a substantial element in total cost and where the nexus between wage changes, price changes, and demand for product is clear and observable.

Enough has been said to indicate that understanding of collective wage determination requires a shedding of any simplified preconceptions about how bargained wages are determined. We turn now to a consideration of the actual factors considered by prudent employers and trade union leaders in formulating wage policies.

THE DETERMINANTS OF WAGE POLICY

What is meant by the term "wage policy"? How are company and union wage policies determined? By whom are they determined? What factors are of the greatest importance? These are some of the principal questions which we now consider.

The term itself is not easy to define. In the broadest sense a company or a union may be said to have a wage policy whenever there is an element of planning and forethought given to wage decisions and wage demands. Policy is the opposite of sheer opportunism. However, a calculated opportunism may be said to represent a form of policy.

No *modern* employer or union leader goes into contract negotiation without being thoroughly prepared in advance. Companies that are large enough to employ specialized industrial relations personnel begin preparing for the next contract negotiation before the ink is dry on the current agreement. This is not an exaggeration. Most major unions now employ staff economists to study continuously the economics of the industry or industries of special significance to their particular union as well as general economic trends. This is the age of the specialist; collective wage determination is no exception to the trend.

Of course, it is not the wage issue alone that requires professional expertise. Current fashions in collective bargaining stress negotiated pension plans, health and welfare programs, and supplemental unemployment benefits that present a technical challenge too forbidding for the average elected union representative or company industrial relations man to meet unaided. The increasing burden of government regulation is another complicating factor in current negotiations, making the use of lawyers virtually obligatory at some stage in negotiations. Smaller companies without the resources to employ specialized talent on a full-time basis are finding it imperative to utilize consulting services or labor reporting services to try to keep abreast of the rapidly shifting scene. Keeping current is not an easy assignment for the specialist. It is an impossible assignment for the operating chief executive of a small company who has to handle contract negotiations as only one of many complex managerial duties.

EMPLOYER WAGE POLICY

The principal determinants of employer wage policy will now be reviewed and analyzed. As to both management and union wage policy, it is dangerous to generalize. It is essential always to ask "which company?" and "which union?" and "under what conditions?" There is no standard approach to wage policy on either side of the bargaining table. The exigencies of the particular situation always will be of substantial influence in bending theoretical or ideal considerations.

A prudent employer in reaching decisions as to the appropriate level of money wages in his business will need to know essentially the same things, whether he is unionized or not. His strategy and actual final decision if he is organized may vary from the policy he might have followed if he were nonunion, but the core of factual material needed for prudent decision-making should be the same in either case.

Among the more important factors that a prudent employer will wish to consider before making up his mind on the level of money wages he thinks appropriate for the coming contract year, we may include the following:

1. The firm's over-all competitive position in the industry and in relation to substitute products.
2. The ratio of labor cost to total cost and the elasticity of substitution of capital for labor.
3. The firm's current market position, with specific reference to its ability to withstand resort to economic force by the union if the latter's wage demands are not met.
4. A measure of its wage costs and rates against those of its principal competitors in the industry and against those of comparable firms in its geographic area.
5. A calculation of its absorption potential under different assumed levels of wage adjustment.
6. A relating of wage demands to its price policy and a relating of the latter to current market conditions. This involves a knowledge of elasticity of demand for the firm's product(s) and some insight into consumer expectations.
7. Appraisal of the equity of its wage-rate structure in terms of a scientific standard developed by job evaluation, etc.
8. Analysis of the general economic picture, including an effort at calculation of the probable impact of federal, state, and local public policy in taxation and other fields.

9. Appraisal of the tightness or looseness of the local labor market in terms of the firm's probable requirements measured against existing and prospective labor supply.

10. Impact upon the firm's labor demand schedule of alternative assumptions as to future wage policy.

11. Weighing the specifics of the local labor market supply and demand picture against the over-all policy of the international union involved and against any uniform employer policy in the industry, if any exists.

12. Appraisal of the probable effects of alternative wage assumptions on the effective utilization of existing labor supply.

The foregoing list of a dozen factors assumes that we are talking about an uncomplicated increase or decrease in the level of money wages alone in a particular enterprise. Collective bargaining life today, however, is not that simple. When we talk about "wages" today, it is understood that from a labor cost standpoint the employer must weight into his calculations the monetary value of a series of "fringe" demands usually made in each negotiation. At a minimum, in addition to a union demand for an across-the-board increase of, say, fifteen cents per hour, there may be a demand to increase benefits under a medical and surgical plan; to increase the value of a group life insurance plan; to raise the value of a negotiated pension plan; to liberalize the paid vacation plan; and to extend shift bonuses by five cents per hour. In addition to all these fairly standard fringe items, there may be a demand for a supplemental unemployment benefit fund and a catastrophe insurance (i.e., extended medical) plan. In other words, when an employer calculates his expectations on "wages" for the coming year, he must consider all possible variables involving additional money outlays. *Package bargaining is a fact of life in most contract negotiations today*. With this notation, we confine our remarks in this chapter to the simplified picture of contemplated changes in the level of money wages in a particular enterprise.

There is no uniform pattern to employer wage policy. Some companies with a number of plants in different geographic areas pursue a policy of uniformity in wage rates and wage changes throughout the chain. Other multi-plant companies prefer to tailor their rate structures at particular plants to the prevailing rates in the community. Some companies attempt to match or exceed rates for comparable work in the area; others do not. Some prefer positions of wage leadership in their industry; others prefer to follow the leader.

Whatever the reasons for a particular policy, no sensible company today formulates a wage policy without full command of all the facts. A thorough knowledge of internal direct and overhead costs, competitors'

But no sensible company today formulates a wage policy without full command of all the facts; internal direct & overhead costs, competitors' cost, state of the product market, etc costs, and the state of the product market is indispensable to sound formulation of wage policy.

In general, employers today enter upon wage negotiations better prepared than they were in the period immediately following World War II. In the earlier period some employers were chagrined to find that the union negotiators were more thoroughly versed in the economics of the industry than they were. In some cases the lesson in the need for thorough preparation for bargaining was an expensive one.

A nonunion employer, armed with the facts, will usually enjoy considerable discretion in reaching his ultimate decision on wage policy. He can decide on the amount of any general increase, and can reach a unilateral decision as to how to distribute that increase among the various occupational classifications in his establishment. He can adjust his wage decision to the short-run condition of the local labor market if he so desires.

An employer dealing with a union obviously does not have this degree of freedom, although the coverage of collective bargaining today is such as to make it unwise for a nonunion employer to ignore policy on any wage issue in unionized sectors.

Several standard policies of unionism must always be taken into account by employers in formulating wage policy. In the first place, most unions are interested in achieving some form of wage uniformity.[17] The growth of pattern or leadership bargaining and multi-employer bargaining arrangements has increasingly shifted the emphasis to an industry orientation. Most employers appear to prefer to gear their wage policy to local or community rates rather than industry rates. The union pressure toward industry-wide uniformity has forced re-evaluation of many employer policies.

In addition to their emphasis on the standard rate unions have been a powerful influence for making "equal pay for equal work" a mandatory feature of wage policy. This factor is of special importance in structural wage problems of intraplant and interplant differentials discussed in the next chapter.

A third effect of unionism has been to increase centralization of authority on the management side. Unionism outlaws individual bargaining. It therefore requires high-echelon participation in both wage policy formulation and administration. Such centralization was not as essential in the pre-union days, when the foreman was likely to be monarch of all he surveyed.

[17] It is essential to keep in mind that "wage uniformity" is not a simple, unitary concept. Thomas Kennedy has analyzed at least seven distinct types of wage uniformity. They are generally not complementary and are often dissimilar. See his *The Significance of Wage Uniformity* (Philadelphia: University of Pennsylvania Press, 1949.)

Finally, the union furnishes management with a highly critical audience for any wage policy the latter may develop. The skepticism with which many unions view job evaluation and incentive methods of wage payment, for example, has brought home to management the necessity for a plausible rationale for its wage policies. Most employers are now aware of the necessity for developing and maintaining a wage policy. They are also aware of the necessity for selling such a policy to their workers.

The bargaining process on wages is becoming more factual and less crude than in former years. The increasing factualization of wage bargaining is due to a number of factors, including the following:

1. The growing complexity of the bargaining agenda, with the accompanying necessity of weighing the total and relative costs of pure wage demands and other income demands such as paid vacations, pensions, paid holidays, paid sick leave, and shift differentials.
2. The growth of centralized bargaining structures, which has been both a product and a cause of an awareness of the need for better-informed negotiation.
3. A healthy fear of greater governmental control, which has induced in some cases a greater emphasis on factual negotiation.

As a consequence, both employers and unions are better informed about the essential economic facts of the plant, industry, or area in question. One index of an increasing employer awareness of the need for complete factual information is the widespread use currently being made of wage surveys as a basis for policy formation. Such private wage surveys by both employers and unions are supplemented by a rapidly improving body of wage data collected by the Bureau of Labor Statistics for key labor markets. BLS since 1956 has made a number of detailed occupational wage surveys in principal labor markets. The bureau also has thorough monthly reports on average hourly and weekly earnings for all types of nonagricultural employment, and makes detailed surveys of wage trends in particular lines such as building and construction and motor truck drivers. The bureau has published informative "wage chronology" studies on particular union-management relationships. Its series on "Current Wage Developments" is also very useful.

The responsibility for formulation of wage policy in most firms today is vested in top management. The problems associated with wage policy under modern conditions are technical and complex. They require an over-all view for an effective solution. No line official is likely to have all the facts bearing on the decisions involved.

In multi-employer bargaining employer formulation of wage policy may rest with a central labor relations association established for joint negotiation with the union or unions. In such instances extensive pre-consultation with the individual employers in the association is essential. There are a great many difficult problems associated with the formulation of a united employer wage policy. Firms differ markedly in their efficiency and operating conditions, even in a fairly homogeneous industry. Also, some firms may prefer to orient wage policy toward their local area, whereas others are interested in an industry orientation. Each employer is likely to have one or more problems that are perhaps unique with him, but for which he wishes recognition when the central policy is formulated. It is no easy task to develop an over-all wage policy that will be a rational reflection of the pooled judgment of the affected firms. Any common program must necessarily involve compromises that may be disappointing in varying degrees to some of the participating employers.

Enough has been said to indicate that employer wage policies cannot be based on a hunch or on intuition. Nor can an employer rely with confidence on a policy of day-to-day opportunism. Sound policy formation depends on possession of all the relevant facts and on a judicious effort at predicting and planning for future events. In this matter of anticipation a thorough knowledge of the needs of the union or unions involved is an indispensable element in the employer's calculations.

Some of the principal conclusions in this section on management wage policy may be summarized as follows:

1. Both large and small employers today are increasingly cognizant of the necessity for having a well-defined wage policy based on a hard core of facts rather than on guesswork.

2. Wage policy formation is the responsibility of top management in most firms. In multi-employer bargaining it is frequently the responsibility of a central body of associated employers.

3. Policy for the individual firm or the industry is necessarily dictated by operating conditions peculiar to the firm or the industry. Generalization is therefore extremely difficult. In all instances, however, it is essential for management to regard wages as a form of cost and to develop policies accordingly. Management is necessarily more concerned with cost-price-quantity relationships than is the union.

4. Under the influence of unionism, more and more companies are developing wage policy with an orientation toward the industry of which they are a part, rather than toward the area in which they are located. There is a continuing employer preference, however, for gearing company wage policy to the pattern of labor rates in their local area.

THE DETERMINANTS OF UNION WAGE POLICY

What are the chief determinants of union wage policy? How are union wage demands formulated, and by whom? Taking the latter question first, it is clear that in actuality (as distinguished from union democratic theory) formulation of wage demands is a function of union leadership. The amount of preliminary reciprocal action between leadership and rank-and-file in formation of such demands, however, varies considerably from one union to another. In situations in which the local union has considerable autonomy, as in the building trades unions, there is perhaps more direct participation and influence of the rank-and-file upon wage policy. In other instances wage policy for the union as a whole is developed exclusively by top international union officials, and the decision is then filtered down to the rank-and-file. The major industrial unions, notably in autos and steel, allow their locals a minimum of discretion on wage policy.

Even when considerable centralized control exists, union wage policy usually evolves after considerable direct or informal investigation of the needs and desires of local union memberships. Some unions have a fairly elaborate prenegotiation apparatus for sounding out the desires and feelings of the local membership on wages and other issues. In others, however, wage policy formation is strictly an oligarchic proposition.

In recent years unions have exhibited an increased tendency toward centralization of authority in wage policy formation. The control of local unions by the international union has steadily increased. There has also been a substantial degree of interunion centralization in the formation of wage policy. The CIO had for some years a central wage policy committee for coordinating the wage demands of its principal international unions. Although the AFL observed international union autonomy to a greater extent than the CIO, there was evidence of coordinated thinking in the older labor organization as well.

Now that the two federations have merged it seems likely that synchronization will increase on wage demands as well as on other union goals such as the shorter work week. The Industrial Union Department of the AFL-CIO, for example, provides on organizational home for coordinated policy efforts among international unions dealing with a common employer. Resolution No. 15 passed at the 1957 convention of the UAW lauded joint efforts of the UAW and the IAM in the aircraft industry, and pledged UAW support to efforts of the Industrial Union Department of the AFL-CIO "to bring together for joint programming the various international unions having contracts with the same companies." The same resolution cites coordinated effort already under way in the case of several companies dealing with two or more international unions. The unions involved "have been meeting to discuss and promote common objectives and thereby bring to bear the full weight of all the workers in such companies behind the goals to be achieved."[18]

[18] *UAW Convention Proceedings,* April 8, 1957.

The dynamics of union wage policy are substantially different from those of management in bargaining. Since unions are political institutions, there must be a degree of responsiveness and interaction between union leadership and rank-and-file that one does not find in most management organizations. This holds true even in the most autocratically administered unions.

Unions cannot operate on a chain-of-command basis as do many business firms. There is more two-way communication in the union hierarchy, notwithstanding the high degree of centralization in many unions. The actual formation of union wage policy in most instances, however, is the function of top leadership. Increasingly, this formulation occurs at the international union level. It is then transmitted for action to the member local unions.

Some factors responsible for increased centralization in policy formation on the union side are similar to those discussed in connection with company wage policy. As noted earlier, wage bargaining has become a technical, complicated process. It demands a degree of expertise and a fund of information not ordinarily available to local union leadership, and certainly not in the possession of the rank-and-file. The need for informed and responsible bargaining has been a powerful stimulant to increased centralization.

Also, certain major goals of union policy such as achievement of the standard rate and industry-wide stability in wage relationships cannot be achieved by uncoordinated local union bargaining. Centralized control is imperative in the interests of uniformity. The consequences to big unionism in this respect are not much different from the consequences to big business. Large-scale organization precludes the tolerance of too much pure democracy in the sense of complete rank-and-file participation.

In most unions, however, the rank-and-file have more of a voice on wage policy and wage demands than may at first appear to be true. For one thing, in most unions agreements negotiated with employers are subject to approval by the membership. In the large, highly centralized unions the right of ratification may actually be only the right to rubber stamp. Nevertheless, the authority to veto is always there and is occasionally exercised. Also, formulators of central union policy must meet the same kind of conflicting internal pressures as an employers' association in multi-employer bargaining. The central union wage policy must reflect as accurately as possible the needs of diverse elements in the union structure of locals. Many locals are powerful enough to enforce their demands without help from the international. Central policy formation must always consider the political necessities of keeping local unions in line.

What determines what unions will ask for in the way of wage demands? What are the real dynamics of union wage policy as distinguished from the rationalizations that might assume a prominent position in wage disputes arbitration? Full understanding of the real forces behind union wage demands depends upon an awareness of the principal implications of the basic fact that the union is a political institution operating in an economic environment.

Because the union is a political institution, such factors as the following are of critical importance in shaping wage demands:

1. The gains made by rival unions in the industry or in the area.
2. The relative strength of the employed and unemployed portions of the union membership.
3. The relative position of the unskilled and semiskilled members of the union, if it is an industrial union.
4. A pragmatic estimate of what is actually obtainable now, weighted with an estimate of what is obtainable in the future.
5. In a partially organized industry, the impact of alternative wage proposals upon the competitive position of the unionized portion of the industry.
6. Considerations of national political strategy that may have a bearing upon the economics of particular demands, such as using a drive for negotiated private pensions as an instrument for securing employer support for an expanded federal Social Security program.
7. An estimate of the employer's *disposition* to concede or to resist union demands.
8. An estimate of the employer's *capacity* to concede or to resist union demands.
9. An appraisal of the union's resources relative to the employer's known strength and disposition, coupled with an appraisal of the temper of the rank-and-file.

In industries in which wage-cost-price relationships are clear-cut and reasonably predictable, such as the ladies' garment industry, the union will give careful consideration to the probable employment effect of alternative wage demands. In some cases local labor market conditions will have a persuasive influence on union wage policy. In others the particular balance of labor demand and labor supply in a local market will have a negligible effect on union wage demands.

For example, the powerful craft unions in the building trades are likely to pay close attention to the labor pricing potential of a tight labor market, and to extract from contractors whatever the traffic will bear. Here the unions might take full advantage of a labor supply shortage to boost hourly rates beyond a "responsible" level. That is to say, they will ignore the ultimate employment effects in favor of a short-run gain.

On the other hand, many industrial unions are largely uninfluenced by local labor supply-demand ratios in determining their over-all wage policies. Their sights are set on the industry as a whole. As noted earlier, the increasing institutionalization of markets and the tendency toward consolidated bargaining structures have markedly reduced the importance of local labor market forces in determining the price of labor. As Kerr has pointed out, wage markets and job markets are frequently disjointed and go their separate ways.

One should not jump to the conclusion, however, that local labor demand and supply factors are no longer of any consequence in shaping either employer or union wage policies. As noted, many employers have a strong preference for area rates as a guide to wage policy. They are making increasing use of area wage surveys in preparation for wage bargaining. Furthermore, many industrial unions with master agreements covering many employers or many plants of a single company agree on the necessity for leaving the determination of occupational wage rates to the locals concerned. Although insisting on the necessity for negotiating over-all wage policy on a centralized basis, such unions often concede the desirability of tailoring occupational rate structures to the requirements of the local labor market picture.

Business unionism is essentially pragmatic in its approach. Consequently, the wage policies of particular unions (both craft and industrial) will be geared to the operating conditions of particular industries or plants when necessary.[19] Whenever this is the case, the influence of local labor demand and supply factors will be of considerable (though not necessarily determinative) importance. Since the union is a political institution, however, the force of comparison is always of tremendous significance in shaping the wage policies of particular unions.

Ross shows the comparison factor as one of the two most significant equalizing tendencies in collective wage determination. The second is the tendency toward consolidated bargaining structures. Among the more compelling factors tending to produce "orbits of coercive comparison" are centralized bargaining within the union, common ownership of establishments, governmental participation in wage determination, and rival union leadership.[20] Each of these factors produces a peculiar pressure for uniformity. Similarly, a pressure toward uniformity in occupational rates and uniformity in wage adjustment patterns develops from consolidated bargaining structures, either of the multi-employer type or multi-union type (an employer dealing with several unions jointly).

The need for institutional security is a powerful influence toward union

[19] For some excellent case studies, see A. Howard Myers, *Crisis Bargaining: Management-Union Relations in Marginal Situations* (Boston: Bureau of Business and Economic Research, Northeastern University, 1957.)

[20] Arthur Ross, *op. cit.*, pp. 45–75.

acceptance of multi-union or multi-employer bargaining. Through multi-union bargaining, as Ross points out, unions "protect themselves against participating in the establishment of inequities. They eliminate the possibility of making what appears to be a satisfactory settlement, and then witnessing another union making a better settlement which renders their own embarrassing or untenable." Similarly, the chief advantage of multi-employer bargaining to the union lies in the institutional security it provides against "the apathy of workers, the hostility of employers, and the inroads of rival organizations."[21]

As already noted, employers appraise their wage structures and wage policies in comparison with those of other firms in their industry or area. Unions, however, usually outdo employers in their interest in comparisons. It is difficult to sell a union's rank-and-file on foregoing a general wage increase or settling for, say, a 5 per cent increase if there is knowledge that other unions are securing 10 per cent general increases. *The union leader is under pressure to deliver at least the average increase being obtained elsewhere.*

Union wage policy thus cannot be guided by purely economic considerations. The compulsion to match gains of other unions is one that cannot be ignored. The rank-and-file is neither informed about, nor interested in, distinguishing features which might make a 10 per cent increase logical in one industry and no increase logical in another. Since they are interested in wages as income, their concern about an employer's competitive position is not as great as perhaps it should be. Furthermore, there is a tendency to have virtually unbounded faith in an employer's capacity to absorb in some manner a succession of wage increments.

It is here that the test of trade union leadership emerges in severe fashion. It has been assumed that a sheeplike rank-and-file is led down a suicidal path of high wage policy by an unscrupulous or uninformed trade union leadership. More frequently the opposite is true. Trade union leaders have often been in the uncomfortable position of enlightening a militant rank-and-file as to why a desired wage adjustment cannot be achieved.

The wartime wage stabilization program provided an outstanding illustration of union leadership having to restrain the rank-and-file in the formulation of wage and other demands. It was the responsibility of trade union leaders during World War II to sell the membership on the importance of wage stabilization. This was done in exemplary fashion by most union leaders, assisted by NWLB policy on approving fringe benefits.

In the postwar inflation period, union leaders similarly were under terrific rank-and-file pressure to secure general wage increases. In not a few instances the demands of the membership were impossible to attain. When

[21] *Ibid*, p. 71.

this was the case, again the union leader had to assume the unpopular role of a curber rather than a stimulator of aggressive action.

Many union leaders are becoming more keenly aware of the external significance of the wage bargain. They are better able than the membership to appreciate the cumulative impact of a series of separate wage bargains. In an inflationary period the membership is likely to be concerned with only one issue—the rising cost of living. They are not going to be impressed with the need for a responsible wage policy when they see their purchasing power being whittled away by mounting prices of consumer goods.

It is worth noting that the succession of postwar rounds of across-the-board wage increases was blunted somewhat in 1949 and early in 1950 by an intensified drive for negotiated pension plans. The new focus was only partially due to intrinsic interest in pensions. Another explanation lay in the recognition by trade union leadership of the relative difficulty of obtaining another round of wage increases. Since union leaders recognized the need to deliver something, their pension drive may be viewed as a statesmanlike diversion of rank-and-file pressure.

Union leaders cannot be too statesmanlike. How quickly the picture can change was illustrated by the impact of the Korean action and increased U.S. mobilization. As the cost of living rose rapidly, and as the probability of wage and price controls increased, the emphasis on pensions was dwarfed by the tremendous rank-and-file pressure for general wage increases to match cost-of-living increases. In the main, employer resistance to such pressure was either weak or nonexistent. As a result, in the latter half of 1950 a remarkable number of general increases were negotiated. In this experience, the force of the comparison factor clearly outweighed any considerations of private responsibility.[22]

The principal conclusions on union wage policy may be summarized as follows:

1. The formation of wage policy in a union is necessarily a leadership function. Although there may be a more direct reciprocal relationship between union leaders and members than there is with a corporation and its stockholders, the rank-and-file are dependent on leadership for making equitable and pragmatic decisions on wage policy.

2. Union wage policy is influenced most strongly by the standard of comparison—the gains made by rival unions. The union leader must also take account of conflicts of interest within his own union's membership.

[22] A more recent illustration is afforded by the generally cold and hostile reception accorded to Richard Gray's suggestion at the 1957 AFL-CIO convention. Gray, head of the federation's Building Trades Department, proposed that unions consider foregoing wage demands in 1958 as a contribution to the fight against rising unemployment and rising prices and costs. He stood virtually alone among his brothers in taking this position.

Thus the function of determining wage policy for a union is primarily a *political* one of reconciling and accommodating a series of external and internal pressures from employers, from other unions, from the government, and from conflicting interests within the union.

3. Local labor market factors are likely to be a less persuasive influence upon unions than upon employers, except when the comparison element is of critical local importance. With both employers and unions, however, the tendency toward increasing centralization and institutionalization of wage determination functions is contributing to the reduced importance of local labor supply and demand factors.

STANDARDS FOR EVALUATING JOINT DECISION-MAKING ON WAGE LEVEL CHANGES

When a union seeks a general increase of fifteen cents per hour for all employees of a particular concern and the employer offers eight cents per hour, and there ensues a two-month strike at the conclusion of which a wage increase of ten cents per hour is put into effect, on what basis is the rightness or wrongness of such an increase to be evaluated? What criteria should be applied to measure the validity of this wage bargain? If the Carpenters' union negotiates a twenty-cent increase for Boston journeymen and at the same time the Des Moines Carpenters' wages are raised ten cents per hour, do we have any valid basis for saying that the Boston increase is "too high" or the Des Moines increase "too low"? If the UAW negotiates a 3 per cent annual improvement factor increase amounting to approximately six cents per hour per employee on the average, plus an SUB fund averaging five cents per hour per employee, is this a greater or lesser increase in "wages" than a Teamster local contract calling for nine cents across the board?

Do we have any objective criteria by which the economic wisdom of particular wage level changes can be measured or tested? The writer suggests that we do not. There is no *scientific* basis for concluding that particular wage decisions are right or wrong. The field of collective wage determination abounds in rationalizations and value judgments. Both union leaders and employers have become skilled in the art of rationalizing whatever decisions they make. Prior to wage negotiations, the particular union is always "behind" some desired point. After negotiations, whatever the size of the increase, a "victory" has been won and the workers are "better off" than they were. Prior to negotiations, employers are always "hard-pressed" to find room for an increase and sometimes say that an increase would "drive us to the wall." After negotiations, whatever the size of the increase, business usually goes on and dire predictions are forgotten.

A value judgment of a particular wage level adjustment depends on the assumptions made. The blunt fact remains that the principal standard for measuring a successful wage bargain is *the standard of mutual acceptability*. This may sound like a cynical basis for judgment. Successful bargains, as thus defined, frequently depart radically from the normative concepts of the economists. Nevertheless, the validity of a private bargain *to the parties* is determined by their respective standards of acceptability and workability. A theoretically responsible bargain which is not a workable one for either or both parties is necessarily an unacceptable bargain. A workable bargain is one that permits the parties to live together for the period of the contract on a relatively harmonious pattern of accommodation. Its terms may or may not be consonant with what the economist might consider economically sound criteria.

The seven principal criteria usually cited by employers and union leaders in justifying their respective claims in wage negotiations are:[23]

1. The minimum necessities of the workers.
2. Changes in the cost of living.
3. The maintenance of take-home pay in the face of reduction in hours.
4. Changes in the productivity of labor.
5. The ability (or inability) of the employer to pay.
6. The alleged effect of higher or lower wages upon consumer purchasing power and employment.
7. The wages paid in other industries or places.

Of these seven, the first and third are used only by unions and the remaining five are used by both employers and unions when it suits their respective purposes. It is evident from the previous discussion that criteria 2, 5, and 7 have the greatest practical relevance to the actual determinants of employer and union wage policy.

These criteria are seldom employed with consistency or objectivity by employers and unions. Their use is conditioned by particular economic circumstances. As economic circumstances change, the choice and use of criteria will change. Both employers and unions employ these criteria as tools or weapons. They function as more or less plausible rationales for wage decisions already determined by more complex and subjective pressures.

This is not to question the good faith of either unions or management. It is essential to keep in mind, however, that most of the criteria are two-edged weapons. Cost of living is a useful lever for union wage demands in a period of rising prices and high employment. But it is rejected

[23] Sumner H. Slichter, *Basic Criteria in Wage Negotiations* (Chicago: Chicago Association of Commerce and Industry, 1947.)

promptly by labor as an invalid test during the downswing. Similarly, inability to pay is pleaded by companies when profit expectancies are dim. When past profits and future expectations are encouraging, however, management will frequently dispute the relevancy of its ability to pay as an argument in wage determination.

Little progress has been made in developing a normative concept of what constitutes a fair wage *per se*. There is not even a consensus as to the true function of a wage.

If we make our generalizations broad enough, we can find a substantial area of agreement on wage policy criteria. For example, virtually everyone subscribes to the "equal pay for equal work" proposition. However, reasonable men differ as to whether particular demands for correction of alleged intraplant occupational rate inequities implement or violate the equal pay for equal work principle. One of the most frequent sources of grievances in contemporary contract administration is the typical dispute as to whether Job *X* should pay the same as Job *Y*, or whether the present rate differential is appropriate. Reasonable argument can also develop over the manner of distributing a negotiated general increase among various occupations in order to correct alleged inequities. These matters are discussed in detail in the following chapter.

Virtually all parties would concede that employees should be entitled to a future expectation of an improvement in their real wage position as well as their monetary wage, and that such an improvement depends on productivity gains. There is often sharp disagreement between union and management, however, as to how the gains from increased productivity are to be allocated and whether wage increases should anticipate or follow increased productivity.

Similarly, both employers and unions would agree in general that both industry rates and area rates are relevant to an appraisal of the merits of particular wage decisions. They often disagree sharply, however, in the emphasis attached to one criterion or the other.

If a union is negotiating with a marginal employer who has proved to the union's satisfaction that he cannot follow the industry pattern without going out of business, should the union make whatever concessions may be necessary to keep this firm going and its members employed? Generalizing in the abstract, most employers and union leaders would probably agree to two basic propositions covering such a situation. One is that unions should forego wage demands where genuine inability to pay exists and loss of jobs is certain. The second proposition is that no employer has a right to stay in business when his only way of doing so is by paying what all would agree are "substandard" wages. In terms of a particular situation sharp disagreement might exist as to which of the two general propositions properly applies to the concrete case. Numerous recent illustrations can be found, notably in the textile industry, of union concessions to marginal firms in "crisis bargaining" situations.[24]

Much progress can be made toward greater mutual acceptability of wage bargains where the company and union can agree on the fundamental purposes of their wage policy, and can agree in particular negotiations on the relevant criteria. As George Taylor has pointed out, selection of relevant criteria is often tantamount to deciding what wages will be paid.[25] The pioneer two-year (1948-1950) and five-year (1950-1955) contracts between General Motors and the United Automobile Workers illustrate Taylor's point. Once the parties had agreed on two essential criteria relevant to the wage issue, the terms of the bargain developed naturally. The essential features of the original GM-UAW formula were: (1) agreement that wage rates should be adjusted quarterly to compensate for changes in the cost of living, with no upper limit but with a floor on reductions; and (2) agreement that the employees' real wage position should be bettered by providing for an annual improvement factor increase related to the average annual rate of increase in physical productivity per man-hour for the economy as a whole.

The same basic formula was renewed in the 1955-1958 and 1958-1961 GM-UAW contracts, and in the years since 1950 has been widely copied in other union-management relationships.[26]

The escalator clause portion of the formula has had its ups and downs in popularity in recent years, depending in large measure on the short-run vagaries of the business cycle. Some unions and companies have borrowed the annual improvement factor idea from GM and UAW without the escalator portion. Others have included an escalator clause but have stuck to conventional bargaining on general wage increases. Still others have combined long-term contracts with scheduled wage adjustments bearing no rational relationship to productivity increase considerations.

Economists are split in their evaluation of the merits of escalator adjust-

[24] See A. Howard Myers, *op. cit.* See also Irwin L. Herrnstadt, "The Reactions of Three Local Unions to Economic Adversity," *Journal of Political Economy*, LXII (October, 1954), 425–39.

[25] George W. Taylor, "Criteria in the Wage Bargain," *New York University First Annual Conference on Labor, Proceedings* (Albany: Matthew Bender & Co., 1948), pp. 65–88.

[26] It is somewhat surprising in view of the growth of long-term contracts in recent years that more empirical analyses have not been forthcoming. For penetrating observations on both administrative aspects and economic effects of long-term contracts, consult the chapters by Jack Stieber and Joseph Garbarino respectively in Harold W. Davey, Howard S. Kaltenborn, and Stanley H. Ruttenberg, eds., *New Dimensions in Collective Bargaining* (New York; Harper & Brothers, 1959.)

ments. Few economists, however, quarrel with the logic of the annual improvement factor rationale, stated contractually as follows:

> The annual improvement factor provided herein recognizes that a continuing improvement in the standard of living of employes depends upon technological progress, better tools, methods, processes and equipment, and a cooperative attitude on the part of all parties in such progress. It further recognizes the principle that to produce more with the same amount of effort is a sound economic and social objective.

From an economist's standpoint, however, one discordant note must be struck before the improvement factor rationale is embraced wholeheartedly. As Garbarino has recently pointed out,[27] the point at which the strict application of the formula has broken down has been at the time of contract negotiations. The theory of productivity wage adjustments has been couched usually in terms of *wages alone*. The pure theory requires that for the economy as a whole all increases in income should be contained within the limits set by increasing productivity if inflation is to be avoided. Yet at every negotiation since 1948 UAW bargaining unit personnel have been accorded other benefits such as pension plans, SUB plans, higher increases for skilled classifications, and so on. This is not to say that UAW pacts in the automobile industry have been "inflationary" since it is probable that productivity increases in that industry have been considerably in excess of the national average.

In the next chapter we turn to a consideration of the problem of relative wage rates, i.e., structural wage problems.

SELECTED BIBLIOGRAPHY

(See also bibliography for Chapters 11 and 12.)

Backman, Jules, "Wage Productivity Comparisons," *Industrial and Labor Relations Review*, VIII (October, 1954) 59–67.

Bakke, E. W. and others, *Labor Mobility and Economic Opportunity*. New York: John Wiley & Sons, Inc., 1954

Bronfenbrenner, Martin, "The Incidence of Collective Bargaining," *American Economic Review*, XLIV (May, 1954) 293–307.

———, "The Incidence of Collective Bargaining Once More," *Southern Economic Journal*, XXIV (April, 1958) 398–406.

———, Potential Monopsony in Labor Markets," *Industrial and Labor Relations Review*, IX (July, 1956) 577–88.

Coppe, John A., "On the Meaning of Monopoly Power in Labor Relations," *Labor Law Journal*, VII (May, 1956) 261–64, 296–98.

[27] See Joseph Garbarino, "The Economic Significance of Automatic Wage Adjustments," in Davey, Kaltenborn, and Ruttenberg, *ibid.*

Douty, Harry M., "Post-War Wage Bargaining in the U. S.," *Economica*, XXIII (November, 1956) 315–27.

Dunlop, John T., ed., *The Theory of Wage Determination*, 1954 Proceedings, International Economic Association. New York: St. Martin's Press, 1957.

Fellner, William, *Competition Among the Few: Oligopoly and Similar Market Structures*. New York: Alfred A. Knopf, Inc., 1949.

Gitlow, A. L., "Wages and the Allocation of Employment," *Southern Economic Journal*, XXI (July, 1954) 62–83.

Herrnstadt, Irwin L., "The Reaction of Three Local Unions to Economic Adversity," *Journal of Political Economy*, LXII (October, 1954) 425–39.

Hicks, J. R., *The Theory of Wages*. New York: The Macmillan Co., 1932.

Kerr, Clark, "Labor Markets: Their Character and Consequences," *Proceedings of the Second Annual Meeting, Industrial Relations Research Association*. Champaign: IRRA, 1950, pp. 69–85.

———, "Trade-Unionism and Distributive Shares," *American Economic Review*, XLIV (May, 1954) 279–92.

Lester, Richard A. and Edward A. Robie, *Wages under National and Regional Collective Bargaining: Experience in 7 Industries*. Princeton: Industrial Relations Section, 1946.

———, *Company Wage Policies*. Princeton: Industrial Relations Section, 1948.

Levinson, Harold M., "Collective Bargaining and Income Distribution," *American Economic Review*, XLIV (May, 1954) 310–21.

———, *Unionism, Wage Trends and Income Distribution*. Ann Arbor: University of Michigan Press, 1951.

Marshall, Howard D., "Unions and Labor Mobility," *Labor Law Journal*, VII (February, 1956) 83–97.

Melman, Seymour, *Dynamic Factors in Industrial Productivity*. New York: John Wiley & Sons, Inc., 1956.

Myers, Charles A., "Trade Unions as Wage Decision-Making Units," *Journal of Personnel Administration and Industrial Relations*, II (Summer, 1955) 39–48.

Palmer, Gladys L., *Labor Mobility in Six Cities*. New York: Social Science Research Council, 1954.

———, *Philadelphia Workers in a Changing Economy*. Philadelphia: University of Pennsylvania Press, 1956.

Peterson, John M., "Employment Effects of Minimum Wages, 1938–50," *Journal of Political Economy*, LXV (October, 1957) 412–30.

Pierson, Frank C., *Community Wage Patterns*. Berkeley and Los Angeles: University of California Press, 1953.

Rees, Albert, "Union Wage Policies," in *Interpreting the Labor Movement*, Industrial Relations Research Association Publication No. 9. Champaign: IRRA, 1952, pp. 130–48.

Reynolds, Lloyd G., "Toward a Short-Run Theory of Wages," *American Economic Review*, XXXVIII (June, 1948) 287–308.

Ross, Arthur, *Trade Union Wage Policy*. Berkeley: University of California Press, 1948.

Rothschild, K. W., *The Theory of Wages.* New York: The Macmillan Co., 1954.

Rottenberg, Simon, "Wage Effects in the Theory of the Labor Movement," *Journal of Political Economy*, LXI (August, 1953) 346–52.

Segal, Martin, "Interrelationship of Wages under Joint Demand: The Case of the Fall River Textile Workers," *Quarterly Journal of Economics*, LXX (August, 1956) 464–77.

Shultz, George P., *Pressures on Wage Decisions.* New York: John Wiley & Sons, Inc., 1951.

——— and C. A. Myers, "Union Wage Decisions and Employment," *American Economic Review*, XL (June, 1950) 362–81.

Sibson, Robert E., "The Logic of Annual Improvement Wage Increases," *Labor Law Journal*, V (October, 1954) 708–16.

———, "Wage Comparisons in Bargaining," *Labor Law Journal*, IV (June, 1953) 423–32.

Slichter, Sumner H., *Basic Criteria in Wage Negotiations.* Chicago: Chicago Association of Commerce and Industry, 1947.

Stevens, Carl M., "Regarding the Determinants of Union Wage Policy," *Review of Economics and Statistics*, XXXV (August, 1953) 221–28.

Taylor, George W., "Criteria in the Wage Bargain," *Proceedings, New York University First Annual Conference on Labor.* Albany: Matthew Bender & Co., 1948, pp. 65–88.

——— and Frank C. Pierson, *New Concepts in Wage Determination.* New York: McGraw-Hill Book Co., Inc., 1957.

Turnbull, John G. and Lloyd Ulman, "An Economic Appraisal of Collective Bargaining," *Labor Law Journal*, IV (February, 1953) 125–29.

Weldon, J. D., "Economic Effects of Collective Bargaining," *Industrial and Labor Relations Review*, VI (July, 1953) 570–78.

Williams, Gertrude, "The Myth of 'Fair' Wages," *Economic Journal*, LXVI December, 1956) 621–34.

Wiseman, Sylvia, "Wage Criteria for Collective Bargaining," *Industrial and Labor Relations Review*, IX (January, 1956) 252-67.

Wootton, Barbara, *The Social Foundations of Wage Policy.* New York: W. W. Norton & Co., Inc., 1955.

Woytinsky, W. S. and Associates, *Employment and Wages in the United States.* New York: Twentieth Century Fund, 1953.

Internal and external wage structures

In this chapter we are concerned with the problem of relative wage rates and their determinants. We are interested in the structure of occupational rates from both an internal viewpoint (i.e., the wage rate hierarchy within a particular firm) and an external viewpoint (i.e., intra-industry, interindustry, and geographical differentials in wage rates and wage levels).

SCOPE OF STRUCTURAL WAGE PROBLEMS

More specifically, we are concerned with such questions as to whether collective bargaining has facilitated or impeded the task of developing and maintaining a rational structure of occupational rates within unionized firms. How has collective bargaining affected personal differentials and occupational differentials within particular firms? After exploring problems in rationalization of the wage structure of a particular enterprise, we shall turn to external structural problems and attempt to draw conclusions as to the probable impact of collective bargaining on intra-industry, interindustry, and geographical differentials.

WAGE RATIONALIZATION IN THE INDIVIDUAL FIRM

A prime concern of modern management is the development and maintenance of a rational wage structure of occupational job rates. The problem of wage rationalization is a continuous one for most business enterprises. It is necessarily a dynamic problem because of the rapid changes in job content resulting from technological improvements and the introduction of new job operations. Constant attention is thus required to the internal relationships among job rates for the various occupational classifications in the modern firm.

Developing an equitable hierarchy of job rates is a task faced by all business concerns. It is chiefly a problem of the larger business units. There appears to be a rather direct relationship between the size of the firm and the scope for inequities among job rates. In smaller firms there are usually fewer distinct job classifications and therefore less opportunity for inequalities in pay to develop without attention being drawn to them quickly.

As noted in the preceding chapter, the negotiation of across-the-board increases in wage rates is a politico-economic phenomenon. In spite of the increasing factualization of the bargaining process with greater reliance on objective data, the negotiation of general increases is likely to be determined on "unscientific" grounds. Whether an increase is granted or a general decrease effected will depend essentially on the status of the company's finances, the power relationships between the parties, and the internal and external pressures operating upon the union leadership.

In attempting to develop an equitable structure of job rates, the possibility of a more objective approach is increased. An intelligent employer appreciates the fact that serious inequalities among job rates are a fertile source of employee grievances. Although he may be interested in keeping his labor costs as low as possible, he will be concerned about developing a balanced internal structure of wage rates. In this respect the employer's motivation coincides with the standard union objective of equal pay for equal work. Management and the union have a common objective here, even though there may be serious conflict as to how to operate a program to correct intraplant inequities.

THE USES OF JOB EVALUATON

The techniques of job evaluation have had increasingly greater appeal to management in recent years as the most satisfactory method of solving the problem of structural inequities. During World War II there was a substantial increase in the number of firms installing and using job analysis and job evaluation systems. In part, the wartime popularity of these methods of scientific wage determination can be attributed to their usefulness as a way of easing the rigors of the wage stabilization program. Continuing interest in these techniques indicates that a substantial segment of employers is convinced that they have merit as methods of bringing order out of chaos among occupational rates.

Unions often oppose job evaluation vigorously. Their opposition has considerable historical justification. In the past job evaluation has sometimes been used as a sophisticated cover-up for a rate-cutting program. In World War II the rationale was exactly the opposite. Job evaluation was used then to boost occupational wage rates. This experience has convinced many unions that it is better to attempt to solve inequity problems by old-fashioned negotiation than by the more impersonal approach of job evaluation, which many workers do not understand and hence fear.

Union opposition frequently has a deeper basis than simple mistrust of management intentions. The union may have difficult problems in reconciling the conflicting internal pressures of a heterogeneous membership. If it is faced with the ticklish task of balancing the interests of skilled and unskilled workers, job evaluation might well upset the union's control over its rank-and-file. Some unions find themselves in the position of condoning existing inequities among job rates because of political necessity. They could not stand an uncompromising application of their own slogan of equal pay for equal work. To do so in some instances would wreck the tenuous balance of political forces within the union.

Many of the larger industrial unions with a more or less polyglot membership face this problem constantly. They prefer to settle such inequities by negotiation and compromise, rather than by more impersonal methods. Craft unions oppose job evaluation out of fear that it may be used with a program to dilute job skills and thus lower existing rates.

In recent years union opposition to job evaluation appears to be lessening considerably. In fact, some unions that formerly fought the introduction of job evaluation have swung around to full acceptance of the technique. They use it as a basis for processing classification grievances with considerable vigor. The writer knows of a number of situations where job descriptions pursuant to job evaluation have been made part of the basic contract, and where a good share of the daily grievance business comes from so-called job slotting disputes as to whether a particular set of job duties are properly classified as Assembler *B* or Assembler *C*, and so forth. Many such disputes reach arbitration under these circumstances where management has taken the administrative initiative in classifying a particular job and the union is attempting to sustain the burden of proving that the classification is improper.

To give the reader a more concrete picture, set forth below is an arbitration case on a classification issue in a relationship where the union has accepted a highly technical management approach to job evaluation and classification, and has sought to utilize the grievance procedure for cases wherein it has felt management to be in error in applying its techniques. After the reader has made his own decision on the following case, he may find out the writer's decision by turning to the Appendix.

CHECKING THE CHECK CHART

Preliminary Recital:

Under the new three-year contract effective August 8, 19—, the Company is using a Machining Check Chart as a means of evaluating and slotting various jobs. The dispute here arises over differing interpretations of the meaning of the Check Chart as applied to Employee *J*'s duties on Operation 90 on Part AM–2010. The dispute concerns whether work on Operation 90 should be regarded as Semi-Automatic Lathe Operator "A" Grade F or as Semi-Automatic Lathe Operator "B" in Labor Grade E....

Essential Facts:

The grievance was initially filed on August 17, 19— protesting that *J* should be classed as a "B" operator rather than a "C", as was then the case. On August 24, 19—, the Company introduced a special snap gage to insure holding tolerance on the operation. In the Company's view, the adding of this gage gave the operation in question a Check Chart rating of ten points, placing it in the "B" Lathe Operator category. Under the Union's interpretation, the Check Chart gives this operation 18 points, placing it in the "A" Lathe Operator category.

Both parties rely upon the Check Chart to sustain their respective positions. Specifically, the Union alleges a violation of Article XVII, Section 8 of the contract and the Machining Check Chart of the master job description book. The Union requests the arbitrator to rule that *J* should be classified under the contract as Semi-Automatic Lathe Operator "A" and be made whole for any loss in pay. Article XVII, Section 8 reads as follows:

> "A schedule of Occupational Rates for incentive occupations marked Exhibit 'B' is attached hereto and made a part hereof. The classifications of the incentive occupations and their occupational rates shall constitute the basis for the computation of earnings under the Company's Standard Hour Incentive Plan."

The Company's Machining Check Chart is based on "three variables which are necessary requirements in the performance of machining operations." These three variables are set forth below:

"1. The number of different types of machining details performed on a part during a particular operation.
2. The number of different very difficult tolerances to be maintained on a part during a particular operation.

3. The number of different tools used in the operation of a machine in order to machine a part during a particular operation."

The Check Chart definitions of the foregoing three variables are reproduced below:

"*Number of Different Types of Details*

Each different type of machining detail performed by a machine actuated tool, within its machine cycle, is to be counted as only one detail irrespective of the number of times it may occur. When more than one detail is accomplished with the same tool, the total number of details performed is to be counted.

"The following is a partial list of details commonly found in machining operations:

Ream	Grind	Chamfer	Form
Bore	Mill	Tap	Spin
Countersink	Face	Turn	Roll
Drill (Inc. Core Drill)	Counterbore	Knurl	Form Radius
	Center	Serrate	

"*Number of Different Very Difficult Tolerances*

Each very difficult tolerance performed by a machine actuated tool, within its machine cycle, is to be counted as only one very difficult tolerance irrespective of the number of times it may occur. A complete list of very difficult tolerances is given in Exhibit 'A'.

"*Number of Different Tools*

Each different tool used is to be counted as only one tool irrespective of the number of times it is used or the number of details it may perform within the machine cycle. A list of tools for which allowances are to be made is given in Exhibit 'B'."

The Check Chart provides a method of scoring each operation for purposes of slotting the work in question. On the particular operation in question, both parties agree that three different machining details, one very difficult tolerance, and five different tools are involved. However, the Union maintains that the machine goes through two complete machine cycles on this operation and therefore urges that the operation must be scored as six machining details, one tolerance, and ten tools. The tolerance is counted only once because it is a width tolerance and the operator holds it on the machine's second pass rather than on the first.

Under the Union's interpretation of the Check Chart, this operation would be scored as 18 points. Under the Company's interpretation, the operation is scored as 10 points. Operations ranging from 9 to 13 points are slotted in the "B" classification and those 14 points and above are slotted as "A" jobs.

The three different machining details on the operation in question are turning, facing, and chamfering. The operation sequence calls for the operator to set up the machine, run the pieces through on one side, remove them and reverse them, and then run them through on the other side. No change in the set-up, machining details or tools is involved.

The Issue:

The sole issue for determination is whether the Company had violated the contract in slotting work on Operation 90, Part AM-2010 as belonging to the Semi-Automatic Lathe Operator "B" classification.

Contentions of the Union:

The Union contends that under a proper interpretation of the Company's own Check Chart the work in question is undoubtedly "A" work. There can be no dispute that on this operation the machine goes through two complete cycles, says the Union. Therefore, it is proper under the chart to multiply the number of details and the number of tools by two in arriving at the proper point score for the operation under the Check Chart formula.

In the Union's view, the phrase "within its machine cycle" applying to details, tolerances and tools is clear and unambiguous. While each different machine detail, tolerance, or tool is only counted once regardless of the number of times it occurs within a particular machine cycle, it must be counted twice when the machine goes through two complete machine cycles as it does in the instant case. The language of the Company's own chart clearly sustains the position now urged by the Union. Furthermore, this operation was paid at the "A" rate under the old contract and should continue to be so paid under the new contract.

For the foregoing reasons, the Union urges that a proper scoring of Operation 90 is 18 points under the Check Chart, bringing this operation within the "A" point range.

Contentions of the Company:

The Company maintains that the Union's interpretation, if adopted, would completely distort a well-established method for arriving at equitable occupational rates for different operations. The Union is attempting to use an isolated phrase out of context as a means of distorting or destroying the procedure for evaluating various operations objectively in terms of differing degrees of skill, responsibility, job knowledge, etc.

Although the Check Chart itself is comparatively new, says the Company, its objective is the same as that of earlier methods of arriving at appropriate rates for various operations. The Check Chart is a more precise and more objective method of evaluating work than the prior method of comparing job descriptions for incentive occupations.

The phrase "within its machine cycle" relied on by the Union could just as well have been left out so far as the obvious purpose of the Check Chart is concerned. That purpose is to inventory the number of *different* machining details involved in a particular operation, the number of *different* very difficult tolerances the operator is required to hold in a particular operation, and the number of *different* machine tools the operator is required to use in a particular operation.

The Check Chart's stress on *different* details, tolerances, and tools—no matter how many times a particular one occurs on a particular operation—

is the key to this case and to the manifest purpose of the chart. The objective is to evaluate fairly the degree of skill, responsibility, job knowledge, etc., required to perform a particular operation.

Obviously, it makes no difference to the amount of skill required of the operator as to how many times a particular tool cuts or how many times a particular machine detail is performed. Occupational rates are set in terms of the relative skill and knowledge required from the operator on a particular operation.

If this principle is kept firmly in mind, it is clear that "machine cycle" can have no meaning other than the work or the period through which the machine goes to do the particular operation on which the rate is being set. That is, the term machine cycle can only refer to the total process the machine goes through in making the piece on this particular operation. What the Union is attempting here is to relate occupational rates to what the machine does rather than what the operator does.

Mr. H, Time Study Supervisor, testified that there are many jobs in the plant where a particular machining detail or tool is used several times in identical fashion on a particular operation. His testimony was undisputed that never in the past has an identical detail performed twice been considered as *two* details in evaluating the job for occupational rate purposes.

The Union's interpretation would require multiplying by two whenever the same work is performed on two sides of a piece. Since there are many such jobs in the plant, under the Union's theory everybody would be an "A" operator. A man on an operation properly scored at 7 points (doubled to 14) would be an "A" operator, whereas a man on a difficult job properly scored at 15 points would also be an "A". The results would be absurd and provide no basis for discriminating between difficult and comparatively simple operations.

The Company does not deny that this particular operation was paid at an "A" rate under the old contract. However, says the Company, there were only two Lathe Operator classifications under the former contract, "A" and "B". The new contract provides for six lathe classifications and permits a more careful distinction among skills required for the various operations to eliminate intraplant inequities that admittedly existed under the old contract.

For the foregoing reasons, the Company submits that the work in question is properly classified as Semi-Automatic Lathe Operator "B" and urges the denial of the grievance.

DETERMINANTS OF EFFECTIVE JOB EVALUATION

There are almost as many types of job evaluation as there are industrial engineering and management consulting firms offering such services to management. Each firm of experts seems to have its own patented twist on basic techniques. Some variant of the point evaluation method appears to be the most widely used today. All job evaluation systems have the following basic steps in common:

1. Preparation of complete job descriptions for all jobs in the plant.
2. Agreement on a list of factors relevant to the rating of all jobs, such as: (a) degree and type of skill required; (b) effort required; (c) responsibility for materials and equipment and safety of others; (d) working conditions surrounding the job; (e) previous training or experience required.
3. An evaluation of all jobs after assigning weights to the various elemental factors common to all.
4. A ranking of all jobs in terms of the evaluation.

A job evaluation expert is not properly concerned with monetary values at all. His concern is with the development of accurate and complete job descriptions for all distinct operations in the plant and with the objective evaluation of these jobs to develop an equitable job hierarchy. Furthermore, he is concerned with rating the job, not the man on the job. Assignment of monetary values *follows* the job evaluation.

Experience indicates that the success or failure of job evaluation depends not so much on the type of plan used as upon the manner of its introduction and administration. Many plans that seemed excellent from a technical standpoint have failed in execution because of improper or insufficient attention to the human aspects of the program.

Whatever the plan, it is imperative that it be developed and introduced with great care, that it have top management's full approval, and that the union involved accept the relationship between the job evaluation plan and wage setting. Of particular importance are the procedures for implementing a job evaluation plan in daily administration. There must be a clear understanding of the procedure to be followed in handling new and changed jobs under the plan. Finally, it is of crucial importance that the plan be sufficiently flexible in administration to take account of "illogical" employee reactions to a "logical" rate structure. Certain intraplant rate differentials, for example, may not jibe with the logic of the job evaluation plan's occupational hierarchy. If these differentials have been in existence for many years, it may not be wise to attempt to force them to conform to the plan's logic on an overnight basis.

The AFL-CIO Research Department has published some advice to unions as to how to make sure that job evaluation plans do not conflict with basic union objectives.[1] This article provides valuable insight into union thinking on the relationship of job evaluation to the collective bargaining function. The general injunction running through the article is a warning against acceptance of management findings as "scientific." The unions are advised to guard the right to challenge and bargain about rates

[1] "Job Evaluation Plans," *AFL-CIO Collective Bargaining Report*, II (June, 1957), 33–39.

resulting from the application of a job evaluation plan. The article is skeptical about the claimed objectivity of job evaluation and cautions about the subjective elements in assigning weights to the various factors. In general, the belief is reflected that bargained wages are preferable to evaluated wages. The unions are cautioned about the temptation to succumb to the management theme that the process is so scientific that its subject matter can safely be removed from the bargaining table.

As this AFL-CIO article makes clear, there is no one official union position toward job evaluation. Some unions continue to oppose job evaluation to the point where it is fruitless for an employer to attempt its introduction. Other unions have accepted it and attempted to use it as a tool of contract administration for processing grievances as to proper slotting. In still other situations genuine joint job evaluation has been conducted with considerable success. One of the more celebrated efforts at joint evaluation was the inequity correction program in basic steel some years ago.[2] Job evaluation appears to be gaining favor with employers (and an increasing number of unions) as an effective approach to the problem of correcting intraplant inequities in occupational rates. It is not, however, the only means for correcting inequities.

OTHER APPROACHES TO THE PROBLEM OF CORRECTING INTRAPLANT INEQUITIES

Assuming that job evaluation, for one reason or another, cannot be used either on a unilateral employer basis, on a consultative basis, or on a joint participation basis, what other approaches can be taken to the problem of eliminating wage inequities under collective bargaining?

One rather common short-cut approach involves reaching mutual agreement on job descriptions and wage rates for a number of key jobs that will serve as benchmarks. The parties then rank or cluster the rest of the jobs in terms of their relative importance measured against these pilot or benchmark jobs. If both management and union negotiators are sincere and well-informed, this approach to the inequities problem can be both fruitful and time-saving. If good faith is absent, however, or if the matter is in the hands of men who are not thoroughly acquainted with all the jobs involved, the process can scarcely rise above the level of orthodox political jockeying.

Assuming that a plant has a fairly large number of distinct job classifications running the gamut from unskilled to highly skilled, the approach suggested involves selection of several key jobs or representative jobs. Labor grades can be developed through such a method. If this is done

[2] See Robert Tilove, *Collective Bargaining in the Steel Industry* (Philadelphia: University of Pennsylvania Press, 1947). See also Ernest Dale, *Greater Productivity Through Labor-Management Cooperation*, AMA Research Report No. 14 (New York: American Management Association, 1949), pp. 33–40.

carefully on the basis of complete information, the rest of the jobs in the plan can easily be clustered in appropriate labor grades.

Another approach to the inequity problem is to attempt to iron out unjustified rate differentials through use of the contract's grievance machinery. In some plants employee complaints under the general heading of unequal pay for equal work form the bulk of all grievances filed during the contract year. In many contracts, however, the raising of grievances over individual job rates is prohibited, for to permit grievances over individual job rates is to invite continuous and perpetual bargaining. A highly unstable labor-management relationship may result. Frequently, under this system, more grievances are provoked than are alleviated. An opportunity is afforded for continuous internal whipsawing by the union. Existing wage distortions may be increased rather than reduced.

There is more merit in the method of compiling a list of apparent or alleged inequities among job rates for settlement and correction when the contract comes up for renewal. Although the negotiations for the correction of inequities are frequently a time-consuming operation, it is more logical and appropriate to handle such problems at a time when the basic contract is up for renegotiation than to conduct guerrilla operations on a continuous basis. A common technique is to negotiate the amount of the general increase, say ten cents per hour, and then allocate a portion of this increase for the correction of inequities in job rates.

One of the most frequent intraplant inequity issues in recent years has been posed by the growing dissatisfaction of skilled trades in manufacturing plants with the narrowing of the differentials between their rates and the rates for semiskilled and unskilled operations. A survey of contracts in manufacturing today will show that in many cases the parties have switched from negotiating general increases in terms of cents per hour to percentage adjustments. A percentage increase across-the-board will, of course, preserve the proportionate differentials instead of narrowing them. Many companies and unions have changed their Annual Improvement Factor increases from so many cents per hour to a percentage increase for this reason. In other cases it will be observed that the skilled trades have received boosts of as much as fifteen or twenty cents per hour whereas the common labor rates have only gone up five cents per hour. In short, it appears that the secular trend toward a narrowing of occupational differentials that has been in progress for some twenty years is now being arrested and partially reversed in a number of cases.

WAGE ADMINISTRATION PROBLEMS

We turn now to a consideration of some specific policy questions in wage administration. These include such troublesome matters as whether to pay on an hourly basis or on some form of incentive related to output;

setting rates on new or changed jobs; proper use of rate ranges for jobs paid on a time basis; equal pay for equal work problems; use of grievance procedure in relation to wage administration; and many others. After some brief comments we shall consider the wage structure problem from the external view.

METHOD OF WAGE PAYMENT: DAY WORK OR PIECE WORK?

When it is difficult to measure the employee's output or performance in quantitative terms, the job is usually paid on an hourly rate basis. For example, such skilled occupations as tool and diemaker, maintenance machinist, and pattern maker could not ordinarily be placed under any incentive plan directly related to measurable output. It is also difficult, though not impossible, to put many forms of indirect labor on a quantitative standard for payment purposes.

On the other hand, most of the semiskilled, highly repetitive machine or hand operations characteristic of American mass production lend themselves readily to a form of compensation that is directly related to output, i.e., an incentive method of wage payment. When physical output can be accurately and systematically measured, management usually inclines toward the incentive type of wage payment rather than an hourly rate.

A wide range of incentive payment plans may be found in American industry. Full analysis is not possible here. Perhaps most prevalent is the use of piece rates set after time study to determine output per hour of the "average normal operator." A performance standard is set upon the basis of time study, and a piece rate is then established that enables the average normal operator with extra effort to achieve earnings higher than normally would be paid for the job on an hourly rated basis.

Most employers would probably agree that an incentive operator should enjoy a piece rate that would enable him to earn premium pay of from 20 to 30 per cent above the guaranteed base rate for the operation. The incentive must be substantial enough to induce increased effort.

Piece-rate systems can be of the increasing, decreasing, or constant type. The first of these, in which earnings increase more than proportionately to output, is exceedingly rare and would be vigorously opposed by most employers. The decreasing type, in which earnings increase less than proportionately to increases in output, was common prior to extensive unionization. Such systems are still in use in situations in which the employer retains unilateral control over wage administration.

In almost all unionized plants some variant of the constant piece-rate system is in use. Most unions will insist on a one for one ratio between earnings and output.

In recent years there has been an increasing amount of experimentation with joint administration of wage incentive systems. Some plants have joint time study operations; others have a joint committee to review production standards and piece rates set in terms of those standards. In the majority, however, the methods analysis and time study operations remain management functions. The establishment of production standards and the setting of piece rates are also usually management functions, with the union reserving the right to challenge the fairness of the standard or the rate through the contract's grievance machinery.

Union opposition to incentive methods of payment is sometimes deep-rooted. The direct relating of earnings to effort works against a major union principle of wage uniformity. However, in situations in which the union's institutional status is secure and in which the job operations clearly lend themselves to an incentive method of payment, there seems to be a lessening of union opposition.

Most unions are not equipped for joint participation with management in administration of a wage incentive plan. Nor do most unions wish to share responsibility for the effective operation of such plans. They prefer to insist upon the right to challenge managerial exercise of administrative initiative. If the right to challenge is secure, most unions are not interested in going further.

Incentive payment plans received considerable stimulus during World War II, for reasons similar to those discussed in job evaluation. Familiarity with their operation, under a situation in which the status of the union was not questioned and in which increased output did not result in unemployment, has provided a postwar impetus to piece-rate systems. Fear of unemployment was always a powerful factor in union opposition.

It is difficult to generalize on best practices in this field. What is fair and equitable depends in large measure on the nature of the operations involved and the specific problems of the industry. However, it is possible to set down a few propositions that may have general validity:

1. In union-management relations a constant piece-rate plan is the most feasible and acceptable. The principle of one for one will produce the least opposition and the best results.

2. The average normal operator should be able to earn approximately 20 to 30 per cent above his guaranteed base rate.

3. The guaranteed base rate should not be set at an unrealistically low figure in order to create an illusion that piece-work earnings are exceptionally high. The guaranteed base rate should be set at the rate for which the job would be compensated on an hourly rate basis.

4. Piece rates should not be reduced unless there has been a substantial change in methods, materials, design, or equipment.

5. Provision should be made for challenging tight rates through the grievance machinery of the contract.

6. The value of joint participation in time study, standard and rate setting, and revision should be carefully explored. Most often, however, interests of efficient and economical operation will be served by management's retaining control over methods analysis, time study, establishment of production standards, fixing of piece rates, and revision of piece rates.

7. When management retains control, every effort should be made to familiarize union officials and rank-and-file workers with the purposes and details of whatever incentive plan is used. Ignorance and misunderstanding are among the most frequent causes of employee opposition to incentive systems.

8. An incentive worker should be paid his guaranteed base rate or his average hourly earnings on piece work, whichever is higher. During lost time or downtime as a result of machine breakdown, materials shortage, etc., the worker should receive not less than his guaranted base rate for such time. If asked to work on an experimental job, or to serve as an instructor, or to do the work of an absent employee when his own regular incentive work is available, scheduled, and can be performed, and other "special cases," the incentive worker should receive his average hourly incentive earnings based on a preceding period of regular work. The principle here is that an incentive worker should not suffer a loss in earnings under circumstances where he is taken away from his regular work for the company's convenience.

9. As in job evaluation, the success of an incentive system depends on continuous attention to daily administration, to preclude its becoming outmoded or unfair due to changing industrial circumstances.

As with job evaluation, no hard and fast rules can be laid down about the extent to which union participation should be encouraged in the installation and administration of an incentive method of wage payment. The precise relationship between the parties will necessarily depend upon conditions in the industry and in the plant, how long and how constructively the parties have been bargaining with one another, and upon the respective views of the employer and the union as to the role of the latter in the operation of an incentive system.

In most instances the principle of managerial administrative initiative, subject to check through the grievance machinery, will have the greatest validity. However, joint participation may sometimes work out satisfactorily. Again, as in job evaluation, it cannot be overemphasized that the success of an incentive system depends almost entirely on *worker acceptance and understanding*.

The principle of incentive compensation, relating earnings directly to effort, is fairly clear-cut and simple. The specific applications of the principle are often difficult and highly technical. Numerous areas of disagreement between management and the union are present. Such problems as selection of operators for time study purposes, estimating proper allowances for job and personal delays in setting production standards, figuring responsibility for scrap, and payment for downtime are frequently a source of fundamental conflict between management and the union.

Most employers (and many unions) are strongly opposed to union participation in time study or the setting and revision of production standards. It is a field in which the consensus clearly favors the principle of managerial administrative initiative.

If an incentive method of wage payment is in use, it is vitally important that the contract language be as clear-cut and unambiguous as possible in setting forth the policies and procedures governing the administration of the system. The most carefully drawn language will not eliminate disputes over interpretation and application, but fuzzy language will produce chaos.

GUARANTEED RATE OR AVERAGE EARNINGS?

A frequent source of controversy concerns the problem of whether an incentive worker gets his guaranteed base rate or his average incentive earnings when not on his regular incentive work. If he is on his regular production work, there is usually no problem. In such cases it is generally agreed that he receives either his guaranteed rate or his incentive earnings, whichever is higher. The critical question is as to how he should be compensated when, for one reason or another, he is not on his regular incentive work or runs into unusual trouble on his regular production work. There is perhaps no consensus on this question.

The reader may wish to evaluate the following contract language setting forth certain "special cases" in which average earnings will be paid when all the conditions set forth in each special case are fulfilled by the factual circumstances involved. The language is from a recent John Deere-UAW contract.

Section 15. In the following special cases, incentive workers will be paid at an hourly rate equal to their average straight-time hourly earnings. The method of computing the incentive employee's average straight-time hourly earnings shall be as follows: Divide the sum of the money paid for all hours worked (excluding the shift differential premium and overtime penalty pay) during the two (2) previous computed work weeks by the sum of the hours worked during such period.

A. When an employee experiences excess stock or hard stock which is outside the material specification, either of which makes it impossible to run an operation at machine speeds and/or feeds used in determining the incentive standard, and his Foreman having been notified, directs the employee to continue at work.

B. When an employee is directed to reclaim his own work when such defective work is because of improper blueprints of operations or wrong instructions by the Foreman or other authorized instructor or to rework returned material.

C. When an employee is taken away from his regular incentive work when such work is available, scheduled and can be performed, and is directed to rework another employee's defective work where circumstances prevent the rework operation from being performed by the original workman.

D. When at the request of Management an employee is temporarily taken off his regular incentive work, when such work is available, scheduled and can be performed to take care of an emergency, to do maintenance work or to do work of an experimental nature on a new or basically modified product. An "emergency" as applying to work assignments for incentive workers may be created by the development of an unforeseen situation, such as power, water, or electric trouble, heavy snowfall or rainfall, fire or explosion, that requires immediate additional help at a given location by an employee or employees from a different work classification.

E. When an employee is taken from his regular incentive work when such work is available, scheduled and can be performed, to do the work of an absent employee.

F. When at the request of Management an employee is temporarily taken from his regular incentive work, when such work is available, scheduled and can be performed, to perform work of a trial nature to try out jigs, dies, and tools for a new product, job or process; the length of time spent or number of pieces to be run on a trial basis to be pre-determined by the Foreman.

G. When an operation is performed at the direction of the Foreman on a machine other than the one on which the standard was established and it is impossible to run the operation at machine speeds and/or feeds established in the standard.

H. When an employee is required to serve as an instructor.

I. If, due to failure of equipment, an operator is unable to continue his work and is not assigned to other incentive work, but is directed by his Foreman to repair the equipment.

J. An incentive standard covering the temporary conditions enumerated in paragraphs A, B, C, and G above may be established provided the conditions so enumerated last for at least (8) hours.

"Scheduled" is assumed to mean that the work is or would be normally machined, made, or used, as the case may be, and is required for use in succeeding operations within the current week, provided, however, that in all circumstances in which an employee's job is in operation during his absence or when he resumes his regular job immediately following a temporary assignment, his job will be considered as scheduled.

"Such work is available and can be performed" is assumed to mean that the material is at hand, in position and condition to be worked upon and it is physically practical to perform the operations listed on regular machines. In the Foundry not "physically practical" would mean that it would not be practical to charge the material in the cupola not required by the Foundry; that the cores not be made unless required by the molding department for the current day's operation. Since the Foundry operates on a daily schedule, it is not practical to store hot metal or cores for but a very short time.

K. In all cases where a condition arises which calls for payment of average straight time hourly earnings, the employee will notify the Foreman immediately. If the Foreman authorizes the employee to perform such work, the time of starting such work and the time of stopping such work shall be shown on the back of the employee's Daily Time Report and approved by the Foreman.

Most students of incentive systems would agree in principle with the policies expressed in the foregoing language. The Deere-UAW provisions on average earnings are explicit and concrete. Notwithstanding this careful effort to articulate precisely each "special" case, these paragraphs have proved over the years to be a productive source of disputes reaching arbitration.[3] The reason appears to be a basic conflict in philosophical approach to incentive payments that finds expression in cases under this language.

Broadly speaking, the company starts from the proposition that an incentive worker should normally be paid incentive earnings only when he is directly engaged in productive incentive work.

The union, on the other hand, starts from the proposition that an incentive worker should have a normal expectation of being able to earn incentive earnings eight hours a day, forty hours a week.

The company is understandably interested in having the contract language strictly and narrowly interpreted. The union is understandably interested in bringing as many situations as possible under the rubric of average earnings.

The typical average earnings case is one wherein the union maintains that *all* the contract conditions of one of the "special cases" are met by a given factual situation, with the company arguing that one or more of the conditions essential to applying the clause are not fulfilled.

The parties agree in principle that average earnings are not due unless all the conditions set forth in the particular "special case" are satisfied by the factual circumstances involved. Thus, in disputed cases, this prerequisite for payment of average earnings stands in the company's favor. In each case the union always must assume the burden of proving that all conditions are met.

Over the years many key words and phrases in these paragraphs have had their meaning definitely settled by arbitration decisions. For example,

[3] This discussion is based on Harold W. Davey, "The John Deere-UAW Permanent Arbitration System," in Jean T. McKelvey, ed., *Critical Issues in Labor Arbitration* (Washington: Bureau of National Affairs, Inc., 1957), pp. 161–92, at pp. 180–81.

a key requirement in a number of special cases is that an employee be taken from his regular incentive work when such work is "available, scheduled, and can be performed." These words are defined in the contract, but their meaning has been further clarified by a series of decisions. Also, such questions as what constitutes an "absent employee," "work of a trial nature," or "work of an experimental nature on a new or basically modified product" have been answered reasonably well by decisions in recent years.

A continuing basis for conflict exists, however, because new or modified factual situations are constantly developing. Many grievances of this type carry considerable "heat." An adverse decision is not always well-received.

Frequently, cases have arisen where equitable considerations would have dictated payment of average earnings, but where contractually one or more of the requisite conditions were not satisfied. Such decisions are difficult to make and even more difficult to accept. In terms of the judicial theory of arbitration, however, the contract itself must always be the touchstone. If contract requirements and equity do not appear to coincide, the contract governs.

DAY WORK PROBLEMS

Payment by the hour, day, or week is usually a simpler, less contentious form of wage payment than an incentive method, although time bases for wage payment create their own knotty policy questions that merit some discussion. One of the most basic questions is whether to establish single rates or rate ranges for day work jobs. As a general rule, employers prefer rate ranges and unions prefer single rates. A great deal depends on the nature of the work and the industry involved. Single rates promote union objectives of uniformity and minimize the possibility of grievances about personal inequities. Employers understandably prefer rate ranges because they afford greater flexibility in wage administration and permit management to reward superior effort and performance on the job.

SINGLE RATES OR RATE RANGES?

The concepts of "union scale" and "standard rate" are historically associated with single rates below which no union man is supposed to work. In the building trades generally, a journeyman's rate for carpenter, electrician, painter, etc., is worked out to apply to all construction projects over which the union in question has jurisdiction in a particular labor market area. Apprenticeship rates leading up to the journeyman rate are graduated in terms of length of service, but at any particular service stage these are also single rates. In the music and entertainment field contract wages are fixed in terms of minima below which no union performer is expected to work. Union scale in the newspaper editorial field is negotiated in terms of weekly minimum salaries below which no American Newspaper Guild member is expected to work.

In manufacturing industries, however, rate ranges for hourly paid occupations are more common than single rates. Where rate changes are in use, the chief area of controversy is over how a worker should progress from the minimum of the range to the maximum. In the typical situation management will argue for progress on merit and the union for automatic step-ups to the maximum at regular intervals. The most frequent compromise between these views is to provide for automatic step-ups to the midpoint of the range, with individual merit increases determining the worker's progress from the midpoint of the range to the maximum.

On many semiskilled and unskilled operations paid on an hourly basis there is a strong case for automatic progression, at least to the midpoint of the range. When the time required to achieve average efficiency on the job is relatively short, there seems no valid objection to automatic raises to the midpoint of the range. This reasoning is based on the assumption that the midpoint of a range is the monetary equivalent of what would be paid if the job were on a single rate basis. The midpoint may be considered as the rate that would be paid to an average worker for average performance. Raises up to the midpoint then could well be automatic at intervals of two, three, or six months. However, progress from the midpoint to the maximum of the range could be a merited rather than an automatic progression. Failure to grant merit increases between midpoint and maximum could be challenged through the grievance machinery.

Employers have always regarded the granting or withholding of merit increases as a managerial function or prerogative. The National Labor Relations Board has held that the statutory obligation to bargain collectively embraces negotiation with the union on merit increases upon request and requires the employer to furnish the union with information as to merit increases granted or withheld.

Many unions have ceded their right to negotiate on merit increases, preferring to leave the matter entirely in management's hands, subject to challenge through the grievance procedure. Others keep a strict and watchful eye on the exercise of employer discretion.

In situations in which the prime union emphasis is on establishing a schedule of job rates, merit increases above the job rate are normally left entirely to management's discretion. When there is an established system of rate ranges, however, the union will normally strive for some variant of automatic progression or will seek to establish a control through the grievance machinery over the granting or withholding of merit increases.

The right answer to the problem depends on the facts of the particular case. As a general proposition, when rate ranges are in use, the following procedure appears best suited to protecting the union's interest in uniformity and management's interest in rewarding individual performance:

1. Establish rate ranges with a reasonable spread for clearly definable job classifications.
2. Hire new employees at the minimum of the rate range, so far as practicable.
3. Provide for automatic progression from the minimum to the midpoint of the range in each classification.
4. Base advancement from the midpoint to the maximum of the range on individual merit.
5. Wherever practicable, establish objective standards of performance for use in determining whether to grant or withhold merit adjustments.
6. Provide that the granting or withholding of a merit increase shall be subject to challenge through the contract's grievance procedure.

In the writer's arbitration experience the challenged denial of a merit increase has been rare. This experience may not be typical. The denial of a merit increase is a discretionary managerial act. It is difficult to challenge successfully unless it can be shown that the action was clearly arbitrary, capricious, or discriminatory. In most situations the burden of proof would be difficult to maintain. Furthermore, many unions do not wish to become embroiled in too many individual disputes. They will not challenge to the point of arbitration unless they feel the company in question is deliberately discriminating in its administration of the merit increase program.

EQUAL PAY FOR EQUAL WORK: SEX DIFFERENTIALS

One of the most difficult applications of the equal-pay-for-equal-work principle is that involving female employees. In many industries prior to World War II, when female labor was employed, wage differentials based on sex alone were not unusual. The wartime labor shortage and the postwar full employment period have greatly increased the number of female employees in industries subject to unionization. Women workers form a substantial percentage of total union membership today.

Most unions support in principle the proposition that there should be no wage differentials based on sex. This is reflected in many recent contractual provisions in a variety of industries. The most common statement requires that equal compensation be paid, regardless of sex, whenever men and women are engaged on work that is comparable in all respects.

When men and women are employed on exactly the same jobs, the principle is clear-cut and easy to apply. Problems arise, however, in many plants in which women are employed exclusively on some operations and men are employed exclusively on others. The distinction between male jobs and female jobs frequently carries with it a wage differential unfavorable to female labor.

Women are especially suited to light assembly work, repetitive machine operations, simple inspection, and other jobs in which manual dexterity is of great importance. In plants in which no men are employed on such jobs the wage rates are likely to be comparatively low.

Sometimes unions find it necessary to condone the maintenance of a differential based on sex, often at the instigation of the female workers themselves. The women may urge the maintenance of a differential since they are aware, or at any rate believe, that if equal pay for equal work were rigorously enforced, the employer would hire men.

When men and women are employed on similar but not identical operations, the problem of defining what constitutes equal work is not always a simple one. There is much less wage discrimination against women in industry today than prior to World War II, but the principle of equal pay for equal work is by no means universally followed, even in union-management relationships.

SETTING WAGE RATES ON NEW OR CHANGED JOBS DURING THE LIFE OF A CONTRACT

No employer likes to be continually negotiating with a union. Labor problems are only one of many phases of the employer's job. Nor do union officials, especially at the international level, have the time to indulge in frequent bargaining sessions with employers over wage rates on particular jobs.

Consequently, many contracts provide a wage schedule containing job rates for all existing jobs, with the understanding that this schedule remains intact for the duration of the contract. The schedule will establish the single rate or rate range for all hourly paid jobs, and will set forth the guaranteed base rate or occupational rate for all jobs on an incentive arrangement.

In any one plant the content of most jobs will not change during the life of a contract. In a dynamic industrial system, however, there always will arise a number of new jobs that cannot be fitted into existing classifications, or the duties on existing jobs may have to be changed. What procedure should be followed in setting rates on new or changed jobs?

Practice varies considerably on this question. In some cases the parties will sit down and negotiate the rate every time a new job appears or an existing job has its duties changed appreciably. In others it is customary for management to set the rate on the new or changed job, subject to challenge by the union through the grievance procedure. Many contracts in effect prohibit management from changing the duties or rate on a job existing at the time of the contract's signing for the life of the contract.

As a general rule, the most practical and efficient approach would appear to be one which permits management to set the rate on a new job, reserving to the union the right to challenge this rate within a specified time period, thirty, sixty, or ninety days. This is a frequent practice on incentive jobs, and has validity for new hourly jobs as well. In plants with well-established job evaluation systems the problem of setting rates on new or changed jobs is not likely to be as troublesome as in plants with no definite system of wage administration.

Even under a job evaluation program, however, disputes may frequently arise, particularly in connection with changes in the content of an existing job. The normal direction of technological change is toward work simplification with the breaking down of complex tasks into simpler, more specialized assignments. Hence, the resultant wage change is likely to be downward and therefore productive of considerable employee and union resistance. As already noted, many contracts protect strictly against reduced wages as a result of job content changes during the life of a contract by carefully spelling out the circumstances under which an employee's rate may be reduced.

An even more difficult issue relates to whether disputes over rates on new or changed jobs should be arbitrable or subject to strike action under the contract. An arbitrator under contracts that exclude such disputes from the arbitration step well might be grateful for the exclusion, since such disputes do not lend themselves to the "judicial" type of arbitration. The proper rate for a new job is essentially a "political" question that should be worked out by the parties. At the same time, there are real advantages in using arbitration as an alternative to economic force for any contract dispute during the life of an agreement. Majority practice seems to favor making such disputes arbitrable.

APPRAISAL OF UNION IMPACT ON INTERNAL WAGE STRUCTURES

The impact of unionism on internal wage structures has been significant. The influence of unionism and collective bargaining in most firms has been in the direction of eliminating or narrowing personal wage differentials and occupational wage differentials.[4] Whether the results are

[4] We now have an impressive number of empirical studies to draw upon in making these summary comments on the impact of unionism on internal and external wage structures. The principal references will be found in the bibliography at the end of this chapter. However, special mention is warranted here of a few studies. See Harry

viewed as favorable or unfavorable depends on one's assumptions and the facts of particular cases. The writer's belief is that in most cases the net impact of collective bargaining on the structure of occupational rates within particular firms has been favorable in the sense that a more logical and equitable relationship among occupational rates has been developed. The results have also been favorable to the degree that unionism has eliminated the wide discrepancies in personal rates for particular types of work. It is necessary to concede, however, that in some cases the effect of union policy has been to maintain rather than eliminate unjustified differentials. In such cases the dispersion of earnings under collective bargaining has been perhaps greater than it would have been under non-union conditions.

In general, union influence on wage and salary administration policies has been beneficial by promoting standards of uniform treatment and consistency. Certainly, there is slight evidence to support the thesis that unionism serves to "distort" previously ideal wage rate hierarchies within particular firms. On the contrary, one might agree with Livernash that "As a broad total influence, collective bargaining appears to be associated with more logical wage-structure policies and improved wage-structure administration."[5]

IMPACT OF COLLECTIVE BARGAINING ON EXTERNAL WAGE STRUCTURE

The discussion up to now has been concentrated on structural wage problems of the individual firm. Attention will be directed now to consideration of the impact of collective bargaining on *external* wage structures, i.e., upon intra-industry, interindustry, and geographical differentials in occupational rates.

Although the union's impact on internal rate structures in a particular plant is frequently observable and significant, such influences become less noticeable as we expand the area of coverage. The influence is still considerable, however, on an intercompany basis in the same industry or area and among plants of the same company.

The approach to inequities within an industry or area will vary substantially, depending on the circumstances. The type of wage uniformity

M. Douty, "Union Impact on Wage Structures," *Proceedings of the Sixth Annual Meeting, Industrial Relations Research Association* (Madison: IRRA, 1954), pp. 61–76; E. Robert Livernash, "The Internal Wage Structure," in George W. Taylor and Frank C. Pierson, eds., *New Concepts in Wage Determination* (New York: McGraw-Hill Book Company, Inc., 1957), pp. 140–72; Arthur M. Ross, "The External Wage Structure," Taylor and Pierson Book, *cit.* pp. 173–205; and Lloyd G. Reynolds and Cynthia H. Taft, *The Evolution of Wage Structure* (New Haven: Yale University Press, 1956), *passim.*

[5] E. Robert Livernash, *op. cit.,* p. 171.

sought, the extent to which the industry is organized, the nature of the product, and the competitive structure of the industry are all highly significant factors. Within a geographical area, the degree to which employers are organized is also of considerable significance.

The logic of multi-employer bargaining leads toward standardization and uniformity in an effort to eliminate labor cost as a competitive factor. Yet such uniformity may be difficult to achieve. Employers within an otherwise homogeneous industry vary widely in managerial efficiency, quality of equipment, and effective utilization of labor supply.

As employers organize for labor relations purposes, and as one or more unions achieve full unionization in an industry, it is possible to look forward to an increased use of joint wage rationalization programs to eliminate inequities. The experience in the basic steel industry is encouraging in this respect. Although there is no reason to expect miracles of accomplishment in the near future, the joint approach on an industry-wide basis to the elimination of unjustified inequities appears to have many fruitful possibilities. Such an approach need not imply a goal of identical wage rates for identical jobs. This would place an intolerable burden on high-cost firms. It should be possible, however, to develop a higher degree of uniformity in job nomenclature and correlation of pay with responsibility than now obtains in most industries. The same approach might have limited application also on an area basis where employers in the area as well as labor are highly organized.

Thomas Kennedy has identified seven basic types of wage uniformity, any one or a combination of which may serve as the objective in multi-employer bargaining arrangements: [6]

1. Uniformity of rate per unit of output.
2. Uniformity of rate per unit of skill and effort required.
3. Uniformity of rate per hour of labor of a particular type.
4. Uniformity of rate ranges.
5. Uniformity of minimum rates.
6. Uniformity of rate changes.
7. Uniformity of total costs.

Clearly, the job of taking labor costs out of competition on a multi-employer basis is not as simple as it might appear at first. Of Kennedy's seven types the second appears to approach most closely the intraplant objectives of job evaluation, even though its accomplishment poses numerous administrative difficulties on a multi-employer basis.

Kennedy's analysis shows conclusively that the seven types of wage uniformity are not complementary to one another, and in some situations

[6] Thomas Kennedy, *The Significance of Wage Uniformity* (Philadelphia: University of Pennsylvania Press, 1948.)

are actually opposed. In most situations it is necessary for management and the union(s) under multi-employer bargaining to effect a pragmatic compromise between two or more types, depending on the circumstances of the industry in question.

In considering approaches to wage uniformity on an inter-firm basis in a particular industry or area (and especially among the plants of a multi-plant company) it would be difficult to overestimate the importance of the standard of equitable comparison. *The comparison factor is of critical significance both as to changes in wage levels and also as to relationships among occupational rates.* Comparison as a wage criterion pushes in the direction of uniformity, whereas the employer's ability to pay pushes in the direction of dispersion. In recent years the comparison factor appears to have been the stronger of the two in most cases. Over the long pull, it seems reasonable to anticipate that differentials will continue to decline (and perhaps, ultimately, disappear) among the several plants of a single firm and among various firms in the same industry.

When we turn to consideration of the impact of collective bargaining on interindustry differentials and geographical differentials, however, the picture is substantially altered. Most students of relative wage rates are inclined to discount or minimize the influence of collective bargaining on such differentials. The gap between high and low wage industries appears to remain substantially the same. High wage industries remain high wage industries and low wage industries continue to be low wage industries, relatively speaking.[7] If collective bargaining has had any impact here, Reynolds and Taft feel that it is in the direction of widening customary interindustry differentials. They would therefore classify the results as "harmful."[8] Their analysis of structural changes in more fully unionized countries shows that a higher degree of unionization may lead to a narrowing of inter-industry differentials. In the United States, however, the influence of unionism (if any) has been to widen rather than to narrow such differentials.

The tendency of unionism probably has been to narrow geographical differentials, but the observable impact has been slight and not always in the same direction. For example, building trades wage rates in the South are further below the level of the North today than they were forty years ago.

While the comparison factor is of greatest importance on an intra-industry basis, it is interesting to note the amazing degree of correspond-

[7] For an excellent critical appraisal and summary of the principal empirical studies in recent years, see George Hildebrand, "The Economic Effects of Unionism," in Neil W. Chamberlain, Frank C. Pierson, and Theresa Wolfson, eds., *A Decade of Industrial Relations Research, 1946–1956*, Industrial Relations Research Association Publication No. 19, (New York: Harper & Brothers, 1958), pp. 98–145.

[8] Lloyd G. Reynolds and Cynthia H. Taft, *op. cit.*, p. 194.

ence in wage developments in the durable goods industries, as shown recently by Ross.[9] His data for fifteen industries on increases in straight-time, hourly earnings from 1939 to 1952 measured in cents per hour show that twelve of the fifteen industries experienced aggregate increases ranging from $1.02 to $1.10 per hour:

Industry	*Increase: 1939-1952, cents/hour*
Basic steel	109.1
Malleable iron foundries	109.8
Steel foundries	102.1
Nonferrous metals (smelting and refining)	104.9
Nonelectrical machinery	103.7
Engines and turbines	109.3
Tractors	106.8
Agricultural machinery (except tractors)	108.0
Machine tools	104.1
Electrical machinery	92.1
Automobiles	105.7
Tires and inner tubes	109.7
Aircraft engines and parts	107.8
Ship and boat building and repairing	99.4
Locomotives and parts	112.2

As Ross points out, the foregoing figures show equalization of wage movement and preservation of differentials with a vengeance. This remarkable flatness of movement disappears, however, in other sectors. Ross found that, for the thirteen-year period covered, the aggregate increase was $.61 per hour in work shirts, $.75 in footwear, $.86 in cigarettes, $1.00 in pulp and paper, $1.17 in petroleum refining, $1.34 in building construction, and $1.40 in bituminous coal.

From another viewpoint, the Ross figures confirm the proposition that the high wage industries continue to be high wage industries and the low wage to be low wage industries.

ARE OCCUPATIONAL DIFFERENTIALS TOO NARROW OR TOO WIDE?

As noted in the preceding chapter, collective bargaining in recent years has contributed to a narrowing of the percentage spread between the rates of skilled and unskilled labor in manufacturing and other areas. This has been accomplished chiefly through securing across-the-board increases in terms of cents per hour rather than in percentage increases.

Many times this has served to iron out long-standing inequities between the rates for skilled and unskilled labor. Prior to the growth of industrial unionism in the '30's and '40's, the highly skilled craft workers (by virtue of union organization and inherent economic strength) had

[9] Arthur M. Ross in Taylor and Pierson, *op. cit.*, p. 194.

established scales of pay far in excess of the rates paid for unskilled and semiskilled operators. A narrowing of the gap by general increases in terms of cents per hour was probably desirable.

In some areas the pendulum may have swung too far in favor of the unskilled and semiskilled. Unless an adequate differential is maintained, the incentive to train for skilled occupations is weakened, and the supply of skilled labor in future years may prove inadequate. Recognition of the problems of skilled trades within manufacturing is being forced upon industrial unions that are faced with the possible defection of craft groups. The demand for separate representation by crafts has a real basis when the industrial union has ignored the economic problems of the skilled minority within its ranks.

If the pendulum has swung too far, the industrial union can take care of the problem in either of three ways:

1. Negotiating general increases on a percentage rather than on a cents per hour basis.
2. Earmarking a certain amount from a general increase for the correction of intraplant inequities.
3. Negotiating a special wage bargain for the skilled workers involved.

By the same token, the craft unions have a serious obligation to avoid policies that will restrict unduly the supply of skilled labor. Although some improvements in recent years must be noted, the fact remains that in many jurisdictions the craft unions have restricted entrance to the trade to the point where the supply of labor in many occupations is grievously insufficient to fill employer requirements. This is notably true in the building trades, in which the "lump of labor" fallacy apparently continues to dominate the policy approach of many local union leaders. Coupled with the failure to institute adequate apprentice-to-journeyman ratios is the continuing union opposition to technological advancement in the building and construction industry.

Failure on the part of craft groups to take cognizance of the future labor supply requirements makes it difficult to avoid the conclusion that in such situations collective bargaining has had undesirable economic effects. The original rationale for such an approach was the desire to conserve limited job opportunities for those who were already union members. In an economy committed to the maintenance of a maximum of employment opportunities such a negative approach appears contrary to the interests of the economy at large, no matter how immediately beneficial it may be to union members already employed.

Restriction of labor supply by control of entrance to the trade, combined with a monopoly on job opportunities in local areas, was the stimulus for the closed shop ban in the Taft-Hartley Act and in many state labor laws. The closed shop contract *per se* is not culpable. Rather it is the closed shop contract combined with a closed union that presents the real difficulty.

In a period of nearly full employment (which could turn into one of overemployment as a result of military exigencies) both craft and industrial unions have an obligation to make certain that their internal policies and collective bargaining demands take full account of the need for maximum utilization of the existing labor supply and the need for adequate future supplies in various occupational classifications. This involves added emphasis on: (1) training an adequate number of apprentices; (2) improved on-the-job training; and (3) the maintenance of open unions. Failure to accomplish these goals necessarily will increase wage distortion in the structure of occupational rates. It also will result in unnecessary unemployment and imperfect utilization of labor supply.

There is no "scientific" answer to the question as to what the gap *should be* between common labor rates and skilled labor rates. What the relationship will be necessarily depends upon the nature of the work involved, the product market, labor supply-demand ratios, employee preferences, historical custom, and many other variables. We do know that the tendency to narrow the spread between unskilled and skilled rates is a world-wide phenomenon in which general inflation has played a more important role than union policy. The spread is greater in the United States than in other countries with fuller unionization, and there are indications that the trend toward narrowing differentials in this country has been arrested and, in some cases, reversed as a result of the "revolt of the crafts."[10]

CONCLUSION

In the first part of this chapter attention was directed to the role of unionism and collective bargaining in relation to internal wage structural problems. Handling such problems on an objective rather than a personal basis is a comparatively recent development in American industrial relations. The growth of collective bargaining itself has been one of the more powerful influences in directing management's attention to the necessity of developing a rational, balanced structure of occupational rates. The increased interest in wage rationalization programs is also related to the increasing size of business units. In a large plant rate-setting by the whim of foremen or by "old-fashioned" bargaining is likely to produce too many inconsistencies and inequities in the wage structure.

The two major techniques for achieving a balanced wage structure and a definite relationship between earnings and effort are job evaluation and

[10] BLS surveys show that the trend toward special wage increases for skilled workers continued in 1957 and 1958.

the incentive method of wage payment. Some of the problems in connection with each have been explored. Unionism has traditionally been opposed to both methods of wage determination. Union opposition has been essentially a compound of fear of resulting unemployment and a remembrance of past abuses by management in the use of such systems. Management has a responsibility to erase any lingering bases for these union fears. Once this has been done, there is no logical reason why the interests of both management and the union cannot be served by effective use of job evaluation and, where appropriate, by incentive wage payments. Properly installed and properly administered, a job evaluation system gives the employer accurate knowledge of his wage costs and supports the union objective of equal pay for equal work. Job evaluation rates the job and not the man. It should reduce the number of grievances. Similarly, an incentive method of payment, properly administered, simultaneously promotes the union objective of uniformity and the employer desire to reward increased effort. The guaranteed base rate for the various jobs on an incentive set-up takes care of the union interest in the standard rate. The piece-rate method of relating earnings to output provides a viable mechanism for rewarding individual performance.

Management can overcome union opposition and worker resentment by observing the following principles:

1. Recognize and accept the union as an integral part of the industrial relations framework.
2. In cases of unilateral administration by management of either a job evaluation plan or an incentive plan make sure that the workers and union officials fully understand the nature and purposes of the plan.
3. Encourage, when feasible, union participation in job evaluation or an incentive system. The potentialities of joint job evaluation committees and joint time study committees should be explored.

In the second part of the chapter attention was directed to the impact of unionism and collective bargaining on external wage structures. Here it was seen that the net effect of collective bargaining has not been substantial. Union policy appears *in general* to have ratified the operation of existing economic tendencies toward a narrowing of interindustry and geographical differentials, but the results have been mixed and sometimes in the opposite direction. Unionism appears to have had little if any effect on the rank ordering of industries in terms of relative wage levels. In some cases collective bargaining up to now has probably widened the gap somewhat between high paying and low paying industries.

The evidence to date compels agreement with the conclusions of Reynolds and Taft that unionism and collective bargaining have not at any rate worsened the wage structure.

SELECTED BIBLIOGRAPHY

Abersold, Paul, *Problems of Hourly Rate Uniformity*. Philadelphia: University of Pennsylvania Press, 1948.

Abruzzi, Adam, *Work, Workers, and Work Measurement*. New York: Columbia University Press, 1956.

Baker, Helen and John M. True, *The Operation of Job Evaluation Plans*. Princeton: Industrial Relations Section, 1947.

Barkin, Solomon, "The Bench-Mark Approach to Production Standards," *Industrial and Labor Relations Review*, X (January, 1957) 222-36.

Cullen, Donald E., "The Interindustry Wage Structure, 1899-1950," *American Economic Review*, XLVI (June, 1956) 353-69.

Douty, Harry M., "Union Impact on Wage Structures," *Proceedings of the Sixth Annual Meeting, Industrial Relations Research Association*. Madison: IRRA, 1954, pp. 61–76.

———, *Wage Structures and Administration*. Los Angeles: Institute of Industrial Relations, University of California, 1954.

Dunlop, John T. and Melvin Rothbaum, "International Comparisons of Wage Structures," *International Labour Review*, LXXI (April, 1955) 347–63.

Eisemann, Doris M., "Inter-Industry Wage Changes, 1939–1947," *Review of Economics and Statistics*, XXXVIII (November, 1956) 445–48.

Garbarino, Joseph, "A Theory of Inter-Industry Wage Structure Variations," *Quarterly Journal of Economics*, LXIV (May, 1950) 282–305.

Gilmour, Robert W., *Industrial Wage and Salary Control*. New York: John Wiley & Sons, Inc., 1956.

Gomberg, William, *A Trade Union Analysis of Time Study*, 2nd ed., Englewood Cliffs, N. J.: Prentice-Hall, Inc., 1955.

International Association of Machinists, *What's Wrong with Job Evaluation? A Trade Union Manual*. Washington: Research Department, International Association of Machinists, 1954.

Kennedy, Thomas, *The Significance of Wage Uniformity*. Philadelphia: University of Pennsylvania Press, 1948.

Kennedy, Van Dusen, *Union Policy and Incentive Wage Methods*. New York: Columbia University Press, 1945.

Lester, Richard A., "A Range Theory of Wage Differentials," *Industrial and Labor Relations Review*, V (July, 1952) 483–500.

Levitan, Sar A., "Incentive Systems and Wage Controls," *Labor Law Journal*, V (February, 1954) 111–118.

Maher, J. E., "Union, Nonunion Wage Differentials," *American Economic Review*, XLVI (June, 1956) 336–52.

Meyers, Frederick and Roger L. Bowlby, "The Interindustry Wage Structure and Productivity," *Industrial and Labor Relations Review*, VII (October, 1953) 93–102.

Myers, Charles A., "Empirical Research on Wages," *Proceedings of the Sixth Annual Meeting, Industrial Relations Research Association*. Madison: IRRA, 1954, pp. 241–51.

Ober, Harry, "Occupational Wage Differentials, 1907–1947," *Monthly Labor Review*, LXVII (July, 1948) 127–34.

Perlman, Richard, "Value Productivity and the Interindustry Wage Structure," *Industrial and Labor Relations Review*, X (October, 1956) 26–39.

Reder, Melvin W., "The Theory of Occupational Wage Differentials," *American Economic Review*, XIV (December, 1955) 833–52.

Reynolds, Lloyd G., "The State of Wage Theory," *Proceedings of the Sixth Annual Meeting, Industrial Relations Research Association.* Madison: IRRA, 1954, pp. 234–40.

———, "Wage Differences in Local Labor Markets," *American Economic Review*, XXXVI (June, 1946) 366–75.

——— and Cynthia H. Taft, *The Evolution of Wage Structure.* New Haven: Yale University Press, 1956.

Ross, Arthur M. and William Goldner, "Forces Affecting the Interindustry Wage Structure," *Quarterly Journal of Economics*, LXIV (May, 1950) 254–81.

Ross, Harold G. and Melvin Rothbaum, "Interplant Wage Inequities," *Industrial and Labor Relations Review*, VII (January, 1954) 200–210.

———————, "Intraoccupational Wage Diversity," *Industrial and Labor Relations Review*, VII (April, 1954) 367–84.

Salkever, Louis R., "Toward a Theory of Wage Structure," *Industrial and Labor Relations Review*, VI (April, 1953) 299–316.

Slichter, Sumner H., "Notes on the Structure of Wages," *Review of Economics and Statistics*, XXVIII (February, 1950) 80–91.

12

Collective bargaining, full employment, and inflation

One of the critical questions of our time is whether unregulated collective wage determination can be compatible with a national objective of maintaining full employment with a stable general level of prices. In the two preceding chapters we were concerned primarily with the determinants of wage policy at the firm or industry level. In this chapter we consider the aggregate impact of collective bargaining on the general level of wages and the general level of prices.

Since 1935 it has been our national policy to encourage unionism and collective bargaining. Since passage of the Employment Act of 1946 we also have been committed to maintaining a "maximum" of employment opportunities. Most of us also endorse the proposition that national policy should work against price inflation.

The question now is, can we have our cake and eat it, too? Can we simultaneously fulfill these three basic objectives of maintaining free collective bargaining, full employment, and stability in the general level of prices?

Economists are split sharply on whether it is realistically possible to do so. A clear majority argue that unregulated collective bargaining will produce mass unemployment, inflation, or both. A minority argue more optimistically that a combination of effective fiscal and monetary policy with self-restraint in wage bargaining can create the possibility of success on all three objectives simultaneously.

We shall summarize the most recent arguments as to the alleged inflationary impact of collective bargaining stemming from the 1957–1958 phenomenon of an inflation-recession. A brief appraisal of the validity of these competing views will then be made. Finally, we shall pull together in summary form some general conclusions as to the economic effects of bargained wages.

Since 1945 we have maintained full employment and free collective bargaining, accompanied by considerable though not runaway price inflation. Wage bargaining was regulated only during the Korean war, and then not very rigorously. On the national level, unemployment has risen above the five per cent level only three times between 1945 and 1958, and then for relatively brief periods. The Consumers Price Index (CPI), however, has risen steadily during this period except for a few occasions. Do we have enough evidence now to answer satisfactorily the question as to whether union wage policies have been a prime factor in inducing the amount of price inflation experienced since the end of World War II?

Spokesmen on both sides of this question were exceptionally vocal during 1957 and 1958, a period when prices rose, employment fell, new investment declined, productivity remained constant, and strike activity was statistically negligible. The battle of name calling was joined most publicly and clearly in the automobile industry. The UAW gave wide publicity to its proposal that the auto manufacturers should reduce prices on 1958 models by $100. All three major automobile concerns categorically rejected the UAW proposal. Ford in particular blamed recent inflation on the rapid increase in the wages of automobile workers since 1947.

It is not our purpose here to probe into the truth or falsity of the welter of statistical charges and countercharges involved in this debate. Rather, an effort will be made to summarize objectively the main points in the respective theses of those who believe that labor cost increases from collective bargaining were a critically responsible cause of recent inflation, and those who believe that this was not the case and that the blame lay elsewhere.

THE WAGE INFLATION THESIS

Those who blame union policies for 1957–1958 inflationary developments have contended that this inflation was essentially a "cost-push" inflation, induced by constant pressure of wages on costs and thus on prices.

Price increases were not caused by the more conventional or "classical" type of inflation, i.e., an excess effective demand competing for a limited supply of goods and services. This is not a case of too many dollars chasing too few goods. Those who blame the wage-cost-price chain as the triggering factor in this inflation have contended that increases in the wage bill in key industries such as automobiles and steel forced price increases that had a multiplier impact on the cost structures of related firms. Productivity gains were not sufficient to match the higher labor cost structure, according to this view. The inevitable result was seen in the 1958 economic picture of abnormally high prices, excessive unemployment, stiffening consumer resistance, and no indication on the union side of a disposition to temper bargaining demands to conform to such harsh economic realities.

The only way out of such a "cost-push" type of inflation, say economists like Theodore Yntema of Ford Motor Company, is for the major unions to stop squeezing and to adopt a more realistic attitude toward the ability of management to absorb continuing increments of additional labor cost. In Yntema's view, ". . . bargaining power has swung so far in favor of the giant unions that wages are bound to outrun increases in productivity, and cost-push inflation is certain to result." [1] The distinguished economist Edward Chamberlin joined forces with Yntema in condemning the monopolistic market power of unions, and suggested curbing union power to raise wages that outstrip productivity gains, thus forcing price increases with resultant decline in output and increased unemployment.[2]

This in brief is the case for those who argue for union wage policy as the primary causative factor in producing the 1957–1958 inflation-recession phenomenon.

THE ADMINISTERED PRICE-INTERNAL FINANCIAL INFLATION THESIS

Turning now to the other side of the argument, we find official union spokesmen arguing that wage increases did *not* outstrip gains in productivity; that price increases were *not* necessitated by increased labor costs; and that continuing price inflation in the face of widespread unemployment was due to policies of administered prices to maintain unreasonably high profit margins. The argument also stresses the impact of huge internal financial resources of the large corporations that obtained "costless capi-

[1] Theodore O. Yntema, statement before the Subcommittee on Antitrust and Monopoly of the Committee on the Judiciary, United States Senate, February 4-5, 1958.

[2] Edward H. Chamberlin, *The Economic Analysis of Labor Union Power* (Washington: American Enterprise Association, Inc., 1958).

tal" for expansion by retained profits, after taxes and dividends, plus high and rising depreciation allowances permitted under federal tax laws.[3]

According to this view, wage and fringe benefit advances *could* have been accommodated under a stable level of prices if business had chosen to share the fruits of industrial progress with consumers. Instead, business elected to follow a high price-high profit policy that produced a serious inflation notwithstanding the fact that *unit* labor costs remained relatively stable. As a consequence, runs the union argument, wage increases were urgently needed in 1958 to improve the relationship between investment and consumption. To achieve balanced economic growth under peacetime conditions, restraints must be imposed on the high price-high profit policies of the dominant corporations in the administered-price industries. According to this view, we also must put an end to governmental policies that encourage and partially subsidize internal financing, supplemented by borrowed funds, as the primary means of raising investment capital.

AN EVALUATION OF COMPETING THESES

The extreme nature of the foregoing conflicting explanations of the 1957–1958 inflation-recession phenomenon is clearly apparent. The product mix of fact and polemics is heavily weighted in favor of the latter. What can one say as an economist attempting to appraise the situation objectively? It might be well to start with a few basic facts. What happened to wages, prices, and productivity in the period after World War II, and more particularly from 1953–1958?

Average hourly earnings for nonsupervisory manufacturing employees were $.63 per hour in 1939, $1.24 per hour in 1947, $2.00 per hour in September, 1956, and $2.10 per hour in February, 1958, according to the Bureau of Labor Statistics. Between 1947 and 1956, average hourly earnings of *all* employees increased by about 59 per cent. Adding in certain fringe items, total compensation per hour for the same period increased by about 61 per cent. To what extent did this constitute an increase in real earnings? BLS data reveals that in the postwar period the CPI increased by about 22 per cent. Converting money earnings to real earnings with constant purchasing power, the increase in real earnings per hour for all employees would have been approximately 30 per cent and, if employer fringe contributions are included, about 33 per cent.

Output per employee man hour increased about 26 per cent during the period 1947–1956, clearly less than the increase in real earnings for the same period. Between 1947 and 1952, however, real earnings did not increase as rapidly as did productivity. According to BLS, "By 1953 real

[3] AFL-CIO, *The National Economy in Review* (Washington: AFL-CIO, 1958).

earnings had nearly caught up with the increase in productivity, they remained in line through 1955, and it was not until 1956 that real earnings appeared to have definitely exceeded productivity. Real earnings, including supplements, overtook productivity somewhat earlier and have remained ahead since 1954." [4]

What about increases in unit labor costs and nonlabor costs and prices? For the 1947–1956 period, the increase was approximately the same, 27 to 28 per cent, for all three measures. It should be noted that "price" here is not the same as in CPI. The price index used for comparison here with indexes of unit labor and nonlabor costs represents the change in price of all final goods and services produced by the private economy, minus the price of the gross farm product.

Was the increase in unit labor costs for the period in question necessarily the cause of price increases during that period? BLS cautions against jumping to such a conclusion, pointing out that the "influence of demand pressures as well as increases in the various non-labor costs may in fact be as important or more important in determining price change." To illustrate this need for caution, BLS points out that the pent-up demand following World War II, the effect of the defense build-up after Korea, strong business demand for new plant and equipment, and maintenance of high employment levels all played a part in influencing the level of prices.

The foregoing admonition points up a salient consideration in analysis of wage-price-cost-productivity-profit-employment relationships. Explanations of causative factors in the 1957–1958 inflation-recession couched in unitary terms are likely to be dangerously oversimplified. It is virtually impossible to isolate from a complex of variables any one factor, such as union wage policy or excessive internal financing, and with any accuracy to lay the *entire* blame for price inflation on this one factor.

Taking the period 1947–1956, it is obvious that prices were affected by *both* increases in labor costs and in nonlabor costs in varying degrees. The net result has been that the relative share of total payments going to labor and nonlabor categories was roughly the same in 1956 as it was in 1947.

In the writer's opinion the available relevant evidence does not provide a basis for accepting either of the conflicting theses described earlier without serious qualifications. If it were realistically possible to isolate and pinpoint the *differential* impact of the various pressures affecting the level of prices, it is probable that *some* causative significance could properly be attributed to *all* of the following: union wage policy, corporate price-

[4] U. S. Department of Labor, Bureau of Labor Statistics, *Productivity, Earnings, Costs and Prices in the Private Nonagricultural Sector of the Economy, 1947–56,* (Revised), May 29, 1957, mimeographed.

profit policy, internal financing of new plant and equipment, governmental monetary and fiscal policy, and so on. But any explanation that attempts to lay sole blame on any one factor should be automatically suspect.

The fact is that there are numerous illustrations of collective bargaining raising unit labor costs with little change in productivity and compensated for by price increases, resulting in declining output and unemployment because the firm had not built into the demand curve for its product sufficient inelasticity to accommodate the increased prices. On the other hand, many case illustrations can be found where prices (and profit margins) have been increased and have evolved a considerable amount of "float," using wage increases as an excuse. The specific impact of a given wage increase on labor cost and company price policy varies considerably from one company to the next and one industry to the next. It is unfortunate that the polemicists on both sides have chosen in their respective arguments the route of assessing total blame and claiming complete innocence. The cause of reasoned economic analysis has not been improved by the recent great debate. Nevertheless, the controversy continues with no perceptible indication that it will diminish in heat or intensity. In the meantime, fortunately, the body of reliable empirical data on the economic effects of unionism and collective bargaining continues to grow.

UNIONISM AND INFLATION

Speaking generally, it seems reasonably clear that union pressure for steadily increasing wages and various fringe benefits involving money outlays introduces an inflationary bias into the economic picture, particularly if one starts from the assumption that full employment is to be maintained at all times. This bias may not be particularly noticeable on the upswing of the business cycle, when factor prices and product prices in nonunion industries actually may rise faster than in the collective bargaining sector. But collective bargaining unquestionably introduces rigidities on the downturns. A decline in demand is customarily met by a decrease in output and employment rather than by lower prices and wages. This tendency was clearly observable in the 1957–1958 recession, where wages and wholesale prices continued to rise, notwithstanding considerable falling off of industrial production and increasing unemployment. The result is that each upswing in wages and prices starts from a higher base than would otherwise be the case.

The contributory impact of bargained wages on secular price inflation is easy to exaggerate, however, even though the inflationary bias must be admitted. One may not ignore the many other factors that can influence an upward movement in prices. For example, it can be logically argued that the main inflationary pressure between 1945 and 1948 came from aggregate money demand rather than upward wage pressure.[5] In any long run consideration, however, it would be difficult to deny that the weight of union policy supports creeping inflation if it is assumed that full employment is to be maintained by an accommodating fiscal-monetary policy.

From a practical standpoint it is both unrealistic and unreasonable to expect unions to forego wage demands when they have no reason to suppose that such sacrificial conduct will improve matters. Unions survive and grow by delivering gains or the appearance of gains. It is illogical to expect them to enforce a policy of restraint upon the rank-and-file except in wartime. The cure for secular inflation cannot be expected to come from enforced union abnegation.

By the same token, it is unrealistic and unreasonable to expect the individual employer to hold back the flood by maintaining or lowering his prices in the face of a rising cost structure. Individual employers and individual unions are in no position by their own unaided actions to underwrite either full employment or stability in the general level of prices. However, there is a cumulative understanding that employers and unions can destroy stability by pursuing wage and price policies that require an increased money supply to accommodate whatever level of wages and prices organized sellers (of products and labor) may choose to enforce.[6] The members of the cost-push school of inflation stress this point, making the wage increase the initiating or triggering factor, with the money supply becoming a residual element determined by wage-price behavior.

IMPORTANCE OF RAISING PRODUCTIVITY

When considering how private efforts by employers and unions might support rather than block the objective of full employment at stable prices, the key must be joint awareness of the need for constantly increasing productivity. In a dynamic economy the most satisfying answer to the threat of secular inflation is a constantly expanding output of goods and services, a progressively higher national income. Most management and union leaders are well aware of the obvious economic fact that increases in the general level of wages cannot outstrip the average increase in pro-

[5] See Walter A. Morton, "Trade Unionism, Full Employment and Inflation," *American Economic Review*, XL (March, 1950) 13–39.

[6] For an excellent, balanced appraisal of "cost-push" versus "demand-pull" arguments, see George H. Hildebrand, "The Economic Effects of Unionism," in Neil W. Chamberlain, Frank C. Pierson, and Theresa Wolfson, eds., *A Decade of Industrial Relations Research, 1946–1956*, Industrial Relations Research Association Publication No. 19, (New York: Harper & Brothers, 1958), pp. 98–145. On the point discussed specifically here, see p. 109.

ductivity for the nation as a whole without causing an increase in the general level of prices. Gains in the level of real wages can only come through increases in the productivity of the economy as a whole.

What can management and union leaders do in a concrete way about the productivity question? As we have just noted, and as Arthur Ross emphasized some years ago,[7] employers and union leaders can do little if anything individually about the cumulative effect of a series of separately determined wage bargains, even though they may appreciate intellectually the macro-economic impact of a multitude of particular agreements. But individual unions and individual employers can do something about promoting productivity consciousness and raising output per manhour.

Unfortunately, there is little evidence up to now of a disposition on the part of union and management leaders to work cooperatively to this end. The traditional union position is that productivity is management's job. The union's role is seen as the indirect one of inducing greater productivity by putting pressure on management through aggressive bargaining for wage increases and other improvements. The traditional management position has been that it is not interested in working jointly with union leaders on production problems which it regards as part of management's exclusive prerogative domain.

As a consequence of these widely held views, union-management cooperation to increase productivity and reduce costs has had mainly a crisis or depression orientation.[8] Early efforts were based on a mutual recognition that such cooperation was essential to the life of the enterprise. In other words, the cooperation was born of joint fear. Management feared bankruptcy. The union feared loss of employment opportunities for its membership. The orientation was thus inevitably negative.

During World War II, when full employment prevailed, union-management cooperation to increase productivity (if not to reduce costs) had a fundamentally different orientation.

Here the necessity for cooperation to increase productivity was based not on the exigencies of the competitive situation but on an overpowering necessity to increase output by any and all methods to satisfy an insatiable market. Nevertheless, the experience with joint labor-management committees during wartime contains many valuable lessons for peacetime experience.[9] Admittedly, many of the labor-management committees set up at the instigation of the War Production Board were little more than publicity gestures. Some functioned effectively on such matters as pro-

[7] Arthur M. Ross, *Trade Union Wage Policy* (Berkeley and Los Angeles: University of California Press, 1948).

[8] Sumner H. Slichter, *Union Policies and Industrial Management* (Washington: The Brookings Institution, 1941).

[9] See Dorothea de Schweinitz, *Labor and Management in a Common Enterprise* (Cambridge: Harvard University Press, 1949).

moting the sale of war bonds, encouraging plant safety, and developing pressure against absenteeism. Such activities, although useful, do not represent union-management cooperation in the sense the term is used here. In some industries, of course, the joint labor-management committees functioned effectively as technical bodies for improving productivity and total output. It is the experience of these latter groups that carries the most important lessons for future application.

In all such instances the effectiveness of the joint committee was made possible by the presence of certain characteristics in the labor-management relationship, notably: (1) a high degree of mutual confidence between the parties; (2) mature and competent leadership on both sides; and (3) effective two-way communication between management and its rank-and-file employees, with the union serving as the principal instrumentality of this communication. These are prerequisites for an effective program of labor-management cooperation at the technical level.

If and when a point is reached at which such cooperation becomes the norm rather than the exception, collective bargaining may be of substantial assistance to national full employment policy. Unfortunately, the controversy over management and union prerogatives, perhaps more than any other one factor, has impeded the logical extension of union-management cooperation. If either of the parties is primarily concerned with guarding prerogatives, it is difficult to achieve the requisite understanding of fundamentally mutual interests upon which an effective program of union-management cooperation must be predicated.

Pragmatically speaking, the answer must be found through private policy reorientation. The probable alternative is government price and wage controls or secular inflation. But the way out of the unsavory dilemma is not an easy one. It involves a basic, radical change in the attitude of both management and unions toward the problem of cost reduction and the importance of gains in physical productivity. Both management and unions will have to become far more cost conscious in prosperity periods.

Changing times call for for new measures. A pressing need of our time is increased management and union emphasis on reduction of costs and on greater productivity. It has been assumed by most economists that individual unions have nothing to gain by a sacrificial wage policy, or by attempting to adapt their local wage policies to changes in the productivity and cost picture of particular plants in a particular industry. This well may have been true in the past under a partially unionized economy. That does not mean it will hold equally true under relatively complete unionization, in which each union leader knows that the survival of private collective bargaining depends in large measure on absolving unionism and collective bargaining from a charge of inducing or being primarily responsible for inflation, chronic unemployment, or both.

There is no valid basis in logic for concluding that a growth of economic power may not add to unionism's sense of responsibility rather than produce irresponsibility. It is unnecessarily defeatist to assume that unions and management can only cooperate on cost reduction and productivity measures in desperation. As a matter of fact, a persuasive case can be made for the opposite contention, that it is easier to start a program of cooperation in a prosperity period than in a depression.[10]

In spite of the real possibilities of union-management cooperation as a joint device to reduce unit costs of operation, there does not appear to be any realistic prospect of wholesale adoption of such practices by practicing employers and unions in collective bargaining today. Yet the major source of hope that extensive governmental controls may be avoided rests on such a reorientation of management and union thinking. *The crucial need is for management and union thinking to become oriented toward cost consciousness and productivity consciousness.* If such a consciousness does not become prevalent, the alternative possibilities are the unpalatable ones of inflation, public resentment, and eventual governmental control of wage-price-profit relationships, as well as of the mechanisms of banking, monetary, and fiscal policy. Monetary and fiscal mechanisms, properly used, might be sufficient to maintain full employment with stable prices if it could be assumed confidently that the participants in private collective bargaining had achieved sufficient insight into the aggregate impact of wage bargains to take concerted steps such as those just outlined.

THE ECONOMIC IMPACT OF THE UNION: CONCLUDING SUMMARY

Unionism and collective bargaining clearly seem to have had greater impact on relative wage rates than on wage levels. The available evidence indicates that unionism in its economic role has not exercised any significant differential impact on labor's share of the national income or diverted profits to wages. Politically, unionism and other pressure groups have aided the leveling process by favoring progressive taxation, low interest rates, increased minimum wages, and so on.[11]

Notwithstanding the fury of the argument over the alleged inflationary impact of collective bargaining, the available evidence does not convincingly substantiate those who deplore the monopoly power of unions as the principal if not sole cause of what is termed a cost-push inflation. Nor is the evidence convincing in behalf of the thesis of union economists that wage policy is not a contributory factor in the recent inflation. There

[10] See Ernest Dale, *Greater Productivity Through Labor-Management Cooperation* (New York: American Management Association, 1949.)

[11] George H. Hildebrand, *op. cit.*, p. 104.

does appear to be adequate evidence to warrant serious concern about the long-run inflationary bias of unregulated collective wage determination, particularly when there seem to be few signs of accelerated joint efforts by unions and management to increase physical productivity per man-hour. However, the picture here is not entirely gloomy. 1958 offers indications that the rank-and-file worker may be more conscious of the nexus between wage increases and price increases. He thus may become more receptive to a policy of restrained bargaining by his leadership. The 1958 "noninflationary" auto contracts are one illustration.

While unionism may have had comparatively little impact on wage levels and distributive shares, the impact of collective bargaining on the structure of relative wage rates has been considerable, as noted in the preceding chapter. The impact has been most significant and observable in the rationalization of internal wage structures. Union policies, however, also have had some effect in reinforcing and ratifying existing economic tendencies toward a narrowing of occupational and geographical differentials. The impact on interindustry differentials in all probability has been slight. At any rate, the results of a considerable number of recent studies on this problem appear to be inconclusive.

The allocative effects of unionism upon labor supply and its utilization have been substantial, but mixed. Again we face a problem in attempting to isolate the differential impact of unionism. This is never an easy task. A considerable number of empirical labor market studies have been undertaken in recent years.[12] It seems evident that unionism has generally improved the organization of labor markets, increased vertical mobility within the firm, and reduced lateral or horizontal mobility for industrial workers. However, craft unionism probably has increased lateral mobility. The lower interfirm mobility of industrial workers cannot be attributed entirely to collective bargaining.

Unions are frequently blamed for uneconomical restriction of labor supply and for contractual restrictions tending to inhibit efficient allocation and utilization of existing supply. The evidence behind such charges is frequently fragmentary and inconclusive. As a general proposition, the number of unions still attempting to enforce restrictive admission policies, make work policies, restrictions on output, and barriers to technological change has been progressively declining in recent years. Full employment has been responsible for the liberalization of many restrictionist policies. Yet there can be cited many current examples of union opposition to what might be deemed optimum allocation and utilization of labor resources.

[12] See, for example, Charles A. Myers and George P. Shultz, *The Dynamics of a Labor Market* (Englewood Cliffs, N. J.: Prentice-Hall, Inc., 1951); Gladys L. Palmer, *Philadelphia Workers in a Changing Economy* (Philadelphia: University of Pennsylvania Press, 1956); and Lloyd G. Reynolds, *The Structure of Labor Markets* (New York: Harper & Brothers, 1951.)

One of the most serious problems in recent years has been the chronic shortages in certain skilled trades, notwithstanding considerable general unemployment. Allegedly outmoded union apprenticeship programs are frequently blamed for such shortages. Yet, more often than not, the heart of the problem lies in the employer's reluctance to train apprentices, or in the inadequate differential between skilled hourly rates and the average earnings of semiskilled production workers.

There is little doubt that union policy has contributed to a reduction in labor supply compared with what the supply of labor might be in the absence of unionism's pressures for reducing hours, opposing immigration, favoring more education, and negotiating pension plans providing for compulsory retirement. Whether a lower labor force participation rate as a result of such policies is good or bad depends on one's assumptions and value judgments. There is no magic in increased output as such, and there are many human values to increased education and added leisure time.

All things considered, it seems reasonably evident that the economic impact of unionism and collective bargaining has been exaggerated by both opponents and friends of organized labor. A survey of the extensive research in the postwar period compels agreement with the following summary conclusion by George Hildebrand: [13]

> "Consider the evidence. Collective bargaining has not captured wages at the expense of profits. It has not greatly disturbed relative wages and the distribution of labor. Nor has unionism altered the rate of economic progress in any large way. True, unionism has helped foster creeping inflation, but even here only with the indispensable support of other more powerful economic groups. So far its main contributions lie elsewhere; shorter hours, a new system of wage compensation, a private social security system, more orderly plant wage structures, and a system of jurisprudence that regulates the employment relationship to reflect the interests of employees as well as those of management and consumers."

FUTURE RESEARCH AREAS

Much additional research remains to be done on the economics of collective bargaining. We need to improve techniques and procedures for isolating and appraising the *differential* impact of collective bargaining on wage levels, relative wage rates, managerial efficiency, investment, and technological innovation. We have much to learn about wage-price-profit relationships in oligopolistic industries where management is typically negotiating with one or more large, multi-industrial unions. We need intensive analysis of the interrelationship between wage-price movements and the money supply. Our sources of data and analytical tools are now reasonably adequate to permit valid explanations of past economic be-

[13] George H. Hildebrand, *op. cit.*, p. 137.

havior, but our abilities as predictors of future wage behavior and patterns are still comparatively limited. As Melvin Reder provocatively suggests, we still do not know how to predict whether a given wage bargain will follow a local, an industry, or an interunion pattern if two or more of these patterns are inconsistent. Nor can we yet formulate satisfactory hypotheses to explain the compromises that are actually made among the various patterns.[14]

In short, much remains to be done before an adequate theory of collective wage determination emerges.

SELECTED BIBLIOGRAPHY

AFL-CIO, *The National Economy in Review*. Washington: AFL-CIO, 1958.

Boulding, Kenneth E., "Collective Bargaining and Fiscal Policy," *Proceedings of the Second Annual Meeting, Industrial Relations Research Association*. Champaign: IRRA, 1950, pp. 52–68.

Broehl, Wayne G., "Trade Unions and Full Employment," *Southern Economic Journal*, XX (July, 1953) 61–73.

Bronfenbrenner, Martin, "A Contribution to the Aggregative Theory of Wages," *Journal of Political Economy*, LXIV (December, 1956) 459–69.

Chamberlin, Edward H., *The Economic Analysis of Labor Union Power*. Washington: American Enterprise Association, 1958.

Christenson, C. L., "Variations in the Inflationary Force of Bargaining," *American Economic Review*, XLIV (May, 1954) 347–66.

Clark, Colin, "An International Comparison of 'Over-Employment' Trends in Money Wages," *Oxford Economic Papers*, IX (June, 1957) 178–89.

Gruenberg, Gladys W., "Union Monopoly?" *Social Order*, VIII (March, 1958) 117–22.

Hildebrand, George H., "The Economic Effects of Unionism," in Neil W. Chamberlain, Frank C. Pierson, and Theresa Wolfson, eds., *A Decade of Industrial Relations Research, 1946–1956* (New York: Harper & Brothers, 1958.)

Lauterbach, AlbertT., *Economic Security and Individual Freedom: Can We Have Both?* (Ithaca: Cornell University Press, 1948.)

Lester, Richard A., "Reflections on the 'Labor Monopoly' Issue," *Journal of Political Economy*, LV (December, 1947) 513–36.

Levitt, Theodore, "The Future of Collective Bargaining in an Age of Inflation," *Labor Law Journal*, V (January, 1954) 7–27.

Lindblom, Charles, *Unions and Capitalism* (New Haven: Yale University Press, 1949.)

MacDougall, G. D. A., "Does Productivity Rise Faster in the United States?" *Review of Economics and Statistics*, XXXVIII (May, 1956) 155–76.

Marshall, Howard D., "The Problem of Depressed Areas," *Labor Law Journal*, VIII (July, 1957) 488–93.

[14] Melvin Reder, "Wage Determination in Theory and Practice," in IRRA Publication No. 19, cited *supra*, note 6, pp. 64–97, at p. 84.

Mason, Edward S., "Labor Monopoly and All That," *Proceedings of the Eighth Annual Meeting, Industrial Relations Research Association.* Madison: IRRA, 1956, pp. 188–208.

McConnell, Campbell R., "Collective Bargaining and the Survival of Capitalism," *Labor Law Journal*, V (May, 1954) 311–22.

Morton, Walter A., "Trade Unionism, Full Employment and Inflation," *American Economic Review*, XL (March, 1950) 13–39.

National Planning Association, *Employment Act, Past and Future*, (Special Report No. 41). Washington: National Planning Association, 1956.

Peacock, A. T. and W. J. L. Ryan, "Wage Claims and the Pace of Inflation (1948–51)," *Economic Journal*, LXIII (June, 1953) 385–92.

Reder, Melvin W., "The General Level of Money Wages," *Proceedings of the Third Annual Meeting, Industrial Relations Research Association.* Madison: IRRA, 1951, pp. 186–202.

———, "The Theoretical Problems of a National Wage-Price Policy," *Canadian Journal of Economics and Political Science*, XIV (February, 1948) 46–61.

———, "The Theory of Union Wage Policy," *Review of Economics and Statistics*, XXXIV (February, 1952) 34–45.

———, "Wage Determination in Theory and Practice," in Neil W. Chamberlain, Frank C. Pierson, and Theresa Wolfson, eds., *A Decade of Industrial Relations Research, 1946–1956.* New York: Harper & Brothers, 1958.

Rees, Albert, "The Economic Impact of Collective Bargaining in the Steel and Coal Industries During the Postwar Period," *Proceedings of the Third Annual Meeting, Industrial Relations Research Association.* Madison: IRRA, 1951, pp. 203–12.

Seltzer, George, "Pattern Bargaining and the United Steelworkers," *Journal of Political Economy*, LIX (August, 1951) 319–31.

Simons, Henry C., "Some Reflections on Syndicalism," *Journal of Political Economy*, LII (March, 1944) 1–25.

Singer, H. W., "Wage Policy and Full Employment," *Economic Journal*, LVII (December, 1947) 438–55.

Turvey, Ralph, ed., *Wages Policy under Full Employment.* London: William Hodge & Co., Ltd., 1952.

Ulman, Lloyd, "The Union and Wages in Basic Steel," *American Economic Review*, XLVIII (June, 1958) 408–26, and reply by Albert Rees, *Ibid.* 426–33.

U. S. Bureau of Labor Statistics, *Trends in Output per Man-Hour and Man-Hours per Unit of Output-Manufacturing, 1939–53*, BLS Report No. 100. Washington: U. S. Government Printing Office, 1955, pp. 301–34.

Weintraub, Sidney, "A Macroeconomic Approach to the Theory of Wages," *American Economic Review*, XLVI (December, 1956) 835–56.

13

Automation and collective bargaining

↳ refers to technological developments that have made possible the use of machines to control other machines as contrasted with the progressive substitution of machine power for muscle power.

Union interest in control and conservation of job opportunities has already been discussed.[1] Notwithstanding sixteen years of comparatively full employment, workers generally remain keenly sensitive to the real or fancied danger of unemployment. Such sensitivity has been magnified recently by the 1957–58 recession and by the actual and contemplated impact of *fundamental* technological change in a number of industries symbolized by the catchword "automation." Some key union demands in recent negotiations are traceable to genuine concern about the dislocations and disruptions that may branch from the current growth of fully or partially automated plants.

A SECOND INDUSTRIAL REVOLUTION?

The literature in a few short years on automation is staggering.[2] Unfortunately, much of it is of the armchair, crystal-ball type. Empirical studies

[1] See Chapter 9, *supra*.

[2] A few of the most helpful references are listed in the bibliography at the end of the chapter. For a comprehensive bibliography on automation, see U. S. Bureau of Labor Statistics, *Automatic Technology and Its Implications: A Selected Annotated Bibliography*, Bulletin No. 1198. (Washington: U. S. Government Printing Office, 1956.) BLS intends to issue periodic revisions of this bibliography.

are still scarce. There can be no doubt that the type of technological change embraced by the term automation is going to exercise a profound impact on the structure of employment and on collective bargaining in the years immediately ahead.

What do we mean by this term "automation"? A survey of the mushrooming literature shows a surprisingly loose and varied use of the term, as well as a sharp difference of opinion as to whether or not a second industrial revolution is in process. Everyone who writes on the subject seems obligated to promulgate his own definition along with detailed justifications for it.

As used here, the term "automation" refers primarily to technological developments that have made possible the *use of machines to control other machines.* This is fundamentally different from orthodox or conventional technological change, for the latter involves progressive substitution of machine power for muscle power, i.e., doing things by machine that were formerly done by hand, or by machine reducing the amount of human effort that goes into any particular operation. When technological development takes the form of utilizing machines to control the functioning of other machines, we have a distinctly new type of technology in the making.

THREE TYPES OF AUTOMATION

In discussing automation it is now customary to distinguish three types or categories: (1) Detroit automation; (2) feedback automation; and (3) computer automation. These types are well-described by George B. Baldwin and George P. Shultz.[3] "Detroit automation" is more accurately called "continuous automatic production," and can be used only in a limited number of industries making huge quantities of consumer durables. It involves the linking together of conventionally separate manufacturing operations into continuous production lines.

Feedback automation has been made possible by the tremendous strides in electronic engineering in recent years in the development of control devices (servo-mechanisms) applying the basic principles of *automatic self-regulation.* The development of self-regulative control machinery is the key to the use of machines to control other machines. This represents the really fundamental development in automation.

Computer automation has its principal application to office work, and involves tremendous savings in manpower and time through the use of general- and special-purpose computers for processing data electronically.

[3] George B. Baldwin and George P. Shultz, "Automation: A New Dimension to Old Problems," *Proceedings of the Seventh Annual Meeting, Industrial Relations Research Association* (Madison: IRRA, 1955), pp. 114–28.

Detroit automation is logically an extension of conventional technological change, involving greater mechanization and less human effort by linking together machine operations to minimize the need for human intervention or control. However, the use of servo-mechanisms with built-in corrective devices to control the operation of other machines, the development of automatic production through programming instructions to machines through printed circuits, and the use of electronic data processing equipment to replace human clerical operations constitute technological developments that are fundamentally new. Their impact on the labor force and on industrial relations policies will be the principal subject of this chapter.

UNION ATTITUDES TOWARD AUTOMATION

As might be expected, unions have reacted rapidly to these new technological developments. Some union spokesmen have viewed them with alarm. Other have expressed confidence in the long-run beneficial potential of automation from the standpoint of increased living standards and increased leisure. There seems to be a fairly close correlation between the union leaders' views on the impact of automation with the favorable or unfavorable short-run impact on the workers in the industries they represent. Walter Reuther and James Carey, for example, have spoken vigorously about the need for advance planning and community responsibility to cushion the impact of automation in displacing workers. Their concern about the short-run adverse effects of automation is understandable. The industries whose workers they represent (automobiles and electrical equipment) are likely to have sharply reduced manpower needs as a result of "automating."

On the other hand, leaders of the Machinists' union are highly optimistic about the impact of automation, since it is obvious that one consequence of the new technology will be to increase sharply the demand for skilled machine maintenance personnel. Similarly, union leaders representing workers in the companies manufacturing electronic instrumentation equipment and the computers themselves are understandably pleased at the new developments.

Perhaps the present controversy over the favorable versus the disruptive effects of automation is simply the latest chapter in the old conflict of men and machines. Certainly, virtually everyone has had his say. The late Pope Pius XII expressed his concern over the social and economic consequences of automation. The International Labour Organization has officially recognized the problem and is particularly interested in the application of the new technology to the problems of industrially underdeveloped countries. The United States Congress has taken an official look at the problem.[4] The Bureau of Labor Statistics is trying diligently to keep up with the mountainous literature by periodically issuing revised editions of a selected annotated bibliography on automatic technology and its implications.[5] BLS has also initiated empirical case studies on the operational effects of the new technology. The bureau's first three studies are: one dealing with a company manufacturing electronic equipment; a second analyzing the effect of the introduction of an electronic computer into a large insurance company; and the third analyzing the impact of automated equipment in a large, mechanized bakery.[6]

We need more operational case studies, but developments are coming so fast that it will be difficult for the researchers to keep pace. The BLS Division of Productivity and Technological Developments is trying to keep tabs on all research work in this area, and will presumably undertake more case studies of its own to the extent that staff and funds permit. New developments in automation are also commanding the attention of many management and union research departments and university industrial relations centers.[7]

Our purpose here is to spell out in general terms some of the leading implications for change in industrial relations and collective bargaining practice that are likely to flow from automatic technology. We shall then appraise the ability of collective bargaining to adapt its policies and procedures to the new technology.

SOME EFFECTS OF AUTOMATIC TECHNOLOGY

Most authorities agree that the initial impact of the new technology will be in the office rather than in the factory.[8] The use of electronic data processing machines will drastically reduce the number of employees

[4] Some valuable factual material, as well as authoritative statements on the probable impact of automation, may be found in the hearings conducted by a subcommittee of the Joint Committee on the Economic Report in October, 1955. See U. S. Congress, Joint Committee on the Economic Report, *Automation and Technological Change* (Washington: U. S. Government Printing Office, 1955), 644 pages. See also more recent hearings by the Joint Committee on the Economic Report, *Instrumentation and Automation* (Washington: U. S. Government Printing Office, 1957), 202 pages.

[5] Cited in note 2, *supra*.

[6] *Studies of Automatic Technology*, Nos. 1, 2, and 3 respectively.

[7] For a thorough, recent academic analysis, amply documented, see Robert L. Aronson, "Automation—Challenge to Collective Bargaining?" in Harold W. Davey, Howard S. Kaltenborn, and Stanley H. Ruttenberg, eds., *New Dimensions in Collective Bargaining*, Industrial Relations Research Association Publication No. 21. (New York: Harper & Brothers, 1959.)

[8] Consult Howard S. Levin, *Office Work and Automation* (New York: John Wiley & Sons, 1955.) The potential of electronic data processing for business use is ably and briefly discussed by Carl H. Rush, Jr., "Implications of Electronic Data Processing for Industrial Relations Research," *Proceedings of Tenth Annual Meeting, Industrial Relations Research Association* (Madison: IRRA, 1958), pp. 63–73.

needed for lower grades of clerical labor. From an absorption standpoint, this is probably fortunate since in recent years there has been a marked shortage of clerical labor in relation to demand. Also, since most of this labor is young and female, there has been a high turnover rate in these classifications.

The focus of this book is "blue collar" rather than "white collar." We shall therefore turn our attention to the impact on the factory work force. Here there seems to be general agreement that the introduction of automatic technology will have substantial effects in a number of areas, including: (1) working conditions; (2) seniority arrangements; (3) changes in the "job mix"; (4) wage structures and incentive systems; (5) managerial responsibilities; and (6) industrial training programs. Of greatest importance will be the net effect on job displacement or increase.

As far as physical working conditions and worker safety are concerned, the net effects of automation should be beneficial. That is, the new technology should facilitate still greater reductions in the expenditure of human effort, and should result in improved employee safety conditions. The net effect will probably be to create a more "pleasant" working environment.

Impact on present seniority arrangements is directly related to probable changes in the job mix, i.e, the composition of the plant's work force. Most writers foresee a *general upgrading of skills* as a result of the necessity for a higher ratio of managers to workers, a higher proportion of engineers, electronic technicians, and maintenance men, and a reduced number of semiskilled and unskilled employees on routine, repetitive assignments.[9] Industrial seniority clauses now stress job rights in narrowly defined occupational or departmental groupings. The logic of industrial organization heretofore has tended to stress division of labor, with each employee trained to do a particular task. It seems likely that introduction of automatic technology will reverse this *by placing a premium on a mobile, versatile, interchangeable work force.* In short, the present concept of seniority according to noninterchangeable occupational groups (a common form in manufacturing) will give way to plant-wide seniority, placing the emphasis on employee adaptability and interchangeability.

The new "job mix" will see the virtual disappearance of unskilled labor and many types of routine, uninspired machine feeding and tending jobs. The demand will increase for technically trained supervisory personnel, for all-around maintenance mechanics, for engineers, and for electronic technicians. Estimates as to the quantitative impact on employment are difficult to make. It is obvious, however, that no individual firm is going

[9] For a recent skeptical view on upgrading of skills, based on considerable first-hand experience, see James R. Bright, "Does Automation Raise Skill Requirements?", *Harvard Business Review*, XXXVI (July–August, 1958), 85–98.

to introduce automatic technology unless it expects to reduce costs by producing the same amount of goods with less labor, or a greater amount of goods with the same labor. It is reasonable to assume that industries adopting automatic technology will employ a smaller and smaller proportion of the total labor force. We shall return to analysis of the labor displacement effects of automation later in the chapter.

Conventional types of incentive systems based on individual effort will be outmoded by the new automatic technology. It seems probable that day work and, in some cases, some form of group incentive are the only logical methods of wage payment for the types of employee performance required. Finally, as automatic technology increases the ratio and value of equipment to men, the level of supervisory skills will be raised, the span of supervision somewhat narrowed, and the training and retraining of employees for new tasks reoriented.

The main responsibility for industrial training has fallen on the firms making and installing automated equipment. Individual firms, the public schools, unions, and universities seem to be awakening slowly to the need for thorough revision in apprenticeship and vocational training objectives and methods in the light of the new technology.[10]

UNION POLICY TOWARD TECHNOLOGICAL CHANGE

Broadly speaking, union reaction toward the rapid advances in automatic technology is consistent with the historical position of the labor movement toward any form of technological change. This reaction is conditioned by concern over the employment effect of such technological change in the short-run in a particular firm or a particular industry. Unions are not impressed by armchair argument that labor-saving devices in the long-run create more jobs than they destroy. Unions represent employees in the short-run, and are thus required to formulate policies in terms of short-run considerations.

Historically, unions have followed one of three basic policies in regard to the introduction of technological change: (1) obstruction; (2) competition; or (3) control.[11] The first approach generally has proved to be ultimately suicidal, although sometimes it has conserved jobs for currently employed union members in the short-run. The policy of competition was occasionally used by unions in the past when faced with severe nonunion competition in the same industry. The great majority of unions follow a policy of *control*, i.e., attempting through collective bargaining to regulate the rate and manner in which the technological change is introduced in a

[10] Bright's analysis, cited in note 9 *supra*, indicates that the training cycle on most automated jobs may be considerably shorter than originally predicted.

[11] See Sumner H. Slichter, *Union Policies and Industrial Management* (Washington: The Brookings Institution, 1941), Chs. 7, 8, and 9.

particular firm or industry. In this context a policy of control may involve any or all of the following measures:

1. Requiring advance notice and consultation before new machinery or equipment is introduced.
2. Making provision for the vocational retraining of workers specifically displaced by a new machine or a new process.
3. Providing plant-wide seniority for workers displaced technologically, permitting them to bump anyone in the plant with less over-all seniority whose job they can perform.
4. Regulating the rate at which the new machinery or new process is introduced in order to insure absorption of workers to be displaced. If the rate of introduction can be accommodated to the normal pattern of labor turnover, the absorption process will be relatively painless.
5. Establishing an adequate program of dismissal or severance pay for workers who cannot be absorbed, retrained, or otherwise accommodated when technological change destroys their regular jobs.[12]

Each of the foregoing suggestions has a valid application to technological change of the automation type. From the standpoint of employee displacement, the major difference between the introduction of automated units and orthodox technological change is one of magnitude, thus making the need for a cushioned adjustment all the more imperative. Furthermore, as noted earlier, the full or partial automation of a particular establishment may involve sweeping changes in skill requirements and the job mix, as well as radical revision of wage and seniority policies. In other words, the nature of displacement is likely to be more complex and intricate with the introduction of automatic technology.

TYPES OF EMPLOYEE DISPLACEMENT BY AUTOMATION

As envisioned and described by Nat Weinberg, head of the UAW's Research Department, four distinct kinds of displacement may be stimulated by automation. In Weinberg's terminology these are: (1) external displacement; (2) internal displacement; (3) competitive displacement;

[12] The human problems of adjustment are frequently serious even where the institution of the technological change is carefully planned in advance. See John W. McConnell and Bernard P. Lampert, "Employee Adjustment to Technological Displacement: The Fifth Avenue Coach Company Case," *Industrial and Labor Relations Review*, II (January, 1949), 219–26. For a more recent empirical study on the impact of worker displacement, caused by International Harvester's shutdown of its facilities in Auburn, New York, see Leonard P. Adams and Robert L. Aronson, *Workers and Industrial Change: A Case Study of Labor Mobility*, Cornell Studies in Industrial and Labor Relations, Vol. 8. (Ithaca: New York State School of Industrial and Labor Relations, Cornell University, 1957.)

and (4) opportunity displacement.[13] The first category involves actual worker separation from employment. The second involves a job transfer, either to higher-rated or lower-rated employment. Weinberg refers to competitive displacement as a situation in which no one loses a job in the automating concern. However, the automated firm's competitive position is improved to the point where its competitors are forced to lay off employees in their plants. Opportunity displacement involves a related type of unemployment, where there is no immediate separation from employment in the automated establishment, but a contraction of job opportunities in the plant and the industry as a whole.

AUTOMATION AND COLLECTIVE BARGAINING DEMANDS

The automation that is now occurring is, fortunately, taking place in a high employment economy where the *net displacement* to date does not appear to be alarming. The employment effects in particular situations, however, are severe. It is these immediate, short-run consequences that are giving the unions in affected establishments considerable concern.[14] We shall note in the next chapter the intensified union emphasis on various forms of negotiated employment security (or income security) plans, and upon bargaining for a shorter basic work week. Such an emphasis is directly related to the anticipated impact of automation. So also are more pointed measures such as severance pay and retraining programs.

Union leaders have not advocated outright opposition to the introduction of automatic technology, for they have become increasingly aware of the vital nexus between increasing real wages and increasing physical productivity. At the same time, most management representatives contemplating fundamental technological innovation are aware of the human implications in such change and are accepting responsibility for cushioning the impact on specific workers. Certainly no responsible person today would argue that the cost and responsibility for such fundamental change should not be shared by industry and government.

Collective bargaining should have the necessary flexibility and adaptability to develop principles and procedures governing the technological transformation of a particular firm or industry. How to do it in a particular situation is not an easy matter upon which to generalize. In some cases the transition may be gradual enough so that the problem of displacement can be handled by the normal attrition rate of labor turnover.

[13] This discussion is based on a paper by Jack Barbash, then research director of the Industrial Union Department of the AFL-CIO, on "The Effects of Automation on Industrial Workers", presented at the Midwest Economics Association meetings, April 12, 1957, in Milwaukee, Wisconsin.

[14] The serious recent unemployment in Detroit, Michigan is a case in point.

In other cases considerable advance consultation and planning will be necessary. A battery of devices for cushioning the impact will need to be employed, including job transfers with vocational retraining, dismissal or severance pay, plant-wide bumping rights for displaced employees, and expanded SUB plans. Whatever the peculiarities of the individual situation, it is imperative that there be close cooperation at all stages between management and the union if the transition is to be effected smoothly and with a minimum of disruptive personal consequences.

Excluding automation of the office, most of the industries that are now introducing automatic technology or contemplating its introduction are unionized. Thus, it is reasonable to look to collective bargaining as the primary mechanism for adaptation to the requirements of change. Much will depend on the nature of the union-management relationship in particular cases. Even under the most favorable auspices, it seems likely that some human suffering and dislocation will occur. Furthermore, it seems imperative that we rapidly develop techniques for improving our publicly conducted vocational training facilities in line with new requirements. We must also improve our informational facilities on the impact of technological displacement so that displaced workers can be located promptly in new lines of employment. Walter Reuther has proposed establishment of a technological information clearing house, one of whose functions would be to provide an accurate running picture of the impact of technological change on employment. As matters now stand, our information on the employment effects of introducing automatic technology is fragmentary and incomplete.

Another consideration worth noting is that automation may accelerate the trend toward plant decentralization that has been going on since the close of World War II. Since automation requires a minimum of labor, there is no longer a need to locate new plants in areas with abundant labor supply. It is frequently more economical to build a new automated plant than to attempt to convert an existing operation. Thus, as Clifford Baumback has pointed out, automation may aggravate our "distressed area" problems by creating or adding to localized pockets of unemployment.[15]

Collective bargaining will certainly be the chief instrumentality for regulating the introduction of automatic technology as far as individual companies are concerned. It seems obvious, however, that the employment displacement problems in particular situations will extend beyond the power of individual union-management relationships to handle. The macro-economic impact on employment and on effective demand well may require extensive state and federal governmental programs of vocational retraining and greatly improved labor market structures.

[15] See Clifford M. Baumback, "Automation," *Iowa Business Digest,* XXVIII (January, 1957).

Intelligent adaptation to technological change, particularly of the type embraced under the rubric of "automation," represents a major challenge to unions and management in the industries immediately and prospectively affected. There must be in such cases a continuing search for a constructive compromise between the need to encourage increases in physical productivity and cost reduction and the human needs of specific groups of workers adversely affected by such improvements.

SELECTED BIBLIOGRAPHY

Abruzzi, Adam, "New Horizons in Labor Dignity: The Power of Automation," *Automation*, III (December, 1956) 38–42.

AFL–CIO, "Adjustment to Technological Change," *AFL–CIO Collective Bargaining Report*, III (April-May, 1958) 25–31.

"Automation: A Brief Survey of Recent Developments," *International Labour Review*, LXXIV (October, 1956) 384–404.

Baldwin, George B. and George P. Schultz, "Automation: A New Dimension to Old Problems," *Proceedings of The Seventh Annual Meeting, Industrial Relations Research Association.* Madison: IRRA, 1955, pp. 114–28.

Bannon, Ken and Nelson Samp, "Impact of Automation on Ford-UAW Relationships," *Monthly Labor Review*, XXCI (June, 1958) 612–15.

Barkin, Solomon, "Human and Social Impact of Technical Changes," *Proceedings of the Third Annual Meeting, Industrial Relations Research Association.* Madison: IRRA, 1951, pp. 112–27.

Bright, James R., "Does Automation Raise Skill Requirements?" *Harvard Business Review*, XXXVI (July-August, 1958) 85–98.

Burtle, James, "Automation, the Guaranteed Wage, and Hours of Work," *International Labour Review*, LXXV (June, 1957) 495–513.

Diebold, John, *Automation: The Advent of the Automatic Factory*. New York: Van Nostrand Company, Inc., 1952.

Einzig, Paul, *The Economic Consequences of Automation.* New York: W. W. Norton, 1957.

Ferguson, Malcolm P., "Automation: The Management Approach," *Michigan Business Review*, IX (July, 1957) 1–10.

Gleason, Richard D., "The Industrial and Economic Impact of Technological Improvement," *Proceedings of the Third Annual Meeting, Industrial Relations Research Association.* Madison: IRRA, 1951, pp. 128–35.

Grabbe, Eugene M., *Automation in Business and Industry*. New York: John Wiley & Sons, 1957.

Hogan, Howard, *Technological Advances and Skilled Manpower: Implications for Trade and Industrial Education*, rev. ed. Washington: U. S. Government Printing Office, 1956.

Hugh-Jones, Edward M., ed., *The Push-Button World; Automation Today*. Norman: University of Oklahoma Press, 1956.

International Labor Office, Library, *Social Aspects of Automation: Preliminary List*, (Bibliographical Reference List No. 81). Geneva: 1956.

June, Stephen A., *The Automatic Factory, A Critical Examination.* Pittsburgh: Instruments Publishing Co., 1955.

Levin, Howard S., *Office Work and Automation.* New York: John Wiley & Sons, 1956.

Macmillan, Robert H., *Automation, Friend, or Foe?* Cambridge: University Press, 1956.

Maier, R. L., "Automation in the American Economy," *Journal of Business,* XXIX (January, 1956) 14–27.

Moos, S., "The Scope of Automation," *Economic Journal,* LXVII (March, 1957) 26–39.

National Manpower Council, *A Policy for Skilled Manpower.* New York: Columbia University Press, 1954.

———, *Improving the Work Skills of the Nation.* New York: Columbia University Press, 1955.

Political and Economic Planning, *Three Case Studies in Automation.* London: Political and Economic Planning, 1957.

Raushenbush, Stephen, *Productivity and Employment, 1955–65.* Washington: Public Affairs Institute, 1956.

Segal, Martin, "Factors in Wage Adjustments to Technological Changes," *Industrial and Labor Relations Review,* VIII (January, 1955) 217–30.

Sluckin, W., *Minds and Machines.* London: Penguin Books, Ltd., 1954.

Stern, James, "A Union View of Automation," *Antioch Review,* XVI (Winter, 1956–57) 419–34.

U. S. Bureau of Labor Statistics, *Automatic Technology and Its Implications: A Selected Annotated Bibliography* (Bulletin No. 1198). Washington: U. S. Government Printing Office, 1956.

———, *Case Studies of Automatic Technology:* No. 1, A Company Manufacturing Electronic Equipment; No. 2, The Introduction of an Electronic Computer in a Large Insurance Company; and No. 3, A Case Study of a Large Mechanized Bakery. Washington: U. S. Bureau of Labor Statistics, 1956.

U. S. Congress, Joint Committee on the Economic Report, *Automation and Technological Change, Hearings.* Washington: U. S. Government Printing Office, 1955.

———, *Instrumentation and Automation, Hearings.* Washington: U. S. Government Printing Office, 1957.

Wiener, Norbert, *The Human Use of Human Beings: Cybernetics and Society.* New York: Doubleday-Anchor Books, 1954.

Woodbury, David O., *Let Erma Do It: The Full Story of Automation.* New York: Harcourt, Brace, & Company, Inc., 1956.

Woods, H. D., ed., *Industrial Relations and Technological Change.* Montreal: McGill University Industrial Relations Center, 1957.

14

Collective bargaining and employee economic security

The search for employee economic security has been a dominant theme in most negotiations since the end of World War II. Comparison of a cross-section of contemporary contracts with those of ten years ago will reveal an astonishing proliferation of contractual provisions dealing with all phases of employee security—negotiated pension plans, group life insurance, health and welfare plans, maternity leave, supplemental unemployment benefit plans, and so on. This is truly an age of security, if current bargaining emphasis is taken to be significant.

The first edition of this book in 1950 was, in a sense, a "pioneer," for it included a chapter on negotiated pension plans; the real drive for private retirement programs had just gotten under way at that time. Today, virtually every union of any consequence has negotiated some form of pension program to supplement the worker's benefits under the federal old-age insurance system. And pension plans are only part of a complex and costly network of security "fringes" that has become an integral phase of contemporary bargaining in most of the key union-management relationships.

Security as a concept in industrial relations has many facets. Employee security against unfair or arbitrary treatment by management was discussed in Chapters 6, 7, and 9. It was noted in this earlier discussion that protection of the individual against arbitrary or discriminatory discipline was one of the most important functions of unionism and collective bargaining. It is a key factor in inducing many workers to become and remain union members.

But there are many other aspects of employee security. The individual worker has many fears, all of which are considered in varying degrees by modern unionism in contemporary bargaining. The worker's most pervasive fear perhaps is that of being unemployed. Consequently, recent negotiations in such key industries as steel and automobiles have placed considerable emphasis on inaugurating and then improving upon some form of supplemental unemployment benefit plan to cushion the impact of prolonged layoffs on low seniority employees. In the glass industry employers and unions have negotiated a plan for individual security accounts to be drawn on in case of layoff.[1]

Another basic fear of the worker is that he will be unable to provide adequately for himself and his family if he is incapacited for work temporarily or permanently by sickness, accident, or occupational injury. A related fear is whether a personal savings program will be sufficient when combined with Social Security benefits to sustain the worker and his family when age requires retirement from the labor market, or when death suddenly strikes the family breadwinner during his productive years.

The pressure of these fears and anxieties is clearly revealed in recent collective bargaining trends. The growth in private pension plans and health and welfare programs has been truly phenomenal since 1950. While management was by no means generally indifferent to such problems prior to 1950, it is fair to state that the main impetus for institution and improvement of private programs in the security field has come from the union side of the bargaining table.[2]

It is difficult to do justice to the entire range of private employee security programs within the compass of one chapter. The comparatively

[1] For a recent analysis of SUB plans in operation, see John W. McConnell, "Initial Experience in Operation of Supplemental Unemployment Benefit Plans," in Harold W. Davey, Howard S. Kaltenborn, and Stanley H. Ruttenberg, eds., *New Dimensions in Collective Bargaining*, Industrial Relations Research Association Publication No. 21. (New York: Harper & Brothers, 1959.)

[2] For a recent analysis of problems in health and welfare bargaining, see Jack Barbash, "The Unions and Negotiated Health and Welfare Plans," in *New Dimensions in Collective Bargaining, supra*, note 1. For a comparative evaluation of public and private programs in the employee security field, see Glenn W. Miller, "Appraisal of Collectively Bargained and Governmental Programs for Employee Security," in *New Dimensions in Collective Bargaining, supra*, note 1.

small amount of space devoted to analysis of negotiated security programs is not indicative of their relative importance. However, developments are coming so rapidly and in such varied form that a primarily factual treatment almost certainly would be dated by the time it appeared in print. Therefore, we shall concern ourselves here with underlining some of the major problems in this highly dynamic field of economic security.

Three substantive aspects of the basic problem of *economic security* will be considered. First, we shall consider recent problems and trends in the negotiated pension plan field. Second, we shall outline recent contractual problems in the "health and welfare" field, defined here to cover such matters as life insurance, accidental death and dismemberment, sickness and accident payments, hospital and medical care, and surgical care. Finally, we shall appraise briefly contemporary union-management approaches to the problem of employment security—principally SUB plans and guaranteed wage plans.

PENSION PLANS AND RETIREMENT SECURITY

The postwar drive for negotiated pension plans was initiated by the United Mine Workers in its 1945 contract demands. In 1949 and 1950 adoption of pension plans in steel and automobiles gave further impetus toward making some form of negotiated retirement plan a "must" item on many collective bargaining agenda. In 1950 it was not clear whether the new enthusiasm for private pension plans was an opportunistic, stopgap bargaining tactic by unions unable to secure another round of across-the-board wage increases because of the 1949-1950 recession, or a permanent change in union emphasis.[3] Developments since 1950 make crystal clear the fact that union interest in securing and improving private pension plans is an enduring one, largely independent of the perennial concern to increase wages. By the middle of 1954 it was estimated that more than seven million workers were covered by negotiated pension plans. The number covered by 1958 probably exceeds ten million.

Interest in private pension plans has not been entirely a union monopoly. There has been substantial employer sentiment favorable to such plans as a means of improving job satisfaction, worker morale, and productivity. A large number of pension plans have been introduced unilaterally by non-union employers since the end of World War II.

SHOULD PENSION PLAN BE CONTRIBUTORY OR NONCONTRIBUTORY?

Many problems associated with the introduction of negotiated pension plans have now been largely resolved by experience. One of these is

[3] See Chapter 9 of the first edition of this book at p. 211.

whether the plan should be contributory or noncontributory. In the great majority of cases the pension aspect of the total economic security package has been made noncontributory. Although sound arguments can be made for a contributory plan, the trend seems strongly and continuously in the direction of negotiating the noncontributory type. Nevertheless, it is desirable to have in mind some of the principal considerations favoring each type.

Among the principal arguments advanced in behalf of contributory pension plans are the following:

1. Such plans are more socially desirable in that they encourage individual thrift. The values of individual participation are also stressed.
2. The size of benefits can be increased with employee participation.
3. Mobility of labor is not impaired, since the employee usually can take his contributions, plus interest, with him in changing jobs.
4. Employers will be more receptive to negotiating this type of plan.
5. Contributory plans are more likely to be sound in an actuarial sense, since the handling of "other people's money" is involved.
6. A contributory plan will exercise a restraining influence on future union demands, since employees have to share the additional burden of an augmented pension program.

Among the principal arguments advanced in behalf of noncontributory pensions, the following may be listed:

1. The net cost in relation to benefits will be smaller to the employer because of the savings he makes from the forfeited benefits of employees leaving before retirement. The gains in the fund accruing from worker separation can be actuarially estimated, and financing costs thus reduced.
2. Under such a plan it is easier for an employer to insist on a compulsory retirement age.
3. A noncontributory plan eliminates many administrative expenses associated with the contributory type such as payroll deduction expenses, keeping individual employee accounts, etc.
4. Cost in relation to benefits is lower as a result of the savings from complete coverage of the work force. Under a contributory plan, the cost may be greater because of incomplete participation by the employees.
5. If the plan is wholly noncontributory, more actual money after taxes will be available for payment of benefits.

Several other considerations may be mentioned. Many employers favor the noncontributory type on the ground that it will insure them more nearly complete control over its administration and operation. They fear that a contributory plan will bring a demand for greater union participation in its administration. On the other hand, this argument is employed in reverse. Many employers tend to favor contributory plans as a means of convincing the worker that he is not getting something for nothing. They feel it will increase the worker's appreciation of the difficulties and cost of keeping such plans on a sound financial footing.

A seemingly plausible argument for the contributory plan is that it encourages individual thrift. Upon closer examination this argument probably will not stand up. A prudent worker will recognize the continuing necessity for individual saving for postretirement years, whether he is under a contributory or a noncontributory plan. Conversely, the economic habits of an improvident worker will probably not be improved substantially by a contributory plan.

The case for an adequate pension plan of either type can be rested on more fundamental grounds than the homely virtues of individual thrift. The logic of amortizing the cost of a worker's postretirement years over the span of his directly productive years affords solid support for the pension principle.

Furthermore, other, more cold-blooded economic arguments may be advanced. These include the potential savings to industry from reduced labor turnover, reduced absenteeism, and generally increased worker job satisfaction. All of these may reasonably be expected to flow from an effective and equitable retirement program.

A larger question arises over a basic disagreement as to whether privately bargained pension programs should be expanded to minimize the necessity for more extensive governmental assumption of the security function, or whether a universally applied and more effective (in terms of size and benefits) government program is logical. Analysis of this major policy question is not attempted here, since our focus is on privately negotiated plans.[4] It may be pointed out, however, that a network of private plans (with wide variation in coverage, benefits, and eligibility requirements) presents serious problems that cannot be dealt with as effectively on a private as on a public basis. One of the most difficult problems is the inability to transfer benefits from one company to another, and from one industry to another, under most private plans. This presents no serious difficulty under a federal program.

NEED FOR FULLY FUNDED, ACTUARIALLY SOUND PLANS

Whether the plan is contributory or noncontributory, there is general agreement that the program must be financed and funded in such a way as to insure the payment of benefits due the employee upon retirement. Disclosures in recent years as to the misuse of pension and health and welfare funds have reinforced employer and union sentiments in favor of fully funded and actuarially sound plans under capable administration.

[4] For a comparative analysis consult the paper by Glenn W. Miller, *supra,* note 2.

One of the major functions of the AFL-CIO's standing Committee on Ethical Practices is the continual policing of pension and health and welfare plans. It is also significant that the AFL-CIO has endorsed the demand for federal legislation generated by the findings of the Douglas subcommittee.[5]

THE PROBLEM OF VESTING

A major problem in private pension plans is the question of vesting. Vesting involves an employee's right to all or some fraction of the pension equities for which the employer has paid if the employee goes to another firm. In the absence of a vesting arrangement horizontal mobility of workers may be seriously inhibited. On the other hand, the cost of full or partial vesting may be prohibitive in many cases. The earlier negotiated plans made no provision for vesting until an employee had reached a reasonably high minimum age and/or had piled up fifteen or twenty years' service with one employer. Some of the more recent plans, however, have worked out more liberal vesting arrangements. There has been a considerable growth of multi-employer and union-wide area pension plans, which make a worker's movement freer as long as he stays within the framework of the plan's coverage. If pension contributions are regarded as deferred wages, it logically follows that any plan is discriminatory which does not permit each employee to preserve his own earned pension allocation. Thus, even though the great majority of negotiated plans are noncontributory, the search for a viable method of providing full vesting may be expected to continue. The absence of a satisfactory vesting arrangement remains the principal point of vulnerability in most negotiated plans today.

TRENDS IN NEGOTIATED PENSION PLANS

It has become plainly evident that the drive for negotiated pension plans is not a transitory phenomenon. We may expect a steady increase in the coverage of pension plans and in the level of benefits. Although earlier plans were rigid and strict on a compulsory retirement age, there has been a tendency in recent practice to work out ways and means of making retirement a more flexible proposition. One of the critical problems today is development of job opportunities for older workers.[6]

There also appears to be a tendency to divorce private plans from federal Social Security payments, in marked contrast to the earlier plans

[5] In 1958, Congress passed a "mild" measure known as the Welfare and Pension Plans Disclosure Act. For a summary appraisal, see Sar A. Levitan, "Welfare and Pension Plans Disclosure Act," *Labor Law Journal*, IX, (November, 1958) 827-34.

[6] See John Corson and John W. McConnell, *Economic Needs of Older People* (New York: Twentieth Century Fund, 1956.)

which were tied directly to what the worker received from OASI. The emphasis on a funded, actuarially sound plan has been intensified by disclosures of maladministration or corruption in some pension funds.

Increasing attention is now being given to the problem of suitable investment outlets for pension funds, and to the need for hedging future benefits against long-run price inflation. Demands are already being made for escalator pensions.

The negotiated pension plan movement is still in the developmental stage. Much remains to be learned about the viability of such programs. We are far from a consensus as to the one best type of private plan. The pension issue is likely to be a fixture on collective bargaining agenda for many years to come.

HEALTH AND WELFARE PLANS

Negotiated health and welfare plans have increased at a remarkable rate in the period since World War II, and especially since 1952. The pace shows no sign of slackening. Virtually all contemporary contracts now contain some "health and welfare" benefit provisions. Many plans involve a large-scale protection of the employee in terms of accident and sickness, hospital and surgical care, life insurance, accidental death or dismemberment, medical care, and (occasionally) optical and dental care. Perhaps in no other area is the dynamic potential of collective bargaining as a mechanism for meeting the changing economic needs of workers more evident than in the health and welfare field. While there is nothing new about the problems that health and welfare plans seek to solve, the extent and rapidity of the growth of negotiated plans in recent years has been truly phenomenal.

No effort will be made here to analyze in any detail the substance of specific health and welfare plans. There is already a considerable body of informational literature available.[7] The greater part of the discussion here will be on some of the more pressing problems from a bargaining standpoint in negotiated health and welfare plans.

PREVAILING PRACTICE ON HEALTH AND WELFARE

Before going on to problem areas of health and welfare bargaining, it may be advisable to summarize *prevailing* practice (unless otherwise indicated) on various aspects of health and welfare planning. The following summary is based on a recent study by Jack Barbash.[8]

[7] The references most helpful to the writer will be found in the bibliography at the end of the chapter.

[8] Cited *supra*, note 2.

Hospitalization and group life insurance are the most frequently found health and welfare benefits, in that order. When cash benefits are specified on hospitalization, $12 to $14 per day is the typical provision, with Blue Cross being specified in a minority of cases. Typical duration provision is 120 days, with $120 for "extras."

Group life insurance frequently provides today for $3,000 and upwards. In a few contracts the amount of insurance is geared to earnings or length of service. Insurance is frequently continuable after retirement, but on a reduced basis.

Provision for accidental death is frequently found as a supplement to group life insurance—generally double indemnity. A schedule of payments is usually provided for in case of dismemberment.

Plans providing payments for accident, sickness, and disability typically will pay $40 per week or more with a twenty-six-week duration, preceded by a waiting period of eight days for sickness and one day for accidents. Some contracts involve supplementation of payments received from workmen's compensation up to the level of benefits to which the worker is entitled under accident and sickness benefits.

Where surgical insurance is provided, a maximum schedule for specific surgical procedures usually runs between $225 and $300.

A minority of contracts provide for in-hospital and out-hospital medical benefits, customarily paying $3 per in-hospital visit and $4 for visits to the doctor's office.

Some contracts provide for other types of health care such as maternity, polio, major medical, dental, and optical care. Some cover dependents' care.

In prevailing practice the employer pays the entire bill for health and welfare programs. Many plans, however, are on a contributory basis in all or some phases. Pension and health and welfare benefits under the 1958-1961 contract in the women's clothing industry are financed by employer contributions amounting to 9 per cent of payroll. The pension or retirement fund takes 3½ per cent, and a "health, welfare and severance fund" takes 5½ per cent.

PROBLEM AREAS IN HEALTH AND WELFARE BARGAINING

As in other money issues in collective bargaining, a focal point of controversy between unions and management concerns the cost of benefits provided under the plan. Health and welfare plans are negotiated on either a level of benefits basis or on a payroll basis. Under the former basis the employer obligates himself to see that specified benefits are provided without binding himself to any fixed monetary contribution.

Under the payroll basis the employer obligates himself to finance a particular program by either a fixed percentage of payroll or by a specified cents-per-working hour sum for each covered employee. As in the case of pensions, the plan may be contributory or noncontributory; this feature may vary with different types of benefits. Group life insurance, for example, is customarily paid for by the employer, whereas hospitalization insurance is frequently financed on a contributory basis. The overwhelming majority of all plans involve unilateral administration by the employer.

A new element injects itself into health and welfare bargaining that is not present in collective bargaining on other issues. The union today faces the problem of negotiating with the "purveyors of health and welfare benefits" as well as with the employer. Once the scope and content of a plan have been agreed upon between the union and the employer, the next step is getting one's money's worth from insurance companies, hospitals, and medical practitioners. Dealing with such problems has been responsible for most of the recent controversy in the health and welfare field. Unions have frequently found themselves at odds with the purveyors of health and welfare benefits as to cost, scope, and quality of benefits. It is this "bargaining" on the second front that seems to be responsible for most of the recent controversy in the health and welfare field.[9]

Unions are increasingly concerned over the rapidly mounting cost of hospital, medical, and surgical care. Also, a full-scale battle has been fought between the United Mine Workers and the American Medical Association over the UMW's dropping of "unsatisfactory" doctors from its approved list and the AMA's encouragement to county medical societies to drop from membership doctors who work for union medical plans.

One thing is certain. Experimentation in the direction of securing more adequate and complete health and welfare programs in the most economical and efficient manner will continue. If private outlets fail to supply this insistent demand, the unions and other groups will certainly turn to government.

The alternatives are tersely stated by Father Leo Brown: [10]

> The American people, however, is determined that all its constituent groups shall have health care at a cost they can afford. There is a growing conviction that prepaid service-type medicine will afford that care at a cost within their reach. If experimentation with such plans becomes a matter of public contro-

[9] Again the writer is indebted to Barbash for some penetrating insights into the difficulties in this "new" kind of collective bargaining.

[10] Leo C. Brown, S.J., "The Economic Future of Medical Practice," *Social Order*, VIII (June, 1958), 269–79, at 277.

versy, an aroused public opinion, stimulated by organized groups including but not confined to labor unions, may lead to legislation at the national level which would modify the structure of medical practice in even more drastic ways. If, however, experimentation is permitted, the verdict on prepaid, comprehensive-type medical service will be rendered by experience; the deciding factors, moreover, will be the quality of care, the satisfaction of patient and doctor and relative cost.

NEW APPROACHES TO EMPLOYMENT SECURITY

Improved employment security has become a vitally important issue in many negotiations, notably in the durable goods industries that are likely to experience considerable fluctuation in employment levels. In steel, automobiles, flat glass, farm equipment, and a number of other industries, the negotiation of supplemental unemployment benefit plans has been one of the more significant bargaining innovations in recent years.

SUB plans first came into prominence in the 1955 negotiations in the automobile and farm equipment industries, followed by the steel plan in 1956. The basic idea of such plans is to provide payments from a private fund to the laid-off worker to supplement his unemployment compensation payments under state law. The rationale of such supplemental payments is the obvious inadequacy of state UC payments in relation to the worker's average weekly pay. The objective in most SUB plans is to provide the worker with benefits while on layoff that, taken together with his UC payments, will approximate two-thirds of his normal weekly take-home pay. Thus, if a worker's normal take home pay is $90 per week and his UC benefits amount to $30 per week, the SUB payments would be approximately $30 a week.

The recession of 1957-1958 put many SUB plans to a rigorous early test. Experience is still too limited, however, to make any firm statements as to their operational validity. Such payments have certainly been a boon to eligible laid-off workers in automobiles and steel, two industries with a heavy incidence of unemployment in the recession.

As might be expected, numerous knotty problems arose soon after the inauguration of SUB plans. Controversy continues as to such matters as the level and duration of benefits; whether payments should be made from a pooled reserve fund or whether each eligible employee should have his own account; the proper level of seniority eligibility requirements; whether benefit payments should be related to gross wages or to wages after taxes; and whether or not to provide for dependents' benefits. These are among the basic policy issues upon which agremeent has to be reached in instituting or improving upon an SUB plan. Once a plan is in effect, other sources of disagreement arise, principally in connection with disqualifications. The type of issue here is similar to that with which we are already familiar in connection with unemployment insurance itself.

Although SUB plans appear to have been accepted in the industries where they originated in 1955 and 1956, other companies and unions have not adopted to any appreciable extent this particular approach to greater employment and income security. The number of workers covered by SUB plans of one kind or another was probably not much more than two million in early 1958.

One result of the new plans has been to focus attention on the need for revising and improving state unemployment compensation systems. Since SUB plans became a key issue in negotiations, many states have raised the level of benefit payments, although seldom to adequate amounts. The concurrent existence of public and private unemployment insurance systems raises serious problems in integration that are beyond the scope of our treatment here. The entire problem of employment stabilization and the best approach to cushioning the impact of unemployment has been under serious re-examination. Union policy may be expected to focus on improving both public and private plans. At this writing, employers appear to be divided between those who favor some form of limited private supplementation and those who believe in continuing to work strictly within the UC framework.

THE PRESENT STATE OF GUARANTEED WAGE PLANS

SUB plans emerged as the end product of sustained union pressure for negotiated guaranteed wage or guaranteed employment plans of an initially more comprehensive nature. What has happened to the drive for "pure" guarantee plans requiring fifty-two paychecks a year, or so many weeks of guaranteed employment with no minimum annual income specified? The answer seems to be that there has been no appreciable increase in pure plans of the conventional type. Although union interest remains high in achieving the ultimate goal of an annual guaranteed wage or guaranteed employment plan, union pragmatism in recent years has dictated a concentration on the obtainable. There is general recognition of the current impracticality of attempting to secure plans with 100 per cent guarantees and unlimited employer liability. The concentration has been on more modest proposals such as SUB plans, which in the auto industry amount to approximately two-thirds of a semiannual guaranteed wage, and in steel to something less than two-thirds pay for up to fifty-two weeks of layoff. It seems reasonably clear at this writing that conventional plans of fifty-two paychecks a year, as in the much-publicized Hormel plan, are not close to adoption in industry generally and are not likely to be for sound practical reasons. The paramount barrier is the prohibitive cost and risk of such plans. There is also the formidable obstacle posed by management fear of additional losses of managerial prerogatives and flexibility under joint administration of such a plan.

As Herbert Unterberger cogently points out, it is probably a healthy development to have our thinking evolving from the concept of guaranteed annual wages to the concept of income security. We are leaving the slogan stage and facing up to the real issue, which is the degree of income security which American industry can feasibly provide.[11]

CONCLUSION

Security in all its phases will undoubtedly continue to be a dominant theme in negotiations for as far into the future as one might care to look. Most of the major substantive areas of security are now being treated with varying degrees of emphasis in all collective negotiations. Income security and employment security, plus protection against the hazards of illness, disability, death, and old age, make up a complex of security problems that command the attention of all union-management relationships today. Although considerable variety in approach and substantive content will be found in contemporary contracts, the nature of the contract of the future is not difficult to predict. Today's variety and the discrepancies between contracts are accounted for primarily by differences in managerial ability to pay and union bargaining power, rather than by basic differences in philosophical approach to the solution of the employee security problem.

The model contract of the future will in all probability contain most if not all of the following features:

1. A noncontributory pension plan providing for full or partial vesting, and containing some kind of escalator hedge against price inflation.
2. A comprehensive health and welfare plan including such features as life insurance with special provisions for accidental death, hospitalization and surgical insurance, prepaid medical care, major medical or catastrophe benefits, and a variety of special benefits such as maternity leave and dental and optical care.
3. A plan providing for unemployment insurance benefits approximating not less than two-thirds of the employee's normal weekly pay for a period of fifty-two weeks.

[11] See S. H. Unterberger, *Guaranteed Wage and Supplementary Unemployment Pay Plans* (New York: Commerce Clearing House, Inc., 1956.)

SELECTED BIBLIOGRAPHY

Negotiated Pension Plans

Ackerman, Laurence J., "Financing Pension Benefits, *Harvard Business Review*, XXXIV (September–October, 1956) 63–74.

Ain, Samuel N., "OASI—Impact on Private Pension Plans," *Harvard Business Review*, XXXIV (May–June, 1956) 101–108.

American Management Association, *Controlling Employee Benefit and Pension Costs* (Special Report No. 23). New York: American Management Association, 1957.

Bers, Melvin K., *Union Policy and the Older Worker*. Berkeley: Institute of Industrial Relations, University of California, 1957.

Blumenthal, W. Michael, *Disability Retirement in Industrial Pension Plans*, (Research Report Series, No. 93). Princeton: Industrial Relations Section, 1956.

Bureau of National Affairs, Inc., *Pensions and Profit Sharing*. Washington: Bureau of National Affairs, Inc., 1956.

Cameron, James C. and F. J. L. Young, *Vesting of Employer Contributions under Industrial Retirement Plans*, (Bulletin No. 14). Kingston, Ont.: Department of Industrial Relations, Queen's University, 1956.

Corson, John and John W. McConnell, *Economic Needs of Older People*. New York: Twentieth Century Fund, 1956.

Cooper, Walter J. and Roger Vaughan, *Pension Planning; Experience and Trends*, (Industrial Relations Monograph No. 16). New York: Industrial Relations Counselors, Inc., 1954.

Daoust, Joseph H., "Area Pension Plans," *Labor Law Journal*, V (January, 1954) 47–58.

Dearing, Charles L., *Industrial Pensions*. Washington: The Brookings Institution, 1954.

Gallenbeck, Curtis B., "Problems and Procedures in Retirement, Continuation, and Recall," *Proceedings of the Fifth Annual Meeting, Industrial Relations Research Association*. Madison: IRRA, 1953, pp. 93–100.

Goldner, William, "Trade Union Structure and Private Pension Plans," *Industrial and Labor Relations Review*, V (October, 1951) 62–72.

Kaye, Seymour P. and Jack B. Levitt, "Bargaining on Compulsory Retirement," *Personnel*, XXXIII (September, 1956) 153–62.

Law Note, "Legal Problems of Private Pension Plans," *Harvard Law Review*, LXX (January, 1957) 490–509.

Lesser, Leonard, "Contribution and Benefits," *Proceedings of the Fifth Annual Meeting, Industrial Relations Research Association*. Madison: IRRA, 1953, pp. 86–92.

McLean, Louis A., "A New Approach to the Retirement Security Problem," *Labor Law Journal*, VII (December, 1956) 765–67.

Myers, Robert J., "Financial Impact of Pension Costs on the Railroad Industry," *Labor Law Journal*, VII (May, 1956) 265–75.

National Bureau of Economic Research, Inc., *Suggestions for Research in the Economics of Pensions*. New York: National Bureau of Economic Research, 1957.

National Industrial Conference Board, *Income and Resources of Older People*, (Studies in Business Economics, No. 52). New York: National Industrial Conference Board, 1956.

Otis, Henry W., "Comparing Pension Costs," *Harvard Business Review*, XXXV (July–August, 1957) 58–66.

Somers, A. Norman and Louis Schwartz, "Pension and Welfare Plans: Gratuities or Compensation?" *Industrial and Labor Relations Review*, IV (October, 1950) 77–88.

Stein, Emanuel, ed., *Proceedings of New York University Ninth Annual Conference on Labor*. Albany: Matthew Bender, 1956.

Rowe, Evan K. and Thomas H. Paine, "Pension Plans under Collective Bargaining," *Labor Law Journal*, IV (August, 1953) 541–64.

Tilove, Robert, "Employee Benefit Plans," in Neil W. Chamberlain, Frank C. Pierson, and Theresa Wolfson, eds., *A Decade of Industrial Relations Research, 1946–1956*. New York: Harper & Brothers, 1958, pp. 146–73.

U. S. Bureau of Labor Statistics, *Employment and Economic Status of Older Men and Women*, (Bulletin No. 1213). Washington: U. S. Government Printing Office, 1957.

———, *Health, Insurance, and Pension Plans in Union Contracts*, (Bulletin No. 1187). Washington: U. S. Government Printing Office, 1955.

———, *Job Performance and Age: A Study in Measurement*, (Bulletin No. 1203). Washington: U. S. Government Printing Office, 1956.

———, *Older Workers under Collective Bargaining, Part 1: Hiring, Retention, Job Termination*, (Bulletin No. 1199–1). Washington: U. S. Government Printing Office, 1956.

———, *Older Workers under Collective Bargaining, Part 2: Health Insurance Plans, Pension Plans*, (Bulletin No. 1199–2). Washington: U. S. Government Printing Office, 1956.

———, *Pension Plans under Collective Bargaining*, (Bulletin No. 1147). Washington: U. S. Government Printing Office, 1953.

U. S. Bureau of Old-Age and Survivors Insurance, *Private Employee Benefit Plans: Selected Annotated References, 1951–1955*. Baltimore: 1956.

U. S. Senate Committee on Labor and Public Welfare, Subcommittee on Welfare and Pension Funds, *Welfare and Pension Plans Investigation*, (Report No. 1734). Washington: U. S. Government Printing Office, 1956.

Negotiated Health and Welfare Plans

Baisden, Richard N. and John Hutchinson, *Health Insurance: Group Coverage in Industry*. Los Angeles: Institute of Industrial Relations, University of California, 1956.

Baker, Helen and Dorothy Dahl, *Group Health Insurance and Sickness Benefit Plans in Collective Bargaining*. Princeton: Industrial Relations Section, 1945.

Brown, Leo C., S. J., "The Economic Future of Medical Practice," *Social Order*, VIII (June, 1958) 269–79.

Davis, Michael M., "Setting up Union Health Centers," *Labor Law Journal*, VIII (February, 1957) 119–22.

Foundation on Employee Health, Medical Care and Welfare, Inc. *Problems and Solutions of Health and Welfare Programs:* Study No. 1, Part A, "Improving Value and Reducing Cost"; Parts B and C, "Service Benefits—and how to Compare Service versus Indemnity Benefits." New York: Foundation on Employee Health, Medical Care and Welfare, Inc., 1957 and 1958.

Fox, Harland, *Trends in Company Group Insurance Programs*, (Studies in Personnel Policy No. 159). New York: National Industrial Conference Board, 1957.

Health Insurance Plan of Greater New York, Committee for the Special Research Project, *Health and Medical Care in New York City: A Report.* Cambridge: Published for the Commonwealth Fund by Harvard University Press, 1957.

Imberman, A. A., "Racketeering in Health and Welfare Funds," *Harvard Business Review*, XXXII (November–December, 1954) 72–80.

Klem, Margaret C. and Margaret F. McKiever, *Management and Union Health and Medical Programs*, Public Health Service Publication No. 329. Washington: U. S. Government Printing Office, 1953.

Leigh, Samuel, "Management of Welfare Funds," *Labor Law Journal*, VIII (August, 1957) 542–48.

MacIntyre, Duncan M., "Regulation of Employee Benefit Programs," *Industrial and Labor Relations Review*, X (July, 1957) 554–78.

Neufeld, Maurice F., *Day In, Day Out with Local 3, IBEW*, (Bulletin No. 28). Ithaca: New York State School of Industrial and Labor Relations, 1955.

Pollack, Jerome, "A Labor View of Health Insurance," *Monthly Labor Review*, XXCI (June, 1958) 626–30.

Rowe, Evan K., "Health Insurance, and Pension Plans in Union Contracts," Monthly Labor Review, LXXVIII (September, 1955) 993–1000.

Slavick, Fred, "Adequacy of Medical Benefits in Collectively Bargained Health Insurance Plans—Recent and Future Research," *Proceedings of the Tenth Annual Meeting, Industrial Relations Research Association.* Madison: IRRA, 1958.

———, *Distribution of Medical Care Costs and Benefits under Four Collectively Bargained Insurance Plans*, (Bulletin No. 37). Ithaca: New York State School of Industrial and Labor Relations, 1956.

Straub, Alfred G., Jr., *Whose Welfare: A Report on Union and Employer Welfare Plans in New York.* New York: New York State Insurance Department, 1954.

U. S. Bureau of Labor Statistics, *Digest of One-Hundred Selected Health Insurance Plans under Collective Bargaining*, (Bulletin No. 1180). Washington: U. S. Government Printing Office, 1954.

Wilmas, Walter F., "New Frontiers in Social Welfare: Health and Welfare Programs," *Labor Law Journal*, VIII (August, 1957) 539–42.

Wade, Leo J., "Needed: A Closer Look at Industrial Medical Programs," *Harvard Business Review*, XXXIV (March-April, 1956) 81–90.

SUB and GAW Plans

Backman, Jules, "Economics of the Guaranteed Wage," *Labor Law Journal*, VII (October, 1956) 623–28.

Blum, Fred H., *Toward a Democratic Work Process*. New York: Harper & Brothers, 1953.

Bowers, Edison L., Paul Craig, and William Papier, *Financing Unemployment Compensation: Ohio's Experience*, (Research Monograph No. 89). Columbus: Bureau of Business Research, Ohio State University, 1956.

Bureau of National Affairs, *Supplemental Unemployment Benefit Plans*. Washington: Bureau of National Affairs, 1956.

Cooper, Lyle, "Wage Guaranties at Hormel: A Comment," *Journal of Business*, XXIX (April, 1956) 141–45.

Craig, Paul G. and W.E. Schlender, "Some Relationships between GAW and Seniority," *Journal of Business*, XXX (January, 1957) 1–11.

Garbarino, J. W., *Guaranteed Wages*. Berkeley: Institute of Industrial Relations, University of California, 1954 .

Hampton, W. C., "Administering an SUB Plan: The Ford Experience," *Personnel*, XXXIV (July-August, 1957) 76–83.

McCarthy, E. J., "Wage Guaranties and Annual Earnings: A Case Study of George A. Hormel and Company," *Journal of Business*, XXIX (January, 1956) 41–51.

McConnell, Campbell R., "Pros and Cons of the Guaranteed Annual Wage," *Labor Law Journal*, VII (July, 1956) 414–24, 432.

McConnell, John W., "Supplementary Unemployment Benefits," *Proceedings of the Eighth Annual Meeting, Industrial Relations Research Association*. Madison: IRRA, 1956, pp. 167–81.

Mullady, Philomena M., *A Selected Bibliography with Notes on Guaranteed Annual Wage and Employment Plans*, (Bibliographical Series No. 1). Ithaca: New York State School of Industrial and Labor Relations, Cornell University, 1952.

Owen, C. F., "Cost Factors in the Integration of Company Unemployment Benefits and Unemployment Insurance," *Journal of Business*, XXX (January, 1957) 50–59.

Papier, William, "Guaranteed Annual Wage Proposals: Their Implications for Unemployment Compensation," *Industrial and Labor Relations Review*, VIII (January, 1955) 265–74.

Pierce, Samuel R., "Legal Problems in Plans for Private Layoff Pay," *Monthly Labor Review*, LXXIX (August, 1956) 895–900.

Ruttenberg, Harold J., "Pay by the Year: Can the Unions Afford It?" *Harper's Magazine*, CCXI (December, 1955) 29–33.

Seastone, Don A., "The Status of Guaranteed Wages and Employment in Collective Bargaining," *American Economic Review*, XLIV (December, 1954) 911–17.

Slichter, Sumner H., "SUB Plans—Their Economic Impact," *Management Record*, XVIII (February, 1956) 45–47.

Unterberger, S. Herbert, *Guaranteed Wage and Supplementary Unemployment Pay Plans*. New York: Commerce Clearing House, 1956.

Wermel, Michael T. and Geraldine M. Beideman, *Supplemental Unemployment Benefit Plans: Their Economic and Industrial Relations Implications.* Pasadena: Industrial Relations Section, California Institute of Technology, 1957.

Wickersham, Edward D., "Legislative Implications of Recent Unemployment Benefits Agreements," *Labor Law Journal*, VII (June, 1956) 339–47.

———, "Repercussions of the Ford Agreement," *Harvard Business Review*, XXXIV (January–February, 1956) 61–73.

15

Fringe benefit trends

Contract provisions now accounting for approximately 20 per cent of the average employer's labor cost are still misleadingly referred to as fringe benefits. Some of the more expensive aspects of these so-called fringes have been discussed in the preceding chapter. The present discussion deals with current trends in important supplementary payment provisions other than pension plans, health and welfare programs, and supplemental unemployment benefit systems.

It is sometimes difficult to realize that many provisions now taken for granted in contemporary bargaining were not even discussed in negotiations prior to World War II. Paid vacations, paid holidays when not worked, reporting pay, call-in pay, shift premiums for work on second and third shift, premium pay for Saturday and Sunday work as such—these are all benefits that today's blue collar worker is accustomed to receiving; his counterpart in 1940 seldom enjoyed any of them.

Although substantial variety still may be seen in the scope and content of fringe complexes in contemporary bargaining, certain broad generalizations as to current practice and future trends can be safely undertaken. In making such generalizations it is important to keep in mind that many unions exhibit a continuing preference for basic gains in wage rates to the near exclusion of advancement on supplementary benefits discussed herein. Most of the major unions, however, have by now developed a considerable institutional stake in maintaining and improving an already impressive pattern of supplemental wage payments. Surprisingly enough, in the worker's mind some of these fringe improvements take on greater importance than their actual cost would appear to warrant. Analysis of contract administration in many union-management relationships shows that a high percentage of grievances involve individual worker complaints as to alleged inequitability or discrimination in administration of such fringe items as distribution of overtime, eligibility for holiday pay, entitlement to vacation earnings upon leaving employment, and so on.

The continued growth and expansion of fringe benefits in contemporary bargaining is evidence of a broadening employer conception of his obligation to the employees beyond a "fair day's pay," and of the pulling power of such benefits on union leadership. There appears to be nothing transitory about the drive for better fringes. Arthur Ross anticipates that so-called fringes may amount to 25 per cent of the average employer's payroll by 1960.[1] This does not appear to be an exaggerated estimate, judging by current bargaining trends.

Many employers are becoming understandably concerned about the mounting cost of fringe compensation, the difficulty in accurately estimating that cost, and the lack of integration or flexibility in the over-all program of benefits beyond basic wages. While in some cases this concern may fairly be said to be exaggerated, in many situations we have reached an opportune time to pause and take stock. A detached examination of benefit patterns would in many cases reveal an urgent need for the development of a better integrated and more flexible program to satisfy employees' differing preferences and the employer's desire for economical, efficient administration. We shall return to this theme at the conclusion of this chapter. It is now appropriate to present a summary analysis of recent developments and problems in connection with the following typical fringe areas:[2]

[1] Arthur M. Ross, "Fringe Benefits Today and Tomorrow," *Labor Law Journal*, VII (August, 1956), 476–82.

[2] The Bureau of Labor Statistics keeps close track of changes in a variety of standard fringe items in contemporary bargaining. The reader should consult the *Monthly Labor Review* for BLS reports on current practice. The AFL-CIO Research Department in its regular publication *Collective Bargaining Report* is also a helpful source on recent developments on various fringe items. The U. S. Chamber of Commerce periodically surveys the cost of fringe benefits. The problem of measuring the cost of fringes is a difficult one. The difficulties are discussed in a BLS Bulletin, No. 1186, *Problems in Measurement of Expenditures on Selected Items of Supplementary Employee Remuneration, Manufacturing Establishments, 1953* (Washington: U. S. Government Printing Office, 1956.)

1. Vacations with pay.
2. Pay for specified holidays when not worked.
3. Reporting pay and call-in pay.
4. Premium pay for Saturday and Sunday work as such.
5. Shift premium pay.
6. Separation or severance pay.
7. Miscellaneous fringe provisions.

VACATIONS WITH PAY

We have already moved a long way from the World War II formula on vacation pay of one week's vacation after one year of service and two weeks' vacation after five years of service. This standard War Labor Board formula has been considerably improved upon in most contracts.

Virtually all contracts today provide for a paid vacation plan of some sort. A negotiation seldom goes by without some effort by the union to liberalize and expand the previous contract's provisions on this subject. Most vacation plans are pro-rated in terms of the employee's length of service. It is increasingly common to find vacation plans calling for one week after six months of service, one and one half weeks for between three and five years' service, two weeks for between five and ten years' service, two and one half weeks for between ten and fifteen years' service, and three weeks for fifteen or more years' service. Four weeks is usually the upper limit on paid vacations, but few contracts are that liberal.

The major union effort in recent years has been directed to shortening the service period required to qualify for two- and three-week vacation periods. The West Coast aircraft industry, for example, now provides for two weeks' vacation after one year's service. A considerable number of contracts now provide for three weeks' vacation after ten years of service instead of the more usual fifteen years.

Paid vacation plans have appeared in some sectors of the construction industry, which historically has exhibited no interest in such plans because of the casual and seasonal nature of employment.

Another union effort in recent years has been to negotiate vacation payments to approximate what the employee would have earned had he been working during his vacation period, instead of the more conventional forty hours multiplied by his occupational rate. Many contracts today provide for vacation pay as a percentage of employee earnings during the previous year. This type of provision is obviously of special value to incentive workers or to day workers who had considerable overtime during the previous year.

Many problems that plagued the early administration of vacation pay provisions have been resolved satisfactorily by the parties. Definition of what constitutes "continuous service," the setting of eligibility dates, problems over when employees should take their vacations or whether they should be permitted to work during their vacation time, the vacation rights of a separated employee, the question of pay for contractual holidays occurring during an employee's vacation period, and so on, all have been settled in most relationships. The writer can recall only one or two arbitration disputes in his own experience over ten years that dealt with a vacation pay issue.

Continued liberalization of vacation pay provisions may be confidently anticipated, but a practical ceiling on expansion can be envisioned. It is unlikely that the present limits of the more liberal vacation pay plans can be substantially exceeded. A considerable number of employees are now on a normal work week of less than forty hours, and very few are regularly scheduled for more than forty hours. Under these conditions it seems unlikely that the four-week maximum vacation will be exceeded. It is probable, however, that the service eligibility requirements for two- and three-week vacation periods will be reduced progressively in future bargaining.

It is now generally accepted that an employee's vacation credits are an earned equity of which he may not be deprived, even if discharged for cause. At the same time, there is a recognition that an employer must maintain considerable discretion in the scheduling of employee vacations in terms of production requirements and that an employee is not entitled to unlimited freedom of choice. Many companies now schedule most employees for vacation during an annual plant shutdown for inventory and maintenance purposes.

PAID HOLIDAYS

Prior to World War II very few blue collar workers received pay for any hours or days not actually worked by them. Although many companies observed six or more holidays during the year, the production employee's enthusiasm for the day off was tempered by the sobering knowledge that for him it was an enforced one day's layoff without pay. Today this picture has been changed completely. Blue collar workers have now achieved "parity" with their white collar brothers, and are entitled by contract to pay for a specified number of holidays not worked during the year, providing they meet the eligibility requirements. Well over 90 per cent of all contracts have some provision for pay for holidays when not worked. The most prevalent provision calls for six such holidays, but an increasing number of contracts provide for eight holidays, and a few for as many as twelve holidays during the year.

As in the case of vacation plans, holiday pay clauses presented some administrative headaches when first introduced, but most of them have been resolved by experience and improved contract language. The chief administrative problem in holiday pay clauses has always been insuring against excessive absenteeism before and after the paid holiday. Most contracts today require that an employee must work the day before and the day after the holiday in order to qualify for holiday pay. Although there is no difficulty in principle with such a provision, problems still arise in attempting to determine whether in specific cases the failure to work the day before or after the holiday was due to legitimate reasons such as *bona fide* illness, death in the immediate family, and so on. In most cases where there is no question about the employee's good faith and no indication that he was attempting to "stretch" the holiday, however, payment will be made unless the clause is so strict as to preclude absence for *any* reason the day before or the day after the holiday.

For a contract holiday not worked, most contracts specify that the employee will receive eight hours' straight-time pay. For work on a contract holiday, double-time is now most common, with a considerable number of contracts now providing for triple time or two and one-half times the regular daily rate.

Employees on layoff during a period in which a holiday falls do not ordinarily receive pay for the holiday. This is proper in line with the theory of holiday pay, since an employee already laid off is not "losing" by not working the holiday. An employee on vacation is in a different category, since his vacation pay is an earned equity for prior service. Many contracts provide an extra day's pay for a holiday falling within the vacation period. It is frequently labeled, however, as an extra day of vacation to be taken on the next scheduled work day following the end of the employee's vacation period.

As in the case of paid vacation plans, future contracts may be expected to be increasingly liberal as to the number of paid holidays provided for, with eight becoming the prevailing figure rather than six. However, it is unlikely that a majority of contracts will ever be liberalized to the point of twelve paid holidays. This is one fringe benefit that has rather obvious upper limits. A considerable number of contracts now provide that an employee may substitute his own birthday for one of the contract-specified holidays. This particular innovation strikes the writer as admirable from an employee morale standpoint, although potentially disruptive of departmental work scheduling in some cases.

REPORTING PAY AND CALL-IN PAY

When employees report for work at their regularly scheduled time without having been notified in advance not to report, it is customary for the contract to guarantee them either four hours' work or four hours' pay without work. The equity of such a provision is so apparent that it perhaps ought not to be regarded as a fringe benefit but as an essential minimal requirement.

Another related provision common in contracts today is that guaranteeing at least four hours' pay to employees who are "called in" or "called back" to work after having completed their regular shift and gone home. Such clauses are usually operative if the worker is called in within sixteen hours after he has completed his regular shift.

Reporting pay provisions usually give the employer an "escape clause" for failure to notify an employee not to report, if the reason for no available work at reporting time is due to causes beyond the employer's control such as a power failure, fire, "an act of God," or a strike.

PREMIUM PAY FOR OVERTIME AND SHIFT DIFFERENTIALS

Technically, premium pay for overtime hours perhaps should not be classified as a fringe benefit. Discussion of current practice on overtime pay seems warranted here, however, since overtime earnings constitute one of the principal sources of additional worker income above basic occupational rates.

Virtually all contracts specify the length of the working day, define the work week, and make special provision for payments on hours worked beyond the normal working day or work week.

For many years now in most industries, eight hours has been prescribed by contract as the normal work day, and forty hours as the normal work week. Recently, however, there has been a perceptible increase in the number of contracts specifying less than eight hours per day and forty hours per week as normal. Gradual reduction of the work day and work week is a continuing objective of union policy in many cases.

The seven-hour day, thirty-five-hour week is now standard in the women's clothing industry, and the bulk of the printing industry is regularly on less than a forty-hour schedule. Brewing, baking, and construction are other industries in which some break-throughs in the forty-hour norm have been effectuated.[3]

The UAW initially began beating the drums for a thirty- or thirty-two-hour week as a major 1958 contract demand, but switched from hours reduction to profit-sharing in the fall of 1957 after the launching of the Russian satellite caused general concern about whether the United States was losing ground to the Soviet Union in the industrial and technical

[3] See "Reduction in Hours," *AFL-CIO Collective Bargaining Report,* I (October, 1956), 67–70.

fields. Shorter hours for the same pay did not appear to be a popular demand under the circumstances.

The eight-hour day and the forty-hour week will probably remain as standard practice in most industries for some years to come. Wherever economically and technically feasible, however, union pressure may be expected to increase the number of situations calling for a seven-hour day and a thirty-five-hour week, or for an eight-hour, four-day week of thirty-two hours. Half days of work are seldom defensible from a productivity and scheduling standpoint.

Premium pay for overtime hours is universal in collective bargaining today, but the premium rates exhibit a considerable variety. The most prevalent standard is still one and one half times the regular hourly rate for hours in excess of eight in any one work day, or in excess of forty hours in any one work week. An increasing number of contracts, however, call for double-time after an employee has worked more than four hours of overtime in any one day. A substantial number of contracts now provide for double-time for Saturday and Sunday overtime *as such*, regardless of whether Saturday and Sunday are the sixth and seventh consecutive work days in a work week.

As already noted, double-time or two and one half times the normal rate (and in some cases triple-time) are frequently paid for work on contract-specified holidays. Many contracts provide for paying an employee double-time if he is called back to work after going home and before his next regular shift.

The pattern of overtime compensation is now fairly complete in most unionized industries. However, those unions who are still under contracts providing for time and one half only may be expected to attempt to achieve double-time and, in the case of worked holidays, triple-time whenever bargaining strategy and bargaining power permit.

Within the overtime compensation area the two most controversial problems continue to be policy on sharing of overtime and the question as to whether an employee can be required to work overtime. To avoid conflict and misunderstanding on these troublesome matters, the contract should be as specific as possible as to policy. Many contracts today provide for a sharing of available overtime work on a round robin basis among employees in a particular classification or department. Such clauses usually contain a qualifying phrase such as "so far as practical" or "as equally as possible," and occasionally these are productive of disagreement. Generally, employees watch the division of overtime by the employer very carefully, and are quick to protest if they feel the division has been inequitable or out of line with contract policy.

Whether employees can be compelled to work overtime is a frequent subject of controversy, and the practice on this varies widely. To minimize disputes and possible disciplinary actions flowing from refusal to work overtime, it is clearly advisable to spell out the contract policy. In many contracts the employee is obligated to work overtime upon request, and subject to disciplinary action for refusal to do so. In others the acceptance of overtime assignments is made optional with the employee and no stigma attaches to him for refusal to accept overtime. The most feasible policy would vary considerably from industry to industry.

Shift premiums for work on second (swing) and third (graveyard) shifts are now virtually universal, with those on the third shift receiving a higher premium than those on the second. Such practice reflects majority worker preference for day shift employment and the consequent greater difficulty in recruiting qualified personnel for work on the less desirable shifts.

Many contracts still have a "five and ten" policy, with a five cents per hour premium for second shift work and ten cents per hour premium for third shift. This has been exceeded in a considerable number of agreements. A fairly typical liberal shift premium clause is quoted below:

Section 18. Premium Pay for Night Shifts.

When two (2) or three (3) shifts per day are being operated in the plant, employees working on the second shift shall receive an additional ten and one-tenth (10.1) cents per hour; and employees working on the third shift will receive an additional fourteen and four tenths (14.4) cents per hour which will be added as a separate item on the Daily Time Report.

Where first shift employees work overtime extending into the second shift, the above ten and one-tenth (10.1) cents per hour will not be added unless the full shift of eight (8) hours is worked, and, where second shift employees work overtime extending into the third shift, they shall not receive the third shift premium unless the full shift of eight (8) hours is worked.

For determining the appropriate night shift premium for shifts scheduled to start at times other than those provided in Article XVI, Section 2, the hours of such shifts will be considered first, second or third depending upon which shift (as set out in Article XVI, Section 2,) a majority of such hours fall.

SEPARATION OR SEVERANCE PAY

Separation allowances, variously called severance pay or dismissal pay, are currently one of the most dynamic areas of fringe activity. Although fairly common in the newspaper, railroad, and communications industries, such agreements are not yet widespread in most manufacturing industries. The rapid introduction of automated equipment in some industries, however, has intensified union pressure for adequate severance pay for workers permanently displaced by technological change. A dismissal pay plan was negotiated in the steel industry in 1956, and the Steelworkers were expected to press for improvements of this plan in 1959 negotiations. A severance pay provision was an important new feature of the 1958-1961 contracts in the automobile industry.

From the union viewpoint, an employee whose performance has been satisfactory develops an equity in his job proportionate to his length of service. Demands for dismissal pay for permanently displaced employees are thus predicated on the assumption that payments should be made in relation to the employee's length of service. Virtually all employers, of course, would concede that an employee should be discharged only for good and just cause. In cases of permanent reduction of force (in contrast to layoff or discharge), however, the average employer will argue that the employee's prior compensation has been adequate payment for services rendered and that no additional payments are warranted.

Although negotiation of supplemental unemployment benefit plans in some industries, discussed in the preceding chapter, perhaps has blunted somewhat union interest in severance pay proposals as such, the union view is that dismissal pay should not be regarded as a substitute for unemployment insurance or SUB benefits. Dismissal pay is regarded by the unions who seek such provisions as an independent equity to which a satisfactory employee is entitled if he is permanently displaced.[4]

Dismissal or severance pay has a logical basis for employees whose jobs are permanently erased by technological change, plant mergers, or permanent curtailment in the scale of a company's operations. From the standpoint of increasing job security, such provisions operate as a powerful incentive for employers to make every effort to find other suitable employment for a worker whose job has been eliminated.

In all dismissal pay plans the amount due the employee upon termination is related to his length of service. In American Newspaper Guild contracts eligibility begins with six months' service, and "dismissal indemnity" runs from a minimum of two weeks pay graduated up to forty weeks' pay for employees with seventeen or more years of continuous employment. The steel severance pay formula is much more modest, requiring three years of service for eligibility and running from four weeks pay for employees with three to five years' service to a maximum of eight weeks' pay for employees with ten or more years of service.

Depending on the trade or industry involved, contemporary contracts exhibit an amazing variety and proliferation of miscellaneous fringes or perquisites too numerous to summarize and discuss here. Among the items that might be lumped under the "miscellaneous fringe" heading would be such matters as paid lunch periods, paid rest periods, wash-up time, clothes-changing time, payment for time spent in grievance process-

[4] See "Adjustment to Technological Change," *AFL-CIO Collective Bargaining Report,* III (April-May, 1958), 25–31.

ing, tool-sharpening time, furnished meals for overtime work, provision of work clothes, safety glasses, and special equipment, pay for travel time, and so on.

CONCLUSIONS: NEED FOR A BALANCED FRINGE PROGRAM

Fringe payments in recent years have been increasing more rapidly than basic wages and will doubtless continue to do so. This is particularly the case in the fringes dealing with employee economic security, discussed in the preceding chapter. In many relationships the point has already been reached where a detached appraisal of the complex of fringe items is urgently called for in terms of logic, cost, balance, and employee preference. In a typical contract the number and extent of fringe items is such as to make it logical and desirable, if not imperative, to consider possible reallocation of the fringe dollar.[5]

The 1955-1958 contract between Pittsburgh Plate Glass and Libby-Owens-Ford and the Glass, Ceramic and Silica Sand Workers inaugurated a security benefit plan involving individual employee accounts which could be a harbinger of things to come in this field. Under this plan employee accounts are financed by a five cents per hour contribution, and the employee can make withdrawals when he is sick, laid off, resigns, or retires. If he dies, any balance in his account goes to his beneficiary. Thus, sick pay, unemployment benefits, separation pay, retirement benefits, and life insurance are combined under one roof, with the individual employee exercising some discretion as to the use of his account fund.

Certainly a time will come when the saturation point on fringe expansion will be reached and a reappraisal will be called for in terms of employee preferences and management cost criteria. Up to now, however, in many cases fringe appears to have been piled on fringe with very little over-all appraisal of the comparative importance of the various components of the fringe package.

SELECTED BIBLIOGRAPHY

Bambrick, James J., Jr. and Albert A. Blum, "Pay for Union Business During Working Hours," *Management Record*, XIX (November, 1957) 391-98.

Bortz, Nelson, "The Measurement of Fringe Benefit Expenditures," *Personnel*, XXXIII (July, 1956) 87-94.

Chamber of Commerce of the United States of America, *Fringe Benefits, 1953*. Washington: Economic Research Department, Chamber of Commerce of U. S., 1954.

———, *Fringe Benefits—1955*. Washington: Economic Research Department, Chamber of Commerce of U. S., 1956.

[5] Arthur M. Ross, *op. cit.*

Crisafulli, Virgil C. and Sidney C. Sufrin, "Fringe Benefits: Are They Related to Wage Rates?" *Personnel,* XXXII (May, 1956) 533-37.

Haas, George H. and Elizabeth R. Floyd, *Company Severance Pay Plans,* (Research Report No. 29). New York: American Management Association, 1957.

Hill, James C., "Stabilization of Fringe Benefits," *Industrial and Labor Relations Review,* VII (January, 1954) 221-34.

Jacobs, S. Ralph, "Glamorous Fringe Benefits," *Boston University Law Review,* XXXVI (Spring, 1956) 151-69.

Mendelsohn, A. I., "Fringe Benefits and Our Industrial Society," *Labor Law Journal,* VII (June, 1956) 325-28, 379-84.

National Industrial Conference Board, *Fringe Benefit Packages.* New York: National Industrial Conference Board, 1954.

Ross, Arthur M., "Fringe Benefits Today and Tomorrow," *Labor Law Journal,* VII (August, 1956) 476-82.

Sargent, Charles W., " 'Fringe' Benefits: Do We Know Enough About Them?" *Personnel,* XXX (May, 1954) 462-72.

16

Centralization, democracy, and the bargaining process

A major problem of our time is the task of devising ways of maintaining and enhancing the status and dignity of the individual in an age of giant institutional entities such as the multi-plant industrial corporation and million-member national unions. Students of our economic and political structures have wrestled with this problem in a variety of ways. William H. Whyte, Jr., has dealt penetratingly with the problems of individual status in large-scale corporate enterprise.[1] David Riesman has contributed some illuminating insights from a sociological standpoint.[2] Clark Kerr has advocated a philosophy of "liberal pluralism" as the only viable approach to genuine individual freedom in modern economic society.[3] J. Kenneth Galbraith deals im-

[1] William H. Whyte, Jr., *The Organization Man* (New York: Simon and Schuster, 1956.)

[2] David Riesman, Reuel Denney, and Nathan Glazer, *The Lonely Crowd* (New Haven: Yale University Press, 1950.)

[3] Clark Kerr, "Industrial Relations and the Liberal Pluralist," *Proceedings of the Seventh Annual Meeting, Industrial Relations Research Association* (Madison: IRRA, 1955), pp. 2–16.

plicitly with this problem in his stimulating exposition of the thesis of countervailing power in contemporary capitalism.[4]

CENTRALIZATION AND THE INDIVIDUAL

A common thread of concern for individual status runs through these and other approaches to the basic dilemma of centralism and freedom in economic society. One of the more knowledgeable union representatives, George Brooks, predicts that by 1977 there will have been a substantial decrease both in the number of significant companies and in the number of unions with which they deal.[5] Many industries will be dominated by a few large companies, and the employees in each of those industries will be represented by one union, in Brooks' view.

We are concerned in this chapter with the implications of the strong centralization trend in both industry and labor applying to policy determination in contract negotiation and also in contract administration. The focus here is on collective bargaining as a mechanism of industrial self-government, rather than on economic implications of centralization.

The fact of increasing centralization in policy determination, contract negotiation, and even contract administration seems no longer open to effective denial. In Chapter 4 we observed the growth in multi-employer bargaining units, multiplying illustrations of company-wide bargaining, union-wide bargaining, and the conformity-inducing influence of pattern bargaining. In most of the major industrial unions control over policy formation is largely vested in the international officers. This was dramatically illustrated early in 1958 when Walter Reuther made headlines in announcing the UAW's negotiation "line" for 1958 well in advance of the UAW's economic policy convention, which presumably was scheduled to formulate policy for the 1958 negotiations. The delegates were presented with a *fait accompli* before they began their deliberations.

Correspondingly, on the employer side, multi-employer bargaining in many cases has involved the surrender of individual employer sovereignty over policy formation in labor relations to a central employer association. Similarly, in company-wide bargaining, the discretion of local plant management in multi-plant concerns appears in many cases to have been progressively conditioned or limited in recent years under master agreements.

Since this trend toward greater centralization appears to be inexorable, its implications and consequences in terms of democratic standards must

[4] J. Kenneth Galbraith, *American Capitalism: The Concept of Countervailing Power* (Boston: Houghton Mifflin Company, 1952.)

[5] For some penetrating comments on "bigness," see George W. Brooks, "Reflections on the Changing Character of American Labor Unions," *Proceedings of the Ninth Annual Meeting, Industrial Relations Research Association* (Madison: IRRA, 1957), pp. 33–43.

be understood and evaluated. The basic problem is one of reconciling effectively the requirements of responsibility and efficiency with those of democracy. No one seriously suggests setting up a pure democracy model for either management or union organization today. In our complex, interdependent, highly institutionalized economy neither the corporation nor the union can be run like a New England town meeting. Both unions and employers face compelling requirements for efficient and responsible bargaining and contract administration. Centralized control over policy formation is sometimes alleged to be a *sine qua non* for insuring efficient and responsible conduct of union-management relations. Where this is felt to be true, the proportionate importance of the local union and the local plant management are apt to decline rapidly. Yet there is no magic in centralization as a technique or procedure. In many cases excessive centralization may create more problems than it solves. It may stifle expressions of individual freedom or dissent in either the union or the management hierarchy to the detriment of the relationship as a whole. The consequences and appropriate limitations of centralization thus deserve searching examination. Before we can critically appraise current developments, it is essential to have in mind a working model of a "democratic" union and a "democratic" corporation.

ESSENTIAL ELEMENTS OF UNION DEMOCRACY

The American labor movement is made up of some two hundred national and international unions, tremendously diverse and protean in their characteristics as to size, structure, patterns of control, economic strategy, and so on. The fact remains that the key unions are the large ones like the UAW, USA, Teamsters, Machinists, Carpenters, and Mineworkers. It is in such large unions that meaningful concepts of working democracy are of critical importance.

Within the framework of this discussion a union can be said to qualify as democratic if it satisfies certain basic requirements. Most important is the ability of a minority within the local union or a minority of local unions within the international to become a majority by peaceful, politically democratic means. Satisfying this criterion requires free, secret-ballot elections, a union press whose columns are open to the opposition, free debate at local union meetings and at international conventions, and an absence of officer reprisals against individual members who disagree with them on policy matters.

Of critical importance in the context of this discussion is the relationship between the local union and the international. The requirements of democracy are not satisfied if the local union is merely the "creature" of the international, with no effective voice in policy formation, contract negotiation, or contract administration. The model relationship is well stated by Seidman as being one wherein the power is distributed among the national organization, the local unions, and the membership in such a way as "... to permit effectiveness in administration and collective bargaining, while protecting the members against autocracy and oppression." [6]

Many students of trade union government would also argue that the local union membership should have final control over the calling and ending of strikes and the ratification of collective agreements, if there is to be meaningful democracy. The centralization trend in many unions today has made this criterion outmoded in fact. The international union is playing an increasingly decisive role in determinations as to the calling of strikes and the ending of strikes. Furthermore, in many cases the ratification of agreements negotiated by international representatives has become a formality as far as the local unions are concerned. The discretion of local unions on such matters is often more apparent than real.

As to internal democracy, the most vulnerable point for the great majority of unions is the absence of an independent judicial procedure for handling problems in connection with fines, suspensions, expulsions, and discrimination in distribution of available jobs. Only two unions at this writing, the Upholsterers and the UAW, have established an outside judicial body for appellate action by individual union members who feel they have been wrongfully suspended or expelled. One of the most valuable institutional reforms that trade unions might make would be to follow the lead of the UAW and the Upholsterers in voluntarily adopting private arbitration as a procedure for suspension and expulsion cases.

The primary emphasis in this chapter concerns relationships between trade union leadership and members as they affect the collective bargaining process. The "civil rights" of individual union members are treated inferentially rather than specifically in the ensuing analysis.

ESSENTIAL ELEMENTS OF MANAGEMENT DEMOCRACY

The modern corporation is essentially authoritarian in structure and organization. In a union authority and responsibility theoretically flow from the membership to the leadership. The corporation operates on a chain of command basis from the top down. Nevertheless, many management executives are keenly aware that, to be effective, administration must rest on consent.[7] Recent literature in the field of general management is replete with *caveats* as to the necessity of democratic policy-making, two-way communication, freedom within management, bottom-

[6] Joel Seidman, *Union Rights and Union Duties* (New York: Harcourt, Brace & Company, Inc., 1943), p. 22.

[7] The seminal work on this important principle was Chester I. Barnard, *The Functions of an Executive* (Cambridge: Harvard University Press, 1938.)

up management, and so forth. Successful executives are being urged to train their successors and encourage initiative and assumption of greater responsibility by middle and line management. On a more technical plane the literature currently deals extensively with such matters as the "span of control," much of it recognizing inherent limits to the effectiveness of overcentralized, authoritarian operations. Kerr's philosophy of "liberal pluralism" is adaptable to enhancement of individual freedom of initiative and choice within the managerial framework, although his remarks are oriented essentially in terms of guaranteeing freedom to the nonsupervisory wage-earner.

Although the specific requisites of a viable system of democracy within management are difficult to pinpoint, the general outlines of the model are reasonably clear. A working management democracy requires freedom to suggest, to disagree, and to take initiative in policy matters, subject of course to the harsh penalties for business failure when the exercise of such initiative boomerangs. In the labor relations context this calls for some degree of discretion both as to policy formulation and execution for middle and lower management.

The ultimate in policy decentralization is advocated by William B. Given, Jr., who would "take the lead strings off" people all along the management line and give to all levels the "freedom to think and plan boldly; freedom to venture along new and untried paths; freedom to fight back if their ideas or plans are attacked by superiors; freedom to take calculated risks; freedom to fail." [8]

Few top managers are likely to be this enthusiastic about democratizing policy-making. Nevertheless, many executives are now concerned about the deadening of individual initiative and imagination that appears to be the inevitable product of excessive centralized control.

With such basic considerations in mind, we shall examine in greater detail the factors producing centralized policy formation and execution in the labor relations field. We will be recapitulating to some extent materials already treated in Chapters 4 and 9. The problem is important enough to merit some judicious repetition.

UNION FACTORS FAVORING CENTRALIZATION IN LABOR RELATIONS

One of the more important reasons for greater union centralization is to facilitate basic union objectives of standardization and uniformity in wages and other conditions of employment. Tight international union control over policy formation can minimize the possibilities of employers

[8] William B. Given, Jr., *Bottom-up Management* (New York: Harper & Brothers, 1949), pp. 5–6.

taking advantage of relatively weak or ineptly led local unions to break a union-desired pattern.

Greater centralization is also correlated with power drives of international union officials interested in consolidating their own positions within the union's institutional hierarchy, in presenting a united front to employers, and in protecting themselves against splinter movements by rival unions.

Union tendencies toward centralized control have been stimulated historically by the need to secure greater economic strength to bargain on a more even footing with better organized and economically more powerful industry groupings. Many industrial unions, notably the Steelworkers, were organized in the 1930's from the top down, and have always had a high degree of centralization in their make-up for just that reason.

Another major factor prompting greater centralization is the enlarged scope of collective bargaining and the increasing professionalization of the negotiation function. In many unions the local officers simply lack the breadth of training and experience to cope with the formidable technical problems associated with contemporary bargaining. The process of negotiation, as noted in Chapter 5, is increasingly one requiring the services of professionally trained personnel. Consequently, many local union officials lacking the requisite information and know-how defer to international union representatives and staff specialists, either by choice or request. Even in contract administration, as noted in Chapter 6, there is a marked trend for international unions to supervise the settlement of grievances and to participate directly in the presentation of arbitration cases.

Among the external influences accelerating centralization within the union movement, in addition to employer organizations, have been the Taft-Hartley Act and the recognition by many unions of their increasingly quasi-public status. Various Taft-Hartley provisions, notably Section 301 sanctioning civil damage suits against unions for breach of contract, have been responsible for many international unions tightening the reins of discretion on their local unions. Many unions are also becoming more sensitive to the public relations impact of their policies, programs, and methods. This has been responsible not only for greater international union control over locals, but also for the greater degree of authority and supervision exercised by the AFL–CIO over affiliated national and international unions. Since the McClellan Committee disclosures, the entire labor movement has become conscious of operating in a continuous bath of publicity. This may have been a contributing factor in stiffening the AFL–CIO Executive Board to facing up to the unpleasant task of expelling the Teamsters, the Bakery and Confectionery Workers, and the Laundry Workers following the December, 1957 AFL–CIO convention.

MANAGEMENT FACTORS FAVORING CENTRALIZATION

On the management side many of the factors operating toward centralization are similar to those just enumerated for unions. One of the most prominent manifestations of centralizing tendencies on the employer side has been the remarkable growth of multi-employer bargaining associations to protect the smaller employers against whipsawing tactics and other economic pressure devices by unions such as the Teamsters, who previously had overmatched single employers in bargaining strength. The principal aim of many multi-plant concerns in centralizing control over local plant labor relations has also been to avoid whipsawing. Finally, the complexity and scope of contemporary bargaining agenda have required participation by top management personnel, just as they have in the union case. The negotiation task is now too technical for handling by a plant manager or works manager who lacks the specialized knowledge and experience to deal competently with skilled international union negotiators.

In short, the pressures favoring centralized policy-making (and centralized contract administration in many cases) on both sides of the bargaining table have a logical, practical origin. There is nothing sinister about the motivations behind this trend. It is a response to changing economic conditions and shifting patterns of organizational strength on both the union and employer side. Centralized control in large industrial unions is a logical response to match the economic strength of a few large firms occupying key positions in many mass production industries. By the same token, the banding together of small employers in such industries as trucking, the needle trades, building and construction, baking, printing, and many others is a logical and practical effort to match the market economic strength of the large and powerful unions with which such employers deal.

SOME CONSEQUENCES OF CENTRALIZED CONTROL IN LABOR RELATIONS

What have been some of the consequences of increasingly centralized control on both sides of the bargaining table? One valuable by-product of multi-employer bargaining, company-wide bargaining, or union-wide bargaining is usually greater stability in labor relations. Master agreements negotiated by specialists are likely to be technically superior and freer from conflict-producing "bugs" than are contracts negotiated by individual employers with individual local unions. The former agreements frequently reflect the more detached and objective treatment of substantive issues that can be given by top management and international union officials. In certain cases, however, such master agreements may not be as easy to administer locally as a contract specifically drawn in terms of local needs and requirements.

Better contract enforcement well may result from placing more control in the hands of international unions and top management. Fewer unauthorized stoppages should result. By the same token, under centralized control management can keep tabs on line supervision to insure that the contract is scrupulously observed and enforced. Uniform interpretation and application is more likely under centralized control.

On the negative side, the status of the local union may well be reduced to that of a dues-collecting unit with little real power, even in grievance administration. Correspondingly, the discretion of local plant management or of individual employers in a multi-employer unit may be minimal. Democratic relations in the shop may have been purchased at the costly price of an absence of democracy in union affairs and a denial to the local of an effective voice in policy formation and execution. Similarly, the incentive of local plant management may be adversely affected by the knowledge of its limited authority to deal with basic problems of employee relations.

Much of the present opposition to multi-employer and company-wide bargaining derives from genuine concern over the possible destruction of the real democratic values to be achieved in localized handling of labor relations problems. It is felt that the more informed and responsible agreements resulting from centralized control may not be worth the price, if that price is the loss of local management or union participation and discretion.

CENTRALIZED CONTROL IS NOT UNIVERSAL

In emphasizing the trend toward greater centralization in labor relations, it is important to note that this trend is by no means universal. Thousands of collective agreements are negotiated each year between individual firms and local unions where both parties are strictly "on their own." Many powerful international unions, notably in building and construction, afford complete discretion to their locals in both contract negotiation and administration. *The logic of market structures is likely to determine the nature and extent of control.* In many craft unions the basic economic policy is to negotiate for what the local traffic will bear. This approach obviously requires local discretion in bargaining. In manufacturing generally, however, the trend toward central control of policy formation is steady and pervasive, for the reasons noted.

Yet even in highly institutionalized multi-employer or company-wide bargaining, the resultant agreements usually bear evidence of an informed awareness of the need for considerable flexibility to accommodate special local situations. Most master agreements will leave room for local diversity on such matters as seniority systems and procedures, methods of wage payment, wage scales for job classifications, correction of local intraplant inequities, and so forth. Such contracts also usually reserve to local parties full discretion on production standards and wage rates on new or changed jobs.

PATTERN DEVELOPMENT AND PATTERN FOLLOWING

Employers (and some local unions) subject to the exigencies of pattern bargaining frequently claim that when negotiations are conducted in terms of a pattern-setting agreement elsewhere in the industry or area, little attention is paid to local requirements that might dictate a different type of settlement. The degree to which master settlements are accommodated to local conditions is a perennial source of controversy in the steel industry.[9] Many small steel-fabricating establishments argue that they have no choice but to accept the big steel pattern. The Steelworkers union, on the other hand, constantly proclaims its willingness to make departures from the pattern where local economic circumstances justify such a departure. Without going into the details of particular situations, it is difficult to discuss intelligently the pros and cons of such a controversy. We must be content here to note that there is an inherent danger of excessive rigidity in the technique of pattern bargaining.

Local unions affiliated with a multi-industry international union frequently experience difficulty occasioned by the international's desire to dovetail negotiations from one industry to another. A case in point is the UAW's negotiations in its automobile and agricultural implement divisions. Auto contracts expire in the spring and farm equipment contracts in the summer. Normally, the basic pattern is set by the automobile negotiations and followed fairly closely in farm equipment on such basic issues as wages, SUB, and duration of contract. This held true in both the 1950 and 1955 negotiations. The farm equipment division of UAW waited for the results from Detroit to use as a point of departure for negotiations with Deere, International Harvester, and other farm equipment concerns. In 1958 the UAW had to begin negotiations with Deere and other farm equipment manufacturers while its automobile division was operating in Detroit without a new contract. Such are the hazards of centralized interdependency in a multi-industrial union.

DRAWING THE LINE BETWEEN CENTRAL CONTROL AND LOCAL OPTION

Where to draw the line between centralized control and local option is difficult to describe in general terms. The diversity of industrial

[9] See George Seltzer, "Pattern Bargaining and the United Steelworkers," *Journal of Political Economy*, LIX (August, 1951), 319–31.

practices and the variety in employer and union structures makes formulation of generally applicable principles a hazardous undertaking. Perhaps it can be stated that *in multi-employer or company-wide bargaining an effort should be made to combine centralized determination of major policy issues with a maximum of decentralization and local option in the administration and implementation of such policies.* The balance of this chapter will be devoted to putting some meat on the bones of this general proposition.

If we are seeking a "judicious mixture" of centralization and decentralization, it is obvious that the substantive content of such a mixture will vary from one situation to another. The basic objective, however, should be the same in all cases. The aim should be to achieve the advantages of uniformity when uniformity appears to be mutually desirable, while maintaining the values of flexibility and diversity on matters that should be subject to local discretion and action.

CENTRALIZATION ON WAGE POLICY

Wage policy lends itself admirably to centralized determination in most cases of multi-employer or company-wide bargaining. As pointed out in Chapter 10, the formulation of wage policy, from the union standpoint, can no longer be a rank-and-file proposition. The factualization of bargaining processes and the increasing use of techniques of scientific wage determination in many industries require specialized knowledge that the rank-and-file workers and local union leaders do not have. Furthermore, the giant bargaining unit implies a necessity for consideration of the external effect of the wage bargain as well as internal requirements.

On the management side in a similar situation the same requirement of specialized knowledge and the necessity of weighing the external impact of the wage bargain make it impossible to leave full discretion to local management (in the case of company-wide bargaining) or to individual employers (in the case of multi-employer or industry-wide bargaining).

Both management and the union in company-wide bargaining have an interest in uniformity. If the company has several plants, the union in seeking a master agreement will press for terms embodying the best practice on all or most issues. It may attempt to whipsaw the company by matching one plant against another in much the same way that a controlling industrial union will operate prior to multi-employer bargaining in an industry in which the employers themselves have not yet organized.

Similarly, the top management of a firm with several scattered plants will wish to maintain tight control over the discretion of its local plant managers. If the manager of a plant in New York City gives a concession in local bargaining on call-in pay that is more liberal than that obtaining in other company plants, top management can be certain that the union will press for adoption of this policy in the next master agreement.

International union officials and top management alike have their thinking in company-wide negotiations focussed on the over-all impact of the contract. They are in some instances not aware of, nor particularly concerned about, the special problems of local situations. Their detached attitude sometimes may be advantageous to local management or labor. On the other hand, it may be injurious to local interests.

Frequently, a master agreement gives the local unions a better contract than they could have obtained by bargaining as locals. If the entire economic strength of the union is mustered behind the negotiation of a single master agreement, the various locals may receive a contract with better economic terms than they could possibly have obtained unaided. The company is prevented from playing off one plant against another and attempting to set the pattern in terms of the plant with the weakest local union. The advantage to unions in uniformity through a master agreement is clear-cut in such situations.

The advantages in uniformity to management are perhaps not as clear. A company with plants in different labor market areas or in different areas of product competition may find a master agreement hampering. It may wish to vary its wage policy to suit local conditions and customs. As noted in Chapter 10, companies usually are concerned about area rates, whereas unions generally are more interested in industry rates. The company usually does not wish to be out of step with practice in the area where its plant is located.

In other instances employers may welcome the relative certainty and predictability that accompanies a master agreement. If the terms and conditions of employment are relatively uniform in all its plants, this factor alone gives top management of a multi-plant company an ideal basis for checking on relative managerial efficiency. Also, some companies prefer to have a uniform labor policy even though it puts them out of line with other employers in some local labor markets. If their wage policy is comparatively higher than that of other employers, they are able to secure the cream of the local labor market.

A desirable consequence flowing from company-wide bargaining or multi-employer bargaining is the impulse often provided for standardization of job titles and coordination of duties with titles. If uniformity of labor costs is aimed at, there is a strong incentive to develop an effective wage rationalization program in the company's plants or in the industry.

Because wage bargaining has become a technical proposition demanding experienced, well-informed negotiators, it will probably be removed increasingly from the discretion of local unions and local plant managers. Even in single-plant bargaining the employer will find himself dealing more and more with the officials of the international union rather than with local officials. The greater intervention of the international here is only in part a function of the more technical, specialized bargaining now required. It is required also by the necessity for the international union to prevent local unions from breaking ranks or from flouting over-all union policy. If various locals in either exceptionally strong or exceptionally weak bargaining positions in relation to the specific employers with whom they deal were allowed to make bargains in terms of their positions, it would be embarrassing to the over-all position of the union. The international might be aiming at a policy of self-restraint in wage bargaining. It could not afford, therefore, to have a powerful local breaking through the proposed ceiling on demands by using its economic strength solely in its own interest. By the same token, the international could not permit an unusually weak local to make an individual deal with a particular employer that would constitute a break-through of minimum standards established generally by the international.

It has been conceded for some time that wage policy cannot be appropriately the function of the rank-and-file. It is increasingly apparent in many instances that neither can it be any longer the function of the local union. All the signs point toward greater international union authority in this area. Furthermore, it is entirely probable that the centralization will proceed to the point of *interunion policy formulation*, with a central committee setting the over-all outlines of the pattern of wage demands for the coming contract year.

Centralized control over wage policy formation is considered by most economists as the only way in which the requisite degree of responsibility can be achieved. It is certain that it cannot be achieved under an atomistic or fractionalized structure of bargaining units. The bargain must have a wide enough coverage so that its external effect can be appreciated and weighed. On economic grounds, therefore, applause is probably justified for centralizing tendencies. In this chapter, however, the concern over increasing centralization is focussed more on the implications for collective bargaining as an instrument of industrial self-government. Judged by criteria of effective democracy, there is cause for some misgiving about the extent to which control over policy formation has become centralized.

A master agreement is likely to be an inflexible agreement. In spite of clauses safeguarding local discretion on specific points, it well may be difficult in practice for a master agreement to fit local needs and special circumstances, even on wage policy in which the argument for uniformity may be more solid than on some other subjects in the modern collective agreement. What should be done, for example, when the central wage policy is set at a level so high as to imperil a marginal firm or a marginal plant? Should there be an accommodation, an exception to the general policy? Practically speaking, how are the union's interest in uniformity and the local employees' interest in continuing employment to be reconciled? The dilemma is equally difficult from the management viewpoint.

WAGE ISSUES REQUIRING LOCAL DISCRETION

While over-all wage policy generally may be suited to centralized formulation, there are a number of wage issues that require local negotiation and local discretion. Even in highly centralized relationships local discretion is usually maintained on methods of wage payment, on wage scales for job classifications, and on rates for new or changed jobs. The master contract may provide for an across-the-board increase of ten cents per hour and an escalator clause as the general wage formula. The local management and the local union, however, will do their own negotiating on intraplant inequities and on the method of wage payment.

To illustrate this point, on method of wage payment there is frequently a sharp conflict between the local union and the international union as to whether payment should be on an hourly basis or on an incentive basis. As an international union, the UAW has historically opposed incentive methods of wage payment. Yet it has not been able to convince many of its locals in the farm equipment industry to resist continuance of incentive pay systems on many production jobs. The rank-and-file in such situations grieve frequently and vigorously about the operation of the incentive system, but they strongly prefer it to an hourly method of payment.

On wage rate inequities the need for local discretion is clear-cut, since job titles and job duties vary considerably from one plant to another, even in the same industry. Union policy, however, is generally aimed at minimizing interplant differentials on similar jobs.

OTHER ISSUES WHERE CENTRALIZED POLICY FORMATION APPEARS DESIRABLE

Among the other basic issues in collective bargaining logically calling for uniformity in policy determination and administration, one can list negotiated pension plans, group life insurance, health and welfare plans, and supplemental unemployment benefit plans. The intrinsic nature of such items demands uniformity and precludes diversity. Furthermore, the technical problems associated with their negotiation and implementation require control by top management and union representatives.

The foregoing generalization applies convincingly to master contracts involving a multi-plant company and to multi-employer contracts with a particular union. It should be noted, however, that in unions where the locals typically do their own negotiating there is a considerable degree of variation in the type of employment or income security plans from local to local. For example, few locals of the IBEW can boast of as impressive a pension and welfare program as Local 3 in the New York metropolitan area. By the same token, few Teamster locals have as advanced a program of medical care as that embodied in the Labor Health Institute of the St. Louis Teamsters.

SENIORITY: AN EXAMPLE OF A "MIXED" ISSUE ON CENTRAL CONTROL VERSUS LOCAL DISCRETION

Seniority is an excellent illustration of an issue that is frequently subject to a combination of centralized policy formation and local discretion. In a master contract or a multi-employer agreement some basic principles as to seniority may be spelled out and applied in uniform fashion. For example, if seniority is a criterion on promotion, the master contract may specify uniform procedures to follow in connection with the posting of vacancies, determination of qualifications, and so forth, with the vacancy being assigned to the senior qualified applicant. In connection with layoffs and recalls, however, the type of seniority (i.e., departmental, classification, or combination) well might vary from plant to plant, depending on local conditions and local customs. In the writer's experience in arbitrating under contracts with a multi-plant company, the seniority article is the one that usually exhibits the most variety from plant to plant, although the basic governing principles may be uniform in all plants.

Effective and equitable administration of contractual seniority provisions requires the preservation of local discretion. Even within a fairly homogeneous industry conditions will vary markedly from one plant to another.

GRIEVANCE MACHINERY AND LOCAL DISCRETION

On many noneconomic issues the superior knowledge and perspective of top management and international union officials will yield most frequently a better product than is likely to result from local negotiation. On such a vital matter as an effective grievance machinery, for example, the negotiation of a master agreement or a multi-employer agreement may result in the establishment of a uniform and well-defined series of steps in the processing of grievances, with arbitration as the terminal point. Local unions or local plant managers, if left entirely to their own devices, might not develop as sound a machinery.

Yet the handling of grievances is, or should be, a prime responsibility of local unions and local management. The adjustment of grievances is at the core of day-to-day institutional relationships between company and union. The procedure should be usable and well-understood by those immediately involved. The uniform procedures established by the contract perhaps need tailoring to local circumstances.

More important than the influence of centralization on the machinery for handling grievances is its influence on the settlement of grievances. In many instances the requirements of a centralized bargaining relationship have virtually erased local autonomy in settling grievances. This has serious implications for democratic industrial relations and merits further consideration at this point.

Fear of setting up an embarrassing precedent is a prime factor in tightening international union and top management control over the processing and settlement of grievances at the local level. In the administration of a uniform agreement the interpretations need to be uniform if one side or the other is not to be discomfited by an out-of-line local settlement.

The resulting watchdog approach to contract administration does not appear calculated to develop responsibility in local management or union officials. All authorities on grievance procedure and the handling of complaints stress the importance of adjusting grievances on the spot, promptly and on the merits. Central supervision of grievance processing, even of the mildest kind, necessarily militates against achievement of such objectives.

The vast majority of grievances should be settled at the foreman-steward level. This may be difficult to accomplish if contract administration is centralized, either formally or informally. Foremen have to check with plant superintendents, and the latter have to check with top corporation officials. Union stewards have to check with local union officials, and the latter have to check with international representatives. If this were necessary in any appreciable number of grievances, contract administration would break down under a welter of red tape, delay, and confusion.

This picture may be overdrawn. Yet a natural consequence of increased central control will be a reluctance of local officials on both sides to take responsibility for prompt and final settlement of grievances. If a grievance arises that shows any sign of being a precedent-breaking or precedent-establishing one for the bargaining system as a whole, the central officialdom of union and management are likely to take a hand in its adjustment.

Any experienced arbitrator can appreciate the advantages of centralized control of grievance adjustment, although from the standpoint of strictly democratic criteria he may deplore the loss of local autonomy. Where the international union maintains strict control over the screening of grievances prior to arbitration, it is rare to find a grievance reaching the arbitration step that does not present a *bona fide* arbitrable issue. On the other hand, too strict a policing of grievances by the international may result in a build-up of pressures and dissatisfaction within the rank-and-file. An international union representative servicing a particular local industrial union has a difficult job in determining just where to draw the line on attempting to "sell" the local on the idea of dropping certain grievances that may lack merit under the contract, but which may have generated considerable "shop heat" prior to the screening stage.

MAINTAINING A BALANCE BETWEEN CENTRAL CONTROL AND LOCAL OPTION

The problem of maintaining an optimum balance between the requirements of uniformity achieved through centralized bargaining and the requirements of local option to meet special considerations is necessarily a dynamic one. It is difficult to generalize about whether centralization has proceeded too far or not far enough.[10]

The questions involved are far from academic. A wise and constructive approach to the centralization phenomenon is imperative if the values of unionism and collective bargaining as ways of democratizing industrial relations are to be preserved. *Democracy in labor relations requires effective participation at all levels.* If participation is to be encouraged and strengthened, there must be a ceiling placed on the degree to which policy formation is centralized in the hands of top leadership. Centralized bargaining is an imperative requirement for many reasons. But decentralized administration and freedom to depart from centrally determined policies when circumstances indicate a departure to be advisable are equally essential.

The importance of day-to-day relationships in the shop has been stressed repeatedly. The building of sound relationships can be done best at this level. It is difficult to impose good relations from the top down. Excessive centralization in policy formation or administration necessarily inhibits the development of cooperative relationships in the shop. The centrally negotiated contract may be a better instrument than the locally negotiated one. But unless there is a recognition of the need for diversity and flexibility, centralized bargaining may result in formalism, legalism, inflexibility, and a lack of democratic participation.

[10] As knowledgeable an individual as Jack Barbash, for example, has argued in a paper at the May, 1958 Meeting of the Industrial Relations Research Association that the national union in certain respects is "not doing enough in collective bargaining." For an abridged version of this paper, see Jack Barbash, "Power and the Pattern of Union Government," *Monthly Labor Review,* XXCI (June, 1958), 605-607.

Benjamin Selekman has stated ably the case for decentralized administration and argued the virtues of the "grassroots shop," correctly stressing the basic fact that democracy everywhere requires *participation and self-regulation.*[11] In addition to the inherent values of democratic participation it is important to note also sound *economic* reasons favoring the maintenance of local discretion. Perhaps chief among these is the relationship to utilization of local labor supply.

DECENTRALIZED ADMINISTRATION AND EFFICIENT UTILIZATION OF LABOR

The impact of collective bargaining on the utilization of labor supply is made at the local level. Solemn pronouncements by international union officials will not insure productivity consciousness nor will they eliminate featherbedding and other forms of restrictionism. Efficient utilization of labor and elimination of restrictive shop practices depend primarily on the development and maintenance of constructive union-management relationships at the local level.

As Selekman points out, both the disciplined requirements of production (effective utilization of labor) and the human requirements of democracy depend upon decentralized administration. In short, if we are to emphasize what might be termed the efficiency effect of collective bargaining, the most fruitful outlet will be in stimulating cooperative union-management relationships at the plant level.

The need for a positive approach to collective bargaining has been stressed. Such an approach calls for a joint emphasis on increasing productivity. Intelligent utilization of the union-management production committee is one illustration in point. Such committees can operate effectively only at the local plant level, since they demand the closest and most cooperative interpersonal relationships.

Fortunately, most contractual provisions with a direct bearing on effective utilization of labor supply are usually left to local negotiation. Specifically, these include: (1) method of wage payment; (2) structure of occupational rates; and (3) seniority. Also left to local option very often are such vitally important matters as the instruction of apprentices and on-the-job training.

Opponents of increasing centralization of power in the hands of international union officials fear that the local union will become vestigial in time, with no significant functions to perform. Of course, the maintenance of strong local unions is essential to a vital trade union democracy. The fear that local unions will wither and die under increasing centralization, however, appears upon thoughtful analysis to be greatly exaggerated.

[11] See Benjamin M. Selekman, *Labor Relations and Human Relations* (New York: McGraw-Hill Book Company, 1947), pp. 246–48.

Even when the international union is in fact making the major decisions on broad policy issues in collective bargaining, the local union should continue to perform at least two major functions: (1) effective contract administration; and (2) negotiation and administration of local agreements that will insure productivity gains rather than losses, and promote effective utilization of labor supply.

CONCLUSION

A proper blend of democracy and efficiency under centralized bargaining relationships requires a dual perspective. On the one hand, the requirements of efficient (and responsible) negotiation favor centralization of policy-determining authority on many major issues in collective bargaining. From another viewpoint the requirements of efficiency in production and utilization of labor (coupled with the requirements for internal democratization of union and management organizations) clearly favor substantial decentralization in contract administration, as well as local negotiation of issues that have a direct bearing on manpower utilization and productivity gains.

It is not yet clear whether the high-water mark in the centralization trend has been reached on either the management or union side. There seems to be a growing awareness of the dangers in excessive centralization, but such awareness seemingly has had no practical impact in terms of reversing the trend. The felt need to give at least lip service to the virtues of democratizing the decision-making process is in itself somewhat encouraging. Furthermore, as has been noted several times, no uniform patterns are present. Although the "organization man" is becoming more important in unions as well as in management, awareness of the inherent threat to individual freedom and diversity is in itself partial insurance against stultifying uniformity and organizational rigidity.

SELECTED BIBLIOGRAPHY

Argyris, Chris, "Organizational Leadership and Participative Management," *Journal of Business*, XXVIII (January, 1955) 1-7.

Baker, Helen and Robert R. France, *Centralization and Decentralization in Industrial Relations*. Princeton: Industrial Relations Section, Princeton University, 1954.

Barbash, Jack, "Power and the Pattern of Union Goverment," *Monthly Labor Review*, XXCI (June, 1958) 605-07.

Berkowitz, Monroe, "The Economics of Trade Union Organization and Administration," *Industrial and Labor Relations Review*, VII (July, 1954) 575-92.

Coleman, John R., "The Compulsive Pressures of Democracy in Unionism," *American Journal of Sociology*, LXI (May, 1956) 519-26.

———, "The Role of the Local Industrial Union in Contemporary Collective Bargaining," *Proceedings of the Eighth Annual Meeting, Industrial Relations Research Association.* Madison: IRRA, 1956, 274-86.

Dubin, Robert, "Power and Union-Management Relations," *Administrative Science Quarterly*, II (June, 1957) 60-81.

Dunlop, John T., "The Industrial Relations Function in Management," *Personnel Management*, XXXVII (June, 1956) 83-91.

Galbraith, J. Kenneth, *American Capitalism: The Concept of Countervailing Power*, rev. ed. Boston: Houghton Mifflin, 1956.

Johnson, Paul V., "Government Regulation of Internal Union Affairs," *Labor Law Journal*, V (December, 1954) 807-18, 858.

Kahn, Robert L. and Arnold S. Tannenbaum, "Union Leadership and Member Participation," *Personnel Psychology*, X (Autumn, 1957) 277-92.

Karsh, Bernard and Jack London, "The Coal Miners: A Study of Union Control," *Quarterly Journal of Economics*, LXVIII (August, 1954) 415-36.

Kerr, Clark, "Industrial Relations and the Liberal Pluralist," *Proceedings of the Seventh Annual Meeting, Industrial Relations Research Association.* Madison: IRRA, 1955, 2-16.

Kovner, Joseph and Herbert F. Lahne, "Shop Society and the Union," *Industrial and Labor Relations Review*, VII (October, 1953) 3-14.

Miller, Glenn W. and Edward J. Stockton, "Local Union Officer: His Background, Activities and Attitudes," *Labor Law Journal*, VIII (January, 1957) 29-39.

Mills, C. Wright, *The Power Elite.* New York: Oxford University Press, 1956.

Myers, Charles A. and John G. Turnbull, "Line and Staff in Industrial Relations," *Harvard Business Review*, XXXIV (July-August, 1956) 113-24.

National Industrial Conference Board, *Handbook of Union Government, Structure and Procedures*, (Studies in Personnel Policy, No. 150). New York: National Industrial Conference Board, 1955.

———, *Source book of Union Government, Structure and Procedures.* New York: National Industrial Conference Board, 1956.

———, *Improving Staff and Line Relationships*, (Studies in Personnel Policy, No. 153). New York: National Industrial Conference Board, 1956.

Ornati, Oscar, "Union Discipline, Minority Rights and Public Policy," *Labor Law Journal*, V (July, 1954) 471-79, 528.

Rose, Arnold, *Union Solidarity.* Minneapolis: University of Minnesota Press, 1952.

Rose, George, "The Relationship of the Local Union to the International Organization," *Labor Law Journal*, IV (May, 1953) 334-43, 346-51.

Rosen, Hjalmar and R. A. H. Rosen, "Decision Making in a Business Agent Group," *Proceedings of the Eighth Annual Meeting, Industrial Relations Research Association.* Madison: IRRA, 1956, 287–97.

Sayles, Leonard R. and George Strauss, *The Local Union.* New York: Harper & Brothers, 1953.

Seidman, Joel, Jack London, and Bernard Karsh, *Union Rights and Union Duties.* New York: Harcourt, Brace and Company, Inc., 1943.

———————, "Leadership in a Local Union," *American Journal of Sociology*, LVI (November, 1950) 229-38.

Shepard, Herbert A., "Democratic Control in a Labor Union," *American Journal of Sociology*, LIV (January, 1949) 311-16.

Strauss, George, "Control by the Membership in Building Trades Unions," *American Journal of Sociology*, LXI (May, 1956) 527-35.

Taft, Philip, *The Structure and Government of Labor Unions*. Cambridge: Harvard University Press, 1954.

Tagliacozzo, Daisy L., "Trade-Union Government, Its Nature and Its Problems," *American Journal of Sociology*, LXI (May, 1956) 554-81.

Tannenbaum, Arnold S., "Control Structure and Union Functions," *American Journal of Sociology*, LXI (May, 1956) 536-45.

Whyte, William H., Jr., *The Organization Man*. New York: Simon and Schuster, 1956.

17

Industrial conflict and industrial peace

It has become customary today to regard the absence of strikes and lockouts as indicative of a "sound" union-management relationship and, conversely, to regard the continued occurrence of strikes or lockouts in a particular relationship as revealing an immature or an unsound stituation. Within such a framework the ideal industrial society is envisaged as one entirely free from conflict.

This is a dangerously naive and oversimplified version of constructive labor relations. It ignores the crucial fact that the threat of a strike (or a lockout) is the most potent inducement for management and union to agree in a free society. It further ignores the critical consideration that conflict between union and management is not necessarily "bad."

The recent literature has stressed so heavily the importance of accommodation, adjustment, maturity, cooperation, and harmony that we are prone to forget or minimize the fact that our industrial society is founded on a premise of individual and group freedom. Under given circumstances conflict may well be "healthier" than the absence of conflict. In fact, the absence of conflict may be evidence of either a coercive or a "sweetheart" relationship, neither of which would qualify under suitable criteria for "constructive, mature" union-management relations.

With the foregoing qualifications in mind, this chapter seeks to explore the determinants of industrial peace within the framework of public policy discussed in Chapter 3, and to assess our progress or lack of progress in reducing "undesirable" industrial conflict to manageable proportions.

DECLINE OF STRIKES

Industrial conflict in the United States in recent years has not been a particularly serious problem, by whatever criteria one wishes to choose. Work stoppages of all kinds were low in both 1956 and 1957 and the first six months of 1958.[1] Obviously, management and organized labor are not yet permanently committed to an abandonment of the strike and the lockout as methods for resolving conflict. At the same time, certain types of strikes and certain types of employer retaliatory conduct during strikes are declining markedly if not disappearing altogether.

The strike to enforce union recognition, for example, has become comparatively infrequent in comparison to the period prior to World War II.[2] Unions organizing new territory customarily resort to NLRB representation case machinery for establishing their legal claim to exclusive bargaining rights.

Other types of strikes are outlawed by federal and/or state legislation. In this category are jurisdictional strikes, secondary strikes, strikes by government employees, strikes by employees of "public utilities," and so on. In most of these situations the legal prohibition of such strike activity is only one factor (although perhaps the most important) in their marked reduction in recent years. Some credit also must be given to a maturing labor movement and to improving relationships between unions and management.

CHARACTERISTICS OF A CONTEMPORARY STRIKE

The great majority of strikes that still occur are *primary* strikes by Union *X* against Employer *Y*, when agreement cannot be reached on the terms of a new contract. In such cases the process of conflict has become institutionalized to the point where the employer in question customarily does not invite violence by initiating back-to-work movements, refusing

[1] As is well-known, strikes in the turbulent post-war year of 1946 accounted for only 1.43 per cent of manhours worked that year. Since then, in all but two years (1949 and 1952) man-days of idleness as a result of work stoppages accounted for less than one half of one percent of all working time, frequently as little as one quarter of one percent. Time lost as a result of strikes in early 1958 was exceptionally low, below that for 1957, which was the lowest of any year since World War II.

[2] Prior to World War II and more particularly prior to the Wagner Act of 1935, union recognition was perhaps the most important single cause of work stoppages. In recent years, union recognition has been a principal cause of only from 7 to 11 percent of all stoppages.

to continue negotiations, or importing strikebreakers, all of which formerly characterized industrial conflict in the prewar period. This is not to say that employers today have become "soft." It is rather an indication that the majority of employers now recognize the right of unions to withhold labor as an economic pressure device in a primary dispute. The relationship between the company and the union is viewed by the employer as a *continuing* one, even though his employees are on strike.

A fascinating illustration of peaceful point-counterpoint was played out in the summer of 1958 by the major automobile companies and the UAW. The parties operated for several months without a contract for the first time since the UAW organized the industry in the late 30's and early 40's. Yet there was no significant strike or lockout during the interim. Many features of the expired contract were administered on the same basis as they were prior to contract expiration. In its refusal to check off dues or to admit grievances to arbitration, automobile management made the road tougher for the union during the interim period. Yet there was never any indication of an effort to "bust" the union or to exploit management's early superior bargaining position. By the same token, the UAW leadership made a concerted effort (not always successful) to prevent sporadic walkouts in a situation that was inherently ambiguous and frustrating from the rank-and-file employee's point of view.

Typically, when a primary strike occurs, the parties lock horns in terms of the application of economic pressure, but there seems to be an underlying confidence in the enduring nature of the relationship between the company and the union. Each strike, in other words, does not become a grim battle for survival. On the contrary, most strikes today resemble more accurately the classic view of a strike as *a continuation of bargaining by other methods.* The union has no intention of breaking the company. The company has no intention of using the strike as a method of ridding itself of the union. Both parties operate on the assumption that they will resume relationships with one another after a few days or a few weeks or, in extreme cases, a few months.

This is a significant change in the basic attitudes of the parties toward industrial conflict. It deserves emphasis even though it is difficult to document objectively. It involves a maturing conception of a union-management relationship that does not rule out the possibility of industrial conflict. There is an acceptance of the proposition that conflict may at times be necessary as a means of resolving a dispute. Both the employer and the union, however, know that the institutional process of living together will be resumed after the resort to economic pressure has produced a new agreement that in the short-run may be "favorable" to the employer or to the union, as the case may be. This attitude may seem hard-headed or even misguided to some purists who equate the absence of conflict with the ideal in union-management relations. But to the writer it seems to be a pragmatic and psychologically sound approach to the realities of labor relations.

The foregoing remarks should not be loosely interpreted as an advocacy of strikes or lockouts. Certainly, mature management and mature union leadership will aim at an avoidance of open industrial conflict wherever possible. We shall review in a moment the characteristics of those union-management relationships that have been conspicuously successful in avoiding conflict. At the same time, it is worth emphasizing that industrial peace as such is not necessarily the ultimate determinant of a constructive and stable union-management relationship.

CAUSES OF EARLIER STRIKES

Students of labor relations history are generally familiar with principal causes of industrial strife. We know that prior to the Wagner Act of 1935 unions usually had to win their spurs by striking for recognition. An employer prior to 1935 would seldom if ever deal with a union that purported to represent his employees until that union had proved its right to bargain the hard way—by striking. We also know that in many industries in years past negotiations as to the terms of a new contract more often than not ended in a deadlock, and were ultimately hammered out by the arbitrament of economic force. In some cases the basic cause of the strike was purely economic. In others the fundamental cause was grounded in deep-seated individual and group frustrations as an end product of years of managerial arbitrariness or authoritarianism.

In short, most of the strikes from 1776 to 1935 had a cause or complex of causes not too difficult to discern. Under contemporary conditions where the right to organize and the right to bargain collectively are protected by law, and where the institution of unionism and collective bargaining as a process have acquired considerable acceptability not only by employers but by the lay public at large, the use of the strike has become comparatively infrequent. At the same time, the very acceptance of unionism and collective bargaining places a higher premium on justification of resort to economic pressure. When one considers the generally favorable legal status of unions since 1935 in comparison to their status prior to that date, it is interesting to note that when a union strikes today, the burden of proof seems to fall squarely on that union. The nation is conditioned to the assumption that industrial peace is the norm. Where conflict arises, the blame attaches to the agency that seemingly initiates the conflict. Most unions are not unaware of this shift in psychological emphasis. Furthermore—and this is a fact worth remembering—unions seldom strike without the preponderant support of the rank-and-file. The party that suffers most by a strike is still the individual worker and his family. This sober truth has not changed over the years, notwithstanding improved strike benefits.

The fact remains that strikes still occur in our economy, and are likely to occur from time to time in future years, even if we should be so shortsighted as to attempt to outlaw the right to resort to economic force entirely. Assuming agreement that economic force should be used only as a last resort, what can we say about the state of our present knowledge as to the determinants of industrial peace on the one hand, and the factors tending to produce "strike proneness" on the other?

THE DETERMINANTS OF INDUSTRIAL PEACE

Shortly after World War II the National Planning Association, under the urging of Clinton Golden, formerly vice-president of the United Steelworkers of America, initiated a series of case studies of companies and unions that had enjoyed conspicuously successful relationships, in an effort to determine whether there were any common denominators in these relationships that made them work especially well.

The principal findings of the NPA series, now well-known, have already been summarized in Chapter 2. What can the NPA findings teach us in terms of our effort to find a durable solution to the problem of industrial conflict? The most important "lesson" seems to be that the vital key to a constructive, successful union-management relationship lies *in the approach and attitudes of the parties themselves.* The causes of industrial strife are not removed by legislation, nor is industrial conflict eliminated by legislation. It is the relationship between Union *X* and Company *Y* with which we must be concerned.

This must be a disappointing conclusion for those hoping to find a panacea for industrial conflict. Unfortunately for the cause of simplicity, in the field of union-management relationships there is not any discoverable formula that will guarantee the absence of industrial conflict. In labor relations as in any other phase of interpersonal behavior, there is no satisfactory substitute for emotional maturity, still a comparatively rare commodity.

The best insurance we can provide against irrational resort to economic pressure is *increasing institutionalization of the bargaining process.* This involves the development of as many built-in procedural safeguards as the parties can be induced to accept. It also involves a governmental policy that will be sufficiently unpredictable that the parties will not know in advance that they can benefit by withholding agreement if they happen to be in the weaker bargaining position.

The key to successful government policy in the so-called emergency dispute field is the "choice of procedures" approach illustrated by the Massachusetts Slichter law.[3] If the parties know ahead of time that a failure to agree will produce governmental intervention, the party with the weaker case will inevitably operate in such a way as to produce government intervention. If the parties know in advance the sequential chain of procedures that will follow government intervention, as is true under the national emergency dispute section of Taft-Hartley, the rigidity and predictability of such procedures will militate against the prompt and successful resolution of the dispute.[4]

WHAT CAN THE PARTIES THEMSELVES DO?

Before considering further the appropriate role of government in relation to labor disputes, let us consider briefly some of the principal ways in which the parties themselves can insure minimal resort to economic force in disputes over future contract terms.

We have already noted in Chapter 7 the important fact that approximately 90 per cent of all contracts provide for arbitration as the terminal step in grievance machinery, thus instituting an effective peaceful substitute for economic force as a method of final resolution of disputes arising *during the life of an existing contract.* How can the parties contribute to insuring against economic force as the answer to disputes over *future contract terms?* There can be no unitary, definitive answer to this question.

The crux of the matter, as noted above, lies in the nature of the relationship between the parties. The findings of the National Planning Association survey (outlined in Chapter 2) as to the critical determinants of a constructive relationship are invaluable. But there are many union-management relationships that do not satisfy the NPA criteria and yet enjoy an enviable record of uninterrupted production. Most of them would be classified by Professor Selekman as "containment-aggression" in type. Nevertheless, they have hammered out contracts year after year, with strikes frequently threatened but never materializing. By the same token, some of the participants in the relationships eulogized in the NPA studies have had their troubles in recent years. Thus, we must conclude that there is no one formula for privately insuring industrial peace.

[3] For a careful evaluation of experience under the 1947 Massachusetts law, see George P. Shultz, "The Massachusetts Choice-of-Procedures Approach to Emergency Disputes," *Industrial and Labor Relations Review,* X (April, 1957), 359–74.

[4] The most comprehensive factual and analytical discussion of Title II of Taft-Hartley and other approaches to handling emergency disputes is Irving Bernstein, Harold L. Enarson, and R. W. Fleming, eds., *Emergency Disputes and National Policy,* Industrial Relations Research Association Publication No. 15. (New York: Harper & Brothers, 1955.)

It can be said fairly, however, that in the overwhelming majority of relationships there appears to be a growing recognition by both management and union leadership of the desirability of avoiding economic force wherever and whenever possible. It also seems safe to conclude that management and unions will turn more to the possibilities of *private* mediation and *private* arbitration for resolution of disputes over future contract terms. If the alternative is a strike which both parties wish to avoid, or government intervention of one kind or another which both parties also wish to avoid, private mediation and/or private arbitration might prove more acceptable or, in any event, less unacceptable.

In principle, the writer opposes using arbitration for final settlement of disputes over future contract terms. There are serious inherent shortcomings in the use of arbitration in such cases. The principal objection is that arbitration in future terms or "interest" disputes, as Professor Gregory has pointed out, is not really arbitration.[5] The arbitrator is required to bring his wisdom to bear in producing a solution which he thinks the parties should have arrived at in the first place by intelligent bargaining. This is a "political" and not a "judicial" function.

Irving Bernstein's research has shown that the actual results of wage arbitration in future-terms cases do not justify the fears of those who are opposed to using arbitration as a mechanism for final resolution of such disputes.[6] Bernstein concluded that the results from disputes determined by arbitration did not differ appreciably from the results that might have been expected from orthodox private bargaining. This is certainly an inferential tribute to the sagacity of arbitrators. The net effect may also have been beneficial to all parties concerned, since where arbitration was used, economic force was avoided.

As to the potential of private mediation in future-terms cases, comments here must be brief. The writer has no first-hand knowledge of how mediation has worked in the comparatively limited number of situations where it has been tried. There have been a number of instances in recent years where the parties have utilized the services of their contract arbitrator to bring them into accord on the terms of a future contract. The utilization of the contract arbitrator in this fashion may be unwise, for he becomes involved in a type of activity that is alien to his proper function. It well might jeopardize his future effectiveness as an arbitrator of grievances under a contract which he helped the parties to negotiate. This view is subject to the criticism that it is unnecessarily circumspect and cautious. Yet caution is warranted before casting the arbitrator in a role that seems basically inconsistent with his normal judicial function.

[5] Charles O. Gregory, *Labor and the Law,* 2nd ed. (New York: W. W. Norton, 1958), at p. 478.

[6] Irving Bernstein, *The Arbitration of Wages* (Berkeley and Los Angeles: University of California Press, 1954), at pp. 112–13.

ALTERNATIVE PROCEDURES FOR GOVERNMENT INTERVENTION

Assuming that private bargaining breaks down and no agreement can be reached on using *private* techniques for supplementing the negotiation process, at what point should government intervene and in what manner? A survey of the extensive literature in this area reveals no convincing agreement among the experts. Rather than attempting to summarize all the various proposed approaches and procedures, the writer has chosen to set forth briefly his thinking. References to many of the pertinent writings in this area will be found in the bibliography at the end of the chapter.

Certain basic assumptions condition these views as to the appropriate role of government in labor disputes. First among these is the proposition that the right to strike or to lock out in *primary* disputes must be preserved. Second, government intervention should not be sought or forthcoming in most strikes unless personal violence or damage to property may be involved. Third, government intervention should never be premature or completely predictable. Fourth, certain types of government intervention should be excluded from consideration on the grounds that they are either inherently undemocratic or likely to prove ineffective and unfeasible.

With these assumptions and limitations in mind, what are the available alternatives? Ideally, government intervention in terms of the stated assumptions would be limited to effective mediation, supplemented where necessary by encouragement of the parties to utilize voluntary arbitration for future-terms cases. Although mediation is properly regarded as an art rather than a science, a great deal of fruitful research has been done in recent years on ways and means of improving the practice of mediation.[7] Considerable progress has been made in raising the stature and level of training of professional mediators. The one cloud on the mediation sky is the enchantment with the technique of "preventive mediation." Preventive mediation is basically inconsistent with a policy of minimal government intervention in disputes. If we agree that public policy should aim to strengthen collective bargaining processes, we should continue to regard the primary function of a government mediator as a *remedial* rather than a preventive one.[8]

If mediation is unsuccessful and a strike is in progress, what government policies should then be used? In terms of our initial requirement that

[7] See, for example, Ann Douglas, "What Can Research Tell Us About Mediation?", *Labor Law Journal*, VI (August, 1955), 545–52.

[8] For a trenchant indictment of preventive mediation, see Allan Weisenfeld, "Some Thoughts on Labor Mediation," *Proceedings of Sixth Annual Meeting, Industrial Relations Research Association* (Madison: IRRA, 1954), pp. 276–83.

the procedures used should be both democratic and effective, it is essential to discard a considerable number of procedures currently in use or proposed. Compulsory arbitration must be ruled out on the basis that it is neither democratic nor effective. Nor is it really feasible, since its use is vigorously opposed by the overwhelming majority of management and union representatives. By the same token, the present procedures in Title II of the Taft-Hartley Act for handling disputes defined by the President as "national emergency" in character do not meet the criteria of democracy and effectiveness. Government seizure of strike-bound plants is frequently effective, but is scarcely democratic and is pragmatically adaptable only to a limited number of situations. Various proposals for nonstoppage strikes, involving placing employer receipts and employee wages in escrow while the dispute and production both continue, are not politically feasible and are unrealistic in terms of union-management compulsions and pressures in an economic force situation. Fact-finding boards *without* power to recommend are not likely to be effective. Fact-finding boards *with* the power to recommend come close to being compulsory arbitrators. Strike votes, injunctions, labor courts, and many other proposals are equally subject to condemnation within the framework of this analysis and its assumptions.

THE PROPER GOALS OF PUBLIC POLICY

If all the foregoing alternatives are eliminated, what do we have left? First, there must be a clear-cut understanding that public policy is designed to strengthen collective bargaining; that the primary role of government is to assist the parties through effective mediation in reaching voluntary agreements; and that government intervention will be neither premature nor automatic and will not be available to further the temporary strategic advantage of either party.[9]

If it is agreed that public policy should avoid relieving management and unions of their crucial responsibility to make collective bargaining work, what specific procedures are suited to achieving this end?[10] First, at federal and state levels concerted attention needs to be given to improving the quality of existing mediation facilities and providing such facilities in the many states where none are now available. Second, the actual procedures used in handling any major dispute should be determined in the light of the particular circumstances of such dispute. It is

[9] These views are similar to the principles enunciated by David Cole, former head of the Federal Mediation and Conciliation Service, in an address before the National Academy of Arbitrators in Detroit, Michigan, May 1, 1953.

[10] The ensuing discussion is adapted from an earlier paper. For fuller treatment see Harold W. Davey, "Government Intervention in Labor Disputes," *Labor Law Journal*, V (November, 1954) 739–42, 800.

generally conceded that one of the principal difficulties of many current procedures is their rigidity and predictability. On the other hand, uncertainty as to the specific course the government may pursue in a particular dispute will prove to be a powerful incentive to the parties to furnish their own solution.

When disputes occur in which government feels compelled to intervene, and efforts at mediation or acceptance of voluntary arbitration have failed, government should have available through a general enabling statute a flexible choice among several procedures. The discretionary choice among alternatives would depend on which appears to be most feasible for the particular crisis at hand. One possibility would be appointment by the President or the Governor, as the case might be, of a public board of inquiry with power to recommend a basis for settlement. Another would be direct personal intervention by the President or Governor, using the prestige of his office to bring the parties into accord. A third alternative might be to seek an injunction accompanied by the appointment of a public board of inquiry with power to recommend. A fourth would be governmental seizure of the struck facilities.

The last two alternatives certainly do not appear to satisfy our criteria of democracy and effectiveness. However, the power of government to act quickly and decisively in a *genuine crisis situation* must be recognized and preserved. The executive branch of government, at either the federal or state level, must be prepared to cope effectively with the rare situation in which the complete intransigeance of one or both parties compels prompt, firm action in the public interest. In such cases injunctions and seizure, distasteful as they may be in a free economy, may have to be employed.

In conclusion, it is pertinent to repeat once more the principal thesis of this chapter. The most durable and satisfactory solutions to the problem of industrial conflict must come from the parties themselves rather than as a product of public intervention.

SELECTED BIBLIOGRAPHY

Bennett, George, "How to Get the Most from Mediation," *Labor Law Journal*, VIII (August, 1957) 534-36, 563.

Bernstein, Irving, Harold L. Enarson, and R. W. Fleming, eds., *Emergency Disputes and National Policy*, Industrial Relations Research Association Publication No. 15. New York: Harper & Brothers, 1955.

————, *The Arbitration of Wages*. Berkeley and Los Angeles: University of California Press, 1954.

Chalmers, W. Ellison, "The Conciliation Process," *Industrial and Labor Relations Review*, I (April, 1948) 337-50.

Chamberlain, Neil W., *Social Responsibility and Strikes.* New York: Harper & Brothers, 1953.

——— and Jane M. Schilling, *The Impact of Strikes: Their Social and Economic Costs.* New York: Harper & Brothers, 1954.

Coser, Lewis A., *The Functions of Social Conflict.* Glencoe, Ill.: Free Press, 1956.

Davey, Harold W., "Government Intervention in Labor Disputes," *Labor Law Journal,* V (November, 1954) 739-42, 800.

Daykin, Walter L., "The Right to Strike," *Labor Law Journal,* VI (June, 1955) 361-75.

Douglas, Ann, "What Can Research Tell Us About Mediation?" *Labor Law Journal,* VI (August, 1955) 545-52.

Feinsinger, Nathan P., "Private Mediation: Its Potential," *Labor Law Journal,* VII (August, 1956) 493-96.

Forkosch, Morris D., "Government Impact on Labor-Management Relations: Past-Present-Future," *Labor Law Journal,* V (August, 1954) 543-48, 589.

——— and Ernest Fleishman, "Objectives in Labor-Management Relations," *Labor Law Journal,* VII (May, 1956) 286–96.

Gouldner, Alvin W., *Wildcat Strike.* Yellow Springs, Ohio: Antioch Press, 1954.

Hammett, Richard S., Joel Seidman, and Jack London, "The Slowdown as a Union Tactic," *Journal of Political Economy,* LXV (April, 1957) 126-34.

Jensen, Vernon H., "Dispute Settlement in the New York Longshore Industry," *Industrial and Labor Relations Review,* X (July, 1957) 588-608.

Kerr, Clark, "Industrial Conflict and Its Mediation," *American Journal of Sociology,* LX (November, 1954) 230-45.

Kleiler, Frank M., "Presidential Seizures in Labor Disputes," *Industrial and Labor Relations Review,* VI (July, 1953) 547-56.

———, "White House Intervention in Labor Disputes," *Political Science Quarterly,* LXVIII (June, 1953) 227–40.

Knowles, K. G. J. C., " 'Strike-Proneness' and Its Determinants," *American Journal of Sociology,* LX (November, 1954) 213–29.

Kornhauser, Arthur, Robert Dubin, and Arthur M. Ross, eds., *Industrial Conflict.* New York: McGraw-Hill Book Co., Inc., 1954.

Levinson, David, "The Westinghouse Strike, 1955–56," *Labor Law Journal,* VII (September, 1956) 543–51.

Marshall, Howard D. and Natalie J. Marshall, "Nonstoppage Strike Proposals —A Critique," *Labor Law Journal,* VII (May, 1956) 299–304.

McDermott, Thomas J., "Ten Years of the National Emergency Procedure," *Labor Law Journal,* IX (March, 1958) 227–43.

Parnes, Herbert S., *Union Strike Votes: Current Practice and Proposed Controls.* Princeton: Industrial Relations Section, 1956.

Porter, Arthur R., "Are Strikes Necessary?" *Labor Law Journal,* V (December, 1954) 803–806.

Rohman, Murray M., "National Emergency Disputes," *Labor Law Journal,* VIII (August, 1957) 523–28, 558.

Sayles, Leonard R., "Wildcat Strikes," *Harvard Business Review*, XXXII (November-December, 1954) 42–52.

Shulman, Harry, "Reason, Contract, and Law in Labor Relations," *Harvard Law Review*, LXVIII (April, 1955) 999–1024.

Shultz, George P., "The Massachusetts Choice-of-Procedures Approach to Emergency Disputes," *Industrial and Labor Relations Review*, X (April, 1957) 359–74.

Stagner, Ross, *Psychology of Industrial Conflict*. New York: John Wiley & Sons, Inc., 1956.

Steiner, Peter O., "Collective Bargaining and the Public Interest," *Labor Law Journal*, IV (June, 1953) 410–16.

Syme, Herbert M., "The Public Emergency Dispute: Its Various Aspects and Some Possible Solutions," *Labor Law Journal*, V (August, 1954) 563–70.

Valtin, Rolf, " 'Preventive Mediation,' Grievance Disputes and the Taft-Hartley Act," *Labor Law Journal*, VII (December, 1956) 768–75.

Wallen, Saul, "Voluntary Mediation," *Proceedings of the Sixth Annual Meeting, Industrial Relations Research Association*. Madison: IRRA, 1954, pp. 284–87.

Warren, Edgar L., "Thirty-six Years of National Emergency Strikes," *Industrial and Labor Relations Review*, V (October, 1951) 3–19.

Weinberg, William and Allan Weisenfeld, "Prosperity versus Strikes," *Industrial and Labor Relations Review*, VII (October, 1953) 123–26.

Weisenfeld, Allan, "Mediation or Meddling?" *Industrial and Labor Relations Review*, VII (January, 1954) 288–93.

———, "Some Thoughts on Labor Mediation," *Proceedings of the Sixth Annual Meeting, Industrial Relations Research Association*. Madison: IRRA, 1954, pp. 276–83.

———, "Public Opinion and Strikes," *Labor Law Journal*, IV (July, 1953) 451–54, 504, 512.

Whyte, William F., *A Pattern for Industrial Peace*. New York: Harper & Brothers, 1951.

Young, Stanley, "Mediation as a Harmonizing Influence in Collective Bargaining," *Personnel Administration*, XX (September-October, 1957) 21–28.

18

Constructive labor relations: a blueprint for the future

In concluding this study of contemporary collective bargaining, what can be said meaningfully in summary form as to the net accomplishments and shortcomings of this vitally important process in both the economic and noneconomic spheres of industrial relations? The next logical question, having taken stock of where we stand today, is, what fundamental developments should be anticipated in the years immediately ahead? This chapter is devoted to the author's own answers to these questions.

The absence of homogeneity and uniformity in today's bargaining relationships requires that any summary statement of accomplishments and failures be qualified in the interest of strict accuracy. The following generalizations are thus subject to this important *caveat.*

BALANCE SHEET ON COLLECTIVE BARGAINING

On the positive side, there have been comparatively few instances where collective bargaining, once introduced, has not been continued and, in the majority of cases, grown generally more stable and harmonious. Although union membership drives in recent years have not been conspicuously successful in organizing new territory, most unionized sectors have remained that way, and relationships with management appear generally to have improved rather than deteriorated. Although it would be a difficult type of assertion to verify statistically, the author's impression is that the proportion of "working harmony" bargaining relationships as compared to the number of "armed truce" relationships has increased considerably in recent years. There seems to have been no perceptible increase, however, in the number of relationships deserving the classification of affirmative union-management cooperation.

If industrial peace, defined as a declining incidence of resort to economic pressure, is regarded properly as a constructive accomplishment, the record in recent years is most encouraging, as shown in the preceding chapter.

Among the *economic* accomplishments and contributions of collective bargaining, one may safely include: (1) rationalization of occupational rate structures within particular firms; (2) improved techniques and procedures for wage and salary administration; (3) some improvement in the organization and structure of labor markets; (4) broadening of the concept of managerial responsibility for the total economic welfare of the employee, above and beyond "fair wages" as such; (5) some improvement and objectification of the wage bargaining process. This may not be regarded as an impressive list. As we noted in the chapters on wage determination (10, 11, and 12), however, the economic impact of unionism and collective bargaining in many areas is much less substantial than the constant din about "labor monopoly," "wage inflation," and "restrictionism" would lead one to believe.

Most supporters of collective bargaining and its principal detractors on economic grounds join in the basic conclusion that *the indisputable values of the process lie in the noneconomic sphere*. It is in protection of individual rights to reasonable, equitable, and nondiscriminatory treatment on the job that collective bargaining probably has made its most important contribution. As a mechanism of industrial self-government, collective bargaining has proved its worth over and over again, and has the most to offer in the future.

THE NEGATIVE SIDE OF THE LEDGER

Unfortunately, collective bargaining as a process has shortcomings and defects that must be listed in any comprehensive accounting. First among these would be certain "pathological" aspects of the labor scene, such as collusive or "sweetheart" contractual relationships of the type exposed by the McClellan Committee in 1957–1958. Next in order of condemnation would be those collective bargaining relationships of the take-it-or-leave-it type that Reynolds some years ago aptly characterized as "collective bludgeoning." Third would be those management-union relationships that are still in the open conflict or industrial warfare stage. Fortunately, there do not appear to be many of the latter type anymore.

In addition to the foregoing extremist classifications, it must be admitted that many orthodox or conventional bargaining relationships today exhibit certain shortcomings or defects when measured against "model" behavior. Among the more important of these faults one must list the following: (1) a tendency to operate strictly in terms of short-run, expedient considerations without due regard for the long-run economic conditions of the firm, the industry, or the economy; (2) an unwillingness to work cooperatively on increasing productivity and reducing costs; (3) a disposition on labor's part to assume an inexhaustible management potential for absorbing additional labor cost increments; and (4) a continuing union insistence in some cases on the maintenance of outmoded concepts of seniority, working rules, and delaying actions against the introduction of technological change. As in the case of our brief analysis of the accomplishments of collective bargaining, it must be noted that the foregoing "defects" are not characteristic of all bargaining situations. Nevertheless, they are, unfortunately, factors to be soberly reckoned with in a good many cases.

One most encouraging attribute of collective bargaining in recent years has been its demonstrated ability to accommodate to changing economic and industrial requirements. There appear to be few signs or examples of labor relations dry rot or stagnation on the contemporary scene. The future ability of collective bargaining to function as a valid mechanism for determining the price of labor and for establishing an equitable system of industrial jurisprudence is completely dependent on a retention of this capacity for dynamic and flexible response to changing requirements.

Many critics of contemporary union leadership complain about the shortsightedness and lack of imagination in the approach of today's unionists at the bargaining table. These critics appear to feel that unionism has about "run out the string" on new ideas and on valid fresh approaches to contemporary bargaining. Even one who is not this pessimistic must be disturbed by the apparent absence of an articulated long-range approach to basic industrial problems by most union leaders. The bargaining philosophy of too many unionists today can still be adequately described by the time-worn Gompers phrase, "More — now".

COMMON GOALS IN A CONSTRUCTIVE RELATIONSHIP

If management and organized labor are to improve their joint ability to bargain collectively in a constructive and forward-looking manner, they need to be in fundamental agreement on certain basic goals. A "constructive" union-management relationship requires joint agreement on the validity and desirability of achieving the following four major goals:

1. An increasingly productive enterprise.
2. Achieving this first goal in a manner that will preserve and enhance the dignity of the individual.
3. A joint determination to minimize sources of conflict and irritation and to maximize opportunities to promote and expand areas of mutual interest and profit.
4. Achievement of a steadily higher level of personal well-being for employee and supervisor alike.

POSITIVE COLLECTIVE BARGAINING DEFINED

The conclusion of the first edition of this book summarized the essential elements in a concept of *positive, affirmative collective bargaining*. In rethinking and re-evaluating these attitudes and beliefs about the collective bargaining process, the author is compelled to conclude after eight more years' experience that the essential elements in this concept remain substantially unchanged. On balance, the potential and future of collective bargaining is about the same as it was eight years ago; the requirements for a constructive relationship remain basically the same.

In summary, *positive collective bargaining* involves shared support by management and labor for seven propositions:

1. Collective bargaining can be a democratic and effective instrument for two-way communication in industrial relations.

2. Management as well as labor can take the initiative in formulating proposals for change, instead of maintaining the more traditional defensive role. Both the contract negotiation machinery and the grievance machinery can be effectively bilateral when the parties have developed confidence in each other's integrity and sincerity of purpose.

3. Collective bargaining in its highest form can become a form of collective planning, going beyond the orthodox confines of the collective bargaining process. This contemplates extensive and continuous union-management cooperation to increase productivity, reduce unit costs, and adjust through joint effort to the impact of technological change. This conviction is not based on an assumption of complete identity of interest between labor and capital. Rather, it implies a more realistic appraisal of those points at which conflict is inevitable (even desirable), and also of those points at which cooperation is desirable but hard to achieve.

4. The prerogative approach must be rejected by management and labor in both contract negotiation and contract administration. As applied to contract negotiation, this requires a willingness to appreciate the need

for flexibility in the scope of collective bargaining. As applied to contract administration, this requires an appreciation of the necessity for unified authority in plant operation, coupled with an understanding of the potentialities of collective bargaining as a method of management.

5. Collective bargaining must constantly seek a proper balance between the requirements of stability and the necessity for dynamic change. This calls for a high degree of rationality and intelligence in the bargaining process. It requires statesmanship that can encompass the necessity for increasing central control over major policy decisions, while at the same time recognizing the wisdom of self-determination and local discretion in contract administration.

6. The area of private decision-making must remain as broad and inclusive as possible, consistent with the over-all requirements of the public interest.

7. *The success or failure of private collective bargaining quite possibly will determine the fate of our economic system as a whole.*

THE FUTURE

If the great majority of union and management leaders were to conduct their relationships in accordance with the foregoing convictions, there would be little need for concern about the future potential and effectiveness of collective bargaining as a way of life in industrial relations. It seems rather obvious, however, that a great many management and union representatives fall considerably short of having achieved this way of looking at the collective bargaining process and their roles in this process. On balance, movement has been more forward than backward in collective bargaining relationships in recent years. Barring total war or disastrous depression, most union-management relationships will continue to develop and mature rather than deteriorate or regress.

As a process, collective bargaining has a demonstrated capacity for adjustment to dynamic economic change. There seems no valid reason to expect a loss in flexibility in the face of continued economic growth and development. Today's bargainers are, generally, better informed and better able to understand the compulsions operating upon the parties than were their counterparts of ten or twenty years ago. There is no reason to suppose that they will become less informed, less skilled, or less responsible in the art of contract negotiation and contract administration.

It is interesting to speculate on what a typical collective labor agreement may contain twenty years hence. A generally optimistic bias leads the author to predict that many of the most troublesome issues in contemporary bargaining will have been fairly well resolved by 1980. The union security issue, the prerogative controversy, and disputes caused by union restrictionism of one kind or another should gradually diminish and eventually vanish as management acceptance of unionism and the quality of union leadership both increase.

In the years ahead, the overwhelming majority of unions should move away from negative, defensive, and frequently self-defeating restrictionism, and move in the direction of *positive programs to earn more by producing more*. Union policy today frequently displays the inheritance of many years of strong job-consciousness, rooted in the fear of unemployment and the desire to conserve a limited number of job opportunities. One might expect the strike, the lockout, and the boycott to become virtually obsolete in the years ahead. The right to resort to legitimate economic pressure, however, must be carefully preserved. It is reasonable to anticipate continued improvement in contract administration as the parties become more adept in the equitable adjustment of grievances and the *proper* uses of arbitration.

In the last analysis the collective bargaining process still stands out in perspective as the most valid institutional approach yet devised for preserving and maintaining the essential components of our private enterprise system, while at the same time contributing to the enhancement of the dignity and freedom of the individual worker in our society. If the goal of our society is to maintain and improve both capitalism and democracy, our wholehearted energies should be devoted to strengthening and perfecting the collective bargaining process. The alternatives to such an emphasis are depressing and ominous.

APPENDIX

ARBITRATOR'S REASONING AND DECISIONS IN ILLUSTRATIVE CASES

CASE 1
Spell-Out Time

ARBITRATOR'S REASONING AND DECISION

Paragraph 13(b) on its face does not support the Union's contention that it constitutes a prohibition against working employees more than three hours without a spell-out in any half day. The paragraph does not say in so many words that employees may not be worked more than three hours at a stretch without a spell-out. The question before the undersigned is whether such a limitation on management discretion may reasonably be implied from Paragraph 13(b).

The Company denies that any such implied limitation can be found in Paragraph 13(b). In order to sanction such a limitation, says the Company, the arbitrator would have to do violence to the contract language itself. He would have to torture the plain meaning of the clause or else add or substitute words. Paragraph 13(b) places no limits whatsoever on management discretion except to say that a spell-out will be allowed in any half day of over three hours. Good practice would dictate that management should give the spell-out at or near the half-way mark in the half day, says the Company. However, the Company is not obligated contractually to follow such a practice. Paragraph 13(b) leaves management discretion unfettered.

The undersigned agrees with the Company's grammatical analysis of the key phrase "in each half day of over three hours." Counsel for the Company is on the firmest grammatical ground in maintaining that the phrase "of over three hours" can only be read so as to modify and limit "each half day". However, acceptance of this grammatical analysis and construction does not lead with automatic simplicity to the conclusion reached by the Company as to the meaning and intent of Paragraph 13(b).

The question remains as to what the parties intended when they mutually contracted that a spell-out or relief period for personal needs should be allowed in each half day of over three hours. Why did they agree on three hours as a figure rather than say, two hours, or four hours?

In my judgment, the only reasonable answer (keeping in mind the obvious purpose of the clause) is that the parties agreed employees should not have to work longer than three hours consecutively without a break. The inference is clearly reasonable that if no spell-out is required in a half day of up to but not more than three hours, a spell-out *is* required to preclude any situation of working more than three hours consecutively in any half day.

This reasoning is supported by past practice of the parties under the contested clause. Three Union witnesses who worked on hog-kill testified that at no time in their recollection had the hog-kill gang ever been worked more than three hours at a stretch without a spell-out, except in the instance now under consideration. This testimony was not refuted by the Company.

Past practice is a helpful, although not necessarily decisive, guide to the intent of the parties in cases such as this where the arbitrator is required to choose between conflicting interpretations as to the meaning of a particular clause. In this case it appears to the undersigned that the past practice of the parties conforms to the reasonably implied intent of Paragraph 13(b) and that the construction of Paragraph 13(b) urged here by the Company is inconsistent with the spirit and purpose of such a clause.

While in the instant case an excess of only 23 minutes more than three hours was involved, the Union correctly emphasizes that the logic of the construction urged upon the arbitrator by the Company would, in the Union's words, "permit violation of the contract by several hours at the whim of the company in other situations." (Union brief, p. 13)

If a "half day" within the meaning of this contract can be as long as 5½ hours (or perhaps longer), the logic of the Company's position would compel a conclusion that the Company is not obligated by contract to provide for more than one spell-out period during the 5½ hours and the Company can set the time of that spell-out anywhere it chooses. While "good practice" would call for scheduling the spell-out within a 45-minute radius around the middle of such a 5½ hour stint, the Company maintains that it is not in any way bound by contract to do so. According to contract, in the Company's view, it can set the spell-out period anywhere it chooses to in any half day of over three hours.

In my judgment, acceptance of the Company's construction would amount to sanctioning the fixing of a spell-out time by the Company at any point during the "half day," even at times that would clearly defeat the obvious purpose of such a clause.

In contract construction, an arbitrator must give serious consideration to the rationale and purpose of a clause. It is my considered judgment that the construction of Paragraph 13(b) urged by the Union conforms more closely to considerations of reasonableness and equity than does the construction of this clause urged by the Company. My conclusion as to the reasonableness and equity of an interpretation holding that Paragraph 13(b) was intended to prevent working employees more than three hours at a stretch in any half day without a spell-out period is strengthened by uncontroverted evidence in the record that such an interpretation is consistent with the past practice of the parties under this paragraph. Therefore, in my judgment, the grievance has merit and should be sustained.

AWARD

1. For reasons stated in the Opinion accompanying this Award, the undersigned hereby finds and awards that working employees more than three hours at a stretch in any half day is not consistent with the spirit, purpose, and intent of Paragraph 13(b) of the contract.

2. Pursuant to the finding in Paragraph 1 of this Award, those employees on the hog-kill chain who worked more than three hours at a stretch on March 15, 19__ should be reimbursed by the Company for the spell-out time to which they are entitled under Paragraph 13(b) of the contract.

HAROLD W. DAVEY
Arbitrator

Ames, Iowa

CASE 2
Sleeping on the Job

ARBITRATOR'S REASONING AND DECISION

The arbitrator's task in the instant case is to determine whether the Company has proved its charge that *A* was "sleeping on the job" on the morning of June 28, 19__.

In carefully reviewing the testimony of the principal witnesses on both sides, the undersigned was impressed with the underlying agreement on a number of critical points. In the first place, *A* admits having his eyes closed at times and admits further that he may have had his head in his hands with his elbows sticking out. These actions would convey to an observer some distance away an impression that *A* was asleep or dozing. Secondly, there is agreement in the record that the crucial time interval is a short one of not more than ten minutes' duration.

Third, while some of the Company witnesses testified to *A*'s head nodding lower until it hit his locked hands, there is no contention that he stayed slumped over but rather his head jerked up each time. Thus, full crediting of Company testimony would not establish that *A* fell completely asleep during this short time interval. The most that the testimony of Company witnesses could be held to establish was that *A* appeared to be in imminent danger of falling sound asleep.

The arbitrator takes judicial notice of what is common knowledge as to overt symptoms preliminary to becoming unconscious in sleep, i.e. eyes closed, head nodding lower and lower, jerking up, and then nodding again. This is a condition which all have experienced at one time or another. The arbitrator's personal recollection of this experience does not lead him to equate it with "sleeping on the job" which is the offense for which *A* was disciplined in the instant case. It may or may not lead to sleeping on the job. It might lead to drifting off into complete unconsciousness which is true sleep. Or, if successfully fought by the person in question, it would lead to completely restored wakefulness.

The record indicates no doubt in the minds of the four Company witnesses who observed *A* between 11:20 A.M. and 11:30 A.M. that *A* was sleeping or dozing in a sitting position. The fact remains that this was an assumption on their part. An assumption does not constitute proof.

The record makes clear that the Company witnesses merely observed *A*. They did not call out to him. Nor were they close enough to him to testify as to whether in fact he was conscious of what was going on and tending to his job. The fact that four rather than two or one reached the same conclusion based on visual observation does not alter the basic fact that the conclusion is based on an assumption.

Following the hearing, the arbitrator visited the scene of the incident and the crane was brought into the same position as it was on the day in question. A man was in the cab at the time of the arbitrator's inspection. The arbitrator stood near the screw machine and also walked directly under the cab of the crane and looked up. The arbitrator would estimate that the cab of the crane was at least fifteen to twenty feet above the floor and the screw machine near the door of the steel shed was, I would estimate, approximately twenty-five to thirty feet away. At such a distance, it is certainly possible to see the operator in the cab, but the arbitrator had some difficulty in seeing the operator's eyes. I note also from the record that at least one Company witness, Mr. *W*, testified that he could not tell whether *A*'s eyes were open or closed.

The combined distances involved are not great, but they are large enough in my opinion to make it impossible to say conclusively whether *A* was in fact asleep or giving the appearance of being asleep. In this connection, it is worth noting that *A*'s duty in the cab was solely that of keeping his foot on the mechanical brake. In order to do so, he was obliged to sit in a leaning forward position. His duties did not obligate him to sit straight with eyes open. He could have performed this duty with his eyes shut and head on his locked hands the entire time, giving every appearance of being asleep when in fact he was not.

A testified that, although drowsy, he was fully conscious at all times and was keeping his foot on the brake. He was indisputably awake at 11:20 A.M. and again at 11:30 A.M. During the interval of ten minutes, his appearance and actions in the cab were apparently such as to convince four observers that he was sleeping or dozing. However, none of these four observers took any action to test the validity of their assumption that he was in fact sleeping or dozing. In cross examining *A* the Company made considerable point of the fact that *A* said nothing to any of the people he says he saw watching him. By the same token, it is curious to me that none of the four Company observers hailed *A* to see whether he would respond. This would have been a simple test of the validity of their assumption that he was in fact asleep which none of them chose to make.

In its opening statement, the Company contended that it would show through witnesses that *A* was in fact sleeping on the job. After careful consideration of the testimony and circumstances and in the light of the considerations advanced in this opinion, it is the considered judgment of the undersigned that the Company has failed to sustain the burden of proving that *A* was in fact sleeping on the job. The Company has at most proved that four witnesses felt on the basis of observation that *A* appeared to be sleeping or dozing. In the face of *A*'s flat denial, corroborated by *B*'s undisputed testimony that *A* responded verbally to him on at least two occasions during the ten minutes in question, the arbitrator is constrained to hold that an assumption based on appearances does not constitute proof of the offense for which *A* was disciplined. Since the Company in the arbitrator's judgment has failed to prove good and just cause for discipline, the grievance must be sustained.

AWARD

1. For reasons stated in the Opinion accompanying this Award and based on the circumstances of this particular case, the undersigned hereby finds and awards that the disciplinary suspension of Employee *A* from June 29, 19__ to July 12, 19__ was not for good and just cause within the meaning of Article IV, Section 1 of the contract.

2. Pursuant to the finding as stated in Paragraph 1 of this Award, Grievance No. 163-H should be and is hereby sustained and the affirmative relief requested therein is hereby granted.

HAROLD W. DAVEY
Permanent Arbitrator

Ames, Iowa

CASE 3
Careless Truck Driver

ARBITRATOR'S REASONING AND DECISION

The grievant was the only witness to the accident. Thus, the Company's case against him necessarily rests on circumstantial evidence. The undersigned's responsibility here is to weigh the Company's circumstantial case against *D* and determine whether it is sufficiently strong to invalidate his denial of personal responsibility for the accident that occurred.

In the abstract, it is impossible to quarrel with the proposition that direct eye-witness testimony is preferable to circumstantial evidence. However, this does not mean that circumstantial evidence may not be regarded as valid proof where the nature of that evidence is such as to make a convincing demonstration of the invalidity of direct testimony. After a careful review of the testimony and evidence in the instant case, the undersigned is convinced that the only explanation for the accident consistent with the known facts about the accident is that *D* did not have his jeep under control at the time.

The Union stressed its argument that the Company had proved only that an accident took place. It seems to me that the record establishes considerably more than the fact of the accident. The Union's own witness, *E*, testified that there was nothing mechanically wrong with the jeep immediately following the accident and that it had not been in for repair since December, two years ago. *D* himself testified that he was already 15 or 20 feet beyond the railroad tracks when the sharp swerve took place, thus eliminating the possibility that the tracks themselves caused the swerving. Testimony shows the road in question to have been concrete, containing no chuckholes or other hazards to smooth driving. The Company's contention that the jeep veered off the road at an angle of approximately 90 degrees was not disputed. Thus, the record reveals considerably more about this accident than the mere facts of its occurrence.

D's testimony that there was something wrong with the steering mechanism and the brakes is not supported by the mechanic's testimony and is inconsistent with his own professed ignorance of what caused the swerve into the parked car. In the light of established facts about the condition of the road, the sharp nature of the swerve, and the absence of mechanical defects in the jeep, the only credible explanation for the accident is that *D* did not have the jeep under proper control at the time.

To put it another way, the weight of the circumstantial evidence is such as to render invalid in my judgment *D*'s internally inconsistent testimony. If he did in fact have the jeep under proper control and was not driving recklessly, then the only possible factors that could have caused an accident such as the one involved here would be obstructions or holes in the road and/or faulty equipment. *D*'s own testimony indicates that there were no chuckholes, stones or other hazards on the road itself. *E's* testimony stands uncontradicted that there were no mechanical faults in the jeep needing repair.

In fact, the only testimony that supports *D*'s argument is the testimony of *E* and *G* to the effect that this large jeep was hard to drive and had a tendency to swerve, especially when empty, when run at the maximum speed allowed by the governor.

I have given careful consideration to this testimony relating to the individual characteristics of this particular jeep. It seems beyond question that this particular jeep, perhaps because of its size, may have been more difficult or trickier to drive than lighter jeeps. However, this large jeep had never been involved in an accident before July 9th. Furthermore, *E* testified that since the new steering axle was put in in December, 19__, the jeep had not been in for repair and that he hadn't heard much about it in quite a while. Also *D* himself had driven the jeep for all but 15 minutes of a full shift without incident. For an experienced driver such as *D*, this would seem adequate time to become accustomed to the individual peculiarities of the jeep in question, even assuming that he did not catch on as rapidly as did *G*.

In another decision involving a similar charge, I have stated that where an employee denies the charge against him, serious disciplinary action should not be sustained unless the record contains substantial evidence in support of the charge.* However, the factual picture in the instant case clearly distinguishes it from the case just cited. In the Waterloo case, there was no accident, the disciplined employee having sufficient control of his truck to avoid a collision. Here, the known facts as to the accident in question and the condition of the jeep involved permit only one credible explanation, namely that *D* did not have his jeep under proper control.

It is therefore my judgment that the Company has offered the requisite quantum of proof to sustain the charge against *D*. The penalty assessed for the offense in question appears to be appropriate.

AWARD

1. For reasons stated in the opinion accompanying this Award and based on the testimony and evidence adduced in this particular case, the undersigned hereby finds and awards that Employee *D* was disciplined for good and just cause within the meaning of Article IV, Section 1 of the contract between the parties.

* In re John Deere Waterloo Tractor Works and Local 838, UAW-CIO, Grievance No. 1365-D, decided June 2, 1953 and reported at 20 *LA* 583 (1953).

2. Pursuant to the finding as stated in Paragraph 1 of this Award, Grievance No. 4-564 should be and is hereby denied.

HAROLD W. DAVEY
Permanent Arbitrator

Ames, Iowa

CASE 4
Checking the Check Chart

ARBITRATOR'S REASONING AND DECISION

The parties disagree as to how the Company's Machining Check Chart should be used in scoring (i.e., evaluating) the work involved on Operation 90 on Part AM-2010. Since this particular operation involves running the parts through twice, first on one side and then on the other, the Union contends that the Check Chart requires counting each machining detail and each tool twice because two machine cycles are involved. The Company urges that such an interpretation would result in evaluation absurdities with every operation becoming "A" work and no possibility of discriminating among operations on the basis of degree of difficulty.

Both parties agree that in this particular operation three different machining details, one very difficult tolerance and five different tools are involved. However, the Union argues in effect that because on this particular operation the parts are run through twice, once on each side, therefore the operation must be scored as though in fact there were six different machining details, one very difficult tolerance and ten different tools. This is admittedly not the case, but the Union interpretation would require scoring the operation as though it in fact were the case.

A careful review of the language of Company Exhibit 1 (the Machining Check Chart) indicates that it is designed to accord a higher evaluation to those machining operations that involve the greater number of different machining details, very difficult tolerances, and tools. The document makes clear that each different type of detail, tolerance and tool is to be counted only once irrespective of the number of times it may occur or be used, as the case may be. The emphasis throughout the document is consistently on the number of *different* details, the number of *different* very difficult tolerances that must be held, and the number of *different* tools used.

This emphasis on differences is clearly related to the chart's purpose of evaluating machining operations in terms of the degree of skill and difficulty involved on the operator's part. In actual application, the Union's interpretation of how points should be scored on the operation in question would completely defeat the purpose of evaluating differences in skill required among various operations for occupational rate purposes.

The Union's entire case rests on the phrase "within its machine cycle" or "within the machine cycle". Since each part on the operation in question is run through twice, first on one side and then on the other, there is a surface plausibility to the argument that literally two machine cycles are involved. However, at no time during the argument did the Union refer to the job in question as *two different operations.* Operation 90 on Part AM-2010 is clearly a "particular operation" within the meaning of that phrase as used in the Machining Check Chart. The Check Chart makes clear that the evaluation is based on the number of different types of machining details performed on a part *during a particular operation.* The same phrase "during a particular operation" appears in connection with tolerances and tools.

In summary, it is the undersigned's considered judgment that the Union has failed to establish that the Company erred in its application of the Check Chart to Operation 90 on Part AM-2010. Furthermore, the method of scoring suggested by the Union as applicable in the instant case would do violence to the manifest purpose and intent of the Chart. It would leave no basis for discriminating between easy and difficult operations. Under the Union's theory, any operation which involved running the pieces through twice with no change in set-ups, machine details, tools, etc., would nevertheless be evaluated as though it involved twice as many different machining details, tools, etc. as in fact were involved. Neither the Check Chart in question nor any other principle of job evaluation known to the undersigned is consistent with such an interpretation.

AWARD

1. For reasons stated in the Opinion accompanying this Award, the undersigned hereby finds and awards that the Company did not violate Article XVII, Section 8 of the contract in slotting Operation 90 on Part AM-2010 as work classified as Semi-Automatic Lathe Operator "B" in Labor Grade E.

2. Pursuant to the finding as stated in Paragraph 1 of this Award, Grievance No. 55-2 should be and is hereby denied.

HAROLD W. DAVEY
Permanent Arbitrator

Ames, Iowa

Index of Authors

Index of Subjects